Ivy Global

SAT
6 Practice Tests

 For automatic scoring and scaling, please visit **cloud.ivyglobal.com**.

SAT 6 Practice Tests, Edition 3.0

This publication was written and edited by the team at Ivy Global.

Editor-in-Chief: Sarah Pike
Producers: Lloyd Min and Junho Suh

Editors: Sacha Azor, Corwin Henville, and Nathan Létourneau

Contributors: Rebecca Anderson, Thea Bélanger-Polak, Stephanie Bucklin, Grace Bueler, Lauren Calvello, Alexandra Candib, Alex Dunne, Alex Emond, Bessie Fan, Ian Greig, Elizabeth Hilts, Lei Huang, Mark Mendola, Geoffrey Morrison, Ward Pettibone, Arden Rogow-Bales, Kristin Rose, Rachel Schloss, Yolanda Song, Nathan Tebokkel, and Isabel Villeneuve

About the Publisher

Ivy Global is a pioneering education company that delivers a wide range of educational services.

E-mail: publishing@ivyglobal.com
Website: http://www.ivyglobal.com

Contents

Introduction

Chapter 1

Section 1
About This Book

Welcome, students and parents! This book is intended to help students prepare for the SAT, a test created and administered by the College Board, and required by many colleges and universities in the United States as part of the application process.

The goal of this book is to provide you first and foremost with practice: it contains 6 full-length practice tests. A breakdown of the key ideas in each section of the test is also provided. With practice, you can turn this challenging admissions requirement into an opportunity to demonstrate your skills and preparation to colleges.

Here is what's inside:

- A breakdown and overview of the content of each section with sample SAT questions
- 6 full-length practice tests
- Answer keys at the back of this book, and full answer explanations and scoring online

The first key to succeeding on the SAT is knowing the test, so the rest of this chapter provides details about its structure, format, and timing. This chapter delves into the question types and content you will encounter in each section. We recommend reviewing this chapter, taking the practice exams in Chapter 2, and then reviewing any challenging material.

Check out our website for additional resources, including review of foundational concepts, extra practice, answer explanations, an analysis of your strengths and weaknesses, and online scoring sheets. You'll also find information about our comprehensive SAT Guide, upcoming tests, tutoring services and prep classes, and other tips to help you do your best. Good luck studying!

 For additional resources, please visit **ivyglobal.com/study**.

Details of the SAT
Part 1

The SAT is a standardized examination designed to measure students' abilities in three areas: reading, writing, and mathematical reasoning. The SAT is written and administered by the College Board. While many American colleges and universities require SAT scores, remember that these aren't the only things that colleges consider when assessing applicants. Your high school grades, course selection, extracurricular activities, recommendation letters, and application essays are also all factors that colleges will use to assess whether you are a good fit for their school.

The Format and Scoring

The SAT is 3 hours long (without the optional Essay) and contains the following sections and scores:

Test	Time	Questions	Scaled Score	Area Score
Reading	65 minutes	52 questions	10 to 40	200 to 800
Writing and Language	35 minutes	44 questions	10 to 40	
Math Calculator	55 minutes	38 questions	10 to 40	200 to 800
Math No-Calculator	25 minutes	20 questions		
Essay (optional)	50 minutes	1 passage	2 to 8	2 to 8

The SAT will also publish cross-test scores and subscores, based on your results. These show up on your report, but aren't a part of your SAT composite score. These are as follows:

Test	Sub and Cross-Test SAT Scoring	
Reading, Writing and Language, Math	Cross-Test Scores (scored from 10 to 40)	• Analysis in Science • Analysis in History/Social Studies
Reading, Writing and Language	Subscores (scored from 1 to 15)	• Words in Context • Command of Evidence • Expression of Ideas • Standard English Conventions
Math		• Heart of Algebra • Problem Solving and Data Analysis • Passport to Advanced Math
Essay (optional)	Subscores (scored from 1 to 4)	• Reading, Analysis, and Writing

Taking the SAT
Part 2

Let's discuss how you go about taking the SAT. The exam is administered at standard testing dates and locations worldwide throughout the academic year. These standard dates fall in March, May, June, August, October, November, and December, but the March test date is only available in the United States. You can see the upcoming dates in your location on the College Board website: sat.collegeboard.org.

How Do I Register?

The easiest way to sign up for the exam is on the College Board website: sat.collegeboard.org. You'll need to fill out a personal profile form and upload a recognizable photo, which will be included on your admission ticket. There is a cut-off for registrations a month before the test date, after which you'll need to contact the College Board to see if late registration or standby testing is an option.

If you chose to register by mail, you'll need to enclose a photo with a paper registration form. To do this, ask your school counselor for *The Student Registration Guide for the SAT and SAT Subject Tests*, which includes a registration form and a return envelope.

When Should I Take the SAT?

Typically, students take the SAT during 11th grade or the beginning of 12th grade, but you should plan to take the exam when you feel most prepared. Keep in mind that almost all colleges will accept scores through December of your 12th grade year. However, if you are planning to apply for Early Admission to any school, you'll need to take the test by November of 12th grade at the very latest.

Can I Retake the SAT?

Yes! The College Board has no limits on how many times you can take the SAT. While many students take the exam two or three times, we don't recommend taking the exam more than this, because you'll get fatigued and your score will start to plateau. In order to give yourself the option to retake the test, it is always wise to choose a first testing date that is earlier than you need. That way, if you decide you'd like to retake the test, you won't miss any deadlines.

How Do I Send My Scores to Colleges?

When you sign up for the SAT, you can select which schools you'd like to receive your scores. You can also do this after taking the SAT by logging onto your account on the College Board website. If you have taken the SAT more than once, some schools allow you to use the College Board's "Score Choice" program, which allows you to choose the test results you would like to report to schools.

However, there are schools that request applicants to send the results of every SAT test they have taken. Even so, most schools have a policy of only considering your highest scores. You can see how your prospective schools consider your scores by visiting their admissions websites.

What's the "Disadvantage Score" on the SAT?

The College Board includes an "Environmental Context Panel" in the information that it sends to schools, which includes a score that you may have read described as a "disadvantage score." This score is not included in the calculation of your overall scores. It is a form of supplementary information presented alongside your scores.

The Environmental Context Panel includes information about your high school and the area in which you live. It's not a direct measure of your achievements; rather, it's intended to help place your achievements in context. The score considers factors like average education levels, household incomes, housing and family stability, and college attendance rates in your area.

Many of the factors considered are correlated with test scores, so students with high disadvantage scores will likely have had to cope with circumstances that make it more difficult to do well on the SAT.

Can I Do Anything to Influence My Disadvantage Score?

No, not really. You should try not to worry about your disadvantage score. Short of making major life changes, like moving to a new school or neighborhood, you can't do much to influence it. It's also not entirely new information. Social context has always factored into admissions processes. Schools have always considered the schools students attend, and personal essays often explore a student's social context. The Environmental Context Panel just provides an organized, standardized panel of information from objective sources.

Test-Taking Strategies
Part 3

Now that you're familiar with the SAT, there are a few strategies that can help you succeed on the test. First, remember that the SAT is a standardized exam and its format is the same every time it's administered. By knowing the time limit, number of questions, and directions for each section, you will be ahead of the game. Review these key details for each portion of the test thoroughly and you'll save time by skipping over the directions on your test day.

Second, to do well on the SAT, you need to know the length of the test, the time allowed for each section, and the time allotted for breaks. Remember that time between sections isn't transferable; you can't proceed to the next section or look at previous sections if you finish early. However, if you have extra time, make sure to use it to go over your answers and confirm that you've entered them correctly.

Third, remember that each question is only worth one point, regardless of its difficulty. Don't waste 10 minutes on a question that stumps you, only to find that you do not have enough time to answer the things you know inside-out. If you aren't sure of the answer, bubble in a guess on your answer sheet, circle the question in your test booklet, and return to it later. There is no penalty for guessing. Before your time is up for the section you're working on, make sure you enter a guess for every question you do not attempt.

Finally, remember that, with the exception of the essay, all of your work on the SAT will be graded by a machine. Before beginning each section, double check that you are working on the correct section of the answer sheet. What you write in your answer sheet determines whether you'll get a point or not, so you don't want to make a mistake when it comes to bubbling your answers!

When you write your essay, write as legibly as you can. Even though you're trying to write quickly, your readers need to be able to read your handwriting in order to give you points. Remember to write your essay only in the lines of the lined pages provided in your answer sheet—your readers won't be able to see anything you write outside of these margins! Don't write any part of your essay in your test booklet, though you can use this space for jotting down notes or an outline for your essay.

The night before you take the exam, make sure to set your alarm and plan a time to leave that allows for delays. You need to be on time, or you can't take the test!

Test Day Checklist

As you plan your test morning, here's a checklist to help you remember what you need to bring:

- ☐ Admission ticket
- ☐ Approved photo ID
- ☐ No. 2 pencils and erasers
- ☐ Calculator with new batteries and back-up batteries
- ☐ Non-beeping watch
- ☐ Snack and water bottle
- ☐ Directions to the test center and instructions for finding the entrance

Take a deep breath and remember: you are smart and accomplished! Believe in yourself and you will do well.

Section 2
Reading

The **Reading Test** requires you to read a variety of passages and to comprehend, analyze, and synthesize information to answer associated questions.

You won't need outside knowledge about the topics, as every correct answer can be supported by evidence found in the passage. While the passages and questions will be different each time, they fall under specific categories that you can learn about below. These will help prepare you for any content you will see on test day.

Anatomy of the Reading Test		
Number of Passages	Number of Questions	Amount of Time
4 full-length passages, 1 pair of shorter passages	52 questions	65 minutes

Reading Passages
Part 1

Rules for Reading Passages

1. *Read the preface*

   These introductory sentences before the passage lay out foundational or background information that is often essential for understanding the passage. This is especially true for Founding Documents and Great Global Conversation passages.

2. *Understand each paragraph*

   Make sure you understand the main idea of each paragraph before moving on to the next. If you go through the entire passage without understanding it and have to read it again, it will ultimately cost you more time. Use the strategies for marking up below to help you.

3. *Come back to details*

   Small details, like exact dates or numbers, are less important in your first read-through. If you are tested on these, you can always revisit the passage and spot them easily.

4. *Pay attention to the first sentence*

   Use the topic sentence of each paragraph to help you predict what the rest of the paragraph will say. Read it closely to help you more quickly and easily understand the paragraph as a whole. This is especially helpful if you are short on time.

Strategies for Marking Up the Passage

1. *Underline main ideas*

   It's important to understand the main ideas of the passage and how they work together. Underline places in the passage where questions like *Who? What? or Why?* are answered. This will help you find the focus of the passage, organize your thoughts, and make it easier for you to refer back to the passage when answering questions.

2. *Summarize*

   Jot down general summaries next to each paragraph so that the passage is easier to manage after you've finished reading. You can use words or phrases you've underlined to help you draft a three- to six-word summary. Use acronyms and abbreviations to keep your summaries brief.

3. *Identify Transitions*

   Circle transition words, which link sentences and paragraphs together. They often indicate important changes in direction, such as a contrasting point, counterargument, or change in time frame or point of view.

See the sample passage below illustrating these strategies for marking up the passage. Main ideas are underlined, summaries are written in the margins, and transition words are circled and explained. Your passages don't need to be marked up this much; this is only an example.

This passage is adapted from "Traveling to Mars with Immortal Plasma Rockets" by Gary Li. ©2016 by Gary Li. [Science Passage]

#1: electronically charged plasma reducing fuel usage

#2: electrical energy injected into fuel, shot out to propel

#3: electric forces destroy chamber wall

While: from describing promising outlook of plasma rockets to the reality of technical problems

#4: need self-repairing wall

#5: ballistic deposition— atoms re-stick onto wall

First: from mention of need to address technical issues to listing potential solutions

#6: manipulate plasma— make displaced particles turn around

Second: from first technique to second technique

However: introducing new and important quality of plasma to be utilized in this technique

#7: manipulate plasma— electric force imitates gravity effects

Result: summarizing the technique and introducing its name

#8: wall surface + plasma manipulation—immortal wall

Next step: possibilities for future

Plasma rockets transform fuel into a hot soup of electrically charged particles, known as plasma, and eject it to propel a spacecraft.
Line Using plasma rockets instead of the traditional
5 chemical rockets can reduce total in-space fuel usage by 90 percent, meaning we could deliver 10 times the amount of cargo using the same fuel mass. NASA mission planners are already looking into using plasma rocket transport
10 vehicles for ferrying cargo between Earth and Mars.

The rocket creates a plasma by injecting electrical energy into a gaseous fuel, stripping negatively charged electrons from the positively
15 charged ions. The ions are then shot out the back of the rocket, pushing the spacecraft forward.

While the future of plasma rockets is bright, the technology still has unsolved problems.
20 Unfortunately, all that energy in plasma does more than propel spaceships—it destroys any material with which it comes into contact.
Electric forces from the negatively charged walls cause the positively charged ions to slam
25 into the wall at very high speeds. These collisions break atoms off the wall, slowly weakening it over time.

It's not enough to use tougher materials to withstand the bombardment: there will always
30 be some amount of damage regardless of the strength of the material. We need to manipulate the plasma and the wall material so that the chamber wall can repair itself.

The first technique is known as ballistic
35 deposition and is present in materials with microscopic surface variations such as spikes or columns. When an ion hits the wall, a piece of these micro-features that breaks off can fly in any direction. Some of these pieces will hit
40 nearby protruding parts of the surface and stick, leaving the wall effectively undamaged.

The second phenomenon is less intuitive and depends on the plasma conditions. Imagine the same scenario where the wall particle breaks off
45 and flies into the plasma. However, instead of being lost forever, the particle suddenly turns around and goes straight back to the wall.

This is similar to how a baseball tossed straight up into the air turns around and drops
50 back to your hand due to gravity. In a thruster, it's the electric force between the negatively charged wall and the wall particle itself. This wall particle comes off neutrally charged, but loses its electron in the plasma, and therefore
55 becomes positively charged. As a result, the particle is pulled back toward the wall, in a phenomenon known as plasma redeposition. This process can be controlled by changing the density and temperature of the plasma.
60 Ballistic deposition depends on the wall's surface structures, while plasma redeposition depends on the plasma. By manipulating the design of the micro-features on the chamber walls, damage can potentially be reduced to by
65 much as 50 percent. On a thruster, this could make the difference between getting to Mars and getting stuck halfway. The next step is to include the effects of plasma redeposition and to determine whether a truly immortal wall can be
70 achieved.

Types of Passages

Passage Type (Number per Test)	Description	Focus Points	Frequent Question Types
Literature (1 per test)	• Classic and contemporary literature from the United States and around the world • Excerpts from novels or short stories • Description of a scene, object, or character • Example: *The Folded Leaf* by William Maxwell	• Characters • Characterization • Passage structure and plot • Rhetorical language • Implied information	• Point of View • Summarizing • Analyzing Word Choice • Implicit Meaning • Relationships • Analyzing Structure • Analyzing Purpose
History and Social Studies (1 per test)	• Recent developments or explanations of concepts in fields including anthropology, communication studies, economics, education, law, political science, psychology, and sociology • Example: "Why You Shouldn't Trust Internet Comments" by John Bohannon for the American Association for the Advancement of Science	• Discoveries • Developments • Claims and facts • Research and evidence	• Quantitative Information • Analyzing Structure • Analyzing Arguments
Founding Document or Great Global Conversation (1 per test)	• Historically important, foundational texts dealing with civic and political life • Mainly from the United States • Excerpts from speeches, essays, or books • Example: "Resistance to Civil Government" by Henry David Thoreau	• Author's arguments • Author's purpose • Author's strategies in persuading his or her audience • Rhetorical language	• Analyzing Purpose • Point of View • Central Ideas • Analyzing Word Choice
Science (2 per test)	• Recent developments or explanations of concepts in the natural sciences, including earth science, biology, chemistry, and physics • Example: "What Tech Is Next for the Solar Industry?" by Kevin Bullis for the *MIT Technology Review*	• Discoveries • Developments • Relationships between variables • Claims and counterclaims • Experiment results • Specific facts, details, and numbers	• Quantitative Information • Relationships • Analyzing Structure • Analyzing Arguments

Question Types
Part 2

Information and Ideas

Explicit Meaning

Explicit Meaning questions ask about something stated directly in the passage. *Incorrect answers* will be something not stated or supported in the text, or that contradict something stated directly in the passage.

This passage is adapted from "How Making Fun Weekend Plans Can Actually Ruin Your Weekend" by Selin Malkoc. ©2016 by Selin Malkoc. [History & Social Studies]

Across thirteen studies, we found that the simple act of scheduling makes otherwise fun tasks feel more like work. It also decreases how much we enjoy them.

Line 4   We think that it has to do with how scheduling
5   structures time. Scheduling, at its core, is about allocating time to activities. There are set beginning and end points.

Such strict scheduling, however, is at odds with people's perceptions of leisure and relaxation, which are associated with unconstrained freedom.

10   On the flip side, structured time is associated with work activities. Meetings start and end at specific times; deadlines loom; the specter of the clock is omnipresent. So when your weekend is structured and planned, even if the activities are fun, they start to take on some of the
15   qualities we tend to associate with work.

Question

According to the passage, the act of scheduling activities

A) makes the activities more enjoyable.

B) fosters a sense of expectation.

C) makes them feel more like work.

D) is only worthwhile if the activities are fun.

Answer

The correct answer is (C), as the passage indicates that "the simple act of scheduling makes otherwise fun tasks feel more like work." It also states that scheduling is "at odds with people's perceptions of leisure and relaxation." (A) is incorrect because the passage indicates that scheduling makes the activity less enjoyable. (B) is incorrect because the passage does not indicate anything about a sense of expectation. (D) is incorrect because the passage does not discuss when scheduling is worthwhile.

Implicit Meaning

Implicit Meaning questions ask about ideas that are implied but not stated directly. Read between the lines and combine clues from different parts of the text to understand what the author is suggesting. *Incorrect answers* will not be supported by enough information from the passage.

This passage is adapted from *Lay Down Your Arms!* by Bertha Von Suttner. First published in 1889. [Literature]

Several days passed without me seeing Tilling again. Every evening, I went to the theatre, and from thence to a party, expecting and hoping to meet him, but in vain.
Line My reception day brought me many visitors, but, of
5 course, not him. But I did not expect him. It was not like him, after his decisive "You really must not expect from me, countess," to present himself after all at my house on a day of the kind. I had offended him that evening— that was certain; and he avoided meeting me again—that
10 was clear. Only, what could I do? I was all on fire to see him again, to make amends for my rudeness on the former occasion, and get another hour of a talk such as I had had at my father's—an hour's talk the delight of which would now be increased to me an hundredfold by
15 the consciousness, which had now become plain to me, of my love.

Question	Answer

The passage most strongly suggests that

A) the main character had only met Tilling once before.

B) Tilling was a friend of the main character's father.

C) the main character had recently fallen in love with Tilling.

D) Tilling and the main character were former enemies.

The correct answer is (C), as the passage states that the main character had become conscious of her love and that she was "on fire to see him again." Therefore, it is reasonable to conclude that she had fallen in love with Tilling sometime since their last encounter. (A) is incorrect because there is insufficient evidence to conclude that their last meeting was their first. (B) is incorrect because the passage does not indicate that Tilling was a friend of the main character's father, only that they had last spoken at the father's house. (D) is incorrect because the passage nowhere indicates that they were former enemies.

Summarizing

Summarizing questions ask you to identify a reasonable summary of parts of a passage or of an entire passage. Review the portion you are asked about and pick out the most important ideas discussed. *Incorrect answers* will focus on details, rather than key ideas, or contain information not found in the part of the passage you are asked about.

This passage is adapted from "Fashion's closed circuit opens up and goes global—next stop cyberspace" by Anthony Kent. © 2016 by Anthony Kent. [History & Social Studies]

Fashion weeks used to be an industry affair: fashion labels presenting their new seasonal collections to prospective buyers. Journalists from fashion magazines
Line and newspapers bridged the gap between industry and
5   consumer, providing information about new looks and trends and summarizing the ups and downs of the well-heeled world to consumers at large.

But fashion weeks are evolving from an exclusive industry function to participatory consumer events.
10 Fashion events are becoming less about fashion cliques and more about opening up to the masses.

The internet has both changed the way fashion weeks are followed by consumers and the way in which products are acquired: there are new communication and
15 shopping channels, particularly mobile, for brands to build an online and offline presence. Interactive software enables the dissemination of fashion—the sharing of looks and styles. New forms of hardware and more powerful software provide the opportunity to interact and
20 engage with fashion brands at any time and place.

These developments have led to the rapid convergence of the physical and digital fashion worlds. The sanctity of fashion time and space is shrinking as consumer empowerment and choice expands.

Question	Answer
Which choice best summarizes the passage? A) The internet has led to exclusivity during fashion weeks. B) Fashion, once an art, has become a commercial undertaking. C) Fashion and journalism have grown hand in hand. D) The internet has allowed for more open access to the fashion world.	The correct answer is (D), as the passage indicates that fashion weeks, which used to be exclusive events, have opened up to consumers all over the world (lines 12-20). The passage also indicates that the internet has provided the opportunity for average consumers to engage with fashion brands quickly and easily. (A) is incorrect because the passage suggests that the internet has led to inclusivity during fashion events. (B) is incorrect because the passage does not discuss concepts of art or commercialism in relation to fashion. (C) is incorrect because the passage does not focus on the growth of journalism.

Relationships

Relationships questions ask you to describe the relationship between two things or people discussed in the passage. Look back at the passage for information about both of the items or people you are asked about. *Incorrect answers* may invert the relationship between the two items or contain information not supported by the passage.

This passage is adapted from "Why We are Willing to Pay for Mega Expensive Things" by Paul Harrison. ©2016 by Paul Harrison. [History & Social Studies]

It may not seem logical or good value for money, but there are plenty of us that will fork out for expensive presents. It may be thousands of dollars on fancy goods
Line like retro-inspired coffee machines or fridges, or a
5 designer purse, or perhaps a pair of designer shoes.

In reality, nobody "needs" a $700 pair of shoes, or a retro $2000 fridge, but these products seem to transcend their rational utility. They have meaning beyond their function. They are objects of desire that help us to
10 communicate to ourselves and others who we are.

Desire, status, and luxury are concepts that have been explored for hundreds of years. Probably one of the best known books about this topic was by sociologist and economist Thorstein Veblen, and was published in 1899.
15 Veblen suggested the act of buying expensive things was a means for people to communicate their social status to others. He suggested that purchasing luxury goods and expensive houses, or attending exclusive soirees was a form of "wealth signaling," or what others have called
20 "peacocking."

Question	Answer
Based on the passage, which choice best describes the relationship between expensive products and social status?	The correct answer is (A). The passage explains the concept of "wealth signaling," the act of buying expensive things to communicate social status. This is clearly described in (A). (B) is incorrect since the passage does not discuss frequency of such purchases, nor does it touch upon economic status. (C) is incorrect: the passage does not indicate that these purchases lower social status. (D) is incorrect because the passage does not touch upon economic status.

Based on the passage, which choice best describes the relationship between expensive products and social status?

A) People buy expensive products to communicate social status.

B) Expensive products are frequently purchased by those with high economic status.

C) Buying unnecessary, expensive products lowers the purchaser's social status.

D) Purchases of expensive products lead to an increase in economic status.

Words in Context

Words in Context questions give you a word or phrase from the passage and ask you to select the answer choice that could best replace it. *Incorrect answers* will still be synonyms of the word or phrase you are asked about, but either will not make sense in the original sentence or will change the meaning of the original sentence.

This passage is adapted from *The Orchid* by Robert Grant. Originally published in 1905. [Literature]

It was generally recognized that Lydia Arnold's perceptions were quicker than those of most other people. She was alert in grasping the significance of
Line what was said to her; her face clearly revealed this.
5 She had the habit of deliberating just an instant before responding, which marked her thought; and when she spoke, her words had a succinct definiteness of their own. The quality of her voice arrested attention. The intonation was finished yet dry: finished in that it was
10 well modulated; dry in that it was void of enthusiasm.

Question

As used in line 5, "deliberating" most nearly means

A) brooding.

B) discussing.

C) reflecting.

D) consulting.

Answer

The correct answer is (C), since the use of the word "deliberating" in this context means "to think about something carefully." Thus, "reflecting" makes the most sense. (A) is incorrect because "deliberating" in this context does not mean to dwell gloomily. Therefore, "brooding" is incorrect. (B) is incorrect since the passage indicates that Lydia Arnold "deliberates" before responding. It is unreasonable to deduce that she "discusses" with a person before responding to that person. (D) is incorrect since the passage does not suggest that Lydia consults anyone or anything.

Command of Evidence

Command of Evidence questions list four selections from the passage and ask which one best supports your answer to the previous question. *Incorrect answers* contain information that does not provide sufficient support for the previous answer.

This passage is adapted from I. Stergiopoulos, A. Drenth, and G. Kema, "With the Familiar Cavendish Banana in Danger, Can Science Help it Survive?" ©2016 I. Stergiopoulos, A. Drenth, and G. Kema. [Science]

Virtually all the bananas sold across the Western world belong to the Cavendish subgroup of the species and are genetically nearly identical. These bananas are
Line sterile and dependent on reproduction via cloning, either
5 by using suckers and cuttings taken from the underground stem, or through modern tissue culture.

The familiar bright yellow Cavendish banana is ubiquitous in supermarkets and fruit bowls, but it is in imminent danger. The vast worldwide monoculture of
10 genetically identical plants leaves the Cavendish intensely vulnerable to disease outbreaks.

Fungal diseases once before severely devastated the banana industry in the past. When a fungal disease called Fusarium whipped through plantations during the 1950s
15 and '60s, it brought the global banana export industry to the brink of collapse and nearly wiped out the species. This could soon happen again if we do not resolve the cause of these problems. Plant scientists are working out the genetics of wild banana varieties and banana
20 pathogens as we try to prevent a Cavendish crash.

Question	Answer

The author uses the phrase "Cavendish crash" (line 20) to suggest that

A) extensive contamination of banana fields can quickly lead to food poisoning.

B) introducing a new species of banana would be detrimental for the banana industry.

C) if a disease breaks out among the Cavendish subgroup, global export could collapse.

D) new technology could give rise to a new banana subgroup and replace the Cavendish.

The correct answer is (C). The passage suggests that since such a significant portion of the exported bananas in the banana industry are genetically identical, a disease devastating the Cavendish subgroup could wipe out the whole species. "Cavendish crash" in context most likely refers to the collapse of either the species or of the global export—or both. (A) is incorrect because the passage does not discuss contamination or food poisoning. (B) is incorrect because the passage suggests the opposite—that introducing variety could help prevent a crash in the industry. (D) is incorrect because the passage does not discuss the potential for a new subgroup, nor does it discuss new technology that can assist in the creation of one. Further, the passage does not discuss replacing the Cavendish subgroup.

Which choice provides the best support for the answer to the previous question?

A) Lines 3-6 ("These bananas … culture")

B) Lines 9-11 ("The vast … outbreaks")

C) Lines 13-16 ("When a … species")

D) Lines 18-20 ("Plant scientists … crash")

The correct answer is (C), since the given lines clearly illustrate the problem with genetically identical plants: vulnerability to disease outbreak, risk of species extinction, and economic crash. The lines illustrate a time in the past when a fungal disease posed a threat. (A) is incorrect because it does not mention disease outbreak or a potential crash—only reproduction techniques. (B) is incorrect because the given lines only discuss the vulnerability of genetically identical bananas to disease, not the risks of species extinction or economic crash. (D) is incorrect because although it mentions the phrase, it does not sufficiently define "Cavendish crash."

Analogical Reasoning

Analogical Reasoning questions ask you to find an answer choice that is similar to an idea or relationship presented in the passage. *Incorrect answers* will not closely mirror the situation from the passage you are asked about.

This passage is adapted from "Here's Why 'Baby Talk' is Good for Your Baby" by Catherine E. Laing. ©2016 by Catherine E. Laing. [History & Social Studies]

Intonation is very important to infants' language development in the first months of life. Adults tend to speak to babies using a special type of register that we
Line know as "baby talk" or "motherese." This typically
5 involves a higher pitch than regular speech, with wide, exaggerated intonation changes.

Research has shown that babies prefer to listen to this exaggerated "baby talk" type of speech than typical adult-like speech: they pay more attention when a
10 parent's speech has a higher pitch and a wider pitch range compared to adult-like speech with less exaggerated pitch features.

For example, a mother might say the word "baby" in an exaggerated "singsong" voice, which holds an
15 infant's attention longer than it would in a monotonal adult-style voice. Words produced in this way also stand out more from the speech stream, making it easier for babies to pick out smaller chunks of language.

Across the vast stream of language that babies hear
20 around them every day, these distinctive pitch features in baby talk help babies to "tune in" to a small part of the input, making language processing a more manageable task.

Question

The effect of "motherese" is most similar to which of the following situations?

A) A performer in a music competition wears a bright yellow dress on competition day.

B) A man raises his voice to speak over a crowd and get the attention of his friend.

C) A student studying abroad speaks the country's language with a foreign accent.

D) A teacher plays classroom instruments during the first class of a music course.

Answer

The correct answer is (B). The passage indicates that "motherese" or "baby talk" is the idea of speaking with higher pitch and wider intonation so that the speaker's voice stands out from the common speech stream. The passage indicates that this way of speaking is preferable to babies and easier for them to understand, since they hear common adult-like speech around them all the time. (A) is incorrect because "motherese" is a strategy that helps babies hear and learn language, while the described situation only indicates that a contestant wears a bright yellow dress, potentially to attract more attention from the judges. This situation does not include applying methods that are more easily understood or preferable. (C) is incorrect because the idea of speaking with an accent is not similar to the technique of language learning described in the passage. (D) is incorrect because this situation does not demonstrate holding attention or being easier to understand.

Rhetoric

Analyzing Word Choice

Analyzing Word Choice questions ask you how specific words, phrases, or patterns shape the meaning and tone of the text. They will often require you to read between the lines and decipher the passage beyond a literal understanding of what is being said. *Incorrect answers* may interpret rhetorical devices too literally or mischaracterize a passage's tone.

This passage is adapted from "Address to the Jury," delivered by Emma Goldman in New York on July 9th, 1917. [Founding Documents/Great Global Conversation]

Gentlemen of the jury, we respect your patriotism. We would not, even if we could, have you change its meaning for yourself. But may there not be different
Line kinds of patriotism as there are different kinds of
5 liberty? I for one cannot believe that love of one's country must consist of blindness to its social faults, deafness to its social discords, inarticulation to its social wrongs. Neither can I believe that the mere accident of birth in a certain country or the mere scrap of a citizen's
10 paper constitutes the love of country.

Question	Answer
The rhetorical effect of lines 1-3 ("Gentlemen … yourself") is to A) win over the jury by appealing to a shared understanding of patriotism. B) flatter the jury by praising their patriotism. C) acknowledge that an idea matters to the jury before clarifying its definition. D) call into question the existence of a widespread concept.	The correct answer is (C). Goldman assures the jury that she and her co-defendant respect their patriotism, and have no desire to alter the jury's private understanding of this concept. Immediately after this, she asks if there may be multiple forms of patriotism, and articulates her own understanding of it using the words "I for one." Thus, the lines referenced set up the expanded definition of patriotism that follows. (A) is incorrect because it's very possible that Goldman and the jury understand the idea differently; the words "we would not...have you change its meaning for itself" certainly allow for this possibility. (B) is incorrect because "respect" in this context means to "acknowledge as valid" rather than "admire," so Goldman is not praising the jury. (D) is incorrect because Goldman doesn't question whether or not patriotism exists.

Analyzing Arguments

Analyzing Arguments questions ask you to identify claims or counterclaims, or assess the author's reasoning or evidence. There are a few specific types, listed below. *Incorrect answers* will misidentify or misinterpret claims or evidence or the role they play in the passage.

Analyzing Claims and Counterclaims questions ask you to identify the claims or counterclaims made in the passage. A **claim** is an idea that the author is aiming to persuade the reader to believe, and is usually supported by evidence. A **counterclaim** is an assertion that goes against a claim previously introduced in the passage.

Assessing Reasoning questions ask you to follow the author's line of reasoning, evaluate its validity, and understand why the author used a certain method of reasoning. How does the author's reasoning line up with what he or she is trying to prove?

Analyzing Evidence questions ask you to identify what evidence the author uses to support his or her arguments, or whether or not he or she includes any evidence at all.

This passage is adapted from Angela Gutchess, "Aging Brains Aren't Necessarily Declining Brains." ©2014 by Angela Gutchess.

Much of our understanding of aging brains has thus far focused on declining cognitive abilities. But there is some evidence that social and emotional abilities are
Line relatively well-preserved with age. Older adults seem to
5 be just as good at forming impressions of others and are even better at regulating or controlling their emotions than younger adults.

This suggests that brain regions underlying these abilities may not exhibit the same downward trajectory
10 with age as those associated with cognitive abilities; these brain areas may show different patterns of reorganization and change.

Should these abilities be better preserved with age, they could be harnessed to develop effective memory
15 strategies. For instance, emphasizing the motivational, personal, and emotional significance of information to be remembered could help older people's memories.

Question	Answer

The author most likely uses the evidence in lines 2-7 ("But there is … than younger adults") in order to support her claim that

A) older adults' brains are better developed in general than younger adults' brains.

B) despite a decline of cognitive abilities, aged brains still retain functional capacity in some areas.

C) as brains age, emotional functions are heightened and memory capacity is improved.

D) brain regions affecting emotional abilities are the same as those affecting long-term habits.

The correct answer is (B). The primary claim of the passage is that, despite declining cognitive abilities in aging brains, certain brain areas may show fewer negative changes or even improvement during the aging process. (A) is incorrect because the passage does not indicate that older adults' brains are generally better developed than those of younger adults. (C) is incorrect because the referenced lines do not mention memory capacity. (D) is incorrect because neither these lines nor this passage indicates that these brain regions are shared.

Analyzing Structure

Analyzing Structure questions ask you about the structure of the text as a whole, or about the relationship between the whole text and a specific part of the text, such as one sentence or paragraph. *Incorrect answers* may mischaracterize the focus or structure of the passage.

This passage is adapted from "A Century After His Death, a Japanese Literary Giant is Returning as an Android—Here's Why" by Philip Seargeant. ©2016 by Philip Seargeant. [History & Social Studies]

The centenary of Natsume Soseki's death this year is being marked by numerous events in his home country. He is one of Japan's most revered writers. But in the
Line English-speaking world he remains comparatively
5 unknown. This is surprising, given the key role that English culture played in his life, and the fact that he spent two formative years living in London.

Soseki came to the UK in 1900. At the time, Japan was going through a period of rapid modernization after
10 two centuries of self-imposed political isolation. In the country's only two universities, classes were all being taught in English by Western professors.

Soseki was sent abroad as part of a government scheme to train Japanese scholars so they could take
15 over these teaching duties on their return. Arriving in England, he studied briefly at UCL, was tutored by the Shakespearean scholar William James Craig, and witnessed the funeral of Queen Victoria.

For the most part, his time in England wasn't a
20 happy one. "The two years I spent in London were the most unpleasant … of my life," he later wrote. "Among English gentlemen I lived in misery, like a shaggy dog in a pack of wolves." He suffered from depression, from isolation, and spent most of his time hidden away in his
25 room, reading.

Yet, it was while living in London that he formulated the ideas for his seminal *Theory of Literature* (1909), which takes a scientific approach to the study of literature, aiming to find universal values by which to
30 evaluate literary works and so "challenge the superiority of the Western canon." Damian Flanagan writes that the "alienation that Soseki initially experienced in London allowed him to view both himself and Japanese society in general with fresh eyes"—and that he channelled this
35 into his later creative work.

Question	Answer

The reference to Japan's "period of rapid modernization" (line 9) primarily serves to

A) explain the popularity of Soseki's work in his home country.

B) help establish why Soseki traveled to London.

C) provide context for Soseki's scientific theory of literature.

D) introduce the main topic of the passage.

The correct answer is (B). The remark about Japan's period of modernization leads directly to a discussion of its educational system at the time, which depended on Western professors. The passage then explains that Soseki was in London to study, ultimately in order to "take over these teaching duties." (A) is incorrect; there's no evidence in the passage that Soseki's popularity was due to modernization in particular. (C) is incorrect because the passage never explicitly links modernization with Soseki's theories. (D) is also incorrect, as the passage is primarily about Natsume Soseki.

Point of View

Point of View questions ask you to analyze the point of view or attitude of the author either toward a specific subject or toward the text overall. *Incorrect answers* will contain views not supported by the text or will overstate the author's point of view by using absolute language like "best" or "always."

This passage is adapted from "The Arrogance of Power," a speech given by Robert C. Byrd in 2003 on the Senate floor. [Founding Documents/Great Global Conversation]

I believe in this great and beautiful country. I have studied its roots. I have gloried in the wisdom of its magnificent Constitution, and its inimitable history. I
Line have marveled at the wisdom of its founders and its
5 framers. Generation after generation of Americans has understood the lofty ideals that underlie our great Republic. I have been inspired by the story of their sacrifice and their strength.

But today, I weep for my country. I have watched the
10 events of recent months with a heavy, heavy heart. No more is the image of America one of a strong, yet benevolent peacekeeper. The image of America, Madam President, has changed. Around the globe, our friends mistrust us; our word is disputed; our intentions are
15 questioned.

Question	Answer
Robert C. Byrd's attitude is best described as A) outraged that the United States is no longer respected by foreign nations. B) distressed that the United States has lost sight of its founding ideals. C) worried that the United States will not be able to maintain peace around the world. D) determined that the United States can stay strong in the face of adversity.	The correct answer is (B). Byrd begins by discussing the United States' "lofty ideals" and his admiration for its history. He goes on to say "I weep for my country" and that he has a "heavy, heavy heart" due to America's current state. (A) is incorrect because there is little indication that he's outraged, and being disrespected by foreign nations is only a small part of his point. (C) is incorrect because Byrd focuses primarily on the nation's past and how it contrasts with the present, not its ability to maintain peace. (D) is incorrect because Byrd does not indicate the United States is facing any particular adversity, nor does he mention that he feels positively about the present state of the nation.

Analyzing Purpose

Analyzing Purpose questions ask you about the purpose of either an entire passage or specific sections of the passage. Consider the goals of the passage you're analyzing, and how different sections relate to each other. *Incorrect answers* will be too specific or too broad, or they won't best indicate the author's purpose.

This passage is adapted from "We Shall Overcome," a speech delivered by Lyndon B. Johnson to Congress regarding the Voting Rights Act of 1965 which prohibited racial discrimination in voting. [Founding Documents/Great Global Conversation]

This bill will establish a simple, uniform standard which cannot be used, however ingenious the effort, to flout our Constitution. It will provide for citizens to be
Line registered by officials of the United States Government,
5 if the State officials refuse to register them. It will eliminate tedious, unnecessary lawsuits which delay the right to vote. Finally, this legislation will ensure that properly registered individuals are not prohibited from
10 voting.

I will welcome the suggestions from all of the Members of Congress—I have no doubt that I will get some—on ways and means to strengthen this law and to make it effective. But experience has plainly shown that
15 this is the only path to carry out the command of the Constitution.

To those who seek to avoid action by their National Government in their own communities, who want to and who seek to maintain purely local control over elections,
20 the answer is simple: open your polling places to all your people.

Question

The main purpose of the second paragraph is to

A) encourage members of Congress to give their input and thoroughly rewrite the bill.

B) deter members of Congress from changing the bill and suggest they not participate.

C) downplay the negative effects of the bill but acknowledge that they are present.

D) welcome feedback on strengthening the bill but stress that it is absolutely necessary.

Answer

The correct answer is (D). As he says in lines 11-12, Johnson will "welcome the suggestions" from Congress. Then in line 15 he says, "But … this is the only path," indicating that although he welcomes suggestions, the bill is strictly necessary. (A) is incorrect because Johnson welcomes input only on ways "to strengthen this law and to make it effective," not ways to entirely change the bill. (B) is incorrect because it directly contradicts lines 11-14. (C) is incorrect because, while Johnson welcomes improvements to the bill, he does not acknowledge any existing flaws.

Central Ideas

Central Ideas questions ask about the ideas that are the focus of the passage. Look for recurring themes throughout the passage, consider the big picture rather than details, and use your paragraph summaries to help you answer these questions. *Incorrect answers* will contain themes or ideas that are only mentioned briefly in a part of the passage, or ideas that go beyond the passage. Be wary of answer choices that include stronger opinions than the ones stated in the passage.

This passage is adapted from "A New Way to Detect Tsunamis: Cargo Ships" by James Foster. ©2016 by James Foster. [Science]

Despite the advances in tsunami monitoring and modeling technology over the last decade, it remains difficult for hazard response agencies to get enough
Line information about potential tsunami threats. The
5 problem is that there are too few observations of tsunamis to provide sufficiently accurate predictions about when, where, and how severely tsunamis might occur. In particular, there are very few sensors in the deep oceans that lie between tsunami sources—usually
10 earthquakes occurring under the ocean trenches that mark where tectonic plates meet—and the distant coastlines that might be threatened. Gaps in the coverage of the network, as well as routine outages of instruments, limit the ability of the current detection system to
15 accurately assess the hazard posed by each event.

Question	Answer

The central claim of the passage is that

A) there is much more to be done to improve the tsunami detection system.

B) tsunamis happen too frequently for response agencies to predict them.

C) tectonic plates are located too far apart to send signals from one to another.

D) tsunami detection cannot be improved by implementing new instruments.

The correct answer is (A). The last sentence mentions the problems that need to be addressed to overcome challenges with tsunami detection. (B) is incorrect because the passage does not indicate that tsunamis happen too frequently, nor does it cite this as the primary obstacle to effective detection and prediction. (C) is incorrect because the passage does not make this claim about tectonic plates; it also does not discuss sending signals between these plates. (D) is incorrect because the passage does not claim that implementing new instruments would be ineffective, only that past technological advances have not been sufficiently effective.

Synthesis

Multiple Texts

Multiple Texts questions ask about the relationship between two paired passages. These questions can be similar to many of the Information and Ideas question types, especially Explicit and Implicit Meaning. *Incorrect answers* will contain information about only one passage instead of both, confuse which passage contains which ideas, or misrepresent the way the two passages are related to each other.

Passage 1 is adapted from Calvin Coolidge, "Speech on Taxes, Liberty, and the Philosophy of Government." Passage 2 is adapted from John F. Kennedy, "Address to the Economic Club of New York." On December 14, 1962, then-President Kennedy made a call for a sharp cut in tax rates and a reform of the tax system for the purpose of economic growth in his address to the Economic Club of New York—an organization dedicated to the study and discussion of social, economic, and political matters. [Founding Documents/ Great Global Conversation]

Passage 1

The costs of government are all assessed upon the people. This means that the farmer is doomed to provide a certain amount of money out of the sale of his
Line produce, no matter how low the price, to pay his taxes.
5   The manufacturer, the professional man, the clerk, must do the same from their income. The wage earner, often at a higher rate when compared to his earning, makes his contribution, perhaps not directly but indirectly, in the advanced cost of everything he buys. Taxes take from
10 everyone a part of his earnings and force everyone to work for a certain part of his time for the government.

The yearly expenses of the governments of this country—the stupendous sum of about 7 billion, 500 million dollars—is difficult to comprehend. I want to cut
15 down public expense. I want the people of America to be able to work less for the government—and more for themselves. I want them to have the rewards of their own industry. This is the chief meaning of freedom.

Passage 2

So long as our national security needs to keep rising,
20 an economy hampered by restrictive tax rates will never produce enough revenues to balance our budget—just as it will never produce enough jobs or enough profits. Surely the lesson of the last decade is that budget deficits are not caused by wild-eyed spenders but by slow
25 economic growth and periodic recessions.
In short, it is a paradoxical truth that tax rates are too high today and tax revenues are too low and the soundest way to raise the revenues in the long run is to cut the rates now. Only full employment can balance the budget,
30 and tax reduction can pave the way to that employment. The purpose of cutting taxes now is not to incur a budget deficit, but to achieve the more prosperous, expanding economy which can bring a budget surplus.

Question	Answer

Which statement best describes the relationship between the passages?

A) Passage 1 argues for cuts in tax rates, while Passage 2 argues for increases in government budgets.

B) Passage 1 focuses on the role of the government in cutting taxes, while Passage 2 focuses on the role of the people in paying them.

C) Passage 1 focuses on recessions in the economy, while Passage 2 focuses on the well-being of consumers.

D) Passage 1 argues for lower taxes for individual freedom, while Passage 2 argues for lower taxes for a prosperous economy.

The correct answer is (D). The final sentence of Passage 1 contends that tax cuts would allow people to "work less for the government—and more for themselves," and that this would be an accurate manifestation of freedom. The final sentence of Passage 2 indicates that the purpose of tax cuts is to "achieve the more prosperous, expanding economy." (A) is incorrect since Passage 2 does not mention an increase in budget. (B) is incorrect because both Passage 1 and 2 focus equally on the role of the government and of the people. (C) is incorrect since Passage 2, not Passage 1, mentions recessions, and Passage 1, not Passage 2, focuses on the well-being of consumers.

Quantitative Information

Quantitative Information questions ask you about information in a graphic, or how the information in a graphic relates to the passage. Take time to understand the labels or legend on the graphic so you know what it represents. *Incorrect answers* will misinterpret or contradict the information in the graphic.

This passage and graphic are adapted from Sean Nee, "How Many Genes Does it Take to Make a Person?" © 2016 by Sean Nee. [Science]

Life has evolved over three billion years from simple one-celled creatures to multicellular plants and animals coming in all shapes, sizes, and abilities. In addition to growing ecological complexity, over the history of life we've seen the evolution of intelligence, complex societies, and technological invention.

It's natural to think of the history of life as progressing from the simple to the complex and to expect this to be reflected in increasing gene numbers. As humans lead the way with superior intellect and global domination, the expectation was that since we're the most complex creature, we'd have the most elaborate set of genes.

This presumption seems logical, but the more researchers discover about various genomes, the more flawed it seems. About a half-century ago the estimated number of human genes was in the millions. Today we're down to about 20,000. We now know, for example, that bananas, with their 30,000 genes, have 50 percent more genes than we do.

As researchers devise new ways to count the genes of an organism, there's a clear convergence between the gene count in what we've always thought of as the simplest life forms—viruses—and the most complex—us. It's time to rethink the question of how the complexity of an organism is reflected in its genome.

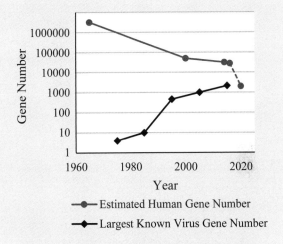

The graph shows the converging estimated number of genes in a person versus a giant virus. The dashed portion of the human gene number shows an estimate for the coming years. Numbers shown for viruses are for MS2 (1976), HIV (1985), giant viruses (2004), average T4 numbers (1990s), and Pandoravirus (2014).

Question	Answer

Data in the graphic best support which of the following ideas from the passage?

A) Viruses, the simplest life forms, have much fewer genes than humans, the most complex.

B) Gene count in humans has been dropping since the mid-1900s due to new illnesses.

C) The increase in number of genes in viruses reflects the growing strength of these life forms.

D) Estimations of human gene count 50 years ago were higher than they are now.

The correct answer is (D). Both the passage and the graphic indicate that, a half-century ago, it was believed that humans had an estimated 1,000,000 genes, but more recent evidence indicates many fewer—20,000. (A) is incorrect because the graph and the passage indicate that viruses have roughly as many genes as humans, if not more. (B) is incorrect because the passage does not indicate that actual gene count has been dropping or mention any new illnesses. The "drop" shown in the graph is due to more advanced research developments and discoveries. (C) is incorrect because like (B), the graph shows that previous estimates were inaccurate, not that viruses now have more genes. Further, the passage does not indicate that the "increase" reflects growing strength.

Section 3
Writing and Language

The Writing and Language section of the SAT tests your ability to review passages written in a variety of styles and correct errors, improve style and tone, and select revisions that best achieve specific writing goals.

The passages in The Writing and Language section cover a specific range of topics: One passage will discuss a topic in Science, one will discuss a topic in Social Studies or History, one will discuss a topic in the Humanities, and one will discuss a career that might be an option for a college-bound student. You will not be tested on outside knowledge of the passage subjects, but you will be tested on the appropriate use of vocabulary in specific contexts.

Anatomy of the Writing Test		
Number of Passages	Number of Questions	Amount of Time
4 passages of 400-450 words each	44 questions	35 minutes

Standard English Conventions
Part 1

Standard English Conventions questions on the Writing and Language section of the SAT ask you to correct grammatical errors in a passage. You'll need to learn and apply the following grammar rules to do your best on these questions. The Writing and Language test includes 20 Standard English Conventions questions, so they account for a little less than half of the 44 questions in this section.

Parts of Speech

The table below provides brief definitions of the main parts of speech as a refresher. If you need a little more practice recognizing these parts of speech in a sentence, check out our supplemental materials online.

Term	Definition	Example
Noun	A word that names a person, place, thing, or idea	The ball is as yellow as a dandelion.
Verb	A word that expresses an action or state of being	Jorge and Frank own a bakery; while Frank bakes, Jorge staffs the sales counter.
Adjective	A word that adds descriptive information to a noun	Blue tokens are worth more than red tokens.
Adverb	A word that adds descriptive information to a verb, an adjective, or another adverb	Miguel sprinted very well, but Priya's lead was too big, so she still won the race.
Pronoun	A word that takes the place of a noun in a sentence*, referring to it instead of naming it again	John liked the spaghetti. He said it was the best spaghetti he had ever eaten!
Conjunction	A word that joins (or "conjoins") words, phrases*, or clauses*	We had pizza and cake at the birthday party, but we forgot the fruits and vegetables.
Preposition	A word that connects a noun or noun phrase* to another word, phrase*, or clause*	I prefer the park by the creek to the one with the baseball diamond.

*Words marked with an asterisk are defined later in this section.

 For additional resources, please visit **ivyglobal.com/study**.

Noun and Pronoun Rules

Term	Definition	Example
Noun	A word that names a person, place, thing, or idea	The <u>ball</u> is as yellow as a <u>dandelion</u>.
Pronoun	A word that takes the place of a noun in a sentence*, referring to it instead of naming it again	John liked the spaghetti. <u>He</u> said <u>it</u> was the best spaghetti <u>he</u> had ever eaten!
Antecedent	The noun that a pronoun refers to	<u>John</u> liked the <u>spaghetti</u>. He said it was the best spaghetti he had ever eaten!
Subject and Object Pronouns	The subject (or subjective) form of a pronoun is used when the pronoun is the subject* of a clause*.	<u>She</u> told him that the test was at 3:00, and <u>he</u> told her that <u>he</u> would be on time.
	The object (or objective) form of a pronoun is used when the pronoun is the object* of a clause*.	She told <u>him</u> that the test was at 3:00, and he told <u>her</u> that he would be on time.
Personal Pronoun	A pronoun that refers to a person, or sometimes an animal or an object that is talked about like a person (e.g., a ship)	Anita likes watching my dog, Frank, honk his horn. <u>She</u> says that <u>he</u> plays it well.
Reflexive Pronoun	A special form of pronoun that should be used only when the antecedent appears in the same clause* as the pronoun, usually as the subject* of the clause* or sentence*	Kate blamed <u>herself</u> for letting the car break down, but I think that some of the blame falls on the car <u>itself</u>.
Grammatical Number: Singular Vs. Plural	Singular nouns and pronouns refer to one thing.	Try rolling the <u>ball</u> towards the pins. <u>It</u> will knock them over.
	Plural nouns and pronouns refer to more than one thing.	Try rolling the ball towards the <u>pins</u>. It will knock <u>them</u> over.
Irregular Noun	A noun whose plural form has a special spelling instead of following the normal rules for making nouns plural	The pond once had one duck and one <u>goose</u>. Now it has dozens of ducks and <u>geese</u>.
Grammatical Person: First, Second, and Third Person	First person pronouns ("I," "we," etc.) take the speaker or narrator as their antecedent.	<u>I</u> like books. Do you? <u>I</u> think that they are wonderful.
	Second person pronouns ("you") take the listener or reader as their antecedent.	I like books. Do <u>you</u>? I think that they are wonderful.
	Third person pronouns ("it," "they," etc.) take anything besides the speaker and listener as their antecedent.	I like books. Do you? I think that <u>they</u> are wonderful.
Possessive Nouns and Pronouns	Nouns and pronouns that express ownership	<u>Indra's</u> plants are always the healthiest. When I heard that only one plant was bearing fruit, I knew it was <u>hers</u>!
Possessive Determiners	A word that modifies a noun to show possession without adding an apostrophe or an "s" to the noun	I like the artist's watercolors, but not <u>her</u> oil paintings.

*Words marked with an asterisk are defined later in this section.

The following table shows the subject, object, possessive, and reflexive forms of the most common pronouns.

Subject Pronouns	Singular	Plural	Object Pronouns	Singular	Plural
First Person	I	we	First Person	me	us
Second Person	you	you	Second Person	you	you
Third Person	he, she, or it	they	Third Person	him, her, or it	them
Possessive Pronouns	Singular	Plural	Reflexive Pronouns	Singular	Plural
First Person	mine	ours	First Person	myself	ourselves
Second Person	yours	yours	Second Person	yourself	yourselves
Third Person	his, hers, or its	theirs	Third Person	himself, herself, or itself	themselves

Pronouns must agree with their antecedents in number.

The store was offering a good deal on the watch that I wanted, so I bought <u>them</u>.

Question	Answer
A) NO CHANGE B) those C) it D) they	The correct answer is (C) because the antecedent of the underlined pronoun is the singular noun "watch." The only choice that is a singular pronoun is (C), "it."

Pronouns with unclear antecedents should be replaced with clearer pronouns or with nouns.

The Senate and the House are the two chambers of Congress. The Senate is composed of 2 senators from each state, while <u>it is</u> composed of 435 representatives from the states, apportioned by population.

Question	Answer
A) NO CHANGE B) they are C) the Senate is D) the House is	The correct answer is (D) because the most logical antecedent in this comparison between the Senate and House is "the House," but the pronoun "it" is too unclear to express that. It looks as though "it" could refer to the Senate, but that doesn't make sense in this context.

A reflexive pronoun should only be used when the most logical antecedent occurs in the same phrase or clause, usually as the subject of the clause.

Peter was so frustrated when he discovered his own mistake that he could've kicked <u>him</u>.

Question	Answer
A) NO CHANGE B) his C) he D) himself	The correct answer is (D) because the underlined pronoun is the object of "kicked." In other words, the pronoun describes the person that "Peter … could've kicked." Based on the context, which explains that Peter was frustrated by "his own mistake," we can infer that Peter is annoyed with Peter. Since Peter is both the subject and the object, we can use the reflexive pronoun "himself."

Nouns should usually agree in number in comparisons or at other times when it would be illogical for noun number not to match.

The teacher asked her assistant to please remind the students to bring <u>their book</u> to school.

Question	Answer
A) NO CHANGE B) their books C) they're book D) they're books	The correct answer is (B). The incorrect answers show a variety of errors. (C) and (D) confuse "they're," which means "they are," with "their," a possessive pronoun. The difference between (A) and (B) is the number of the noun, and to answer correctly you must consider the logic and context: it does not make sense to imagine that the students all share one book. Even though each student may only have one book, collectively the students are more likely to have "books," so the plural noun is a better way of completing this phrase.

A personal pronoun should be used whenever the antecedent is a person.

> Carlo didn't win the race because he was fastest: he won the race because <u>it</u> had the most stamina.

Question
A) NO CHANGE
B) its
C) he
D) him

Answer
The correct answer is (C) because the antecedent is Carlo. It wouldn't make sense to say that the race had the most stamina. That's a personal characteristic, so Carlo is the most logical antecedent, and the correct choice is "he," a personal pronoun.

To make most nouns possessive, add an apostrophe and an "s," even to singular nouns that already end in "s." Plural nouns that end in "s" are different: add an apostrophe, but no extra "s." Possessive pronouns should use their possessive forms without apostrophes. Apostrophes should not be added to plural nouns that are not possessive.

> Never try to take a strange dog's food! While most <u>dog's</u> are friendly, some can become very defensive of their food, and may bite a stranger who attempts to take it from them.

Question
A) NO CHANGE
B) dogs
C) dogs'
D) dog

Answer
The correct answer is (B). In context, the verb "are" gives us a strong clue that the underlined noun should be plural. It also makes more sense to imagine that the word "friendly" describes "dogs" rather than their food. (B) is the only choice that correctly creates a plural non-possessive noun.

Possessive determiners should be used to modify other nouns to show possession rather than in place of possessive nouns or pronouns.

Mary I of England began <u>hers</u> reign as Queen of England and Ireland in 1553, and died just five years later in an influenza epidemic. This was much longer than the reign of Lady Jane Grey: <u>her</u> lasted just nine days before Mary deposed her!

Question	Answer
A) NO CHANGE B) her C) she D) she's	The correct answer is (B) because "her" is a possessive determiner. It can be used to modify the word "reign" in order to show that, in this sentence, the "reign" belongs to Mary I of England. (A), "hers," is a possessive pronoun, but it should be used on its own—not to modify another word. (C), "she," is a subject pronoun, is not possessive, and is not a possessive determiner, so it's not correct in this context. (D), "she's," might look possessive, but is a contraction of "she" and "is," not a possessive pronoun.
A) NO CHANGE B) her's C) hers D) she's	The correct answer is (C). In this sentence, the pronoun doesn't modify another word to show ownership—it stands in for "Lady Jane Grey's reign," so the possessive pronoun "hers" is the correct choice. (A), "her," is a possessive determiner—not the possessive pronoun. (B), "her's," incorrectly uses an apostrophe to try to make a pronoun possessive. (D), "she's," is not a possessive pronoun—it's a contraction of "she" and "is."

Irregular plural nouns usually don't end in "s," so it's necessary to add an apostrophe and an "s" to make them possessive. It's not necessary to add an "s" to make them plural.

The <u>children</u> were very happy to help with the cooking, but they were less enthusiastic about doing the dishes. They agreed to at least do their own dishes, but by bedtime all of the children's dishes were still in the sink.

Question	Answer
A) NO CHANGE B) childs C) child D) childrens	The correct answer is (A). (B), "childs," is incorrect because "child" is an irregular verb and cannot be pluralized by adding an "s." (C) is incorrect because "child" is a third person singular noun that doesn't agree with the verb "were." (D) is incorrect because "children" is plural without an "s."

Verb Rules

Term	Definition	Example
Subject	The noun that is executing the action expressed by a verb	Jorge and Frank own a bakery; while Frank bakes, Jorge staffs the sales counter.
Object	The noun that receives the action of a verb	Jorge and Frank own a bakery; while Frank bakes, Jorge staffs the sales counter.
Verb Number	Verbs use different forms to match the number of their subject.	Jorge's shoes are black, and his hat is white.
Verb Person	Verbs change forms to match the person of their subject.	Jorge is on the phone. He and Frank are baking crullers. I am going to the bakery. Are you?
Action and Linking Verbs	Linking verbs connect the subject to the object without expressing an action on the part of the subject.	Miguel is full.
	Action verbs express an action carried out by the subject.	Miguel ate a big lunch.
Verb Tenses	Past tense verbs indicate action in the past.	Darrell ran to the store.
	Present tense verbs indicate action in the present or routine action.	Darrell runs to the store.
	Future tense verbs indicate action in the future.	Darrell will run to the store.
	Perfect verb tenses express a completed action.	Darrell has run to the store.
	Progressive verb tenses express ongoing or continuous action.	Darrell is running to the store.
	Perfect and progressive tenses can be combined with past, present, or future tenses to make more complex verb tenses.	By this afternoon, Darrel will have been running to the store for hours.
Verb Moods	The indicative mood expresses a simple statement of fact.	I am bad at soccer.
	The subjunctive mood expresses a hypothetical statement.	If I were good at soccer, I would be happy.
	The conditional mood expresses an idea that depends on some other condition.	If I were good at soccer, I would be happy.
	The imperative mood expresses a command. Sentences in this mood often leave out the subject, in which case the subject is "you."	Be my soccer teacher.

Verbs must agree with their subjects in number and person.

Archaeologists who discover a new site typically <u>excavates</u> only a portion of the site, leaving the rest to be explored by future archeologists, who will likely have better tools and methods.

Question	Answer
A) NO CHANGE B) is excavating C) has excavated D) excavate	The correct answer is (D). Remember that the subject of a verb isn't necessarily the closest noun: "site" is a singular noun that's very close by, but if you actually ask "who is doing the excavating?" then it becomes clear that the word "archeologists" is the subject. (A), (B), and (C) all use verbs that only agree with singular subjects.

Verb tense and verb mood must be logical and consistent.

Buy milk from the store, but <u>you should buy</u> fruit from the corner stand. Don't forget the bananas.

Question	Answer
A) NO CHANGE B) you should have bought C) buy D) bought	The correct answer is (C). It maintains the present tense and imperative mood of the first part of the sentence. (A) is incorrect because it shifts the sentence from the imperative mood to the indicative mood. (B) is incorrect because it shifts the sentence to the indicative mood and the past tense. (D) is incorrect because it shifts to the past tense.

Clause and Sentence Rules

Term	Definition	Example
Clause	A verb and its subject, plus any objects and modifiers	Jude likes the soft cheese.
Phrase	A group of words that go together but don't form a whole clause	the soft cheese
Independent Clause	A clause that can stand on its own as a sentence because it expresses a complete idea	Jude likes the soft cheese.
Dependent Clause	A clause that can't stand on its own as a sentence because it does not express a complete idea	because it's easy to spread on a cracker.
Coordinating Conjunction	Conjunctions that connect other words, phrases, or clauses of equal importance in a sentence	Jude likes soft cheese <u>and</u> water crackers, <u>but</u> Moe bought cheddar <u>and</u> saltines.
Subordinating Conjunction	Conjunctions that connect a clause that provides additional but less important information to a main clause	Jude likes the soft cheese <u>because</u> it's easy to spread.
Dependent Marker Word	A subordinating conjunction, preposition, or pronoun that implies a subordinate relationship to another clause	Jude likes the soft cheese <u>because</u> it's easy to spread.
Sentence	A group of one or more clauses that includes at least one independent clause	Jude likes the soft cheese. Jude likes the soft cheese because it's easy to spread on a cracker.
Sentence Fragment	A phrase or dependent clause that's not attached to an independent clause	The soft cheese. Because it's easy to spread.
Run-on Sentence	A sentence that combines two or more independent clauses without proper punctuation or with a coordinating conjunction but no comma	Jude likes the soft cheese and it's easy to spread.
Comma Splice	A type of run-on sentence that uses a comma but no conjunction	Jude likes the soft cheese, it's easy to spread.
Fused Sentence	A type of run-on sentence that puts clauses together without any conjunctions or punctuation	Jude likes the soft cheese it's easy to spread.
Verb Voice	Clauses in the active voice have the action they describe as the main verb and the "doer" of the action as the subject.	The wind tore up my tent.
	Clauses in the passive voice have the "doer" of the main action as an object and the recipient as the subject, and usually use a linking verb as the main verb.	My tent was torn up by the wind.

Avoid fragments. Phrases can be connected to sentences in a variety of ways when they would otherwise be fragments.

The Little Ice Age. It was a period of climatic cooling in the Northern hemisphere for about 300 years.

Question	Answer
A) NO CHANGE B) The Little Ice Age it was. A C) The Little Ice Age it was a D) The Little Ice Age was a	The correct answer is (D). "The Little Ice Age" is a noun phrase, so it can serve as the subject of a sentence. "It" is a pronoun that refers, in this context, to "The Little Ice Age." In (A), the phrase is left as a fragment. (B) makes matters worse by removing the verb "was," thereby turning the other sentence into a noun phrase and leaving us with two fragments. (C) does put the fragment into the sentence, but it squeezes the noun and the pronoun together incorrectly. Only (D) corrects the problem by replacing the pronoun "it" with the noun to which it refers, creating one whole sentence.

One of the most potent tools of international relations is economic. The embargo, a ban on trade.

Question	Answer
A) NO CHANGE B) economic: the embargo, C) economic the embargo: D) economic the embargo	The correct answer is (B). Even though the second "sentence" in (A) has two elements, it's still a fragment because neither of them has a predicate, the part of the sentence with a verb. They're just two noun phrases that mean the same thing. (C) is incorrect because it incorrectly squeezes "the embargo" onto the end of the sentence with no punctuation before it, even though it places a colon after it. (D) is incorrect because it squeezes the whole phrase onto the sentence with no extra punctuation at all. Only (B) correctly uses a colon to attach the phrases, which specify the "tool" to which the sentence refers, to the end of this sentence.

Dependent clauses must be correctly connected to independent clauses to avoid fragments. Squishing two dependent clauses together doesn't make a whole sentence. Removing a dependent marker word can change a dependent clause into an independent clause.

Though Fulgencio Batista was broadly perceived as a corrupt dictator, <u>while he was</u> also staunchly pro-American.

Question	Answer
A) NO CHANGE B) though he was C) he was D) DELETE the underlined portion.	The correct answer is (C). "Though," at the beginning of the first clause, is a dependent marker word—and so is "while." That makes both clauses in (A) dependent clauses, which doesn't make a complete sentence. (B) replaces "while" with a different dependent marker word, which doesn't solve this problem. (D) removes "while," but it also deletes the verb, turning the clause into a phrase. A phrase and a dependent clause don't make a whole sentence: there must be at least one independent clause to make a complete sentence. Only (C) leaves an independent clause by removing "while" but leaving the verb "was."

Independent clauses must be connected to or separated from one another correctly to avoid run-on sentences.

Washington College is nearly three hundred <u>years old, George Washington was himself</u> part of its Board of Visitors and Governors, although he had no college education.

Question	Answer
A) NO CHANGE B) years old, George Washington; was himself C) years old. George Washington was himself D) years old, George Washington was himself:	The correct answer is (C). The clause ending with "years old" and the clause beginning with "George Washington" are both independent clauses. (A) connects them using only a comma, which is called a "comma splice" and is incorrect. (B) repeats the error and inserts a semicolon between a verb ("was") and its subject ("George Washington"). (D) repeats the error, but moves the colon to instead come between the verb and its object. Only (C) correctly splits these independent clauses into two whole sentences.

Coordinating conjunctions must come between the clauses that they connect, while subordinating conjunctions can come at the beginning of either the first or second clause. However, only one conjunction is needed to combine two clauses.

While credit cards were originally intended to be used primarily for large purchases, <u>though</u> they are now used for everyday expenses.

Question
A) NO CHANGE
B) but
C) although
D) DELETE the underlined portion.

Answer
The correct answer is (D). "While" and "though" are both subordinating conjunctions, or dependent marker words, so (A) has two dependent clauses—and two dependent clauses don't make a whole sentence. (C) repeats this error with a different subordinating conjunction. (B) uses a coordinating conjunction instead of a subordinating conjunction, but that doesn't work here; a coordinating conjunction connects two clauses of "equal rank." Since the first clause is a dependent clause, you can only connect it to another clause with a coordinating conjunction if that clause is also dependent.

The rule of law requires that all parties respect the outcomes of legal processes. <u>And that is</u> easier to do when the other side loses, it's just as essential when your own side loses.

Question
A) NO CHANGE
B) For that is
C) That is
D) While that is

Answer
The correct answer is (D). (A) and (B) both put coordinating conjunctions before the two independent clauses they are supposed to connect, but coordinating conjunctions can only connect two clauses by appearing in between them—that is, at the start of the second clause. Where they are now, they leave the sentence as a comma splice. (C) eliminates all the conjunctions, likewise leaving us with a comma splice. Only (D) corrects the problem by using a subordinating conjunction to make the first clause a dependent clause. An independent clause can come after a dependent clause with nothing but a comma to connect them.

Sentences or parts of sentences that have a parallel logical relationship should also have a parallel structure. The parts of speech and features like tense, mood, and voice should match closely between the two parts of the sentence.

Selling records, performing live, and <u>merchandise sales</u> are the main ways that bands make money.

Question	Answer
A) NO CHANGE B) selling merchandise C) the sale of merchandise D) merchandise being sold	The correct answer is (B). There are many ways that a sentence's structure can be made parallel: in this case, the first two items in a three-item list are gerund phrases. In other words, they use "-ing" forms of verbs as nouns. (A) uses a different kind of noun phrase, so it isn't quite parallel. (C) repeats this error. (D) uses a noun phrase with "merchandise." Although it does contain a word ending with "-ing," that word only modifies the noun rather than creating a parallel gerund phrase. Only (B) successfully matches the structure of the other two items in the list.

You should put clauses and sentences in a consistent voice, and you should generally avoid the passive voice.

While John answered customer calls and processed transactions, <u>packing and shipping the orders was done by me.</u>

Question	Answer
A) NO CHANGE B) packing orders was done by me, and shipping them as well. C) I packed and shipped the orders. D) done by me was the packing and shipping of orders.	The correct answer is (C). In this phrase, which is in the first person, the speaker (using the pronoun "I") is the one doing the action of packing the boxes. (A), (B), and (D) all make "packaging and shipping" the grammatical subject of the verb "was," which shifts the second clause of this sentence into the passive voice. Only (C) uses the active voice by making the doer of the action being described the grammatical subject of the compound verb "packed and shipped." Not only is it generally better to use the active voice rather than the passive voice, but in this sentence the first clause is in the active voice and the second clause should match.

Adjective, Adverb, and Conjunction Rules

Term	Definition	Example
Adjective	A word that adds descriptive information to a noun	<u>Blue</u> tokens are <u>worth</u> more than <u>red</u> tokens.
Adverb	A word that adds descriptive information to a verb, an adjective, or another adverb	Miguel sprinted <u>very</u> <u>well</u>, but Priya's lead was <u>too</u> big, so she <u>still</u> won the race.
Conjunctive Adverb	An adverb that links ideas by expressing the relationship between them	The bank offers a credit card with generous cash-back deals. <u>However</u>, the card also has high service fees.
Conjunction	A word that joins (or "conjoins") words, phrases, or clauses	We had pizza <u>and</u> cake at the birthday party, <u>but</u> we forgot the fruits <u>and</u> vegetables.

Memorize the coordinating conjunctions. You can use the acronym FANBOYS to help you remember them.

For, And, Nor, But, Or, Yet, So = FANBOYS

Coordinating conjunctions should always be preceded by a comma when they are used to connect independent clauses, but a coordinating conjunction should not be preceded by a comma when it connects two words or phrases rather than whole clauses.

The government is empowered to conduct warranted <u>searches but it is also</u> restrained from conducting unreasonable searches. No government official may search your <u>person, or, your</u> possessions unless there is a reasonable basis for the search.

Question	Answer
A) NO CHANGE B) searches, but it is, also C) searches but, it is also D) searches, but it is also	The correct answer is (D). The words that come after "but" form an independent clause, with "it" as the subject and "is" as the main verb. A comma is therefore needed before "but," and we can eliminate (A) and (C). There's no reason to put a comma before "also" in this sentence, so we can also eliminate (B).
A) NO CHANGE B) person or C) person, or D) person; or	The correct answer is (B). The conjunction "or" serves to connect two words: "person" and "possessions." Neither of these words makes a whole clause, so no comma is needed. (A) and (C) are both incorrect because they insert unnecessary commas. (D) is incorrect because it unnecessarily inserts a semicolon.

Memorize the most common conjunctive adverbs.

> also, besides, finally, however, indeed, instead, next, otherwise, still, then, further, likewise, moreover, thus

Be careful not to confuse conjunctive adverbs with conjunctions: conjunctive adverbs describe the connections between ideas, but they cannot be used alone to connect independent clauses. They can be the first word of new sentences, or they can be used at the beginning of an independent clause that is connected to the preceding clause by a colon or semicolon.

> Tokyo's population is about 50% larger than the population of <u>New York City, however New York City</u> occupies a much smaller area, so it has a higher population density than Tokyo.

Question	Answer
A) NO CHANGE B) New York City however, New York City C) New York City. However. New York City D) New York City. However, New York City	The correct answer is (D). "However" is being used as a conjunctive adverb in this context: it tells you about the logical relationship between the two sentences but doesn't connect them in the same way that a conjunction does. (A) is incorrect because it incorrectly treats "however" like a coordinating conjunction by using it to connect two independent clauses. (B) repeats the error but changes the placement of the comma. (C) sets the adverb "however" off as though it were a sentence, creating a sentence fragment.

> After the Revolutionary War, some called for George Washington to become the King of our young <u>nation; instead,</u> he resigned his post and retired to civilian life.

Question	Answer
A) NO CHANGE B) nation, instead, C) nation instead D) nation instead,	The correct answer is (A). "Instead," like "however," is a conjunctive adverb—not a conjunction. It therefore cannot be used to connect two sentences with only a comma. (B) and (D) use only commas, while (C) uses no punctuation at all.

Punctuation Rules

Term	Definition	Example
Period	A punctuation mark used at the end of a sentence that makes a statement or expresses a command	Trees, like houses, are made of wood.
Comma	A punctuation mark used within a sentence to separate parts of the sentence from one another for a variety of purposes	Trees, like houses, are made of wood.
Colon	A punctuation mark used within a sentence to introduce a list of items, a quotation, or a definition or direct explanation of the preceding clause	Trees are like houses: they are made of wood.
Semicolon	A punctuation mark used either between two related independent clauses or to set off lists that have internal punctuation from the rest of a sentence	I don't see why I should live in a house rather than a tree; they are both made of wood.
Quotation Mark	Punctuation marks used to indicate that a word or phrase is being quoted from another source, that the text is discussing a word rather than the thing it means, or that the writer has doubts about whether the word being used accurately describes the thing that it is intended to describe	The "experts" all tell me the same thing: "Human beings cannot live in trees."
Question Mark	A punctuation mark used at the end of a sentence that asks a question	Do you suppose that any of those experts have ever tried living in a tree?
Exclamation Point	A punctuation mark used at the end of a sentence that expresses strong feelings or shouting	The hypocrites tell me that I cannot do what they have not tried to do!
Apostrophe	A punctuation mark used to create the possessive form of a noun or pronoun, or to indicate a contraction	Doesn't a tree's canopy make a fine ceiling? Aren't a tree's roots a firm foundation?
Contraction	A word formed from two other words by omitting some letters and replacing them with an apostrophe	Do not try to tell me that a tree is not the same as a house—don't say it, it isn't necessary!
Dash	A punctuation mark used to set off an abrupt interruption	I know that a tree is not the same as a house—it is better than a house!
Essential Clause	A clause that modifies or specifies another part of the sentence in a way that is essential to understanding the meaning of the sentence	The tree that I live in is more beautiful than a mansion.
Nonessential or Parenthetical Clause	A clause that provides extra information that is not essential to understanding the meaning of the sentence	My tree, who I have named Enoch, is also my friend.

A period, question mark, or exclamation mark must be used to end a complete sentence, and the punctuation must match the meaning and tone of the sentence.

> Did you see who won the game <u>last night?</u> I wasn't watching.

Question
A) NO CHANGE
B) last night!
C) last night.
D) last night,

Answer
The correct answer is (A). The sentence is phrased as a question, so a question mark is an appropriate form of punctuation. (B) and (C) wouldn't make sense at the end of a question, and (D) creates a comma splice by using a comma to connect two independent clauses.

Lists should be correctly punctuated with commas or sometimes semicolons. Commas should come between each of three or more list items, and semicolons should be used if one or more of the list items has its own commas for other reasons. A comma before the word "and" at the end of a list is called a "serial comma" or an "Oxford comma," and while we use them in this book, the SAT does not directly test on the use or omission of serial commas.

> We'd like <u>two hamburgers, a meatball sub a gyro and three frankfurters</u>.

Question
A) NO CHANGE
B) two hamburgers; a meatball sub; a gyro, and three frankfurters
C) two hamburgers a meatball sub a gyro and three frankfurters
D) two hamburgers, a meatball sub, a gyro, and three frankfurters

Answer
The correct answer is (D) because it correctly uses commas between list items. (A) is incorrect because it omits a comma between "a meatball sub" and "a gyro." (B) is incorrect because it uses a mix of commas and semicolons to divide list items of equal importance. You can have a "list inside of a list" by separating less important items with commas, and larger categories with semicolons—but here, all the list items are in the same basic category. (C) is incorrect because it uses no punctuation at all to separate the items in the list.

Possessive nouns should make correct use of apostrophes as appropriate. Apostrophes should not be used to punctuate non-possessive plural nouns or possessive pronouns. Apostrophes should also be used to punctuate contractions.

> I like my wife's song's, but I don't like your's.

Question	Answer
A) NO CHANGE B) I like my wife's songs, but I don't like yours C) I like my wife's songs', but I don't like your's D) I like my wifes' songs', but I don't like yours'	The correct answer is (B). (A) is incorrect because it uses apostrophes in the non-possessive plural noun "songs" and in the pronoun "yours." (C) is incorrect for the same reasons as (A); it just moves the apostrophe on "songs" to make it look like a plural possessive, which doesn't make sense in context. (D) is incorrect for the same reason, because it moves the apostrophe on "wife's" to the end, and because it adds an apostrophe to "yours." The correct plural form of "wife" is "wives," so this is incorrect. Only (B) correctly uses apostrophes only on those words that require them.

Parenthetical clauses should be set off from the rest of the sentence using commas, dashes, or parentheses on both sides. The punctuation must match: if a comma is used on one side, a comma must be used on the other. If a parenthetical clause comes at the end of a sentence, then you can use a comma or dash at the beginning and a period at the end.

> The pirate waved her hook—the very same hook her mother had worn, and growled menacingly.

Question	Answer
A) NO CHANGE B) her hook—the very same hook her mother had worn; and growled C) her hook—the very same hook her mother had worn— and growled D) her hook, the very same hook her mother had worn and growled	The correct answer is (C). You can use either dashes or commas to set off parenthetical elements, but you have to use the same punctuation on both sides of the parenthetical element. (A) mixes a dash with a comma, (B) mixes a dash with a semicolon (which doesn't belong there in the first place), and (D) uses a comma at the beginning of the parenthetical but nothing at the end. Only (C) correctly uses a dash at the beginning and a dash at the end (commas in both places would've been fine, too).

Unnecessary punctuation should be removed. There are some places where the conventions of English indicate that punctuation is optional or requires a judgment call about the clarity of the sentence. The SAT doesn't have questions that will require you to make judgment calls about optional, stylistic punctuation; rather, it requires you to spot punctuation that plays no grammatical role and get rid of it.

It was, a difficult day: for all of us.

Question	Answer
A) NO CHANGE B) It was a difficult day for all of us. C) It was a, difficult, day, for all of us. D) It was a difficult day: for all of us.	The correct answer is (B). There's no need for punctuation in this sentence. None of the punctuation in (A), (C), or (D) serves any grammatical purpose.

Other Rules

Term	Definition	Example
Modifier	A general term for words and phrases that change other parts of the sentence by acting as adjectives or adverbs	Having finished my project, I'm going to play games with John, who's coming over tonight.
Misplaced Modifier	A modifier that is placed so that it seems to modify the wrong part of a sentence	I'm going to play games with John, who's coming over tonight, having finished my project.
Dangling Modifier	A modifier that is intended to modify a word or phrase that is not clearly stated in the sentence	Having finished my project, tonight is game night.
Comparative	An adjective or adverb that sets up a comparison by indicating that something has more or less of a property than another thing or things; usually ends in "-er"	My console is newer than John's.

Phrases used in comparisons must be logical and agree in terms of their structure and meaning. Keep parallel structure and noun number agreement in mind, but also make sure that comparisons involve like objects. Look for comparative words like "more" or "better," and match the words they describe.

I'm proud of how well I raise my livestock, but I have more work to do. The pigs on my farm are bigger <u>than my neighbor's farm,</u> but they're still not the biggest pigs in the county.

Question	Answer
A) NO CHANGE B) than my neighbor C) than my neighbor's pigs D) than the neighboring farm	The correct answer is (C). The comparative "bigger" describes "the pigs on my farm" or just "pigs," and "than" sets up a comparison that should include a like object. (A), (B), and (D) all compare pigs with something else—a neighbor or his farm. (C) compares one group of pigs to another, and therefore continues a logical comparison.

Modifiers should be placed directly next to the objects they modify to avoid misplaced and dangling modifiers.

Aiming carefully at the target, <u>the archer's bow was motionless as he held his breath</u>.

Question	Answer
A) NO CHANGE B) the archer's breath was still as he kept his bow motionless C) holding his breath, no movement shook the archer's bow D) the archer kept his bow motionless as he held his breath	The correct answer is (D). Notice the first phrase: "aiming carefully at the target." That's a modifier. It should be placed next to the object that it modifies, which, in this case, is most logically the archer. (A) places it next to the bow, and (B) places it next to breath—so those are both misplaced modifiers. (C) takes the archer out of the sentence altogether, mentioning only his breath and his bow—so that's a dangling modifier. Only (D) correctly places the object of the modifier right next to the modifier.

Some common words are easily confused with one another. Some commonly confused words have different meanings but similar spellings, and some have similar meanings but are used in different grammatical contexts.

	Definition	Correct Usage
Accept vs. Except	Accept: to receive or take as payment Except: with the exclusion of, or to exclude	We <u>accept</u> credit cards for purchases, <u>except</u> those under five dollars.
Affect vs. Effect	Affect: to influence or change, with the thing that is changed as the object of this verb; or (rarely), a physical display of emotion or feeling Effect: a result; or, to cause a change, with the change as the object of this verb	The rain did not <u>affect</u> our crop yield. This was not the expected <u>effect</u>. Bill sought to <u>effect</u> changes in environmental policy. Laura claimed indifference, but displayed an excited <u>affect</u>.
Its vs. It's	Its: the possessive form of "it" It's: contraction of "it is"	<u>It's</u> hard to tell when the baby will start crying. <u>Its</u> arched brows make it always appear upset!
Less vs. Fewer	Fewer: a smaller number of countable things Less: a smaller amount of something that can't be counted, doesn't have a plural form, or is referred to as a collective amount	<u>Fewer</u> people are opening their own businesses these days. Unfortunately, this means <u>less</u> money is being spent locally. <u>Less</u> local commerce also means <u>fewer</u> tax dollars for local government.
Precede vs. Proceed	Precede: to come before Proceed: to move forward	A loud noise <u>preceded</u> the fireworks. The officers told us to <u>proceed</u> with caution.
Their vs. They're vs. There	Their: the possessive form of "they" They're: contraction of "they are" There: at or in a place or position	The team practiced all year, and <u>their</u> hard work paid off. <u>They're</u> going to the statewide championship. <u>They're</u> the first team we've sent <u>there</u> in years.
Than vs. Then	Than: a conjunction used to compare Then: next or soon after	I told her I liked peas more <u>than</u> candy. <u>Then</u> she really thought I was lying!
Too vs. To	Too: in addition, also, or excessively To: a preposition used to show direction toward a point	Please drive <u>to</u> the market this afternoon. Make sure you bring the coupons, <u>too</u>: you don't want to spend <u>too</u> much.
Whose vs. Who's	Whose: the possessive form of "who" Who's: contraction of "who is"	<u>Who's</u> going to the store with me? Judy is. Now, <u>whose</u> car should we take?
Your vs. You're	Your: the possessive form of "you" You're: contraction of "you are"	<u>You're</u> too talented to give up acting. Plus, <u>your</u> voice is incredible!
Who vs. Whom	Who: a pronoun referring to a person, used when the pronoun is a subject Whom: a pronoun referring to a person, used when the pronoun is an object	<u>Who</u> brought the salad? To <u>whom</u> should I return the bowl?

Correct sentences that misuse commonly confused words.

The children looked inside the bucket, but <u>there marbles weren't their</u>.

Question	Answer
A) NO CHANGE B) their marbles weren't there C) their marbles weren't their D) there marbles weren't there	The correct answer is (B). There are two different words from a set of frequently confused words here: "their" and "there." "Their" is the possessive form of "they," and "there" refers to the location of a thing, or the fact of its existence. (B) correctly uses "their" to identify the children's marbles, and "there" to indicate that they weren't in the place the children looked (that is, inside the bucket).

Prepositions have specific meanings and must be used logically. Pay attention to preposition use in questions that also include other problems of grammar or usage.

The bard told us many <u>tales of</u> adventure, evoking powerful feelings in all of us.

Question	Answer
A) NO CHANGE B) tales as C) tails of D) tails as	The correct answer is (A). A "tale" is a story; a "tail" is the part of an animal that sticks out behind it. It makes more sense that the bard told stories than that he told animal parts, so (C) and (D) are incorrect. "Of" is a preposition that can specify the type of a thing, and "as" (when used as a preposition) indicates that something is being used in a certain way, has a certain function, or is occurring during a certain time. It makes more sense that the bard told the type of stories that are about adventures than that he told stories that had the function of being an adventure, so (B) is incorrect.

Expression of Ideas
Part 2

Expression of Ideas questions on the Writing and Language section of the SAT ask you to correct errors of logic, style, and tone in the context of the passage. You'll need to learn and apply a variety of rules for good writing and pay attention to the logical progression of ideas in the passage to do your best on these questions. The Writing and Language test includes 24 Expression of Ideas questions, so they account for a little more than half of the 44 questions in the Writing and Language section.

Rules for Organization

Sentences should come in a logical order. Pay attention to chronological order of events, the introduction and development of ideas, and pronouns, which should usually come after the antecedent to which they refer.

> [1] Before any large building can be constructed, there must be an extensive planning and design phase. [2] Once budgets and work plans are in place, construction can begin. [3] The planning stage of any large project involves budgeting for the project and creating work plans that will allow the project to be completed within the budget. [4] During the construction phase, however, things don't always go as planned.

Question	Answer
To make this paragraph most logical, sentence 3 should be placed A) where it is now. B) before sentence 1. C) before sentence 2. D) after sentence 4.	The correct answer is (C). Consider the ideas in sentence 3, and their relationships to other ideas in the paragraph. (A) and (D) are both incorrect because they put the events in the passage out of chronological order. Overall, the paragraph is discussing the phases of a construction project, and it makes the most sense to discuss those phases in the chronological order in which they occur. Sentence 3 discusses "the planning stage," and explains what that entails: budgeting and work planning. Sentence 1 begins "before" the project, and introduces the idea of a planning stage, so sentence 3 should not come before sentence 1, and (B) is incorrect. Sentence 2 describes what can happen after budgets and plans are in place, so sentence 3—which discusses the creation of budgets and work plans during the planning phase—should come before sentence 2.

[1] When work doesn't go as planned, cost overruns can occur and cause serious problems. [2] Either option is likely to make investors unhappy. [3] If costs run much higher than the planned budget for a project, then managers must either raise additional funds or scale back their plans. [4] In the worst cases, concerned investors may actually withdraw from failing projects, making funding problems even worse.

Question	Answer
To make this paragraph most logical, sentence 2 should be placed A) where it is now. B) before sentence 1. C) after sentence 3. D) after sentence 4.	The correct answer is (C). Consider the language of sentence 2, which refers directly to other ideas: the sentence begins with "either option." Such a reference should generally come right after the "options" to which it is referring. Neither sentence 1 nor sentence 4 discuss "options;" instead, they focus on problems and possible consequences. Only sentence 3 discusses a pair of options, so it makes the most sense to place sentence 2 after sentence 3.

Paragraphs should also fall in a logical order. Pay attention to the chronological order of events and references to ideas that are discussed in other paragraphs. If an idea is introduced in one paragraph, then paragraphs that provide detailed information about the idea should come later. If a paragraph draws a conclusion or contrast, then paragraphs providing details about the ideas upon which the conclusion is based should usually come earlier. If a paragraph begins or ends with transitional language that suggests a direct contrast or comparison, then the contrasting paragraph should come directly before or after the paragraph that contains the contrasting language—before an initial sentence that suggests a comparison, or after a final sentence that suggests a comparison.

— 1 —

There are around 100 living species of marine reptiles. Most living marine reptiles are easily recognized as relatives of terrestrial reptiles who have adapted to life in the ocean, including sea turtles, saltwater crocodiles, and sea snakes.

— 2 —

Most living marine reptiles spend some time on land. Sea turtles, for example, return to land to lay eggs. Marine iguanas and saltwater crocodiles also come onto land to lay eggs and to rest and bask in the sun.

— 3 —

During the Mesozoic era, the seas were filled with a variety of huge marine reptiles. These huge, highly specialized animals looked as remote from their terrestrial cousins as whales and dolphins do from terrestrial mammals today. Large, predatory reptiles like plesiosaurs and mosasaurs were the dominant marine predators. While those great beasts have gone extinct, reptiles still have a place in the world's oceans.

— 4 —

There are, however, some marine reptiles that spend their entire lives in the water. The Olive Sea Snake mates and gives live birth in the sea, and spends its entire life hiding and hunting in the reefs around Australia.

Question	Answer
To make the passage most logical, paragraph 3 should be placed A) where it is now. B) before paragraph 1. C) before paragraph 2. D) after paragraph 4.	The correct answer is (B). Consider the final sentence of paragraph 3: it suggests a contrast between the extinction of the Mesozoic marine reptiles—discussed in this paragraph—and the place that reptiles still have in the world's oceans. That suggests that the following paragraph should discuss the contrasting idea of the place that marine reptiles have in the oceans today. Paragraph 1 best discusses the overall place of marine reptiles in the world's oceans today, so the best choice is to place paragraph 3 before paragraph 1.

An introduction should focus on the main idea that will be discussed in a paragraph or essay. It should not focus on a single detail that is not the focus of the paragraph or essay, nor should it focus on ideas that are not discussed further in the body of the passage.

<u>Anacreon was a Greek lyric poet who composed works that were intended to be accompanied by instruments like the lyre.</u> The music of the national anthem, "The Star Spangled Banner," was actually taken from a British song called "To Anacreon in Heaven." This earlier piece was the song of the Anacreontic Society, a club of wealthy men who met in taverns for concerts and parties. It contained references to Greek gods associated with revelry, romantic love, satire, and mockery—worlds away from the stirring, patriotic imagery of "The Star Spangled Banner."

Question	Answer
Which choice most effectively sets up the main idea of the paragraph? A) NO CHANGE B) The "Star Spangled Banner" is the national anthem of the United States of America. C) Gentlemen's clubs, which would assemble for members-only social events, were once a common part of British and American social life. D) The national anthem of the United States is regarded with patriotism and reverence, but it may have a surprisingly irreverent history.	The correct answer is (D). The paragraph discusses the history of the music of the national anthem as the song of a group of men who met for parties, and describes the lyrical references to satire, mockery, and revelry—all irreverent themes. It contrasts this history with the "stirring, patriotic imagery" of "The Star Spangled Banner." (D) best introduces the overall idea of this contrast. (A) focuses on providing information about Anacreon, who is only a minor detail in the rest of the paragraph. (B) explains that "The Star Spangled Banner" is the national anthem, but the next sentence also explains that, and while understanding that detail is important, it does not introduce the broader focus of the paragraph. (C) provides a detail that is largely irrelevant.

Transitional sentences should connect the ideas that come before and after them. They should not focus on just one of the ideas or on unrelated details.

[1] The role of selective breeding in animals is quite clear to anyone who has spent time reading about the staggering array of dog breeds available as pets. [2] There are nearly 1,000 varieties of banana in the world, and they are produced in 135 countries. [3] For example, the banana strains grown for food today bear little resemblance to their wild ancestors, which are packed with hard seeds and mostly inedible.

Question	Answer
Which choice provides the most effective transition between sentences 1 and 3? A) NO CHANGE B) However, selective breeding has also had a profound effect on many familiar plants. C) These artificially selected breeds can have unusual characteristics. D) Dogs are commonly kept as pets, but may also be used as work animals.	The correct answer is (B). Sentence 1 discusses the role of selective breeding in animals, while sentence 3 provides an example of a plant that has been shaped by selective breeding. The correct answer must provide a transition between animals and plants. (A) provides information about bananas, which are discussed in sentence 3, but provides no transition from ideas about animals. (C) offers a general comment on how natural selection can lead to "unusual" characteristics, but offers no clear transition from animals to plants. (D) discusses the role of dogs, but offers no transition to plants.

Conclusions should focus on the main idea of a paragraph or passage, and may provide a summary of the argument or explain the overall connection between the ideas. They should not introduce totally new ideas or focus excessively on a specific detail rather than the main idea.

Not all of us take color-coding very seriously, but it's a common habit of some very serious people. Lawyers often use color-coded highlighting to categorize their notes, and intelligence analysts for the Air Force and other organizations use color-coding systems when taking notes to distinguish between sources of intelligence and forms of information. Many successful businesses also use color-coded filing systems to help employees stay organized in the complex world of business. You can also buy color-coded sticky notes and color-coded tabs to add to the pages of books.

Question	Answer

Question

Which choice provides the most effective conclusion for the paragraph as a whole?

A) NO CHANGE

B) Color is also believed to influence mood and behavior, and taking color-coded notes may also influence memory.

C) In addition to being well-organized, most successful businesses use effective planning to set and achieve goals.

D) Given its important role in the lives of high-achieving people, maybe we should all take color-coding a little more seriously.

Answer

The correct answer is (D). The paragraph begins by observing that some of us do not take color-coding seriously, but then provides several examples of professions generally regarded as "serious" in which professionals frequently use color-coding. (D) brings these things together, and clearly summarizes the purpose of the paragraph: to suggest that we should all take color-coding more seriously than some of us do. (A) and (B) merely introduce new pieces of information, rather than offering any conclusion or even clearly following from a preceding sentence. (C) does build on an idea in the preceding sentence, which is about how businesses use color-coding as an organizational tool, but by branching off into a discussion of tools other than color-coding it moves away from the central theme of the paragraph.

Transition words and phrases should express appropriate logical relationships between the elements of a passage that they link.

A standard barcode must be visible in order to be scanned. <u>Likewise,</u> an RFID chip can be scanned even when it's hidden from view.

Question

A) NO CHANGE

B) However

C) Thus

D) Indeed

Answer

The correct answer is (B). The first sentence indicates that a barcode must be visible to be scanned; the second sentence indicates that an RFID chip does not need to be visible when scanned. There's a contrast between these ideas, and "however" is the only option that expresses that contrast. (A) suggests a similarity, (C) suggests a cause-and-effect relationship, and (D) suggests a relationship in which the second sentence confirms or expands upon the first.

Rules for Interpreting Graphs

Pay attention to titles, legends, data labels, units, and axis labels in the graph, so that you know what information the graphic shows and how it shows it. Some answer options will be incorrect because they use the wrong units or otherwise misread these keys parts of the graphics.

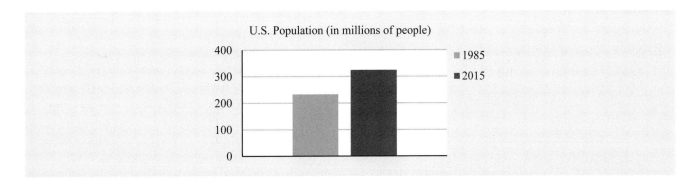

Question	Answer
Which choice offers the best interpretation of information in the graph? A) The population of the United States grew by about 100 between 1985 and 2015. B) The population of the United States declined by about 100 between 1985 and 2015. C) The population of the United States grew by about 100 million between 1985 and 2015. D) The population of the United States declined by about 100 million between 1985 and 2015.	The correct answer is (C). According to the legend, the darker bar represents the population in 2015, and the lighter bar represents the population in 1985. The bar for 1985 is just above 200 while the bar for 2015 is just above 300, and the title indicates that the graph shows U.S. population "in millions," so the chart shows an increase of about 100 million between 1985 and 2015. (A) is incorrect because it ignores the unit (millions) stated in the title. (B) ignores the unit and confuses the bars. (D) includes the unit but confuses the bars.

Correlation does not imply causation, so you should avoid picking a choice that states that one thing causes another only because they seem to be statistically connected on a graph. Always look for additional evidence of a cause-effect relationship in the passage before selecting an answer choice that suggests such a relationship.

Julian opens his concession stand on Friday afternoon and closes it on Sunday afternoon. After looking at average sales from his concession stand, Julian noticed that, on average, <u>eating more corndogs caused people to buy more soda.</u>

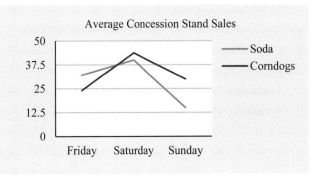

Question	Answer

Question

A) NO CHANGE

B) drinking more soda caused people to buy more corndogs.

C) sales of both corndogs and soda were lowest on Sunday.

D) customers bought the greatest amounts of both corndogs and soda on Saturday.

Answer

The correct answer is (D). It offers a straightforwardly correct reading of the chart without making assumptions that go beyond the scope of the question. (A) and (B) are incorrect because they both speculate about one thing causing another without any support from the passage. While corndog sales and soda sales both increase on Saturday, we can't determine from the information provided whether one increase caused the other. (C) is incorrect because it misreads the data: while soda sales are at their lowest point on Sunday, corndog sales are at their lowest on Friday.

Percentages and rates don't tell you everything that you need to know to figure out total amounts, so if you only have a chart that shows percentages, you can't make assumptions about total amounts.

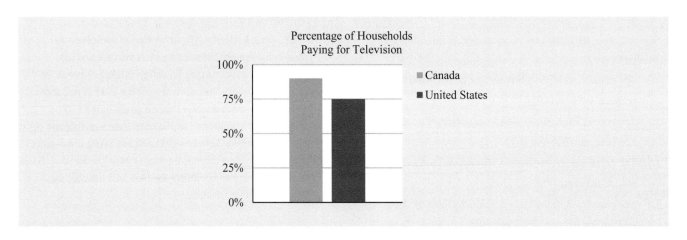

Question

Which choice offers the best interpretation of information in the graph?

A) There are more Canadians paying for television than Americans doing so.

B) A higher percentage of households pay for television in Canada than in America.

C) A higher percentage of Canadians than Americans watch television.

D) Canadians watch more television than Americans.

Answer

The correct answer is (B). The data in the chart show that ~75% of U.S. households pay for television, while ~90% of Canadian households do so. (A) is incorrect because a higher percentage of a different population doesn't necessarily mean a larger number of people. In fact, the U.S. population is about nine times as large as the Canadian population, so this statement is not only unsupported by the information provided but also untrue. (C) and (D) are incorrect because they discuss television viewing habits, which are not addressed by the graphic.

Rules for Word and Phrase Choices

Word and phrase choices should be precise: the best word or phrase means exactly what is intended. It's not better to use a word or phrase that's fancier but less precise.

As a child, I thought that orange juice and cranberry juice tasted better <u>synthesized</u> than on their own.

Question	Answer
A) NO CHANGE B) coalesced C) united D) blended	The correct answer is (D). "Blended" best captures the sense of being mixed together as juices might be. All the other word choices mean something like "blended," but have specific connotations that make them imprecise in this context. Something that is "synthesized" is made from a combination of other things, but that word generally connotes new chemical compounds, ideas that are put together, or sounds that are mixed together. Something that is "coalesced" is a combination of once-separate things, but the word suggests that the mixed elements came together on their own by some natural process. Something that is "united" is brought together, but that word generally refers to groups of people brought together by a shared purpose.

Word and phrase choices should be concise: when given a choice between options that mean the same thing, it's usually better to pick the shortest option. However, sometimes the shortest option omits important information, so look out for choices that leave out important information.

Jett unfolded her map and tried to figure out <u>which direction to follow in order to proceed in the desired orientation.</u>

Question	Answer
A) NO CHANGE B) which way to go C) which way led the way she would go D) which way to go using the map	The correct answer is (B) because it does not include any unnecessary words or phrases that repeat information from elsewhere in the sentence. (A) is incorrect because it uses wordy phrases like "in order to," and because "which direction to follow" is redundant with "the desired orientation." (C) is incorrect because "way" is unnecessarily repeated. (D) is incorrect because the first part of the sentence already tells us that she's using the map, and that does not need to be restated.

The style and tone of words and phrases should match the overall style and tone of the passage.

> The prisoner lay shaking on the pallet. He was almost in tears. Memories of home flickered in his mind's eye. It was <u>super depressing</u>.

Question	Answer
A) NO CHANGE B) a real downer C) the most gruesome, woesome, horrible fate D) a miserable situation	The correct answer is (D). The short sample of text available has a sad, negative tone and a simple, but formal style. (A) uses the intensifier "super," which is very colloquial and informal. (B) uses an informal idiom. (C) uses a list of several adjectives to describe the prisoner's "fate," which conflicts with the simple style of the other sentences.

The way that words and phrases are organized and connected within a sentence should be logical and clear. Sentences with oddly ordered elements or elements that are connected in a confusing way should be revised so that they are clearer: modifiers should be next to the elements that they modify, pronouns should be positioned so that it's easy to identify their antecedents, and parenthetical elements should sometimes be changed into subordinate clauses or other forms that don't interrupt the flow of the sentence.

> <u>The phalanx, pointing their spears forward, was a formation of heavily armed soldiers at different angles, *hoplites*.</u>

Question	Answer
A) NO CHANGE B) *Hoplites*, heavily armed soldiers, in a formation with their spears at different angles, pointing forward, were what a phalanx was. C) The phalanx was a formation of *hoplites*, heavily armed soldiers, who pointed their spears forward at different angles. D) The phalanx was, in formation, *hoplites*, heavily armed soldiers, who, with their spears at different angles, pointed their spears forward.	The correct answer is (C) because it orders the elements of the sentence in the way that most clearly expresses the relationships of the elements to one another and the overall idea of the sentence. (A), (B), and (D) are all made from roughly the same phrases as (C), but the phrases are placed in orders that make it difficult to sort out their relationships. For example, (D) uses the phrase "in formation" in between "phalanx" and "*hoplites*" in an attempt to express the idea that the phalanx was a formation of *hoplites*, or a group of *hoplites* in formation—but it's unclear whether it describes the phalanx or the *hoplites*.

Section 4
Math

The Math Test will test certain topics in math as well as your ability to use reasoning and critical thinking to solve real-world problems in science and in the social sciences. The Math Test includes one section where you may use your calculator and one where you may not. These questions are further divided into four subject areas, as detailed below.

Anatomy of the Math Test		
Section	Number of Questions	Amount of Time
No-Calculator Section	20 questions	25 minutes
Calculator Section	38 questions	55 minutes
Total	**58 questions**	**80 minutes**

Subject Area	Topics Covered	Number of Questions	
		Calculator	No-Calculator
Heart of Algebra	Fundamental concepts in algebra involving linear equations and inequalities	11	8
Passport to Advanced Math	More advanced concepts in algebra involving polynomial and other nonlinear equations	7	9
Problem Solving and Data Analysis	Interpreting qualitative and quantitative data and analyzing relationships	17	0
Additional Topics in Math	Geometry, trigonometry, and complex numbers	3	3
Total		**38**	**20**

Heart of Algebra
Part 1

The **Heart of Algebra** questions on the Math Test require you to analyze, solve, and create linear equations, inequalities, and systems of equations and inequalities. There are 11 Heart of Algebra questions in the Calculator portion and 8 Heart of Algebra questions in the No-Calculator portion, representing approximately 33% of the Math Test. While this section will focus on linear expressions and equations, the terms and techniques that you will find here can also be used on quadratic and higher-order expressions and equations.

Linear Expressions and Equations

This section covers fundamental algebraic tools, terms, and mathematical principles that you need to know on the Math Test.

Term	Definition	Examples
Variable	An unknown number, usually represented by a letter	x, y, z, N, or A
Constant	An unchanging number in an expression	$-987, -2, -0.56, 0, \frac{3}{4}, 1, 382.9$
Coefficient	The constant in front of any variable	2 in $2y$, -5 in $-5u$, 1 in x*, -1 in $-g$ *Any variable by itself has a coefficient of 1
Term	A single variable or number, or variables and numbers multiplied together	$6x, 89g, -2bvc$
Like Terms	Terms that have the same variable raised to the same power	x and $8x$, y^3 and $-7y^3$, $-t$ and t
Expression	A mathematical "phrase" containing numbers, variables, and operations ($+, -, \times, \div$)	$9x, 7y - 2x, -abc + 2 + \frac{45x}{5} - 6h$
Equation	A set of two expressions that are equal to each other	$9x = 36, -5uc + 21 = 7y$
Polynomial	An expression with multiple terms	$-abc + 2 + \frac{45x}{5} - 6h$

	Mathematical Principles	
Distributive Property	Multiplying a number by the sum of numbers in parentheses is the same as multiplying it by each number separately and then adding the results. This also works for division.	$a(b+c) = ab + bc,$ $\dfrac{b+c}{a} = \dfrac{b}{a} + \dfrac{c}{a}$
Factoring Linear Expressions	The opposite of distributing: pulling out a number that multiplies into every term in an expression	$5x + 5y - 10 = 5(x + y - 2)$ $-2y - 4c - 6x = -2(y + 2c + 3x)$
Isolating Variables	Getting a variable by itself on one side of an equation	$4x - 33 = 3$ $4x = 36$ $x = 9$

Essential Techniques

You can **simplify an algebraic expression** by adding or subtracting like terms. To add or subtract like terms, add or subtract their coefficients. You can also simplify expressions by multiplying and dividing.

$$5x + 6x = 11x \qquad\qquad \frac{4x}{2x} = 2 \qquad\qquad \frac{6x}{3} = 2x$$

Remember to use the distributive property to help you factor, multiply, and divide expressions with more than one term:

$$\frac{8x + 4y + 12c}{2x} = \frac{4(2x + y + 3c)}{2x} = \frac{2(2x + y + 3c)}{x}$$

If on the SAT you are asked to "**solve for x**," you need to find a value for x that makes the equation true. For more complicated algebraic equations, you will need to manipulate the equation before you can solve for the unknown variable.

Sometimes you will see an equation that has two different variables in it, such as $y = 2x + 6$. You will not be able to find a value for x or y without more information, but you can solve for one variable in terms of the other. This means that your answer will still contain a variable. To solve for one variable in terms of the other, use the same steps as for single-variable equations and treat the second variable as if it were a number.

Question	Answer
$3y - 15xy + 21x = a(y - 5xy + 7x)$ What is the value of a in the equation above that satisfies all values of x and y?	The correct answer is 3. The greatest common factor of all terms on the left side of the equation is 3: $3y = 3(y)$, $-15xy = 3(-5xy)$, and $21x = 3(7x)$. Since this factor is represented by a in the question, a is equal to 3.

Questions 1 and 2 refer to the following information.

The number of cows, c, and the number of ducks, d, a farmer has in her 4 acres of land is represented by the equation $\dfrac{2c}{3} + \dfrac{4d}{12} = 4$.

1

Given the equation above, what is $6c$ in terms of d?

A) $2d$

B) $36 - 3d$

C) $3d$

D) $48 - 4d$

The correct answer is (B). You need to get $6c$ on one side of the equation. To do this, multiply each side by 9, then isolate $6c$:

$$9 \times \left(\frac{2c}{3} + \frac{4d}{12}\right) = 36$$

Simplify the equation and isolate $6c$:

$$6c + 3d = 36$$
$$6c = 36 - 3d$$

2

If the farmer has 6 ducks, how many cows does she have?

A) 2

B) 3

C) 4

D) 5

The correct answer is (B). You solve for the number of cows by plugging 6 into the original equation, where the variable d is, and then solving for c:

$$\frac{2c}{3} + \frac{4(6)}{12} = 4$$
$$12 \times \frac{2c}{3} + 12 \times \frac{24}{12} = 12 \times 4$$
$$8c + 24 = 48$$
$$c = 3$$

Inequality and Absolute Value Equations

Linear inequalities and absolute value equations are extensions of linear equations. While inequalities and absolute value equations occur less frequently on the Math Test directly, understanding their underlying logic is essential to quickly solving many questions on the test.

Term	Definition	Example
Inequality	A mathematical statement comparing two quantities that are not the same, or that might not be the same	$3 > -1$, $3d \le x$
Absolute Value	The distance from zero of a number on a number line, which is always positive or equal to zero	$|5| = 5$, $|-4| = 4$
Number Line	A line on which consecutive numbers are marked at intervals	

>	greater than This is represented by an unshaded circle with a shaded arrow pointing right on a number line.	$0 > -1$ $7 > 6$ $5x > 9ay$
<	less than This is represented by an unshaded circle with a shaded arrow pointing left on a number line.	$0 < 1$ $-3 < -1$ $u < 8$
≥	greater than or equal to This is represented by a shaded circle with a shaded arrow pointing right on a number line.	$8 \geq 7$ $8 \geq 8$ $-1 \geq 6x$
≤	less than or equal to This is represented by a shaded circle with a shaded arrow pointing left on a number line.	$8 \leq 9$ $8 \leq 8$ $8 \leq -y$

Essential Techniques

To **solve an inequality**, manipulate the inequality to isolate your variable. Just as with an equation, you can add or subtract the same number from both sides of an inequality and the inequality will still be true. However, be careful when multiplying or dividing. Multiplying or dividing both sides of an inequality by a positive number does not change the inequality, but multiplying or dividing by a negative number reverses the inequality: $-x < 3$ is equivalent to $x > -3$.

For example, the number line below shows the possible solutions for $x > 1$:

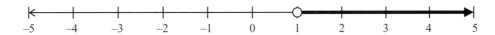

All numbers greater than 1 are possible solutions for this inequality, so a shaded line extends to the right of 1. The number 1 is not a possible solution for this inequality, so there is an unshaded circle over the number 1.

On the SAT, you may need to solve an absolute value equation using algebra. Here is an important rule to remember:

$$\text{If } |x| = a, \text{ then } x = a \text{ or } x = -a.$$

You may also need to solve an absolute value inequality on the SAT. Here are two rules for absolute value inequalities:

$$\text{If } |x| < a, \text{ then } -a < x < a.$$
$$\text{If } |x| > a, \text{ then } x < -a \text{ or } x > a.$$

You can always check your answer by making sure that a value from your possible solutions for the variable makes the original inequality true.

Question	Answer
If $-2a + 10 > 4b$, and a is an integer, what is the maximum value of a if b is 1?	The correct answer is 2. First plug in $b = 1$: $$-2a + 10 > 4$$ $$-2a > -6$$ Divide both sides by -2, and remember to reverse the inequality: $$a < 3$$ Since a is an integer, the maximum value for a is 2.
$$\lvert b - 9 \rvert \le 0.2$$ A construction company produces cold-drawn steel bars with a length, in inches, of b. The inequality above is used to determine whether the bars' lengths conform with the company's requirements. What is a possible length, in inches, for one of the company's steel bars that meets these requirements?	The correct answer is any value for b where $8.8 \le b \le 9.2$. You can solve this problem by solving for the range of b, using the rule above: $$-0.2 \le b - 9 \le 0.2$$ $$8.8 \le b \le 9.2$$

Systems of Equations and Inequalities

Every Math Test will have several questions that require you to solve a system of equations or inequalities. These questions will appear both in algebraic and in text form and can be solved using either substitution or elimination methods, which are detailed below.

Term	Definition	Example
System of Equations	A group of equations that share like terms	$x + 3y = 5$ $y - x = -1$
System of Inequalities	A group of inequalities that share like terms	$x + 3y \ge 5$ $y - x < -1$
Transform	To multiply or divide both sides of an equation by the same quantity	$4x = 2y$ to $8x = 4y$, $\times 2$ $4x = 2y$ to $-2x = -y$, $\div -2$

Mathematical Principles		
Substitution Method	First, isolate a variable in either equation. Next, substitute the value of the variable into the second equation, and solve this equation for the other variable. Finally, plug the value of the solved variable into either one of the original equations, and solve for the remaining variable.	$x + y = 3$ and $2x - y = 12$ $x = 3 - y$ $2(3 - y) - y = 12$ $y = -2$ $x = 5$
Elimination Method	This allows you to cancel variables by adding or subtracting the two equations. For example, if you add these two equations together, the y in the first will cancel out the y in the second.	$x + y = \ \ 3$ $+ (2x - y) = 12$ $3x = 15$

Question	Answer
A pet store sells puppies for $400 each and adult dogs for $300 each. If the store collected $5000 from a total of 15 puppies and adult dogs last month, how many adult dogs did the pet store sell?	The correct answer is 10. Since the total number of puppies and dogs sold is 15, you can express the relationship between the pets as $p + d = 15$. Because puppies are sold for $400 and dogs for $300, you can set up a second equation where the total amount collected is $400p + 300d = 5000$. Next, isolate d by multiplying the first equation by 400, and subtract the second equation from the first equation: $$400p + 400d = 6000$$ $$- (400p + 300d = 5000)$$ $$100d = 1000 \text{ so } d = 10$$

Linear Functions

In this section, linear functions and their notation are explained; once you get used to the notation, solving linear functions on the Math Test is usually straightforward.

Term	Definition	Example
Function	A function is a relationship between an input, often x, and an output, often $f(x)$. Linear functions take the form of linear equations.	$f(x) = 2x$ $g(x) = -5x$ $A(x) = 9x - 2$
Evaluate	To replace the variable in the function with the given input and find the value of the function	If $f(x) = 2x$, then $f(3) = 2 \times 3 = 6$
Domain	The domain is the set of all values for which the function generates an output. On a graph, this is all the x values for which there is a corresponding y-value.	If $f(x) = x - 1$, x can be any real number
Range	The range is the set of all values that could be the output of the function. On a graph, this is all the y-values for which there is a corresponding x value.	If $f(x) = x - 1$, $f(x)$ can be any real number If $f(x) = |x| - 2$, $f(x)$ must be ≥ -2

Essential Techniques

The chart below represents the value of the input, x, and output, $f(x)$, for the function $f(x) = 2x - 3$. You can see how the function acts as a rule for what happens to the input to generate the output. You multiply each input by 2 and then subtract 3.

x	1	2	3	4
$f(x)$	−1	1	3	5

As noted in the terms above, functions can also be graphed on a coordinate plane; this will be discussed in the next section. For now, you need to know that the input, x, of a function generates its output.

On the SAT, you might see **compound functions**, where a function is embedded in another function, such as the one in the sample question below:

Question	Answer
If $f(x) = 3x - 4$ and $g(x) = 8x$, what is the value of $f\left(g\left(\frac{1}{2}\right)\right)$?	The correct answer is 8. First, find $g\left(\frac{1}{2}\right)$. Then, use that answer and plug it into $f(x)$: $$g\left(\frac{1}{2}\right) = 8\left(\frac{1}{2}\right) = 4$$ $$f(4) = 3(4) - 4 = 8$$

Graphing Equations

Linear equations, inequalities, and absolute value equations can all be graphed on a coordinate plane. In this section, we will explain how to identify and graph them.

Type	Description	Example
Standard Line Equation	$y = mx + b$ y is the y-axis value, m is the slope of the line, x is the x-axis value, and b is the y-intercept value.	$y = -2x + 3$ $y = \frac{1}{2}x - 7$
Slope	Slope is how steep a line is. It is represented by m in the standard equation of a line.	$y = -2x + 3$: $m = -2$ $y = \frac{1}{2}x - 7$: $m = \frac{1}{2}$
Parallel Lines	Two lines whose slopes are equal	$y = 2x + 4$ and $y = 2x - 5$
Perpendicular Lines	Two lines whose slopes are the negative reciprocals of each other, which means their product is -1	$y = 3x + 7$ and $y = -\frac{1}{3}x - 1$

y-intercept	The *y*-intercept is the point where the line crosses the *y*-axis. This is *b* in the standard equation of a line.	$y = -2x + 3: b = 3$ $y = \frac{1}{2}x - 7: b = -7$
Horizontal Line Equation	This equation is $y = b$, where b represents the point where the line crosses the *y*-axis.	$y = 5, y = -2, y = 0$
Vertical Line Equation	This equation is $x = a$, where a represents the point where the line crosses the *x*-axis.	$x = \frac{2}{3}, x = 2, x = -2$

Mathematical Principles

Calculating the Slope of a Line	Slope is calculated according to: $$m = \frac{y_2 - y_1}{x_2 - x_1}$$ Where one point on the line has the coordinates (x_1, y_1) and a second point on the line has the coordinates (x_2, y_2).	Slope facts: • Vertical lines have undefined slopes. • Horizontal lines have slopes of 0. • A slope is positive if the line goes up from left to right. • A slope is negative if the line goes down from left to right.

Graphs of Equations and Inequalities

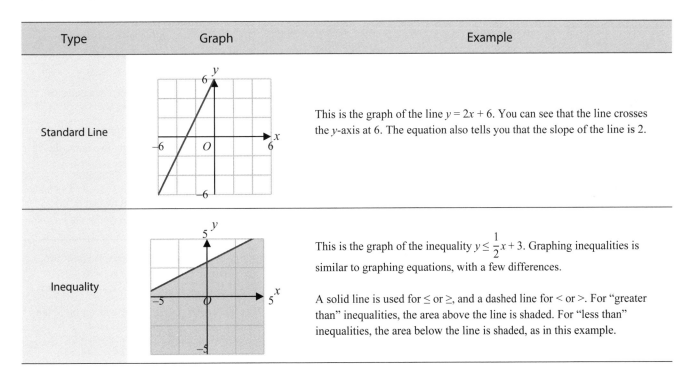

Type	Graph	Example
Standard Line		This is the graph of the line $y = 2x + 6$. You can see that the line crosses the *y*-axis at 6. The equation also tells you that the slope of the line is 2.
Inequality		This is the graph of the inequality $y \leq \frac{1}{2}x + 3$. Graphing inequalities is similar to graphing equations, with a few differences. A solid line is used for $\leq$ or $\geq$, and a dashed line for $<$ or $>$. For "greater than" inequalities, the area above the line is shaded. For "less than" inequalities, the area below the line is shaded, as in this example.

Absolute Value	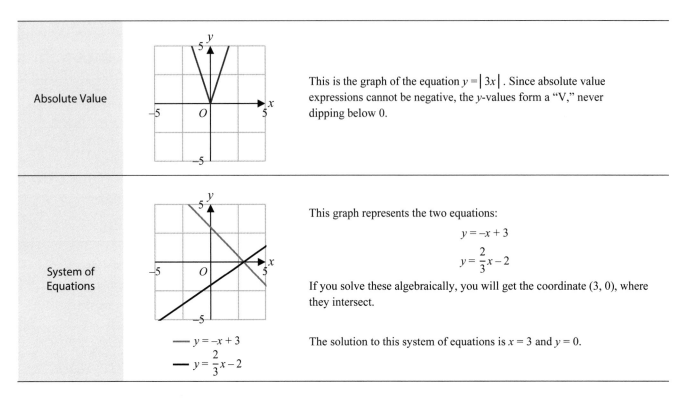	This is the graph of the equation $y = \lvert 3x \rvert$. Since absolute value expressions cannot be negative, the y-values form a "V," never dipping below 0.
System of Equations		This graph represents the two equations: $$y = -x + 3$$ $$y = \frac{2}{3}x - 2$$ If you solve these algebraically, you will get the coordinate $(3, 0)$, where they intersect. The solution to this system of equations is $x = 3$ and $y = 0$.
	—— $y = -x + 3$ —— $y = \frac{2}{3}x - 2$	

Mathematical Principles		
Shift Up or Down	If you start with the function $f(x) = ax$, you can shift the function vertically b units by adding b to the right side of the function: $$f(x) = ax + b$$ If b is positive, the function shifts b units up. If b is negative, the function shifts b units down.	If $f(x) = 2x + 8$ is shifted up two units, the resulting function is $f(x) = 2x + 10$. If $f(x) = 2x + 8$ is shifted down two units, the resulting function is $f(x) = 2x + 6$.
Shift Left or Right	If you start with the function $f(x) = ax$, you can shift the function horizontally b units by taking the function of $x + b$: $$f(x + b) = a(x + b)$$ If b is positive, the function shifts b units to the left. If b is negative, the function shifts b units to the right.	If $f(x) = 2x + 8$ is shifted right two units, the resulting function is $f(x) = 2(x - 2) + 8$. If $f(x) = 2x + 8$ is shifted left two units, the resulting function is $f(x) = 2(x + 2) + 8$.
Stretching a Function	If you start with the function $f(x) = ax + b$, you can stretch the function by multiplying by c: $$c \times f(x) = cax + cb$$ This means that all the y-values are stretched by a factor of c. The x-intercept coordinates are the only pair that remain the same.	If $f(x) = 2x + 8$ is stretched by a factor of two, the resulting function is $2 \times f(x) = 4x + 16$. If $f(x) = 2x + 8$ is stretched by a factor of $\frac{1}{2}$, the resulting function is $\frac{1}{2} \times f(x) = x + 4$.
x-axis Reflection	To reflect a function about the x-axis, multiply the whole function by -1.	If $f(x) = 2x + 8$ is reflected about the x-axis, it becomes $-1 \times f(x) = -2x - 8$.
y-axis Reflection	To reflect a function about the y-axis, take the function of $-x$.	If $f(x) = 2x + 8$ is reflected about the y-axis, it becomes $f(-x) = -2x + 8$.

Essential Techniques

Linear equations and functions are graphed in the same way; you simply treat $f(x)$ as your y-value. Therefore, the graph of $f(x) = -2x - 3$ is the same as the graph of $y = -2x - 3$.

Some questions on the SAT will require you to create or recognize the transformation of a linear function.

Question	Answer

Line L has an equation of $3 - 5x = 2y$. If Line M is drawn perpendicular to Line L, what is the slope of Line M?

The correct answer is 2/5 or 0.4. In order to solve this problem, first put Line L in $y = mx + b$ form:

$$2y = -5x + 3$$
$$y = -\frac{5}{2}x + \frac{3}{2}$$

You now can find that the slope of Line L is $-\frac{5}{2}$. Since Line M is perpendicular to Line L, you can find the slope of Line M by taking the negative reciprocal:

$$-\frac{1}{\left(-\frac{5}{2}\right)} = \frac{2}{5}$$

If the graph below is reflected about the x-axis, what is the y-intercept of the new line?

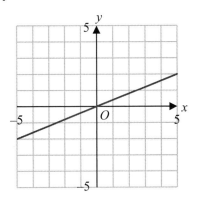

The correct answer is 0. If a line $f(x) = mx + b$ is reflected about the x-axis, it becomes $-1 \times f(x) = -mx - b$, meaning that the y-intercept changes from b to $-b$. However, the original y-intercept of this line is 0, so the y-intercept of this line remains 0 after being reflected about the x-axis.

Passport to Advanced Math
Part 2

The **Passport to Advanced Math** questions cover important topics for college-level math, focusing on expressions, equations, and functions. This content is similar to Heart of Algebra, but with one major difference—every question uses nonlinear math. There are 16 Passport to Advanced Math questions, representing about 28% of the Math Test: 7 in the Calculator Section and 9 in the No-Calculator Section. This section will focus on polynomials and quadratic equations, as well as their graphs.

Polynomial Expressions

This section covers basic polynomial operations such as adding, subtracting, multiplying, and dividing, as well as factoring polynomials. Here is a list of terms and techniques that you should know for this section:

Term	Definition	Example
Degree	The degree of a polynomial is the highest exponent that appears in it.	The degree of $4x^2 + 7x - 3$ is 2, because $4x^2$, the highest term, has an exponent of 2.
Linear, Quadratic, and Cubic Polynomials	A linear polynomial has degree 1.	$x + 5$
	A quadratic polynomial has degree 2.	$x^2 - 7x - 2$
	A cubic polynomial has degree 3.	$-2x^3 + x^2 - x + 5$
Rational Expression	An expression consisting of one polynomial divided by another	$\dfrac{x^2 + 8x - 4}{x + 6}$

Mathematical Principles		
Adding or Subtracting Polynomials	Group the like terms and then simplify.	$(3x^2 - 12x + 11) - (2x^2 - 5x + 6)$ $= 3x^2 - 2x^2 - 12x + 5x + 11 - 6$ $= x^2 - 7x + 5$
Multiplying Polynomials	Use the distributive property to ensure that each term in the first polynomial is multiplied by each term in the second.	$(a + b + c)(x + y + z)$ $= ax + ay + az + bx + by + bz + cx + cy + cz$ All the terms in the second bracket are first multiplied by a, then by b, and finally by c.
	When multiplying terms with the same base, add the exponents.	$(x^2 + 2x)(x - 5)$ $= x^3 - 5x^2 + 2x^2 - 10x$ $= x^3 - 3x^2 - 10x$
Dividing Polynomials	Use synthetic division, explained below.	$\dfrac{x^4 + 3x^3 - 11x^2 - 3x + 10}{x - 2} = x^3 + 5x^2 - x - 5$

Factoring polynomials—rewriting them as the product of smaller-degree polynomials—is an important skill for the Math Test. Here is a table outlining the most common methods to factor polynomials:

Mathematical Principles		
Factoring Quadratic Polynomials if $a = 1$	The answer will look like: $$x^2 + bx + c = (x + p)(x + q).$$ Make sure that $pq = c$ and $p + q = b$.	$x^2 - 7x + 12 = (x - 3)(x - 4)$
Factoring Quadratic Polynomials if $a \neq 1$	The answer will look like: $$ax^2 + bx + c = (mx + p)(nx + q).$$ Make sure that $pq = c$, $mn = a$, and $mq + np = b$.	$3x^2 - 13x - 10 = (3x + 2)(x - 5)$ In this example, $pq = -10 = c$, $mn = 3 = a$, and $mq + np = -15 + 2 = -13 = b$.
Factoring a Difference of Squares	Use the formula: $$a^2 - b^2 = (a - b)(a + b)$$	$25x^2 - 9y^2$ Here a is $5x$ and b is $3y$, so $(a - b)(a + b) = (5x - 3y)(5x + 3y)$.
Factoring a Sum of Cubes	Use the formula: $$a^3 + b^3 = (a + b)(a^2 - ab + b^2)$$	$8x^3 + y^6$ Here a is $2x$ and b is y^2, so $(a + b)(a^2 - ab + b^2) = (2x + y^2)(4x^2 - 2xy^2 + y^4)$.
Factoring a Difference of Cubes	Use the formula: $$a^3 - b^3 = (a - b)(a^2 + ab + b^2)$$	$27y^3 - 64$ Here a is $3y$ and b is 4, so $(a - b)(a^2 + ab + b^2) = (3y - 4)(9y^2 + 12y + 16)$.
Factoring Higher-Degree-Polynomials	Find a value $x = r$ that makes that polynomial equal to 0. Then divide the polynomial by $x - r$ using synthetic division, explained below. Repeat this process until the polynomial cannot be factored further.	$x^3 - 4x^2 + x + 6$ You need an x-value that will make $x^3 - 4x^2 + x + 6 = 0$. Using basic trial and error, this value could be -1. Next, use synthetic division, explained below, and factor to get the answer: $$x^3 - 4x^2 + x + 6 = (x + 1)(x - 2)(x - 3)$$ When applying trial and error, use only factors of the constant term, in this case ± 1, ± 2, ± 3, or ± 6. $x^3 + 2x^2 + x - 2 = (x - 2)(x^2 + 1)$ In this example, $x^2 + 1$ cannot be factored further, so this is the final answer.
Simplifying Rational Expressions by Factoring	Factor the numerator and denominator as much as possible and then cancel out any common factors.	$\dfrac{x^2 + 7x + 12}{x^2 - 9} = \dfrac{(x + 3)(x + 4)}{(x + 3)(x - 3)} = \dfrac{x + 4}{x - 3}$

Essential Techniques

Sometimes you will be required to divide a higher-degree polynomial by a linear polynomial as a step in factoring it. The easiest way to do this is through synthetic division. Let's say you want to divide the polynomial $x^4 + 3x^3 - 11x^2 - 3x + 10$ by the polynomial $x - 2$. Set up the synthetic division like this:

$$
\begin{array}{c|ccccc}
 & 1 & 3 & -11 & -3 & 10 \\
2 & & & & & \\
\hline
 & & & & &
\end{array}
$$

Write the coefficients of the polynomial you are dividing in the top row in order, starting with the highest term. As you work down to the lowest term, if the polynomial skips a term, then write a 0 for that term's coefficient. For example, if there is no second-degree term but there are third- and first-degree terms, then you would write the coefficient for the third-degree term, followed by 0 for the second-degree term, and then the coefficient for the first-degree term. If you are dividing by $(x - a)$, write a in the bottom left. In this case, $a = 2$. The first step is easy: just bring down the first coefficient to below the horizontal line.

$$
\begin{array}{c|ccccc}
 & 1 & 3 & -11 & -3 & 10 \\
2 & & & & & \\
\hline
 & 1 & & & &
\end{array}
$$

Now, multiply the number below the line by the 2 on the left, and write that number below the second coefficient. Add the numbers vertically, and write their sum below the line:

$$
\begin{array}{c|ccccc}
 & 1 & 3 & -11 & -3 & 10 \\
2 & & 2 & & & \\
\hline
 & 1 & 5 & & &
\end{array}
$$

Now, multiply the 5 by the 2 on the left, and write the result below the -11. Continue this process as you work your way to the right:

$$
\begin{array}{c|ccccc}
 & 1 & 3 & -11 & -3 & 10 \\
2 & & 2 & 10 & -2 & -10 \\
\hline
 & 1 & 5 & -1 & -5 & 0
\end{array}
$$

If the polynomial expression is divisible by the linear expression, the rightmost number below the line will be 0. If you don't end with a 0, then you are left with a remainder and you know that the polynomial is not divisible by the linear expression. The numbers below the line simply give the coefficients for the solution: $x^3 + 5x^2 - x - 5$. This means that $\dfrac{x^4 + 3x^3 - 11x^2 - 3x + 10}{x - 2} = x^3 + 5x^2 - x - 5$.

Because you are dividing, the degree of the resulting polynomial will always be one less than you started with. If you start with a 4th degree polynomial, the solution will start with an x^3 term instead of an x^4 term.

Question	Answer
Which of the following is equal to $2x^2 + x - 3$? A) $(2x + 3)(x + 1)$ B) $(2x + 3)(x - 1)$ C) $(x + 3)(2x + 1)$ D) $(x + 3)(2x - 1)$	The correct answer is (B). Since you know that $mq + np = b$, you can eliminate both (A) and (C), because $mq + np$ is greater than 1 in these two expressions. Calculating $mq + np$ in (D) gives you 5, so the correct answer is $2x^2 + x - 3 = (2x + 3)(x - 1)$.
If $2x^3 + 3x^2 - 5x - 6$ divided by $x + 1$ is $(ax + b)(cx - d)$, what is the value of $\dfrac{bd}{ac}$?	The correct answer is 3. Use synthetic division to divide the third degree polynomial by $(x + 1)$ to get $(2x^2 + x - 6)$. Next, factor the quadratic polynomial normally to get $(x + 2)(2x - 3)$. Since bd is 6 and ac is 2, $\dfrac{bd}{ac} = 3$.

Quadratic Equations

Like linear functions, there are unique terms and techniques that you need to know in order to quickly solve, rewrite, and interpret quadratic equations.

Term	Definition	Example
Quadratic Equation	An equation involving a quadratic polynomial	$2x^2 - 4x + 3 = 0$
Root	A solution for x in a quadratic equation	$x^2 - 2x - 15 = 0$ factors to $(x - 5)(x + 3) = 0$. Solving for x, the roots of this equation are 5 and −3.
Extraneous Solution	A solution that works mathematically, but that doesn't make sense in a real-life context or A solution found through the normal process of solving a problem, but that is mathematically invalid	For example, length and time can never be negative. In the expression $y = \dfrac{1}{x}$, there is never a solution where x equals 0, because $\dfrac{1}{0}$ is undefined.
Quadratic Formula	The formula used to find the roots of a quadratic equation	$x = \dfrac{-b \pm \sqrt{b^2 - 4ac}}{2a}$

Solving Quadratic Equations		
Concept	Rules	Example
Solving Quadratic Equations by Factoring	If a quadratic polynomial is equal to 0 and you can factor it, you can find the possible values for x by setting each of the factors to 0 and solving for x.	$x^2 + x - 6 = 0$ $(x + 3)(x - 2) = 0$ $x = -3$ or $x = 2$
Solving Quadratic Equations using the Quadratic Formula	If a quadratic polynomial is equal to 0 and you cannot factor it, you can use the quadratic formula to find the possible values for x. There may be 0, 1, or 2 solutions.	$x^2 - x - 1 = 0$ $x = \dfrac{1 + \sqrt{5}}{2}$ or $x = \dfrac{1 - \sqrt{5}}{2}$
Solving Higher-Degree-Polynomial Equations	Factor the polynomial and find the possible values for x by setting each of the factors to 0 and solving for x.	$x^3 - 4x^2 + x + 6$ $= (x + 1)(x - 2)(x - 3)$ $x = -1$ or $x = 2$ or $x = 3$
Solving Rational Equations	Manipulate the equation so that one rational expression is equal to 0, then factor the numerator to find when it is equal to 0. Remember to test all your solutions to make sure that they do not make the denominator equal to 0. If they do, they are not solutions to the equation.	$\dfrac{x^2 + 3x + 2}{x + 1} = 0$ $\dfrac{(x + 1)(x + 2)}{x + 1} = 0$ $x = -1$ or $x = -2$ However, $x = -1$ is impossible because it makes the denominator 0. So $x = -2$ is the only solution.

Graphing Quadratic Equations and Functions

Quadratic functions are functions that take the form of a quadratic equation. For example, $f(x) = x^2 + 3x - 5$ is a quadratic function. When these functions are graphed on an xy-plane, it is understood that $y = f(x)$.

The simplest quadratic function is $f(x) = x^2$. Its graph is shown below:

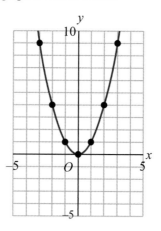

The type of curve created by graphing quadratic functions is called a **parabola**. Parabolas can move up or down, be wider or narrower, or flip upside down, but they will always retain this basic shape. Notice that the parabola above is symmetric about the y-axis. All parabolas are symmetric about a vertical line drawn through their vertex, which is the highest or lowest point. The vertex of the parabola above is $(0, 0)$.

Transformations of Quadratic Functions

Manipulating a function algebraically will move or stretch the graph of the function on the coordinate plane. Below is a summary of various algebraic transformations of quadratic functions and their graphs. The basic parabola is given by the equation $f(x) = x^2$.

Geometric Transformation	Equation After Modification
Shift the parabola up by a units.	$f(x) = x^2 + a$
Shift the parabola down by a units.	$f(x) = x^2 - a$
Shift the parabola left by a units.	$f(x) = (x + a)^2$
Shift the parabola right by a units.	$f(x) = (x - a)^2$
Stretch the parabola by a factor of a. (Note that if $a > 1$ this will make the parabola thinner, and if $0 < a < 1$ this will make the parabola wider.)	$f(x) = ax^2$
Flip the parabola so it opens down.	$f(x) = -x^2$

Below are some examples of parabolas with the functions associated with them. Note that you can also combine shifts, stretches, and flips.

$f(x) = (x - 1)^2$

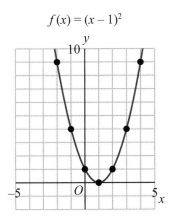

$f(x) = 2x^2$

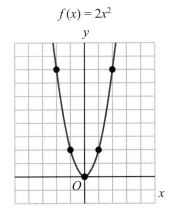

$f(x) = -x^2$

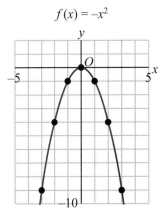

You can tell a lot about the shape of a parabola from its equation. Below is a chart to help you determine key features of a parabola. The equation for the sample parabola is $f(x) = ax^2 + bx + c$. Here are its features:

Geometric Feature	Algebraic Expression
x-coordinate of the vertex	$-\dfrac{b}{2a}$
y-coordinate of the vertex	$f\left(-\dfrac{b}{2a}\right)$
x-intercept(s)	Solutions to $ax^2 + bx + c = 0$ (if they exist)
y-intercept	c
Stretch Factor	a
Vertical Axis	$x = -\dfrac{b}{2a}$
Direction of Opening	Upward if $a > 0$, downward if $a < 0$

Essential Techniques

Sometimes you will be required to solve a system of equations involving one linear equation and one quadratic equation. The best way to do this is to use substitution and then solve the resulting quadratic equation. There may be 0, 1, or 2 solutions. Let's see this technique in action.

Question	Answer
$y + 30 = x^2 + 3x$ $y - 5x = 90$ If the solutions to the system of equations above are (a, b) and (c, d), what is $a + b + c + d$?	The correct answer is 192. You can rearrange the second equation to solve for y and then substitute this into the first equation to get $5x + 90 + 30 = x^2 + 3x$. You can rearrange this quadratic equation and solve it to get $x = -10$ or $x = 12$. Plugging these values into the second equation and solving for y, you get $y = 40$ or $y = 150$. Therefore, the solutions are $(-10, 40)$ and $(12, 150)$. Now $a = -10$, $b = 40$, $c = 12$, and $d = 150$, so $a + b + c + d = 192$.

Exponential, Rational, and Radical Equations

Exponential, rational, and radical equations can also be quickly solved if you are clear on their basic principles and how to manipulate them.

Term	Definition	Example
Exponential Equation	An equation with a variable as part of an exponent	$3^x = 27$
Rational Equation	An equation with a variable as part of a rational expression	$\dfrac{15}{2x-1} = -3$
Radical Equation	An equation with a variable under a radical	$\sqrt{x+2} = 4$

Below is a list of helpful tricks to use when working with these equations. These techniques will help you manipulate these equations until they are in the form you want.

Principles for Operations on Exponents and Radicals		
Concept	Rule	Example
Multiplying Expressions with the Same Base	Add the exponents. If they have a different base, first convert the terms to the same base.	$(2^x)(2^{x+1}) = 2^{2x+1}$
Dividing Expressions with the Same Base	Subtract the exponents. In general, $x^{-a} = \dfrac{1}{x^a}$	$\dfrac{3^{3x}}{3^x} = 3^{2x}$
Taking the Exponent of an Exponent	Multiply the exponents.	$\left(2^x\right)^5 = 2^{5x}$
Multiplying Radicals	Multiply all terms under the radicals.	$\sqrt{a} \times \sqrt{b} = \sqrt{ab}$
Equality of Expressions with the Same Base	When two expressions with the same base are equal, this means that their exponents must be equal.	$3^x = 3^7$ Therefore, $x = 7$.
Eliminating a Radical in an Equation	Square both sides of an equation to eliminate the radical. Make sure to isolate the radical first.	$\sqrt{x-4} = 5$ $x - 4 = 25$
Checking Extraneous Solutions	When solving a rational or radical equation, always check your solutions by substituting them into the original equation.	$\dfrac{6x-6}{x-1} = 0$ $x = 1$ is not a solution because it makes the denominator 0. This equation has no solution.

Question	Answer

Question

If $4^{2x+3} = 2^x 2^{4x}$, what is the value of x?

Answer

The correct answer is 6. You can use many of the exponent rules discussed above to manipulate this equation as follows:

$$4^{2x+3} = 2^{5x}$$
$$(2^2)^{2x+3} = 2^{5x}$$
$$2^{4x+6} = 2^{5x}$$
$$4x + 6 = 5x$$
$$x = 6$$

Question

If $2\sqrt{x+8} - 4 = x + 1$, what is the value of x?

Answer

The correct answer is 1. You can rearrange this equation so the radical is alone on the left side, and then square both sides, as follows:

$$2\sqrt{x+8} = x + 5$$
$$4(x+8) = x^2 + 10x + 25$$
$$x^2 + 6x - 7 = 0$$
$$x = -7 \text{ or } x = 1$$

Remember to check your answers by plugging them back into the original equation.

$$\text{Check: } 2\sqrt{-7+8} - 4 \neq -7 + 1$$
$$\text{Check: } 2\sqrt{1+8} - 4 = 1 + 1$$

Therefore, the only solution is $x = 1$.

Applications of Functions

The functions discussed in this chapter have several real-world applications. In this section you'll get a look at applications of quadratic and exponential functions that you might see on the SAT. Below is a table of some useful things to remember about how to interpret the equations of various functions:

Concept	Algebraic/Graphical Interpretation
The x-value(s) when a quantity being modeled by a quadratic equation (e.g. height) is equal to 0.	The solution(s) for x when the quadratic is set equal to 0. These are the x-intercept(s) of the graph.
The value of a quantity being modeled by a quadratic when the x-value (e.g. time) is equal to 0.	The solution for y when $x = 0$. This is the y-intercept of the graph.
The initial amount of a quantity (e.g. population) being modeled by an exponential equation	The value of a when $y = a(r)^{tx}$. This is the y-intercept of the graph.
The growth factor of a quantity being modeled by an exponential equation	The value of r when $y = a(r)^{tx}$.
The number of times a quantity changes by the growth factor during one unit of time, x, in an exponential equation	The value of t when $y = a(r)^{tx}$.

Below are two examples of situations that can be modeled by exponential growth:

Situation	Equation
A colony of bacteria that begins with 100 cells doubles in size every hour. What function models the colony's rate of growth, if y is the size of the colony and x is the number of hours that have passed?	$y = 100(2^x)$
The half-life of a certain compound is 5 years, meaning that after a period of 5 years passes, half of any sample of this compound will have decayed. A scientist has 3 kilograms of this substance. What equation models the amount of the substance remaining in kilograms, y, if x is the number of years that have passed?	$y = 3\left(\dfrac{1}{2}\right)^{\frac{x}{5}}$

Exponential functions create graphs that look like this:

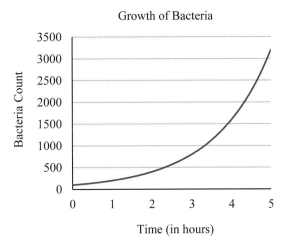

Linear, quadratic, and exponential functions can all be used to model situations. In the long run, exponential functions will grow faster than quadratic functions, which will grow faster than linear functions. The following graph compares these three equation types:

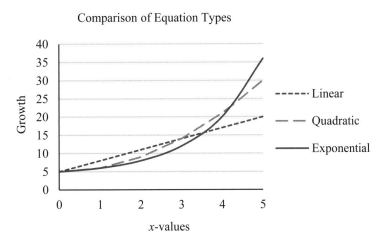

Below are some questions that require you to use your understanding of applications of quadratic and exponential functions.

Question	Answer

Questions 1 and 2 refer to the following information.

Juana throws a paper airplane. Its height h meters above the ground at time t seconds after she releases it is given by the equation $h = -t^2 + 3t + 10$.

1

After how many seconds does the airplane fall to the ground?

The correct answer is 5. The plane hits the ground when $h = 0$, since it will be 0 meters above the ground. You can now substitute this, and solve the quadratic equation normally.

$$0 = -t^2 + 3t + 10$$
$$t = -2 \text{ or } t = 5$$

However, since time can never be negative, the solution $t = -2$ is extraneous. Therefore, $t = 5$.

2

How many meters above the ground was the airplane when Juana released it?

The correct answer is 10. You know that Juana releases the plane at $t = 0$, so you can substitute this into the equation and solve for $h = 10$.

3

The population of minnows in a pond doubles every six months. If there are 500 minnows in the pond at the start of 2010, which of the following equations models the number of minnows in the pond, m, if x is the number of years that have passed since 2010?

A) $m = 500\left(2^{2x}\right)$

B) $m = 500\left(2^{\left(\frac{1}{2}\right)x}\right)$

C) $m = 500(2^x)$

D) $m = 2(500^x)$

The correct answer is (A). The initial population is 500, so you know $a = 500$. The growth factor is 2, so $r = 2$. The number of times the population doubles in one year is 2, so $t = 2$. Therefore, the equation is $m = 500\left(2^{2x}\right)$.

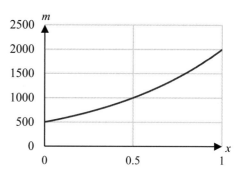

Problem Solving and Data Analysis
Part 3

Problem Solving and Data Analysis deals with how to measure and convert information, how to look at it in various forms, and how to interpret its meaning. This section will show you how to analyze ideas and theories using numbers, text, tables, and different types of diagrams. There are 17 Problem Solving and Data Analysis questions (including problem sets) in the Calculator section and none in the No-Calculator section. Problem Solving and Data Analysis represents about 29% of the Math Test.

Ratios, Percentages, Proportions, and Rates

Ratios, percentages, proportions, and rates compare two or more quantities, either by comparing parts to a whole or by representing a relationship between quantities. Some of the problems involving these topics will require more steps or more complex algebra than the examples we have seen so far.

Term	Definition	Example
Ratio	Comparison of two numbers or two values that is often represented with a colon: this can be parts to parts, parts to wholes, or whole to wholes	1 inch : 5 miles 5 books : 41 games
Proportion	A ratio stated as a fraction, or a comparison of two ratios	If there are 5 green marbles and 10 blue marbles in a bag, then: 1 : 2 (ratio of green to blue) $\frac{1}{3}$ (proportion of marbles that are green)
Percent	A ratio expressed as parts per one hundred, where one hundred is the whole	2 is 20% of 10 because $\frac{2}{10} = \frac{2}{10} \times \frac{10}{10} = \frac{20}{100} = 20\%$
Rate	Comparison of two values with different units, often a rate of change over time	5 km/h 10 words/line
Percent Change	Comparing new and old values via percentage, which can be an increase or a decrease: $\frac{\text{new} - \text{old}}{\text{old}} \times 100\%$	If you had 4 cats and now you have 5, the percent change in number of cats is $\frac{5-4}{4} = \frac{1}{4} = \frac{25}{100} = 25\%$
Growth Factor	The portion of a number by which that number increases or decreases, usually expressed as a decimal	If you have $50 and you make $10 every hour, then in the first hour your wealth increases by: 20% (percent change) 1.20 (growth factor)

Conversion Factor	The ratio between two different units, expressed as a fraction where the numerator and the denominator must be equal	$$\frac{60 \text{ seconds}}{1 \text{ minute}} \quad \text{or} \quad \frac{1 \text{ meter}}{100 \text{ centimeters}}$$ **Note:** While the Math Test gives you most units of conversion, they expect you to know seconds in a minute and centimeters in a meter.

Essential Techniques

To convert between ratios, rates, and units, you need to set up your problem so that you can isolate the ratio or variable that you are solving for. In some cases, you will sometimes need to set up conversion factors in order to cancel units so that only the desired units to answer the question are left, as shown below:

Question	Answer
John runs 2 miles in 15 minutes. How fast does John run, in kilometers per hour? (1 mile is approximately 1.6 kilometers.) A) 5 km/h B) 12.8 km/h C) 16 km/h D) 720 km/h	The correct answer is (B). To solve this problem, set up conversion factors for kilometers to miles and minutes to hours. This way, you will be left with kilometers per hour, your desired result: $$\frac{2 \text{ miles}}{15 \text{ minutes}} \times \frac{1.6 \text{ km}}{1 \text{ mile}} \times \frac{60 \text{ minutes}}{1 \text{ hour}} = 12.8 \text{ km/h}$$

Data Distributions, and Measures of Center and Spread

Measures of center and spread, namely mean, median, mode, range, and standard deviation, will help you interpret data and draw conclusions from it.

Term	Definition	Example
Set	A group of things, often numbers	$\{1, 3, 9\}$
Element	A number or thing in a set	3 is an element of the set $\{1, 3, 9\}$
Frequency	The number of times an element occurs in a data set	The value 5 has a frequency of 3 in the set $\{5, 7, 1, 4, 5, 5, 9, 10, 6\}$
Range	The difference between the biggest and smallest values in a set of data	The range of $\{1, 4, 8, 11\}$ is $11 - 1 = 10$.
Mean	The average of a set of data: $$\text{Mean} = \frac{\text{Sum of all values in the set}}{\text{Total number of elements in the set}}$$	The mean of $\{2, 4, 7, 7\}$ is 5, since $2 + 4 + 7 + 7 = 20$; $$\frac{20}{4} = 5$$

Median	Median is the value that is exactly in the middle of an ordered data set. If there is an even number of elements, the median is the average of the two middle values.	The median of $\{6, 9, 11, 15\}$ is $\dfrac{9 + 11}{2} = 10$.
Mode	The value or values that occur most frequently in a set of data	The set $\{1, 2, 2, 5\}$ has a mode of 2.
Standard Deviation	Standard deviation represents how much the values in a set of data vary from its mean. While you will not need to calculate standard deviation on the SAT, you can use the following expression to conceptualize it, where m is the mean of the data set, n is the number of data points, and each value of x represents an individual data point: $$\sqrt{\dfrac{(x_1 - m)^2 + (x_2 - m)^2 + (x_3 - m)^2 + \ldots + (x_n - m)^2}{n}}$$	List A: 1, 2, 3, 17, 18, 19 List B: 7, 8, 9, 11, 12, 13 Both have a mean of 10, but List A has a higher standard deviation as the points are more spread out.
Outlier	A value that varies substantially from the rest of the values in a data set	In the set $\{1, 2, 3, 4, 1000\}$, 1000 is an outlier.
Box Plot	A box plot is a graphical representation that helps visualize the center and the spread of a set of data. The maximum is the greatest value that occurs in the set, and the minimum is the smallest value. The upper quartile is the value above which only 25% of the data are found (and below which 75% of data are found), and the lower quartile is the value above which 75% of the data are found (and below which only 25% of the data are found). The "box" (shaded) is therefore the "interquartile range."	
Frequency Table	A table representing the elements of a set of data and the number of times they occur	
Histogram	A histogram is a graphical distribution of data, grouped by values or ranges of values, which allows you to graphically calculate range, mean, median, and mode. Note that while they look similar, histograms show frequency distributions of variables while bar graphs compare magnitudes of variables.	

Essential Techniques

To save time, practice different ways of closely estimating measures of center and spread so that you don't have to calculate them directly. For example, given a large set of random data and asked to find the median, you don't have to re-order the set from smallest to largest number. Instead, you can simply eliminate the largest and smallest numbers until only one or two numbers remain.

Question
Five students have an average age of 14 years. When two of these students leave, the remaining three students have an average age of 13 years. What is the sum of the ages, in years, of the two students who leave?

Answer
The correct answer is 31. The five students' ages must add to 70 years in order to have an average age of 14 years. Similarly, the three remaining students' ages must add to 39 years in order to have an average age of 13 years. Taking the difference, the two remaining students' ages must add to 31 years.

Which of the following statements is true for the set {2, 4, 5, 7, 9, 9}?

A) The mode is equal to the mean.

B) The mean is equal to the median.

C) The median is equal to the range.

D) The median is greater than the range.

The correct answer is (B). The range is 7; the mean is 6; the median is 6; and the mode is 9.

Probability

In order to determine how likely an event is, you need to understand probability:

Term	Definition	Example
Probability	How likely something is to happen	$\text{Probability} = \dfrac{\text{Number of ways to get a certain outcome}}{\text{Number of possible outcomes}}$
Venn Diagram	A diagram that uses overlapping circles to demonstrate relationships between sets of numbers	Set A Set B Intersection
Intersection	The portion of two or more sets that share elements	The intersection of {1, 2, 3, 4} and {3, 4, 5, 6} is {3, 4}
Union	All the elements of two or more sets	The union of {1, 2, 3, 4} and {3, 4, 5, 6} is {1, 2, 3, 4, 5, 6}

Question	Answer

Instruments that Students Play

Instrument	Number of Students
Piano	52
Violin	30
No Instrument	24

Several students were surveyed about what instrument they played. No students played any instrument other than the piano or violin. If there were 100 students surveyed, how many students play both the piano and the violin?

The correct answer is 6.

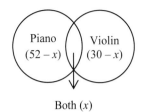

Both (x)

You can let x represent the number of students who play both the violin and the piano. Then, as you can see from the diagram above, the total number of students who play at least one instrument is $52 - x + x + 30 - x = 82 - x$. On the other hand, since 24 students play neither instrument, you know that the number of students who play at least one instrument is $100 - 24 = 76$. Since $82 - x = 76$, you can solve to get $x = 6$.

Conditional Probability and Dependence of Events

Probabilities are written as fractions or decimals between 0 and 1, or as percentages between 0% and 100%. The lower its probability, the less likely an event is to occur. The higher its probability, the more likely an event is to occur. Events may be independent of or dependent on one another, which affects how you calculate their probability.

Mathematical Principles		
Conditional Probability	The probability that an event occurs given that another event has already occurred	Usually phrased in questions as "What is the probability of X given P?" or "If P has happened, what is the probability of X?"
Independent Events	Events whose outcomes do *not* depend on each other	Rolling a fair die twice. Rolling a 1 the first time has the same probability as rolling a 1 the second time.
Dependent Events	Events whose outcomes depend on each other	Picking a card from a standard deck, and then picking another without replacing the first card.

For the purposes of the SAT, a probability of 0 means an event is impossible and will never occur. A probability of 1 or 100% means that an event is certain to happen. If A and B are independent events, then the probability of both A and B occurring is simply $P(A) \times P(B)$. If A and B are dependent events, then the probability of both occurring is conditional: $P(A) \times P(B \mid A)$, where $P(B \mid A)$ is the probability of B given A.

The weatherman of Romley County predicts that there is a 20% chance that rain will fall on Tuesday if the northern winds increase beyond 15 miles per hour on Monday. If his satellite imagery indicates there is a 75% chance that the northern winds will increase beyond 15 miles per hour, what is the percentage chance that rain will fall on Tuesday in Romley County? (Note: Ignore the percent sign when gridding your answer.)

The correct answer is 15. The 20% chance of rain is conditional on winds surpassing 15 miles per hour, which has a 75% chance of happening. 75% times 20% is 15%.

Analyzing Two-Way Tables

Two-way tables can be analyzed to determine conditional probability. This is by far the most frequent use of probability on the SAT exams.

	Classical	Rock	Pop	Total
9th grade	50	21	39	110
10th grade	63	22	20	105
11th grade	3	90	19	112
12th grade	47	12	44	103
Total	163	145	122	430

The table above summarizes students' preferences for music. What is the percent probability that a student prefers rock music, given that he is in the 11th grade? (Note: Ignore the percent sign when gridding your answer.)

The correct answer is 80. This is a conditional probability question, since you are only looking at the students in 11th grade. There are 90 students who prefer rock music out of the 112 students in 11th grade, so the probability is $\frac{90}{112} = \frac{45}{56}$, or approximately 80%.

Graphing Data

Data in the Math Test is frequently displayed as a chart or graph. Here are the various types that you will find:

Term	Definition	Example
Pie Chart	A chart that compares different sections of data as fractions out of a whole	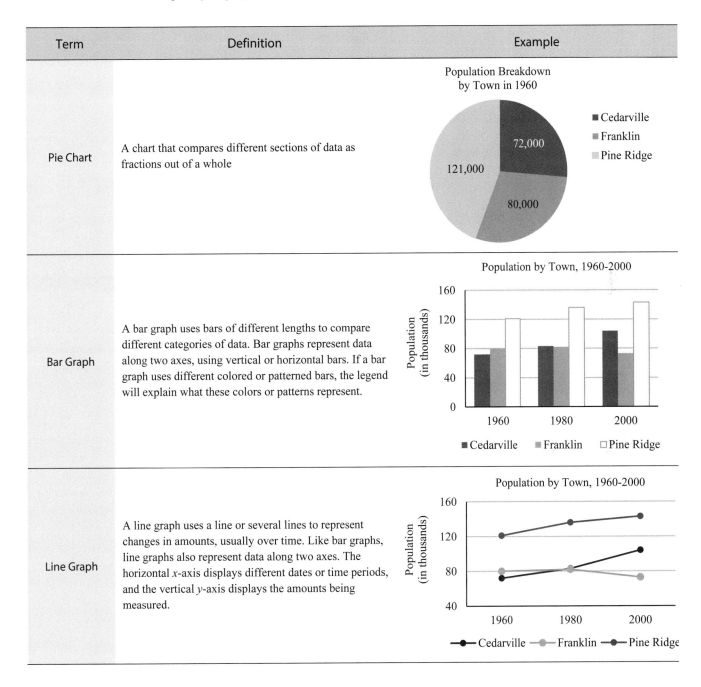
Bar Graph	A bar graph uses bars of different lengths to compare different categories of data. Bar graphs represent data along two axes, using vertical or horizontal bars. If a bar graph uses different colored or patterned bars, the legend will explain what these colors or patterns represent.	
Line Graph	A line graph uses a line or several lines to represent changes in amounts, usually over time. Like bar graphs, line graphs also represent data along two axes. The horizontal x-axis displays different dates or time periods, and the vertical y-axis displays the amounts being measured.	

Essential Techniques

Each type of graph typically corresponds to a specific type of information on the Math Test. While line graphs represent data across a time period, bar graphs and, less frequently, pie charts are used to represent grouped data. As the previous section noted, histograms represent data expressing frequency. Finally, scatterplots, often used in statistical analysis, represent samples of data, as covered later in this part, under Modeling Data.

Question	Answer

Question

Survey of 200 Students' Favorite Sports

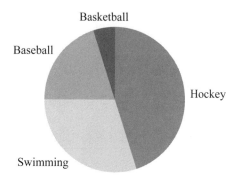

According to the diagram above, approximately how many surveyed students reported either hockey or basketball as their favorite sport?

Answer

The correct answer is 100. Together, the sections representing basketball and hockey make up half, or 50%, of the chart. The chart represents the responses of 200 students. 50% of 200 is 100.

Reading and Interpreting Charts and Graphs

To solve graphical data analysis problems on the Math Test, first make sure that you understand the purpose of the graph. Ask yourself which quantities are being measured and compared, and know the scale and units of those quantities. Make sure that you are familiar with all the types of charts and graphs discussed earlier.

Question

Mary's Driving Speed

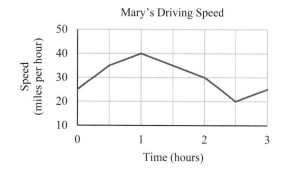

What is the difference between Mary's fastest and slowest speed over the three-hour period, in miles per hour?

Answer

The correct answer is 20. Mary's fastest speed was 40 miles per hour (at 1 hour on the x-axis), and her slowest speed was 20 miles per hour (at 2.5 hours). $40 - 20 = 20$.

Interpreting Data

In some cases, you will need to use data in the chart or graph to find information that is not part of the data you are given. You will have to do calculations with the data you are given or make estimates and predictions based on data or trends.

Question	Answer
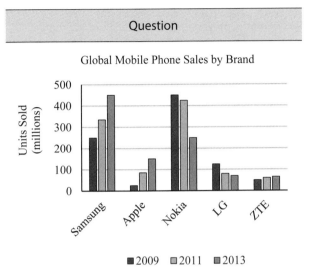 Based on the graph above, what is a reasonable prediction for the number of phones sold by Samsung in 2015? A) 200 million B) 450 million C) 500 million D) 550 million	The correct answer is (D). Every two years from 2009 to 2013, Samsung sold approximately 100 million more phones. Since Samsung sold approximately 450 million phones in 2013, it is reasonable to infer that 550 million phones would be sold in 2015.

Modeling Data

You can use samples of data to make predictions about larger populations or groups. The accuracy of these estimates depends on properties of the sample data, such as size, and on the selection process. In order to make an estimate for a population based on sample data, you treat the sample data as proportional to the entire population. This allows you to use proportions and percentages to make estimates for the whole population.

Term	Definition	Example
Scatterplot	A graph of two variables compared against each other	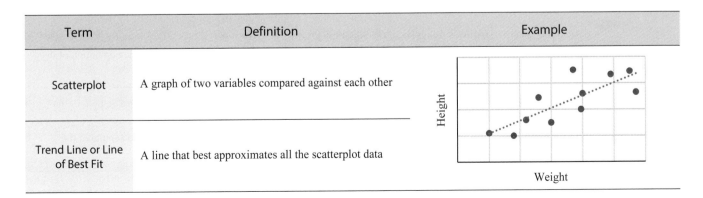
Trend Line or Line of Best Fit	A line that best approximates all the scatterplot data	

Essential Techniques

When researchers collect data, they look for relationships between different variables. One way to find trends in data is to create a scatterplot. Scatterplots are the most common means of analysis because they allow you to easily see trends. The trend is rarely a perfect line or curve, but you can model data through an equation that will approximate these data. Modeling data allows you to find an equation for the relationship between two pieces of information and to make estimates or predictions. The Math Test will mostly feature linear models, but they could also be quadratic, polynomial, exponential, or anything else.

A trend line should be as close to *all* the points as possible, but it does not have to pass through all—or any—of the actual data points. You can calculate the equation of the trend line by using two points on the line. Remember *not* to use the experimental data/real data points unless they fall exactly on the trend line.

Question	Answer

Question

Temperature (°C)	20	24	28	32	36	40
Reaction Time (s)	13.5	11	7.9	3.6	2.1	1.3

A chemist measures the reaction time of an experiment at different temperatures. The results are summarized in the chart above. If the chemist displays these data in a scatterplot, what is true about the slope of the trend line?

A) It is positive

B) It is negative

C) It is zero

D) Not enough information given

Answer

The correct answer is (B). You can see that as temperature increases, reaction time decreases. Therefore, the slope of the trend line would be negative.

Data Collection Methods

Researchers look at samples of populations to determine trends or information for the populations as a whole. The Math Test will test whether you understand this process and a few of the potential issues that arise when data is sampled.

Term	Definition	Example
Population	An entire pool of individuals from which a sample can be drawn	All the people in a town make up the population of people in the town. All of the deer in a forest make up the population of deer in the forest.
Sample	A part of a population which is used to represent the population	25% of the people in a town make up a sample of the population in this town. 15% of the deer in a forest make up a sample of the population of deer in this forest.

Margin of Error	A measure that represents the maximum amount that a population may deviate from a specific sample of that population, given a confidence level	A margin of error of 3 units means that the actual data may vary 3 units in either direction from the sample data.
Confidence Level	The probability with which the observed results from a survey or experiment are predicted to fall within the survey or experiment's confidence interval	A confidence level of 95% means that 19 times out of 20, you can expect your results to fall within your margin of error.
Confidence Interval	A confidence interval is a range, equal to twice the margin of error, covering both the lower and upper ends of acceptable deviations in a population from a specific sample of that population. Both of these are calculated using the survey or experiment's confidence level, defined above.	A confidence interval of 6 units means that the sample data may vary 3 units above or 3 units below the mean of the actual data.
Survey	The collection of a sample, representing facts, figures, or opinions, which is analyzed and used to approximate a representation of a population	A selection of people representing a city's population were surveyed to determine the city's preference for one electoral candidate over another.
Census	An official, systematic, and often reoccurring recording of information of a population	The United States government collects a census of its population every 10 years, counting the total population as well as other information.
Experiment	A scientific examination undertaken to test a hypothesis	A virologist performs an experiment to determine whether a certain kind of mouse is immune to the virus.

Essential Techniques

The goal of data collection is to get information that accurately reflects the entire population. When a question on the SAT asks you to evaluate a data collection method, consider factors like how participants are selected, the size of the data set, and the characteristics of the larger population to which you are comparing your sample.

A sample group that includes only college students, for example, is not a good sample group to represent the entire population of the U.S. Similarly, a sample group that only frequents a certain store is not a good sample group to represent the population of a city. When evaluating a sample selection, consider how well it represents the population that you are trying to represent and how that may affect the results of the sample that is selected.

The size of the sample also affects the accuracy of data. If you only collect a few data points, they will not reflect the entire population as well as many data points. When evaluating questions on the Math Test, a general rule is that more data is better.

Measuring Error

Researchers can estimate the accuracy of their data with a margin of error, a confidence interval, or both. Margins of error and confidence intervals can also be represented visually on a graph. Confidence intervals are shown as vertical bars like the ones in the following graph.

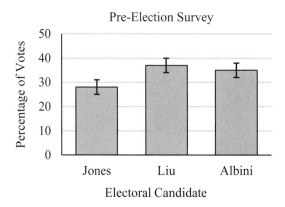

Question	Answer
A lab technician is testing the resilience of bacteria in a petri dish. She selects 10% of the colonies of bacteria at random from the dish and finds that the average life expectancy of bacteria outside of the petri dish is between 54 and 72 minutes, with a 95% confidence interval. Which of the following conclusions is the most reasonable based on the confidence interval?	The correct answer is (C). The technician has found that bacteria from a specific petri dish, when taken out of the petri dish, live between 54 and 72 minutes. This is based on a 95% confidence interval. Since she is estimating the population of bacteria in the petri dish from that sample, (B) and (D) are not reasonable assumptions because they are based on other populations of bacteria, which may not be the same as that of the bacteria in the petri dish. Since the technician is testing bacteria outside of the petri dish, (A) is not reasonable because it is estimating the bacteria's life in the petri dish.

A) 95% of all of the bacteria in the petri dish will live between 54 and 72 minutes.

B) 95% of all bacteria in the lab technician will live between 54 and 72 minutes.

C) It is probable that the bacteria in the petri dish will live, on average, between 54 and 72 minutes outside of the petri dish.

D) It is probable that most bacteria in the lab will live between 54 and 72 minutes outside of a petri dish.

Additional Topics
Part 4

The **Additional Topics** questions on the SAT test various advanced topics in geometry, trigonometry, and complex numbers. Although a variety of material falls under this content area, Additional Topics makes up approximately 10% of the Math Test questions, the smallest proportion of any subject area. You'll only see a total of 6 questions on these topics: 3 in the Calculator Section and 3 in the No-Calculator Section. You'll want to ensure you understand the introductory concepts of lines, triangles, quadrilaterals, polygons, and circles.

Angles and Lines

This section covers fundamental terms and mathematical principles that you need to know about angles.

Term	Definition	Examples
Acute Angle	Less than 90°	
Right Angle	Exactly 90°	
Obtuse Angle	Between 90° and 180°	
Straight Angle	Exactly 180°	
Reflex Angle	Between 180° and 360°	
Full Circle	Exactly 360°	
Complementary Angles	Angles that add up to 90°	
Supplementary Angles	Angles that add up to 180°	

Congruent Angles	Angles that have equal measures	
Bisect	To divide an angle into two equal parts	Line $\overleftrightarrow{BD}$ bisects $\angle ABC$ and divides it into two congruent angles, $\angle ABD$ and $\angle DBC$:
Perpendicular	Two lines at right angles to each other	
Parallel	Two lines that never intersect	
Vertical Angles	When two or more lines intersect, the angles directly opposite each other are congruent.	$a = c$ and $b = d$
Transverse Angles	When a line intersects two parallel lines, eight special angles are formed.	$a = c = e = g$ and $b = d = f = h$

Essential Techniques

To help you solve questions quickly, always look for relationships between complementary, supplementary, vertical, and transverse angles, and between perpendicular and parallel lines.

Question	Answer
In the figure above, what is the value of a, in degrees? (Ignore the degree symbol when gridding your response.)	The correct answer is 32. The two marked angles are supplementary, since the angle they add up to is half of a full rotation, or half of 360°: $$2a - 15° + 3a + 35° = 180°$$ $$5a + 20° = 180°$$ $$5a = 160°$$ $$a = 32°$$

In the figure: angles labeled $3a + 35$ and $2a - 15$.

Triangles and Trigonometry

This section covers important terms and mathematical principles that you need to know about right triangles and trigonometry. If you need more information, refer to our online SAT review.

 For a fundamental review, please visit **ivyglobal.com/study**.

Term	Definition	Examples
Sine	The ratio of the side opposite an angle to the hypotenuse of the triangle: $$\sin(\theta) = \frac{\text{opposite}}{\text{hypotenuse}}$$	
Cosine	The ratio of the side adjacent to an angle to the hypotenuse of the triangle: $$\cos(\theta) = \frac{\text{adjacent}}{\text{hypotenuse}}$$	
Tangent	The ratio of the side opposite an angle to the side adjacent to the triangle: $$\tan(\theta) = \frac{\text{opposite}}{\text{adjacent}}$$	

Triangle diagram with vertices B, A, C; side opposite, hypotenuse, adjacent; angle θ at C; right angle at A.

Pythagorean Theorem	The square of the hypotenuse of a right triangle is equal to the sum of the squares of the legs.	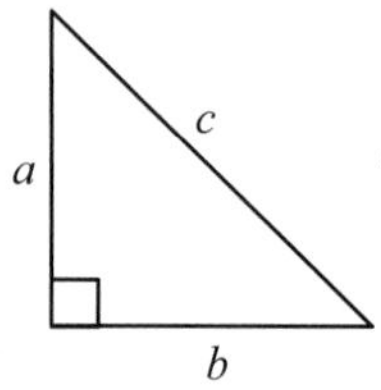 $a^2 + b^2 = c^2$
Pythagorean Triples	Right triangles whose side lengths are in integer relationships	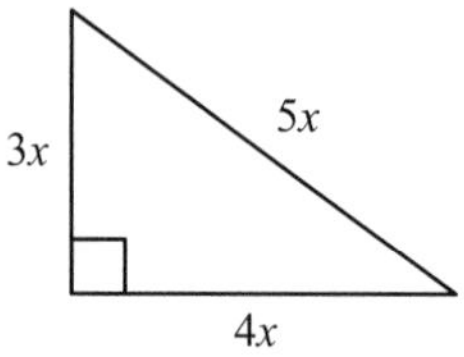 3-4-5 triangle 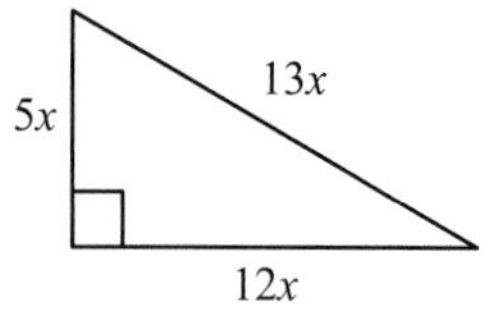 5-12-13 triangle
Special Triangles	Right triangles whose three angles are integers, and whose three sides lengths correspond with integers or the radicals of integers	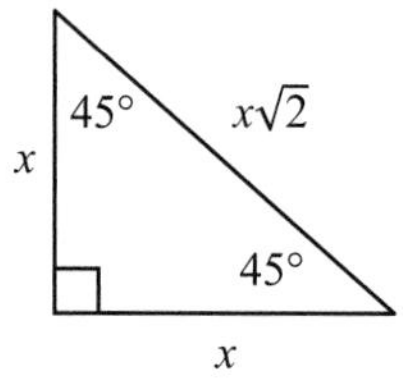 45°-45°-90° triangle 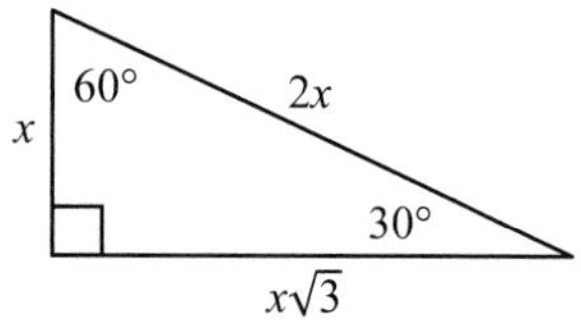 30°-60°-90° triangle

Essential Techniques

Many problems on the Math Test deal directly or indirectly with triangles, so it is helpful to recognize the different ways in which triangles may occur: as similar triangles, as special triangles, as parts of different shapes, and as the space formed when lines intersect. Some triangles are very common on the Math Test and have side lengths that can be easily memorized. The four triangles shown above, 3-4-5, 5-12-13, 45°-45°-90° (side lengths of 1-1-$\sqrt{2}$), and 30°-60°-90° (side lengths of 1-$\sqrt{3}$-2), are worth committing to memory for the SAT. No matter what the value of x is, the side lengths of these triangles will always be in the same ratio.

When evaluating right triangles using trigonometry, a simple way to remember the trigonometric functions is the acronym **SOHCAHTOA**. SOH means that $\sin(x) = \dfrac{\text{opposite}}{\text{hypotenuse}}$, CAH means that $\cos(x) = \dfrac{\text{adjacent}}{\text{hypotenuse}}$, and TOA means that $\tan(x) = \dfrac{\text{opposite}}{\text{adjacent}}$.

Question	Answer

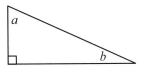

In the triangle above, the cosine of ∠a is 0.55. What is the sine of ∠b?

The correct answer is 0.55. From the diagram, you know that cos(a) is equal to the vertical side of the triangle divided by the hypotenuse (since this vertical side is adjacent to ∠a). On the other hand, sin(b) is also equal to the vertical side of the triangle divided by the hypotenuse (since this vertical side is opposite ∠b). Therefore, cos(a) = sin(b). In general, if two angles are complementary, then the sine of either one of them is equal to the cosine of the other.

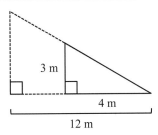

12 m

Note: Figure not drawn to scale.

A farmer owns three pigs and wants to purchase at least six more. To do so, she must extend her small triangular pigpen as shown in the figure above. What is the total length, in meters, of additional fencing material she will need?

A) 12

B) 15

C) 24

D) 36

The correct answer is (C). You can see that the small triangular pen is a Special Triangle, so you know that its hypotenuse is 5 m. If the small pen is extended as shown, then the big triangle is similar to the small triangle. Since the base is now 12 m, three times the previous base, then all the new side lengths must be three times the small side lengths. Therefore, the height is 9 m and the hypotenuse is 15 m.

However, the question asked you for the *additional* fencing material. The additional material for the height is 9 – 3 = 6 m, for the base is 12 – 4 = 8 m, and for the hypotenuse is 15 – 5 = 10 m. Finally, add these together to get 6 + 8 + 10 = 24 m.

Radians and Circles

You need to know these key terms and mathematical principles when you work in radians and degrees to solve problems involving circles:

Term	Definition	Examples
Radian	A unit of measure for angles: 180° = π radians	$30° = \dfrac{\pi}{6}$ radians $45° = \dfrac{\pi}{4}$ radians $60° = \dfrac{\pi}{3}$ radians $90° = \dfrac{\pi}{2}$ radians

Circle	The set of all points at a given distance r (radius) from a center point $$\text{Diameter} = 2r$$ $$\text{Circumference} = 2\pi r = \pi d$$ $$A = \pi r^2$$	
Chord	A line segment that connects two different points on the circumference of a circle, but does *not* pass through the center of the circle $$\text{Chord length} = 2\sqrt{r^2 - t^2}$$	
Arc	A continuous portion of the circumference of a circle	
Arc Length	The distance along an arc	
Sector	The area enclosed by two radii and the arc that they create	$$\frac{x \text{ radians}}{2\pi \text{ radians}} = \frac{\text{Arc Length}}{\text{Circumference}} = \frac{\text{Sector Area}}{\text{Circle Area}}$$
CAST Rule	With angle x in the fourth quadrant, only **cos(x)** is positive; in the first quadrant **all** of the trigonometric functions of x are positive; in the second quadrant only **sin(x)** is positive; in the third quadrant only **tan(x)** is positive.	

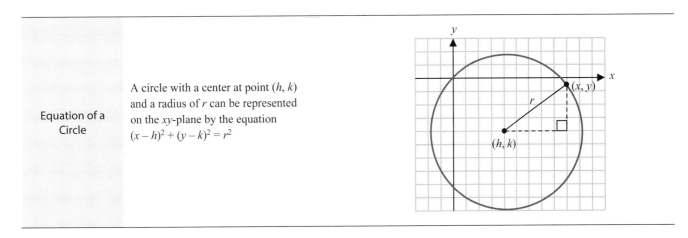

| Equation of a Circle | A circle with a center at point (h, k) and a radius of r can be represented on the xy-plane by the equation $(x - h)^2 + (y - k)^2 = r^2$ |

Essential Techniques

The SAT will occasionally ask you to use the unit circle to find a point or a trigonometric ratio. A **unit circle** is a circle drawn on the xy-plane, centered at $(0, 0)$, with a radius of 1 unit. Angles (usually in radians) are calculated counterclockwise from the point $(1, 0)$. To do so, you will use a combination of the CAST Rule, special triangles, and trigonometry. To draw an angle using the unit circle, draw a line segment from the origin to the circumference of the circle, with the given angle between this line segment and the x-axis. The length of this line segment is 1, since it's the radius of the unit circle. You can then draw a line perpendicular to the x-axis, connecting the x-axis to the point on the circumference of the circle, and determine the side lengths and thus the point on the circumference using the appropriate special triangle:

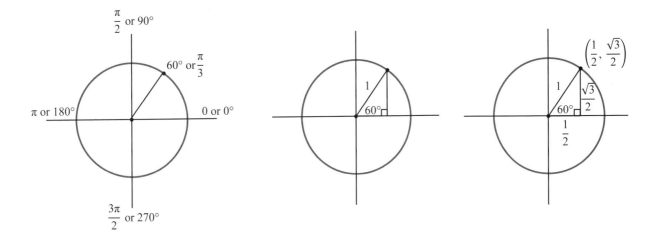

You are also required to know how to complete the square, which is shown in the second sample question on the following page.

The circle below has a radius of 4. The shaded sector represents $\frac{1}{16}$ of the total area of the circle. What is the length of arc AB?

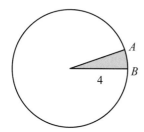

A) 2π

B) π

C) $\frac{\pi}{2}$

D) $\frac{\pi}{4}$

The correct answer is (C). You know that the ratio of arc length to circumference is equal to the ratio of sector area to total area, and since the area of the sector is $\frac{1}{16}$ of the area of the circle, you can find the arc length as follows, where $r = 4$:

$$\frac{\text{Arc Length}}{\text{Circumference}} = \frac{\text{Sector Area}}{\text{Circle Area}}$$

$$\frac{\text{Arc Length}}{2\pi r} = \frac{1}{16}$$

$$\text{Arc Length} = \frac{8\pi}{16} = \frac{\pi}{2}$$

$$x^2 + y^2 - 10x + 8y = 1$$

The equation of a circle in the xy-plane is shown above. What are the coordinates for the center of the circle?

A) $(5, -4)$

B) $(4, -5)$

C) $(-4, -5)$

D) $(-5, -4)$

The correct answer is (A). To solve this problem, you must complete the square. First, group the x^2 and x terms in parentheses, and the y^2 and y terms in parentheses. Next, add the square of half the coefficient of the x term to the x parentheses, and do the same to the y parentheses. This addition will give you two easily factorable quadratics. Since you added these numbers to the left side of the equation, you must also add them to the right side of the equation. Finally, factor the parentheses and simplify to find the equation of the circle in standard form:

$$x^2 + y^2 - 10x + 8y = 1$$
$$(x^2 - 10x) + (y^2 + 8y) = 1$$
$$(x^2 - 10x + 5^2) + (y^2 + 8y + 4^2) = 1 + 5^2 + 4^2$$
$$(x^2 - 10x + 25) + (y^2 + 8y + 16) = 42$$
$$(x - 5)^2 + (y + 4)^2 = 42$$

In standard form, $(x - h)^2 + (y - k)^2 = r^2$, the coordinates of the center are (h, k), or $(5, -4)$.

2D and 3D Shapes

This section covers fundamental terms and mathematical principles that you need to know about shapes, area, and volume. More detail about basic shapes, including 2D area and perimeter, can be found online.

 For a fundamental review, please visit **ivyglobal.com/study**.

Term	Definition	Examples
Solid	A three-dimensional shape	
Prism	A solid with two congruent polygons as bases joined by perpendicular rectangles, named after its base (e.g. rectangular prism)	
Face	Exterior surface of a solid, bounded by edges	
Edge	Line where faces intersect	
Vertex	Point where edges intersect (plural: vertices)	
Surface Area	The sum of the areas of all the faces of a solid	Surface area = $2 \times (4 \times 2) + 2 \times (5 \times 2) + 2 \times (5 \times 4) =$ 76 units^2
Volume	Volume is the space contained within a solid. For any prism, the volume is simply the area of the polygonal base multiplied by the length.	Volume = area of base × length = $\dfrac{6 \times 5}{2} \times 10 = 150$ units^3
Cube	A prism composed of six equal squares Surface area = $6a^2$ Volume = a^3	

Pyramid	Square-based pyramids, the only type that are tested on the SAT, are formed by connecting the vertices of a square base to a single point, the apex. $$\text{Volume} = \frac{1}{3}lwh$$	 slant height h w l
Cone	A shape formed by drawing angled lines between a vertex and every point on the circumference of a circle $$\text{Volume} = \frac{1}{3}\pi r^2 h$$	slant height h r
Cylinder	A shape like a prism but with bases that are circles instead of polygons $$\text{Surface area} = 2\pi r^2 + 2\pi rh$$ $$\text{Volume} = \pi r^2 h$$	h r
Sphere	A round object containing the surface area and volume of a ball $$\text{Surface area} = 4\pi r^2$$ $$\text{Volume} = \frac{4}{3}\pi r^3$$	r

Essential Techniques

All the 3D shapes given on the SAT, with the exception of the sphere, are **right-angled**: their heights are perpendicular to their bases. This means you can find Pythagorean relationships between the height, slant height, and radius of a cone, or the height, slant height, and base dimensions of a square-based pyramid.

To find the volume or surface area of a compound shape, find the volume or surface area of each of its parts and then add them together. You can often divide a shape in different ways, so always take a moment to think about the fastest way for you.

Question	Answer
A trucking company stores diesel in the tank with a radius of 3 feet, as shown above. If the volume of diesel in a half-full tank is 36π cubic feet, what is the total length l of the tank, in feet?	The correct answer is 10. First, you can break the shape into two distinct solids: a sphere (two half-spheres) and a cylinder. The volume of the cylinder is $\pi r^2 h = \pi(3)^2 h = 9\pi h$. The volume of the sphere is $\frac{4}{3}\pi r^3 = \frac{4}{3}\pi(3)^3 = \frac{4}{3}(27)\pi = 36\pi$. If the volume of a half-full tank is 36π cubic feet, then the volume of a full tank is 72π, which is equal to the sum of the volumes of the cylinder and sphere: $$72\pi = 9\pi h + 36\pi$$ $$36\pi = 9\pi h$$ $$\frac{36\pi}{9\pi} = h$$ $$h = 4.$$ However, the question asked you for the *total* length, which is equal to the sum of the radii of each half-sphere, and the height of the cylinder: $4 + (3 \times 2) = 10$.

Complex Numbers

Complex numbers usually appear on 1 or 2 questions of a test. After understanding what they are, you can solve them using basic algebra.

Term	Definition	Examples
Imaginary Number	The square root of negative one, or multiples of it, which do not exist in the set of real numbers	$i = \sqrt{-1}$
Complex Number	The sum of a real number and an imaginary number, which has the form $a + bi$, where a and b are real numbers	$3 + 2i$ $5 - 10i$
Pattern of Powers	Values of i raised to exponents follow a four-part pattern: $i^1 = i, i^2 = -1, i^3 = -i, i^4 = 1$	$i^5 = i^1 = i$ $i^{5055} = i^3 = -i$

Essential Techniques

When working with complex numbers, you are required to know how to use differences of squares and FOIL to simplify expressions. This is shown in the sample question below.

Question	Answer
If $i = \sqrt{-1}$, what is the value of $\dfrac{1}{2+i}$? A) $\quad -\dfrac{i}{2}$ B) $\quad -\dfrac{2-i}{5}$ C) $\quad 1$ D) $\quad \dfrac{2-i}{5}$	The correct answer is (D). You can simplify a complex number, particularly when it occurs in the denominator of a fraction, by multiplying it by an expression that will result in a difference of squares. Since you know that $i = \sqrt{-1}$, and therefore that $i^2 = -1$, this difference of squares will allow you to substitute -1 for i^2: $$\frac{1}{2+i} \times \frac{(2-i)}{(2-i)}$$ $$= \frac{2-i}{4-i^2}$$ $$= \frac{2-i}{4-(-1)}$$ $$\frac{2-i}{5}$$

Section 4
Essay

The Essay is the last section of the SAT. It's optional, which means the colleges you're applying to might not require it—you should check their admissions policies to be sure. Even if you don't *have* to write the Essay, it can help keep your options open for later in the application process, so it's a good idea!

The Essay prompt consists of a set of instructions, which are always the same, and a passage, which changes from test to test. The instructions ask you to analyze how the author of the passage builds an argument to persuade an audience.

In other words, your task is to write a rhetorical analysis, focusing on how the author uses specific techniques and elements to create effects. You will not be asked to take a stance on or form an opinion about an issue. Rather, the focus is on your ability to comprehend source material, analyze how the author presents her argument, and use textual evidence from the passage to support your position.

Anatomy of the Essay		
Length of Prompt Passage	Length of Essay	Amount of Time
650–750 words	Up to 4 lined pages	50 minutes

Rules for Writing the Essay
Part 1

Although there are many ways to write a great SAT essay, there are a few basic principles you should always follow.

1. **Make notes in your test booklet.** As you prepare for the test, you can develop your own symbols, acronyms, and abbreviations to note key elements in the source text—such as circling stylistic devices and underlining arguments. Key elements include language use (rhetorical questions, hyperbole, figurative language, comparisons and contrasts, etc.), reasoning (claim, causality, analogy, appeals to authority, nature, or emotion, etc.), and evidence (data, numbers, sources, etc.).

2. **Outline your essay.** Before you write, briefly organize your essay in the test booklet using short forms and doodles. This outline will only take a minute or two, but it will help keep your essay well-structured as you write.

3. **Write your essay only in the designated section of the exam booklet.** The graders will only see what you write within the available lines. They won't see anything you write in the margins, so don't put clarifying notes there.

4. **Write neatly.** You're not graded for handwriting, but unlike the other sections of the SAT, which are graded by a computer, the essay must be read by another human being. If the readers can't tell what you've written, they won't be able to give you the grade that you deserve.

5. **Write as much as you can,** so long as everything you write is well-organized and meaningful. Longer essays do tend to get better scores, but it's not simply because they have more words. Rather, they use the space to develop their analysis thoroughly. Try to put down as much as you can clearly organize into a sensible essay, but don't add distracting fluff just to fill in blank pages.

6. **Make explicit connections between your ideas and the source text.** The connection between your main point and supporting arguments must be clear to your graders. To make the connection clear, back up every point you make about the text with specific examples, and then explain how each example supports your point. Quoting from the passage and explaining how your quotations support your ideas will prove to the graders that you *know* your points are correct—they weren't just lucky guesses.

7. **Read your essay and make small revisions.** You should try to finish your essay with a little bit of time left over. Use that time to review your essay, making small revisions to fix grammar errors or improve on style and word choices.

How to Structure Your Essay
Part 2

The overall structure of your essay should make it easy for your graders to follow your argument. The chart below illustrates the structure you should aim for and provides estimates of how much time you should spend on each section, including reading and analyzing the passage and proofreading your essay. Remember that these times are just estimates. For example, if it's clear while you're reading the passage that it's going to be an especially tricky essay to write, don't give yourself a full five minutes to proofread. Use that time for writing instead.

Essay Structure
Read and analyze the passage (~10 minutes)
Introduction (~5 minutes)
Yvon Chouinard argues that thousands of so-called "deadbeat dams," meaning dams that have outlived their usefulness as power sources and flood barriers, should be torn down. He develops his argument using three important tools: he weighs the costs and benefits of keeping dams open, uses data to show the good results of previous dam removals, and makes several vivid word choices.
1-4 body paragraphs (~25 minutes)
Chouinard repeatedly compares the cost and benefit of keeping the dams open, presenting readers with a choice and using claims and evidence to urge them to choose dam removal. He states that "the benefits that dams have historically provided...can now be met more effectively" in other ways, and follows this claim with the statement that dams "degrade water quality, block the movement of nutrients and sediment, destroy fish and wildlife habitats" to name just a few examples. This reasoning is meant to convince the reader that keeping dams open would cause needless environmental harm. Chouinard makes a similar claim again when he cites a study by the River Alliance of Wisconsin that "removing dams in that state is three to five times less expensive than repairing them." Again, he wants to show how there is no value in keeping the dams.
	To back up his more general points, Chouinard uses specific data from times when dams were removed. This data is intended to show that removing dams has positive effects. For instance, he cites a group called American Rivers who found that "more than 500 miles of streams" were restored by dam removals. This figure is intended to show a positive benefit of dam removal. Furthermore, he refers to the numbers of salmon spawning on the Elwha River in Washington before, during, and after the existence of a dam. Before the dam, Chouinard states that 400,000 salmon came up the river to spawn, but only 3,000 did so afterwards. This dramatic loss of fish shows the harm done by the dam. To show that the problem was solved by removing the dam, he states that after removal, salmon "returned to the river in numbers not seen in decades."
	Chouinard's final important tool is vivid diction which helps the audience connect to his argument. The phrase "Deadbeat Dams" in his title sounds like "deadbeat dads," or in other words fathers who don't pull their weight in supporting their kids. Making the comparison between the two is a metaphorical way to describe the dams as unhelpful. Chouinard uses this kind of diction again in his final sentence, when he states that he has never heard anyone say, "Gee, I wish we had our dam back." The comical word "gee" casts the idea of missing the dam as especially absurd.
Conclusion (~5 minutes)
Chouinard's goal is to urge his audience to join him in opposing the continued existence of dams that have overstayed their welcome. First, he presents his audience with a choice: they can keep the dams, at an environmental and financial cost, or they can remove them—helping the environment while also saving money. To support this point, he uses data about recovered streams and returning salmon. Finally, he uses diction that is colorful and sometimes funny to try to bring readers around to his point of view. He uses these three tactics together to educate and persuade his readers of a position they might not have given any consideration to before.
Proofread and revise (1-5 minutes)

The next section will discuss how to write introductions and conclusions, and it will also address the internal structure of the essay. An effective internal structure—in other words, the organization of your individual paragraphs—is integral to writing an essay that expresses your argument in a clear and straightforward manner.

Introduction

Your introduction will set the tone for your essay and provide graders with their first impression of your writing. Your introduction must be clear. It's hard to structure a good, coherent essay if the introduction doesn't make any sense.

The best way to make your introduction clear is to keep it brief and straightforward. Your goal is to get to your point as quickly as possible so you can spend the bulk of your time on your body paragraphs.

Start with a brief statement or two relevant to the prompt, demonstrating that you've read the passage and understood the author's claim. It's a good idea to refer to the title of the passage and introduce the author (by full name the first time and by *last name only* every other time), paraphrase the author's central claim, and describe the evidence the author uses to support that claim. Next, state your thesis. Your thesis will lay out the main point of your essay: a claim about the author's use of evidence, style, and reasoning to try to persuade an audience.

Body Paragraphs

In your body paragraphs, you will elaborate on the different points that you mentioned in your thesis statement and link them together to create your overall analysis.

Each body paragraph is like a mini-essay. Every paragraph should start with a **topic sentence**, which is like a mini-thesis statement: it states what the rest of the paragraph is going to discuss.

Following the topic sentence should be 3-4 **supporting sentences**. In these sentences, analyze evidence from the passage (including appropriate quotations) and explain how it supports the argument you made in your topic sentence. To help your reader follow your argument, use transitions that link your ideas together effectively. In the following sentences, the words in italics are examples of transitions:

> *However*, the author does not rely on personal experience alone.
> The author *also* builds her argument by using scientific evidence.
> *Furthermore*, the author uses vivid language to appeal to her readers' emotions as well as their intellect.

Finally, use a **concluding sentence** to summarize the point you have made in your body paragraph. This ensures that your reader has a solid foundation for going on to your next point.

Conclusion

Your conclusion sums up the argument you have been making throughout your entire essay so that your graders know exactly what your argument is. Therefore, it is very important that your conclusion be clear and, like your introduction, brief. Resist the urge to add new arguments in your conclusion; instead, just summarize the arguments you have already made.

The first sentence of your conclusion should rephrase the thesis statement you wrote in your introduction. Don't rewrite it word-for-word (your graders will notice), but restate the ideas in your thesis in a general way. The purpose of this sentence is to show that you have proven your thesis statement.

Essay Scoring
Part 3

The SAT Essay grading rubric is broken down into three domains: Reading, Analysis, and Writing. Each of these domains will be scored on a scale of 1-4 by two graders, for a combined score of 2-8 on each section and 6-24 on the whole essay. Below is a breakdown of what each of these scores means and what the College Board expects to see in your essay.

Reading

The best way to prove that you read the passage and understood all of its nuances is to quote and paraphrase the author's words. Remember, though, that quotation and paraphrase are just one part of a good essay—simply summarizing or restating the source text will not yield a high score. You should also show that you understand the author's ideas by commenting on the significance of your chosen quotations.

Score	Summary	Essay Features
1	Lack of comprehension of the source text	Many mistakes about the passage's main idea or supporting facts, misinterpretation of details, few or no quotations or paraphrases
2	Some comprehension of the source text	Understanding of the passage's main idea, but not its details; some factual errors or ineffective use of quotations or paraphrases
3	Comprehension of the main idea and important details	No significant errors of fact or interpretation; appropriate quotations or paraphrases
4	Thorough comprehension of the main idea, important details, and their relation to one another	No errors of fact or interpretation; skillfully chosen quotations or paraphrases

Analysis

Analysis comes from a Greek word which means "to break apart." This means that your job when writing the SAT Essay is to break apart the different pieces of your source text in order to understand how the passage works as a whole. It might even help to look at the text as you would an unfamiliar machine you wanted to learn more about. The main idea is like the function of the machine; the author's rhetorical devices, word choices, and uses of logic and evidence are like the parts that make the machine go.

There are a couple of ways to frame your analysis. A simpler method, which is often your best bet under pressure, involves picking three important, consistently-used elements from the source text—an important use of evidence, an important rhetorical strategy, and some important word choices—and showing how each contributes to the author's main goal.

A more complex method, which you can try if you've practiced a lot or are particularly confident in your writing, involves weaving your chosen elements into a single analysis. First, identify several techniques that figure prominently in the passage or that are used in an order that develops the main idea. You can then frame your analysis in terms that relate the techniques to one another, showing how they build the essay together.

Score	Summary	Essay Features
1	Misunderstanding of the analytical task or a lack of analysis	Claims without support, summary without analysis, or identification of rhetorical techniques without explanation of their intention, purpose, or effect
2	Limited analysis	Identification of some important rhetorical features or uses of evidence, but without sufficient explanation; too much focus on relatively unimportant elements
3	Effective analysis	Inclusion of important rhetorical features and uses of evidence, explanation of their importance, and adequate support for claims
4	Insightful analysis	Focus only on important rhetorical features and evidence, thorough explanations of their importance, and strong support for claims

Writing

To get a good score on your essay, you need to do more than just come up with a good analysis. You must also convey it to your reader effectively. Your graders will evaluate your ability to write clear sentences, organize your writing, vary your sentence structure, and make effective word choices. The best way to prepare yourself for this part of the test is to read material that challenges you in the weeks and months before you take the SAT. Reading good journalism, essays, fiction, and other accomplished prose will boost your vocabulary and help you gain a more instinctive sense of what works well on the page.

Organization is also an aspect of your Writing score. This means paying attention to the progression of ideas in your essay: if you say you're going to argue something in your introduction, you need to follow through on that promise in the body of your essay. You also must ensure that your conclusion doesn't state something completely different from your introduction. Finally, you should try to arrange your body paragraphs in a way that serves your argument. If the author immediately follows an important statistic with a crucial appeal to emotion, order your analysis of these elements the same way rather than putting unrelated material between them.

Score	Summary	Essay Features
1	Little or no organization and inadequate skill with language	Lack of an introduction, conclusion, or clear progression of ideas; possibly a single long paragraph; grammar or spelling errors that make the essay hard to understand
2	Little or no organization and limited skill with language	Lack of a main idea, or one that changes midway through the essay; ineffective or unfocused introduction and conclusion; insufficiently clear progression of ideas throughout the essay; unclear or repetitive writing, with some errors that occasionally impede understanding
3	Mostly clear organization and effective use of language	Adequate central claim, an introduction and conclusion, a progression of ideas from start to finish, precise use of some challenging words, errors that do not impede understanding
4	Very clear organization and use of language	Skillfully written introduction and conclusion, clear arrangement of ideas, thoughtful progression that furthers analysis, varied sentence structure, skilled use of complex sentences, precise use of sophisticated words, a small number of minor errors

Practice Tests

Chapter 2

Practice Test 1

SAT

Directions

- Work on just one section at a time.

- If you complete a section before the end of your allotted time, use the extra minutes to check your work on that section only. Do NOT use the time to work on another section.

Using Your Test Booklet

- No credit will be given for anything written in the test booklet. You may use the test booklet for scratch paper.

- You are not allowed to continue answering questions in a section after the allotted time has run out. This includes marking answers on your answer sheet that you previously noted in your test booklet.

- You are not allowed to fold pages, take pages out of the test booklet, or take any pages home.

Answering Questions

- Each answer must be marked in the corresponding row on the answer sheet.

- Each bubble must be filled in completely and darkly within the lines.

Correct ●   Incorrect

- Be careful to bubble in the correct part of the answer sheet.

- Extra marks on your answer sheet may be marked as incorrect answers and lower your score.

- Make sure you use a No. 2 pencil.

Scoring

- You will receive one point for each correct answer.

- Incorrect answers will NOT result in points deducted. Even if you are unsure about an answer, you should make a guess.

DO NOT BEGIN THIS TEST

UNTIL YOUR PROCTOR TELLS YOU TO DO SO

For printable answer sheets, please visit **ivyglobal.com/study**.

Section 1

	A B C D		A B C D		A B C D		A B C D		A B C D
1	○ ○ ○ ○	12	○ ○ ○ ○	23	○ ○ ○ ○	34	○ ○ ○ ○	45	○ ○ ○ ○
2	○ ○ ○ ○	13	○ ○ ○ ○	24	○ ○ ○ ○	35	○ ○ ○ ○	46	○ ○ ○ ○
3	○ ○ ○ ○	14	○ ○ ○ ○	25	○ ○ ○ ○	36	○ ○ ○ ○	47	○ ○ ○ ○
4	○ ○ ○ ○	15	○ ○ ○ ○	26	○ ○ ○ ○	37	○ ○ ○ ○	48	○ ○ ○ ○
5	○ ○ ○ ○	16	○ ○ ○ ○	27	○ ○ ○ ○	38	○ ○ ○ ○	49	○ ○ ○ ○
6	○ ○ ○ ○	17	○ ○ ○ ○	28	○ ○ ○ ○	39	○ ○ ○ ○	50	○ ○ ○ ○
7	○ ○ ○ ○	18	○ ○ ○ ○	29	○ ○ ○ ○	40	○ ○ ○ ○	51	○ ○ ○ ○
8	○ ○ ○ ○	19	○ ○ ○ ○	30	○ ○ ○ ○	41	○ ○ ○ ○	52	○ ○ ○ ○
9	○ ○ ○ ○	20	○ ○ ○ ○	31	○ ○ ○ ○	42	○ ○ ○ ○		
10	○ ○ ○ ○	21	○ ○ ○ ○	32	○ ○ ○ ○	43	○ ○ ○ ○		
11	○ ○ ○ ○	22	○ ○ ○ ○	33	○ ○ ○ ○	44	○ ○ ○ ○		

Section 2

	A B C D		A B C D		A B C D		A B C D		A B C D
1	○ ○ ○ ○	10	○ ○ ○ ○	19	○ ○ ○ ○	28	○ ○ ○ ○	37	○ ○ ○ ○
2	○ ○ ○ ○	11	○ ○ ○ ○	20	○ ○ ○ ○	29	○ ○ ○ ○	38	○ ○ ○ ○
3	○ ○ ○ ○	12	○ ○ ○ ○	21	○ ○ ○ ○	30	○ ○ ○ ○	39	○ ○ ○ ○
4	○ ○ ○ ○	13	○ ○ ○ ○	22	○ ○ ○ ○	31	○ ○ ○ ○	40	○ ○ ○ ○
5	○ ○ ○ ○	14	○ ○ ○ ○	23	○ ○ ○ ○	32	○ ○ ○ ○	41	○ ○ ○ ○
6	○ ○ ○ ○	15	○ ○ ○ ○	24	○ ○ ○ ○	33	○ ○ ○ ○	42	○ ○ ○ ○
7	○ ○ ○ ○	16	○ ○ ○ ○	25	○ ○ ○ ○	34	○ ○ ○ ○	43	○ ○ ○ ○
8	○ ○ ○ ○	17	○ ○ ○ ○	26	○ ○ ○ ○	35	○ ○ ○ ○	44	○ ○ ○ ○
9	○ ○ ○ ○	18	○ ○ ○ ○	27	○ ○ ○ ○	36	○ ○ ○ ○		

Section 3 (No-Calculator)

	A	B	C	D		A	B	C	D		A	B	C	D		A	B	C	D		A	B	C	D
1	○	○	○	○	4	○	○	○	○	7	○	○	○	○	10	○	○	○	○	13	○	○	○	○
2	○	○	○	○	5	○	○	○	○	8	○	○	○	○	11	○	○	○	○	14	○	○	○	○
3	○	○	○	○	6	○	○	○	○	9	○	○	○	○	12	○	○	○	○	15	○	○	○	○

Only answers that are gridded will be scored. You will not receive credit for anything written in the boxes.

16   17   18   19   20

/	/	/	/	/
.	.	.	.	.
0	0	0	0	0
1	1	1	1	1
2	2	2	2	2
3	3	3	3	3
4	4	4	4	4
5	5	5	5	5
6	6	6	6	6
7	7	7	7	7
8	8	8	8	8
9	9	9	9	9

Section 4 (Calculator)

	A	B	C	D		A	B	C	D		A	B	C	D		A	B	C	D		A	B	C	D
1	○	○	○	○	7	○	○	○	○	13	○	○	○	○	19	○	○	○	○	25	○	○	○	○
2	○	○	○	○	8	○	○	○	○	14	○	○	○	○	20	○	○	○	○	26	○	○	○	○
3	○	○	○	○	9	○	○	○	○	15	○	○	○	○	21	○	○	○	○	27	○	○	○	○
4	○	○	○	○	10	○	○	○	○	16	○	○	○	○	22	○	○	○	○	28	○	○	○	○
5	○	○	○	○	11	○	○	○	○	17	○	○	○	○	23	○	○	○	○	29	○	○	○	○
6	○	○	○	○	12	○	○	○	○	18	○	○	○	○	24	○	○	○	○	30	○	○	○	○

Only answers that are gridded will be scored. You will not receive credit for anything written in the boxes.

31

32

33

34

35

Only answers that are gridded will be scored. You will not receive credit for anything written in the boxes.

36

37

38

Important: Use a No. 2 pencil. Write inside the borders.

You may use the space below to plan your essay, but be sure to write your essay on the lined pages. Work on this page will not be scored.

Use this space to plan your essay.

START YOUR ESSAY HERE.

_____

_____

_____

_____

_____

_____

_____

_____

_____

_____

_____

_____

_____

_____

_____

_____

_____

_____

_____

_____

_____

_____

_____

_____

_____

Continue on the next page.

Continue on the next page.

_____

_____

_____

_____

_____

_____

_____

_____

_____

_____

_____

_____

_____

_____

_____

_____

_____

_____

_____

_____

_____

_____

_____

_____

_____

Continue on the next page.

_____

_____

_____

_____

_____

_____

_____

_____

_____

_____

_____

_____

_____

_____

_____

_____

_____

_____

_____

_____

_____

_____

_____

_____

STOP.

Reading Test

65 MINUTES, 52 QUESTIONS

Turn to Section 1 of your answer sheet to answer the questions in this section.

DIRECTIONS

Every passage or paired set of passages is accompanied by a number of questions. Read the passage or paired set of passages, then use what is said or implied in what you read and in any given graphics to choose the best answer to each question.

Questions 1-10 are based on the following passage.

This passage is adapted from Elizabeth Evitts Dickinson, *The Last Bullet.* ©2015 by Elizabeth Evitts Dickinson.

The Trouble began when Millicent Virginia Dunville failed to post for the 117th Annual Ladies' Auxiliary Hunt Cup Tea. The Chairwoman of the
Line Social Committee later claimed that Millicent had
5 RSVP'd in the affirmative, but under scrutiny that assertion came into question. No one could put hands on the reply card (and it was so very nice that year, letterpress on 80-pound crème stock with the signature gold grosgrain ribbon).
10   That Millicent had returned the RSVP card was never in question; she was a stickler for protocol. It was the nature of her reply—carefully inked in her signature blue fountain pen, no doubt—that was at issue. Could she have regretfully declined? In over
15 five decades, Millicent had never missed a Hunt Cup Tea. Not when she was nine months pregnant. Not when she suffered a broken leg from a riding accident. Not during The Unfortunate Incident of '82, when everyone would have understood her
20 absence. This year, at age seventy-three, Millicent would have surpassed the late Sylvia Smith for the honor of longest running attendee. Bunny Walters was to have presented her with a sterling silver mint julep cup with "M.V.D." engraved in Old Maryland
25 script.

The seating arrangement further complicated matters. As the recent Past President of the Ladies' Auxiliary, Millicent was meant to sit with the current officers on the stage at the front of the Green Spring
30 Mansion's Steeplechase Room. Now, all eyes faced the void.
    "Like a missing tooth," Bunny whispered.
    "More like a black eye," Shelby Burke replied.
    Shelby advanced what would become one of
35 several theories that day. Millicent's absence was a purposeful slight, an act of political power wrangling over the Auxiliary's bylaws. After tallying their losses at the last Membership Committee meeting— members dying off at an alarming rate; new
40 memberships anemic—Millicent had proposed a rewrite of the rules. Bloodlines, she suggested, should no longer matter for entry into the Ladies' Auxiliary. "We must evolve or die," Millicent had said.
45   "Imagine," Shelby now said, "watering down standards after 117 years for the sake of warm bodies."
    As the wait staff slid tomato aspic onto Wedgewood plates, Bunny volunteered another
50 hypothesis. Little Sorrel had sidetracked Millicent that day. The three-year-old bay gelding was the favorite in Saturday's Hunt Cup steeplechase, and Millicent had a financial stake in the horse. Bunny had heard a rumor that Little Sorrel had suffered an

CONTINUE

55 ankle injury practicing the course that morning. "Hit
the Number 14 fence," she said. Millicent must have
stayed behind to consult the equine veterinarian.

When pressed to name her source, Bunny
objected. "A lady never tells," she said, which was
60 Bunny's modus operandi whenever an unsupported
theory sprang from her own imagination.

Besides, everyone, particularly Bunny, knew that
Millicent cared more for her English hounds and the
fox hunt season than she did for the horses and this
65 annual spring steeplechase competition. Once, the
otherwise punctilious Millicent had been late to the
tea because her prize hound was whelping a litter.
Bunny and her driver had agreed to fetch Millicent
that day, and after a good wait in the idling car,
70 Bunny had marched around the main house, beyond
the guest cottages, to the kennels (ruining her freshly
polished riding boots), to find Millicent crouched in
the dirt over a whimpering dog, while a perfectly
fine vet stood idle.

75 The ladies at the tea were not alone in wondering
about the empty chair. The wait staff also puzzled
over Ms. Dunville's absence. Every year, at the end
of the event, she was known for shadowing the
Ladies' Auxiliary Treasurer and slipping the
80 headwaiter an extra envelope of cash to make up for
the meager tip. "When you have too much money,
it's easy to forget yourself," she would say.

After the Earl Grey had been steeped and sipped,
the finger sandwiches consumed, and the pastries
85 diligently ignored, the room was electric with
another theory. Millicent was not at the tea because
Millicent was dead. Women leaned across aisles to
confer about the last time Millicent had been seen in
public. No one could recall.

90 It was only as the women slipped on belted
trench coats to face the overcast March afternoon
that someone finally reached Millicent's daughter,
Evelyn, by phone in New York. Evelyn deflected
questions of her mother's absence with two words:
95 "She's indisposed."

The rumor was quickly amended. Millicent
Dunville was not dead, but she was most certainly
dying.

1

Which choice best summarizes the passage?

A) The attendees of an event speculate reasons for
   someone's absence.

B) A group of friends mock and ridicule a friend
   behind her back.

C) A distinguished guest skips out on a tea held in
   her honor.

D) The traditions of the annual Hunt Cup Tea are
   broken for the first time.

2

As presented in the passage, Millicent Dunville is
best described as

A) friendly and talkative.

B) meticulous and orderly.

C) intimidating and unapproachable.

D) aggressive and narrow-minded.

3

Which choice provides the best evidence for the
answer to the previous question?

A) Lines 10-11 ("That Millicent … protocol")

B) Lines 35-37 ("Millicent's absence … bylaws")

C) Lines 62-65 ("Besides … competition")

D) Lines 81-82 ("When you … say")

4

The passage indicates that Millicent's absence at the
Hunt Cup Tea was surprising because she

A) had RSVP'd in the affirmative.

B) had attended the Tea for fifty consecutive years.

C) was set to present an award that day.

D) was the current President of the Auxiliary.

CONTINUE

5

Which of the following was a proposed theory explaining Millicent's absence?

A) Millicent was unhappy with the seating arrangement.

B) Millicent was demonstrating her influence over the Membership Committee.

C) Millicent had been injured in a horse-riding accident.

D) Millicent was acting out of disrespect for the wait staff.

6

The author includes the series of sentences in lines 16-20 ("Not when … absence") most likely to

A) demonstrate that Millicent was no longer concerned with her attendance record at the Hunt Cup Tea.

B) characterize Millicent as uncompromising about all aspects of the Ladies' Auxiliary.

C) show that Millicent had consistently maintained a full schedule throughout her life.

D) contrast the current situation to past ones when her absence would have been more understandable.

7

As used in line 34, "advanced" most nearly means

A) accelerated.

B) achieved.

C) introduced.

D) improved.

8

It can be most reasonably inferred that upon learning of Millicent's absence the wait staff were

A) relieved because she was often a demanding and troublesome guest.

B) disappointed because Millicent previously treated them well.

C) unmoved because they were expecting her absence.

D) angry because they had made extensive preparations for her arrival.

9

Which choice provides the best evidence for the answer to the previous question?

A) Lines 14-16 ("In over … Tea")

B) Lines 27-30 ("As the … Room")

C) Lines 75-76 ("The ladies … chair")

D) Lines 77-81 ("Every year … tip")

10

As used in line 85, "diligently ignored" most nearly means

A) accidentally overlooked.

B) unsympathetically shunned.

C) thoughtfully disregarded.

D) intentionally resisted.

CONTINUE

Questions 11-21 are based on the following passage.

This passage is adapted from Atul Grover, "Should Hospital Residency Programs Be Expanded to Increase the Number of Doctors?" © 2013 Dow Jones & Company.

Thanks to baby boomers, the population over 65 will have doubled between 2000 and 2030. And when the Affordable Care Act takes full effect, up to
Line 32 million new patients will seek access to medical
5 care, many of whom will need treatment for ailments that have gone undiagnosed for years, such as cancer, diabetes, arthritis, and heart disease. This surge in demand means the U.S. will have a shortfall of at least 90,000 doctors by the end of the decade,
10 according to the Association of American Medical Colleges Center for Workforce Studies. Many parts of the country have too few doctors already.

A small, vocal minority of researchers suggest we don't need more doctors. That minority clearly is
15 having an impact: many clinicians and policy makers say there is 20% to 30% "waste" in our health-care system. Elliott Fisher, a Dartmouth professor, says those numbers are backed up by Dartmouth research.

20 The Dartmouth studies base their conclusions about waste on comparisons of health-care spending in different geographic areas. But other studies have shown that differences in the health status of patients in the different regions explain the majority of
25 variations in spending. In other words, urban areas, with their high concentrations of poor people, tend to have a higher disease burden and thus higher medical needs. Sicker patients, along with high labor costs, explain the higher levels of spending found in
30 these urban areas—not too many doctors.

There is no question that delivery of care needs to be better organized, and that some current reforms are likely to improve patient outcomes. That's true, for example, with experiments in team-based care.
35 However, these improvements in patient care have not translated to any reduction in the need for physician time.

Another new experiment—accountable-care organizations, which allow groups of providers to
40 share any savings gained by keeping their patients healthy—also hasn't been shown to reduce the number of physicians needed. Indeed, there is a lot of wishful thinking associated with ACOs, just as there was with HMOs* in the 1990s—that everyone
45 would be cared for in a way that would cost less and would prevent people from ever getting sick. Unfortunately, that didn't turn out to be the reality.

Primary care and prevention will increase the need for doctors. An 8-year-old girl with acute
50 leukemia today has an 80% chance of survival. If she survives, in the years that follow, she is likely to get a vaccine to avoid cervical cancer, take cholesterol-lowering drugs, and undergo multiple screenings for breast cancer. She may still develop heart disease or
55 cancer. And as she and millions of other people continue to age, their risk for other conditions like Alzheimer's will increase dramatically. But she, like everyone else, deserves first-rate care every step of the way. We need more doctors, not fewer.

*Health maintenance organizations

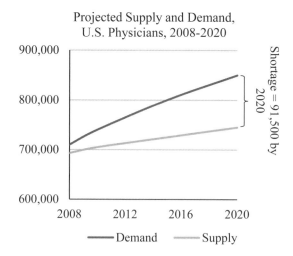

Projected Supply and Demand, U.S. Physicians, 2008-2020

CONTINUE

11

What is the author's main point about the US health care system?

A) The US health care system is about to suffer a significant collapse and hundreds of hospitals will have to be shut down.

B) There is too much wasteful spending in the current health care system, which additional doctors cannot correct.

C) The US needs to prepare for increasing health care demands by training a larger number of doctors.

D) Accountable-care organizations (ACOs) will improve the current health care system and reduce unnecessary care.

12

The author argues that the US will experience a shortfall of doctors because

A) a large portion of doctors are choosing to retire early.

B) new legislation and an aging population will increase the demand for health care.

C) many doctors waste time on non-essential treatments rather than more important ailments.

D) many medical programs have closed and fewer doctors are being trained.

13

Which choice provides the best evidence for the answer to the previous question?

A) Lines 2-7 ("And when … disease")

B) Lines 14-17 ("That minority … system")

C) Lines 25-28 ("In other … needs")

D) Lines 50-54 ("If she … cancer")

14

The passage most strongly suggests that

A) primary care and prevention, while important, will not solve the issue of a doctor shortage.

B) preventing diseases via primary care will help reduce health care costs by reducing early death.

C) relocating doctors from urban to rural areas will reduce US medical costs.

D) the first step in resolving the doctor shortage is conducting more extensive research on its causes.

15

Which choice provides the best evidence for the answer to the previous question?

A) Lines 22-25 ("But other … spending")

B) Lines 28-30 ("Sicker patients … doctors")

C) Lines 35-37 ("However these … time")

D) Lines 48-49 ("Primary care … doctors")

16

As used in line 13, "vocal" most nearly means

A) blunt.

B) outspoken.

C) oral.

D) melodic.

CONTINUE

17

The passage suggests that the "waste" (line 16) in the health care system is

A) likely to result in a reduction in the demand for physician time.

B) a significant expense, but still less expensive than the cost of training enough new doctors.

C) mostly explained by differences in patient health, rather than wasteful spending.

D) best explained by the fact that affluent patients tend to spend more on health care.

18

The primary purpose of the fifth paragraph (lines 38-47) is to

A) discuss another potential option to mitigate the coming shortage of physicians.

B) offer a historical account of physicians' various organizations.

C) provide evidence that the government is coming up with multiple ideas to address problems in health care.

D) support the author's claim that new experiments in patient care will not prevent the coming doctor shortage.

19

As used in line 36, "translated to" most nearly means

A) interpreted.

B) changed.

C) created.

D) expressed.

20

What information discussed in the first paragraph (lines 1-12) is represented by the graph?

A) The number of people seeking medical care will grow quickly in the next decade.

B) Many areas of the US are already suffering from a lack of physicians.

C) The increase in demand for physicians will largely come from individuals with previously undiagnosed conditions.

D) There is already a shortage of doctors, and the shortfall will continue to grow.

21

Which of the following claims is best supported by the graph?

A) There will be more doctors in 2020 than at any time since 2008, but also a greater shortage of doctors.

B) The doctor shortage will continue to grow until there are 91,500 fewer doctors in 2020 than there were in 2008.

C) By 2020, around 850,000 patients will need a doctor, but only about 750,000 will receive any form of treatment.

D) An increase in the supply of doctors over time will cause an even greater increase in the demand.

CONTINUE →

Questions 22-32 are based on the following passages.

The following passages are adapted from Chensheng Lu and Janet H. Silverstein, "Would Americans Be Better Off Eating a Mostly Organic Diet?" © 2014 by Dow Jones & Company.

Passage 1

Is there definitive scientific proof that an organic diet is healthier? Not yet. Robust scientific studies comparing food grown organically and food grown
Line conventionally don't exist, thanks to a lack of
5 funding for this kind of research in humans.

But let's be clear: some convincing scientific work does exist to suggest that an organic diet has its benefits. What's more, it only makes sense that food free of pesticides and chemicals is safer and better
10 for us than food containing those substances, even at trace levels. This was illustrated in a study published in the journal *Environmental Health Perspectives* in 2006. That study, which I led, showed that within five days of substituting mostly organic produce in
15 children's diets for conventional produce, pesticides disappeared from the children's urine.

Many say the pesticides found in our food are nothing to fear because the levels fall well below federal safety guidelines and thus aren't dangerous.
20 Similarly, they say the bovine growth hormone used to increase cows' milk yield is perfectly safe. But federal guidelines don't take into account what effect repeated exposure to low levels of chemicals might have on humans over time. And many
25 pesticides were eventually banned or restricted by the federal government after years of use when they were discovered to be harmful to the environment or human health.

Organic skeptics like to cite a meta-analysis
30 study published in the *Annals of Internal Medicine* last year that suggested organic foods are neither healthier nor more nutritious than their conventional counterparts. Left out of that analysis, however, were recent field studies showing that organic
35 produce, such as strawberries, leafy vegetables, and wheat, not only tastes better but contains much higher levels of phenolic acids than conventional

produce. Phenolic acids are secondary plant metabolites that can be absorbed easily through the
40 walls of the intestinal tract, and can act as potent antioxidants that prevent cellular damage, and therefore offer some protection against oxidative stress, inflammation, and cancer. Knowing that we could reduce our exposure to pesticides and increase
45 our exposure to antioxidants by eating organic food, it makes great common sense to consume more of it.

Passage 2

There is no definitive evidence that organic food is more nutritious or healthier than conventional food, but there is proof that eating more fruits and
50 vegetables and less processed food is.

Therefore, our focus as a society should be to eat as much fresh food and whole grains as possible— regardless of whether it is organically grown or not.

It is difficult to compare the nutritional value of
55 organic versus conventional food because the soil, climate, timing of harvest, and storage conditions all affect the composition of produce. Still, published studies have found no significant differences in nutritional quality between organic and nonorganic
60 produce or milk. Similarly, there is no evidence that giving bovine growth hormone (BGH) to cows changes the composition of milk or affects human health. BGH is inactive in humans and degrades in the acidic environment of the stomach.

65 As for pesticide exposure, the U.S. in 1996 established maximum permissible levels for pesticide residues in food to ensure food safety. Many studies have shown that pesticide levels in conventional produce fall well below those
70 guidelines. While it's true that organic fruits and vegetables in general contain fewer traces of these chemicals, we can't draw conclusions about what that means for health as there haven't been any long-term studies comparing the relationship between
75 exposure to pesticides from organic versus nonorganic foods and adverse health outcomes. It may seem like "common sense" to reduce exposure to these chemicals, but there are currently no good evidence-based studies to answer the question.

CONTINUE

80   We would like to think that organic food is
grown locally, put in a wheelbarrow, and brought
directly to our homes. However, much of it comes
from countries where regulations might not be as
tightly enforced as in the U.S., and labeling of the
85 foods might be misleading. And just because food is
labeled organic doesn't mean it is completely free of
pesticides. Contamination can occur from soil and
ground water containing previously used chemicals,
or during transport, processing and storage.
90 Organochlorine insecticides were recently found in
organically grown root crops and tomatoes even
though these pesticides haven't been used for 20
years.
    Given what we know, the best diet advice we can
95 give families is to eat a wide variety of produce and
whole grains. Whether they want to buy organic is
up to them.

22

The author's main purpose in Passage 1 appears to
be to

A) discuss the implications of new research into
    the health effects of organic foods.

B) persuade readers that eating organic food has
    potential health benefits.

C) critique research which claims to show that there
    are no health benefits from eating organic food.

D) argue that more funding is required to perform
    better research about organic food.

23

The first passage most strongly suggests that

A) study results conflict on some points, but agree
    that it is healthiest to eat an all-organic diet.

B) organic diets have unique health benefits,
    despite incomplete studies that don't address
    these benefits.

C) all studies conducted on humans show that
    organic diets are essential to health.

D) studies are inconclusive regarding the benefits
    of an organic diet, except when it comes to the
    diets of children.

24

Which choice provides the best evidence for the
answer to the previous question?

A) Lines 2-5 ("Robust scientific ... humans")

B) Lines 13-16 ("That study ... urine")

C) Lines 24-28 ("And many ... health")

D) Lines 33-38 ("Left ... conventional produce")

25

In Passage 2, the author's attitude toward health claims
about organic foods would best be described as

A) derisive.

B) skeptical.

C) enthusiastic.

D) quizzical.

26

As used in line 47, "definitive" most nearly means

A) conclusive.

B) consummate.

C) accepted.

D) specific.

CONTINUE

27

As used in line 76, "adverse" most nearly means

A) harmful.

B) antagonistic.

C) unlucky.

D) contrary.

28

The author's purpose in lines 80-82 ("We would … homes") is most likely to

A) provide a detailed description of the process that most people believe is implied by organic labeling.

B) characterize the organic food industry as inefficient and unsophisticated.

C) caricature misconceptions about organic food to help create a stark contrast with reality.

D) offer a vision for how organic agriculture could operate if the author's recommendations are adopted.

29

Passage 1 differs from Passage 2 in that

A) Passage 1 argues that only organic foods should be eaten, while Passage 2 argues that only non-organic foods should be eaten.

B) Passage 1 argues that people should consume more organic foods, while Passage 2 argues it is more important to eat a less processed diet.

C) Passage 1 argues that organic foods are important for health, while Passage 2 argues they could prove harmful.

D) Passage 1 argues that organic foods are overemphasized in the media, while Passage 2 argues they are not emphasized enough.

30

The authors of both passages would most likely agree with which of the following statements?

A) It is reasonable to conclude that exposure to even low levels of pesticides has a negative effect on human health.

B) No decisions can be made about organic foods, as research findings often conflict with one another.

C) Food labels are highly variable and therefore questionable, making it better to select foods based on their freshness.

D) There is information available about the health impacts of various foods that should inform decisions about diet.

31

Based on the two passages, which best describes the relationship between organic food and health risks?

A) Organic foods offer nutritional benefits that more than offset their health risks.

B) Organic foods clearly protect against a variety of known health risks.

C) Organic foods have a reputation for being healthy, but actually increase certain risks.

D) Organic foods may reduce exposure to possible but unconfirmed health risks.

32

Which choice provides the best evidence for the answer to the previous question?

A) Lines 51-53 ("Therefore, our … not")

B) Lines 70-76 ("While it's … outcomes")

C) Lines 80-82 ("We would … homes")

D) Lines 90-93 ("Organochlorine insecticides … years")

CONTINUE

Questions 33-42 are based on the following passage.

This passage is adapted from Lynne Peeples, "Moths Use Sonar-Jamming Defense to Fend Off Hunting Bats." © 2009 by Scientific American.

An insect with paper-thin wings may carry much the same defense technology as some of the military's heavy-duty warships. The finding that a
Line species of tiger moth can jam the sonar of
5 echolocating bats to avoid being eaten seems to be the "first conclusive evidence of sonar jamming in nature," says Aaron Corcoran, a biology PhD student at Wake Forest University and the lead author of the paper reporting the discovery. "It demonstrates a
10 new level of escalation in the bat-moth evolutionary arms race."

Before Corcoran's study, scientists were puzzled by why certain species of tiger moths made sound. Some speculated that the moths use it to startle bats.
15 A few pointed to its potential interference with their echolocation. General consensus, however, fell with a third hypothesis: clicks function to warn a predator not to eat the clicking prey because it is toxic, or at least pretending to be.

20 To test these hypotheses, Corcoran and his team pitted the tiger moth *Bertholdia trigona* against the big brown bat *Eptesicus fuscus*, a battle frequently fought after sundown from Central America to Colorado. High-speed infrared cameras and an
25 ultrasonic microphone recorded the action over nine consecutive nights. The process of elimination began. If moth clicks served to startle, previous studies suggested the bats should become tolerant of the sound within two or three days. "But that's not
30 what we found," says Corcoran, explaining the lack of success bats had in capturing their clicking prey even through the last nights of the study.

How about the toxic warning theory? If this were the case, according to Corcoran, bats would not find
35 the moths palatable or, if they were indeed tasty, they would quickly learn they'd been tricked. Either way, bats should start to ignore the moth's unique ultrasonic clicks. Also, bats partook readily when offered *B. trigona* that lacked the ability to click, and
40 they kept coming back for more. This attraction also

held true for clicking *B. trigona*: the predators persisted after their prey despite only reaching them about 20 percent of the time. Bats actually launched four times as many successful attacks against a control group of silent
45 moths. These findings are "only consistent with the jamming hypothesis," Corcoran notes. "But the most distinctive evidence was in the echolocation sequences of the bats."

Normally, a bat attack starts with relatively
50 intermittent sounds. They then increase in frequency— up to 200 cries per second—as the bat gets closer to the moth "so it knows where the moth is at that critical moment," Corcoran explains. But his research showed that just as bats were increasing their click frequency,
55 moths "turn on sound production full blast," clicking at a rate of up to 4,500 times a second. This furious clicking by the moths reversed the bats' pattern—the frequency of bat sonar decreased, rather than increased, as it approached its prey, suggesting that it lost its target.

60 The biological mechanism behind the moth's defense strategy is still unclear to researchers. "Most likely, moth clicks are disrupting the bat's neural processing of when echoes return," Corcoran says. Bats judge how far away a moth is based on the time delay between making
65 the cry and its audible return. This "blurring" of the bat's vision, he explains, "may be just enough to keep the moth safe."

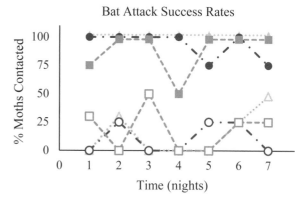

Bat Attack Success Rates

······▲······ Silent moths (bat 1)   — ●— Silent moths (bat 2)

—■— Silent moths (bat 3)   ·····△····· Clicking moths (bat 1)

— ○— Clicking moths (bat 2)   —□— Clicking moths (bat 3)

Adapted from Corcoran, Barber, and Conner, "Tiger Moth Jams Bat Sonar" © 2009 *Science*.

CONTINUE

33

The passage is primarily concerned with

A) the ways *Eptesicus fuscus* bats capture moths.

B) the discovery that tiger moths can jam bats' sonar.

C) how the tiger moths' clicking defense works.

D) why tiger moths developed defenses against bats.

34

The author describes alternate hypotheses of the moths' clicking defense in order to

A) support her claim that researchers need more evidence before they can draw any conclusions.

B) show how the researchers' experiment disproved all but one of these hypotheses.

C) signal to the reader that the researchers' data shows only one side of the debate.

D) explain the multiple reasons that this defense is effective for the moths.

35

According to Aaron Corcoran's research, which of the following represents the tiger moths' most effective defensive countermeasure?

A) Poisonous bodies

B) Defensive maneuvering

C) Clicking ultrasonically

D) Hearing ability

36

Which choice provides the best evidence for the answer to the previous question?

A) Lines 9-11 ("It demonstrates ... race")

B) Lines 16-19 ("General consensus ... be")

C) Lines 27-29 ("If moth ... days")

D) Lines 43-45 ("Bats actually ... moths")

37

According to the passage, the bats would not attack some tiger moths because

A) they lost "sight" of the moths via sonar when pursuing them.

B) they realized the moths were toxic after a few nights.

C) they preferred to focus their attention on easier prey.

D) the moths' ultrasonic clicks startled them, frightening them away.

38

Which choice provides the best evidence for the answer to the previous question?

A) Line 14 ("Some speculated ... bats")

B) Lines 33-36 ("If this ... tricked")

C) Lines 56-59 ("This furious ... target")

D) Lines 63-65 ("Bats judge ... return")

39

As used in line 38, "partook readily" most nearly means

A) ate without difficulty.

B) enjoyed without reluctance.

C) shared happily.

D) participated immediately.

CONTINUE

40

As used in line 50, "intermittent" most nearly means

A) sporadic.

B) random.

C) alternating.

D) unsteady.

41

Which concept is supported by the passage and by the information in the graph?

A) Silent moths are much less likely to become prey than clicking moths.

B) Silent moths are much more likely to become prey than clicking moths.

C) Bats have much less success hunting clicking moths than hunting silent moths.

D) Bats make numerous more attempts to hunt silent months than to hunt clicking moths.

42

Information from the graph best supports which of the following statements?

A) Bats were more effective at hunting silent moths at the end of the study than they were at the start.

B) Bats devoured half as many clicking moths as they did silent moths.

C) Bats became increasingly effective at hunting clicking moths with each subsequent night.

D) Silent moths were consistently more likely to be captured than clicking moths.

Questions 43-52 are based on the following passage.

This passage is adapted from a speech given by President Richard Nixon when he resigned his office on August 9, 1974. His decision followed the 'Watergate' scandal, in which five men connected to the Nixon administration were caught breaking into the headquarters of the opposing political party. At the time of Nixon's resignation, proceedings had already begun in Congress to impeach him and seemed likely to succeed.

Good evening. This is the 37th time I have spoken to you from this office, where so many decisions have been made that shaped the history of this Nation. Each
Line time I have done so to discuss with you some matter
5 that I believe affected the national interest. Throughout the long and difficult period of Watergate, I have felt it was my duty to persevere—to make every possible effort to complete the term of office to which you elected me. In the past few days, however, it has
10 become evident to me that I no longer have a strong enough political base in the Congress to justify continuing that effort. As long as there was such a base, I felt strongly that it was necessary to see the constitutional process through to its conclusion; that to
15 do otherwise would be unfaithful to the spirit of that deliberately difficult process, and a dangerously destabilizing precedent for the future. But with the disappearance of that base, I now believe that the constitutional purpose has been served. And there is no
20 longer a need for the process to be prolonged.

I would have preferred to carry through to the finish, whatever the personal agony it would have involved, and my family unanimously urged me to do so. But the interests of the nation must always come before any
25 personal considerations. From the discussions I have had with Congressional and other leaders I have concluded that because of the Watergate matter I might not have the support of the Congress that I would consider necessary to back the very difficult decisions
30 and carry out the duties of this office in the way the interests of the nation will require.

I have never been a quitter. To leave office before my term is completed is abhorrent to every instinct in my body. But as President, I must put the interests of
35 America first. America needs a full-time President and

CONTINUE ➡️

a full-time Congress, particularly at this time with
problems we face at home and abroad. To continue
to fight through the months ahead for my personal
vindication would almost totally absorb the time and
40 attention of both the President and the Congress in a
period when our entire focus should be on the great
issues of peace abroad and prosperity without
inflation at home. Therefore, I shall resign the
Presidency effective at noon tomorrow. Vice
45 President Ford will be sworn in as President at that
hour in this office.

By taking this action, I hope that I will have
hastened the start of that process of healing which is
so desperately needed in America. I regret deeply
50 any injuries that may have been done in the course of
the events that led to this decision. I would say only
that if some of my judgments were wrong, and some
were wrong, they were made in what I believed at
the time to be the best interest of the Nation.

55 As I recall the high hopes for America with
which we began this second term, I feel a great
sadness that I will not be here in this office working
on your behalf to achieve those hopes in the next two
and a half years. But in turning over direction of the
60 Government to Vice President Ford, I know, as I told
the nation when I nominated him for that office ten
months ago, that the leadership of America would be
in good hands.

So let us all now join together in affirming that
65 common commitment and in helping our new
President succeed for the benefit of all Americans. I
shall leave this office with regret at not completing
my term but with gratitude for the privilege of
serving as your President for the past five and a half
70 years. These years have been a momentous time in
the history of our nation and the world. They have
been a time of achievement in which we can all be
proud, achievements that represent the shared efforts
of the administration, the Congress, and the people.
75 But the challenges ahead are equally great. And they,
too, will require the support and the efforts of the
Congress and the people, working in cooperation
with the new Administration.

May God's grace be with you in all the days
80 ahead.

43

Nixon's primary purpose in delivering this speech
was most likely to

A) ask the American public for their forgiveness for
his mistakes.

B) announce his resignation and offer an
explanation to the public.

C) condemn the press for trying him in the court of
public opinion before all the facts were available.

D) express his full confidence in Vice President
Ford.

44

Which choice provides the best evidence for the
answer to the previous question?

A) Lines 5-9 ("Throughout the ... me")

B) Lines 34-35 ("But as ... first")

C) Lines 37-43 ("To continue ... home")

D) Lines 64-66 ("So let ... Americans")

45

Nixon's tone in the passage can best be described as

A) regretful.

B) excited.

C) livid.

D) uncertain.

CONTINUE

46

Which of the following is NOT a reason Nixon gives for resigning the presidency?

A) He no longer feels he has enough congressional support.

B) He can't fulfill his obligations as President while also fighting for his personal vindication in the Watergate scandal.

C) Vice President Ford stated he was ready to take on the duties of the presidency.

D) The United States faces great challenges in the coming years and requires a cooperative government to face them.

47

The passage implies that Nixon

A) wanted to continue in his office, but felt obligated to resign.

B) was in fact relieved to resign the presidency.

C) resigned in order to spend more time with his family.

D) was tricked into resigning by Congress.

48

Which choice provides the best evidence for the answer to the previous question?

A) Lines 1-3 ("This is ... Nation")

B) Lines 23-25 ("But the ... considerations")

C) Lines 59-63 ("But in ... hands")

D) Lines 66-70 ("I shall ... years")

49

Nixon uses the phrase "dangerously destabilizing precedent for the future" (lines 16-17) to describe

A) encouraging Congress to initiate impeachment proceedings.

B) permitting the President's party to commit crimes.

C) resigning too easily after difficult events occur.

D) finishing out his term in the face of serious accusations.

50

Which of the following is an issue that Nixon states Americans must address in the coming years?

A) A potential economic collapse

B) An overly powerful Congress

C) A trial of those involved in Watergate

D) A struggle for peace

CONTINUE

51

As used in line 33, "abhorrent" most nearly means

A) pitiful.

B) shocking.

C) obscene.

D) objectionable.

52

As used in line 64, "affirming" most nearly means

A) stating.

B) defending.

C) upholding.

D) swearing.

STOP

If you complete this section before the end of your allotted time, you may check your work on this section only. Do NOT use the time to work on another section.

Writing and Language Test

35 MINUTES, 44 QUESTIONS

Turn to Section 2 of your answer sheet to answer the questions in this section.

DIRECTIONS

Every passage comes with a set of questions. Some questions will ask you to consider how the writer might revise the passage to improve the expression of ideas. Other questions will ask you to consider correcting potential errors in sentence structure, usage, or punctuation. There may be one or more graphics that you will need to consult as you revise and edit the passage.

Some questions will refer to a portion of the passage that has been underlined. Other questions will refer to a particular location in a passage or ask that you consider the passage in full.

After you read the passage, select the answers to questions that most effectively improve the passage's writing quality or that adjust the passage to follow the conventions of standard written English. Many questions give you the option to select "NO CHANGE." Select that option in cases where you think the relevant part of the passage should remain as it currently is.

Questions 1-11 are based on the following passage.

A Marine Biologist's Day in Maine

Lucy is up by eight in the morning and out the door by nine. By nine thirty, **1** she's on the beach—but she isn't there to tan. Lucy is a marine biologist. She got her PhD last year, and she's now doing post-doctoral research on the coast of Maine.

[1] She meets the other researchers out by the tide pools. [2] They're focused this month on the effects of an **2** intrusive green crab population that has been harming

1

A) NO CHANGE
B) she's on the beach—but she isnt
C) shes on the beach—but she isnt
D) shes on the beach—but she isn't

2

A) NO CHANGE
B) encroaching
C) invasive
D) infringing

CONTINUE

the balance of the coastal ecosystem. [3] This loss of clams affects other species as well as the economy: the Maine clam industry typically makes $17 million annually, and the lost profits will affect fishermen, distributors, and consumers. [4] The crabs eat soft-shell clams, so the clam population is plummeting. **3** [5] Today, the research team will gather samples of both crabs and clams. **4**

3

At this point, the writer is considering inserting the following sentence:

> Soft-shell clams and green crabs are both invertebrates.

Should the writer make this insertion?

A) Yes, because the sentence serves the passage's overall purpose of providing information about marine animals.

B) Yes, because the information in the sentence explains why researchers are collecting both species.

C) No, because information in the sentence contradicts information elsewhere in the passage.

D) No, because the sentence distracts from the paragraph's focus on explaining why the researchers are collecting crabs and clams.

4

To make this paragraph most logical, sentence 3 should be placed

A) where it is now.

B) before sentence 1.

C) after sentence 4.

D) after sentence 5.

CONTINUE

Arriving at the work **5** <u>cite</u>, Lucy feels a misty spray on her arms as breakers crash on the rocks. The air is chilly; it's early June, but it still feels more like spring than summer. She hears another researcher say, "I love everything about this job except having freezing fingers first thing in the morning." Plunging her hands into a tide pool, she can't help but disagree. **6** <u>The cold is a welcome shock to the system, instantly making Lucy feel more alert and invigorated.</u>

The team spends the morning collecting specimens. Crabs scuttle around, and clams lie still in their respective buckets. Lucy works up a sweat chasing crabs across the warm sand. Compared to sitting at a desk, **7** <u>the animals are lively.</u> By noon, Lucy and her colleagues are gathering up their specimens and equipment to head indoors. **8**

5

A) NO CHANGE

B) sight

C) sleight

D) site

6

The writer is considering deleting the underlined sentence. Should the sentence be kept or deleted?

A) Kept, because it helps to maintain a clear chronology of events in the story.

B) Kept, because it helps to explain why Lucy disagrees with the other researcher.

C) Deleted, because Lucy's opinions about cold water are not statements of fact.

D) Deleted, because it doesn't provide relevant information about the qualifications necessary to become a marine biologist.

7

A) NO CHANGE

B) working with the animals is a lively activity.

C) the biologists are livelier.

D) the animal is lively.

8

The writer wants to insert another sentence here to wrap up the events of this paragraph and provide an effective transition to the next. Which of the following choices best accomplishes these goals?

A) Lucy is sad, because working on the shore is her favorite part of the day.

B) After depositing their specimens in holding tanks and breaking for lunch, they get to work in the lab.

C) They work quickly, because it's almost lunchtime and everyone has worked up an appetite.

D) The equipment will be stored for later use, and the specimens will be placed in holding tanks.

CONTINUE

Lucy spends the afternoon entering and analyzing data on a computer, tagging crabs for an experiment the following day, and monitoring the results of an ongoing experiment on the birthrate of phytoplankton, which the soft-shell clams eat. She wraps up in the lab a little after 5:00 pm, but her work for the day isn't done when she leaves the lab. **9** She will have to do more work in the lab tomorrow. Tomorrow will again start with a trip to the field station as the team of researchers continues to study the changing ecosystem.

When we hear about problems in the ocean, it's easy for us to think that they won't impact **10** ourselves. However, changes in ocean populations **11** effect animal populations at land, ocean fisheries, and ecotourism. No scientists are more engaged in addressing these oceanic environmental concerns than marine biologists.

9

Which choice most effectively supports the idea that Lucy's work continues after she leaves the lab?

A) NO CHANGE

B) Lucy needs to get an early night, because she has to get up early for work the next day.

C) After dinner at home and a call from her sister, she spends the night working on a paper.

D) Lucy works on many experiments, and they all somehow relate to soft-shell clams.

10

A) NO CHANGE

B) we.

C) us.

D) them.

11

A) NO CHANGE

B) affect animal populations at

C) effect animal populations on

D) affect animal populations on

CONTINUE

Questions 12-22 are based on the following passage.

Comets, Briefly Brightening Our Skies

[12] Blazing through the sky for short periods of time before disappearing into the galaxy, humans have long been fascinated by comets. Comets are balls of dust and ice composed of leftover materials that did not become planets during the formation of our solar system.

Comets travel around the sun in highly elliptical orbits. When far from the sun, a comet consists of only its nucleus, which is a few kilometers wide. As the nucleus gets closer to the sun (about as close as Jupiter), some of its ice sublimates, which means it turns directly into gas without melting into liquid first. The coma, a cloud of gas created by the process of sublimation, is very large compared to the initial size of the nucleus. [13] Solar winds disrupt the [14] rock particles; dust, and gas in the coma, sending tails of particles streaming out behind the comet.

12

A) NO CHANGE

B) Before disappearing into the galaxy, humans have long been fascinated by comets, blazing through the sky for brief periods of time.

C) Comets, blazing through the sky for brief periods of time before disappearing into the galaxy, have long fascinated humans.

D) For brief periods of time, humans have long been fascinated by comets, blazing through the sky before disappearing into the galaxy.

13

At this point, the writer wants to insert a sentence that will provide additional support for the preceding sentence. Which choice best accomplishes this goal?

A) On the surface of Mars, frozen CO_2 sublimates in warmer months.

B) Comas vary in size, depending on the initial size of the nucleus and environmental factors.

C) The coma can reach up to 10,000 kilometers in diameter, which is close to the size of the planet Earth.

D) At least one comet's tail was longer than 320 million kilometers.

14

A) NO CHANGE

B) rock particles, dust, and gas in the coma,

C) rock particles dust and gas in the coma,

D) rock particles, dust, and, gas in the coma

CONTINUE ►

These tails can exceed 150 million kilometers in [15] length are visible from Earth. [16] Because tails are caused by solar winds, they always point away from the sun. Thus, if a comet is moving away from the sun, then it's following its own tail. Comets are among the fastest objects in our solar system, [17] lumbering through space at speeds up to 160,000 kilometers per hour.

15

A) NO CHANGE

B) length, are

C) length and are

D) length, further are

16

Which choice most clearly explains why comet tails move away from the sun?

A) NO CHANGE

B) Tails, because of their cause, solar winds, are always pointing away from the sun.

C) They are being caused by solar winds, and tails always point away from the sun.

D) Tails are always pointing away from the sun, being caused by solar winds.

17

A) NO CHANGE

B) lurching

C) cavorting

D) hurtling

CONTINUE

Comets travel very differently around the sun than Earth does. Earth has an almost perfectly circular orbit with the sun at its center. By contrast, a comet has a long elliptical orbit with the sun far off at one end. As the comet approaches the sun its speed [18] increases, and as it moves farther away from the sun its speed stays the same. Some comets [19] conduct an orbit around the sun in a few years, while others take thousands of years to do so.

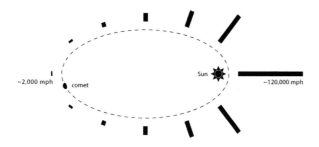

The chart above shows the approximate speed of Halley's comet at various points in its orbit. The length of each bar represents the relative speed of the comet at that point in its orbit.

18

Which choice completes the sentence with accurate information based on the graphic?

A) NO CHANGE

B) increases as the length of its tail decreases, which decreases as it moves away from the sun.

C) increases, and as it moves farther away from the sun its speed decreases.

D) decreases, and as it moves closer to the sun the length of its tail decreases.

19

A) NO CHANGE

B) make an orbit of

C) orbit

D) complete a whole entire orbit around

CONTINUE

Although it is a rare occurrence, sometimes [20] comets collide with another celestial body. In fact, a collision with a comet may have brought water to Earth. The last known collision on Earth was 65 million years ago, when a comet or an asteroid hit Earth just south of the Yucatan peninsula, creating a massive crater. The impact raised a global dust cloud, which blocked the sun and cooled the entire planet.

[21] When Halley's Comet last neared the Earth in 1986, scientists determined that it is made up of carbon, hydrogen, oxygen, and nitrogen in proportions similar to those of the human body. As distant and as different as comets may seem from us as they trail across the sky, we humans are [22] composed of the same elements as they are.

20

A) NO CHANGE

B) comets collides with another celestial body.

C) a comet collides with other celestial bodies.

D) comets collide with other celestial bodies.

21

The writer is considering deleting the underlined clause, and capitalizing the next word. Should the writer make this change?

A) Yes, because this information is irrelevant to the idea that comets are made of the same elements as humans.

B) Yes, because this information contradicts information from the preceding paragraph.

C) No, because it is important to explain when scientists made their discovery in order to convey its significance.

D) No, because the following clause would be unclear and confusing without this introductory clause.

22

A) NO CHANGE

B) constituted with

C) arranged among

D) produced through

CONTINUE

Questions 23-33 are based on the following passage.

Hamilton's Essential Contributions to the United States' Economy

[23] Of all the Founding Fathers, Alexander Hamilton's contributions were the most significant to the establishment of the United States' economy. A trusted advisor of George Washington during the Revolutionary War, Hamilton devoted considerable thought to the kind of government the new country needed. He studied European economies and governments and concluded that strong federal power was necessary for the nation's survival. When delegates [24] summoned in 1787 to create a Constitution for the new country, Hamilton was active at the Convention and instrumental in the Constitution's ratification. He convinced states to approve it through speeches and the influential Federalist Papers, which he co-authored.

23

A) NO CHANGE

B) Of all the Founding Fathers, Alexander Hamilton made the most significant contributions

C) Alexander Hamilton's contributions, compared with all of the other Founding Fathers, were the most significant

D) Alexander Hamilton's contributions, more than any Founding Father, were significant

---

24

A) NO CHANGE

B) consorted

C) convened

D) fraternized

CONTINUE

[1] **25** President Washington decided on the choice of Hamilton as the first Secretary of the Treasury. [2] Washington and his cabinet had no example to follow: they set the **26** preceding for how the executive branch of the government, including the Department of the Treasury, would operate. [3] Thus, Hamilton himself was largely responsible for establishing the United States' early economic policies. [4] Thomas Jefferson was also influential as Secretary of State, a role in which he handled matters of foreign policy. [5] Without sound economic policies, the country might not have survived. **27**

28 Hamilton knew the United States needed to have strong businesses and industries, which could not form without a strong national economy. The country was deep in debt from the war and needed additional revenue to initiate national projects. Although taxes were **29** unpopular—British Taxes having been a major cause of the Revolutionary War, Hamilton argued for their necessity. Without money, how could the government accomplish anything?

25

A) NO CHANGE

B) President Washington chose Hamilton

C) President Washington chose Hamilton to be the first Secretary

D) President Washington made his choice and decided on Hamilton as first Secretary

26

A) NO CHANGE

B) precedent

C) proceeding

D) president

27

Which sentence should be removed in order to improve the focus of this paragraph?

A) Sentence 1

B) Sentence 2

C) Sentence 3

D) Sentence 4

28

A) NO CHANGE

B) Hamilton knew: the United States

C) Hamilton knew, the United States

D) Hamilton, knew the United States,

29

A) NO CHANGE

B) unpopular, British taxes having been a major cause of the Revolutionary War Hamilton

C) unpopular British Taxes having been a major cause of the Revolutionary War, Hamilton

D) unpopular—British taxes having been a major cause of the Revolutionary War—Hamilton

CONTINUE

[30] Virginians and New Yorkers wanted the nation's capital to be in their respective states. Hamilton's "Report on Credit" stated that the government needed to repay its war bonds, take on the war debts of the states, and place a tax on imported goods. Many **[31]** members of Congress thought covering states' war debts expanded the central government's power too much, but Hamilton pointed out the difficulties of each state repaying war bonds independently. Virginia was strongly opposed to Hamilton's proposal, so Hamilton met secretly with Virginia Congressman James Madison. They agreed that Virginia would support the measure if the nation's new capital would be just outside Virginia rather than in New York. With Virginia's support, the measures of the "Report on Credit" passed.

[32] Hamilton was therefore instrumental in the process of relocating the nation's capital. Many states thought a federal bank would place too much power in the hands of the central government. **[33]** Additionally, for the sake of efficiency and to establish credit for the federal government, the nation needed a centralized bank. In 1790, the idea was approved.

30

Which choice most effectively establishes the main topic of the paragraph?

A) NO CHANGE

B) On January 14, 1790, Hamilton presented Congress with a plan of action for jumpstarting the economy.

C) President Washington relied on Hamilton.

D) Hamilton threw himself into his work, becoming increasingly obsessive as he developed his plans.

31

A) NO CHANGE

B) members' of Congress thought covering states war debts

C) members of Congress thought covering state's war debts

D) members of Congress thought covering states war debts

32

Which choice most effectively establishes the main topic of the paragraph?

A) NO CHANGE

B) Hamilton also proposed a national bank, and once again met resistance.

C) Eight cities had served as temporary capitals before this permanent capital was established.

D) There have been three national banks in the history of the United States.

33

A) NO CHANGE

B) However,

C) Therefore,

D) Likewise,

CONTINUE

Questions 34-44 are based on the following passage and supplemental material.

Artistic Game-Changer: Marcel Duchamp

Marcel Duchamp was a pioneer of the twentieth-century Conceptual Art Movement, which prompted a major expansion of the definition of "art." Conceptual Art broke with the main tenets of most of the world's earlier artistic schools, which had tended to emphasize formal elements and elegant aesthetics. The Modern Art Movement of the second half of the nineteenth century had already begun to move away from these conventions by experimenting with color and form to produce striking visual effects rather than aiming to represent their subjects directly. By **34** swelling the scope of what the public accepted as art, the Modern Art Movement laid the groundwork for the twentieth century's Conceptual **35** Art Movement. Conceptual artists shifted the focus even further, from visual effects to ideas. They rejected the notion that a piece of art must be beautiful or demonstrate artistic skill—proclaiming, **36** rather, that it should be considered art as long as it expresses, an artistic concept.

34

A) NO CHANGE

B) broadening

C) building

D) deepening

35

A) NO CHANGE

B) Art Movement and conceptual artists

C) Art Movement, conceptual artists

D) Art Movement: and conceptual artists

36

A) NO CHANGE

B) rather: that it should be considered art as long as it expresses, an artistic concept.

C) rather, that it should be considered art as long as it expresses an artistic concept.

D) rather, that it should, be considered art as long as it expresses an artistic concept.

CONTINUE

[1] Duchamp was born in France in 1887 and lived and worked as an artist in both France and the United States. [2] Many critics claimed that the piece was not legitimate, but he maintained that it was the provocative, **37** trendy nature of his act that made it art. [3] Disenchanted with the commercial art world, he refused to engage in practices generally seen as necessary for financial success and recognition: developing an identifiable aesthetic, frequently showing his work publicly, or creating pieces similar to each other for the sake of profit **38** , and in 1955 he became a U.S. citizen. [4] He developed the notion of a "Readymade," a pre-existing object that an artist finds, chooses, and claims as art, **39** modifying the object only by signing it. [5] Famously, Duchamp's 1917 submission to an art exhibition, *Fountain*, consisted of a urinal that he rotated ninety degrees and signed with a pseudonym. **40**

37

A) NO CHANGE

B) gimmicky

C) traditional

D) innovative

38

The writer is considering deleting the underlined portion of this sentence. Should the writer make this change?

A) Yes, because it occurs later in time than other events mentioned later in the paragraph.

B) Yes, because it distracts from the sentence's focus on the practices that Duchamp rejected.

C) No, because the fact that Duchamp was not a U.S. citizen explains why critics disliked him.

D) No, because the fact that Duchamp became a U.S. citizen shows that he rejected the artistic establishment.

39

A) NO CHANGE

B) modifying the object by signing it by the artist.

C) modifying the object, the piece of art, signing it.

D) modifying the object only by applying his or her, the artist's, signature.

40

To make the paragraph most logical, sentence 2 should be placed

A) where it is now

B) before sentence 1

C) before sentence 5

D) after sentence 5

CONTINUE ▶

When Duchamp was asked in an interview about his disregard for public opinion, he **41** says, "You should wait for fifty . . . or a hundred years for your true public. That is the only public that interests me." **42** Because he did not receive critical acclaim for much of his career, over fifty years later Duchamp is seen as one of the most influential artists of the twentieth century. Duchamp's influence can be seen in the work of later conceptual artists: Andy Warhol, with his pop art images and prints of everyday objects; Jackson Pollock, with his canvases covered in splattered paint; Sol LeWitt, **43** who made cubic steel "structures." Thus, Duchamp achieved the respect of the public he cared **44** about, Duchamp and the Conceptual Art Movement permanently changed ideas about art's definition, its scope, and its possibilities.

41

A) NO CHANGE
B) will say
C) is saying
D) said

42

A) NO CHANGE
B) Considering that
C) Although
D) However

43

A) NO CHANGE
B) with his
C) in making
D) by making

44

A) NO CHANGE
B) about. Duchamp
C) about Duchamp
D) about? Duchamp

STOP

If you complete this section before the end of your allotted time, you may check your work on this section only. Do NOT use the time to work on another section.

Math Test – No Calculator

25 MINUTES, 20 QUESTIONS

Turn to Section 3 of your answer sheet to answer the questions in this section.

DIRECTIONS

Questions **1-15** ask you to solve a problem, select the best answer among four choices, and fill in the corresponding circle on your answer sheet. Questions **16-20** ask you to solve a problem and enter your answer in a grid provided on your answer sheet. There are detailed instructions on entering answers into the grid before question 16. You may use your test booklet for scratch work.

NOTES

1. You **may not** use a calculator.
2. Variables and expressions represent real numbers unless stated otherwise.
3. Figures are drawn to scale unless stated otherwise.
4. Figures lie in a plane unless stated otherwise.
5. The domain of a function f is defined as the set of all real numbers x for which $f(x)$ is also a real number, unless stated otherwise.

REFERENCE

$$A = \frac{1}{2}bh$$

$$a^2 + b^2 = c^2$$

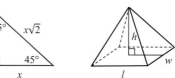

Special Triangles

$$V = \frac{1}{3}lwh$$

$$V = \frac{1}{3}\pi r^2 h$$

$$A = lw$$

$$V = lwh$$

$$V = \pi r^2 h$$

$$A = \pi r^2$$
$$C = 2\pi r$$

$$V = \frac{4}{3}\pi r^3$$

There are 360° in a circle.

The sum of the angles in a triangle is 180°.

The number of radians of arc in a circle is 2π.

CONTINUE

1

If $42 = 3(x - 4)$, what is the value of x?

A) 4

B) 10

C) 18

D) 20

2

For what value of k does $x^2 + kx + 9 = (x + 3)^2$?

A) 0

B) 3

C) 6

D) 9

3

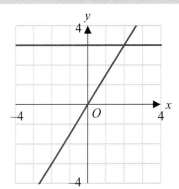

If (x, y) is the solution to the system of equations graphed above, what is the value of x in terms of y?

A) y

B) $\dfrac{2}{3}y$

C) $\dfrac{1}{3}y$

D) $-\dfrac{1}{3}y$

4

A barrel of crude oil is extracted from shale at a cost of $51, and is then transported to and from the refinery at a cost of $6 each direction. Oil is processed three times at the refinery plant, at a cost of $9 each time. What is the profit, in dollars per barrel, if one barrel is sold for $93? (Profit is equal to revenue minus expenses.)

A) 1

B) 2

C) 3

D) 4

CONTINUE

5

If $c - 1 = 3$, what is the value of $(c \times c) - 1$?

A) 3

B) 8

C) 10

D) 15

6

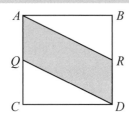

Note: Figure not drawn to scale.

The square above has an area of 100. If Q is the midpoint of $\overline{AC}$ and R is the midpoint of $\overline{BD}$, what is the area of the shaded region?

A) 40

B) 50

C) 60

D) 75

7

If $2(3a - b) = 4b$ and $b = 6$, what is the value of a?

A) 6

B) 5

C) 2

D) −6

8

$$\frac{2x}{x - 1} - \frac{3x}{x + 1}$$

Which of the following expressions is equivalent to the expression above?

A) $-\dfrac{x}{x^2 - 1}$

B) $\dfrac{5x - x^2}{x^2 - 1}$

C) $-\dfrac{x}{x - 1}$

D) $-\dfrac{6x}{x^2 - 1}$

9

Joel is a years older than Luca. In b years, Joel will be twice as old as Luca. What is Joel's present age, in terms of a and b?

A) $-2(a - b)$

B) $-2a - b$

C) $2a - b$

D) $a - b$

10

$$\left| x - 3 \right| \leq 5$$

Which of the following inequalities is equivalent to the absolute value inequality above?

A) $-2 \leq x \leq 8$

B) $-8 \leq x \leq 2$

C) $x \leq -2$ or $x \geq 8$

D) $x \leq -8$ or $x \geq 2$

CONTINUE

11

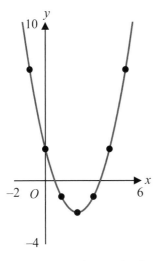

The figure above shows the graph of a quadratic function f in the xy-plane, with a minimum point at $(2, -2)$. Which of the following is equal to $f(5)$?

A) $f(-2)$

B) $f(-1)$

C) $f(0)$

D) $f(1)$

12

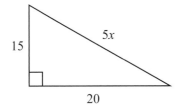

What is the value of x, given the triangle above?

A) 5

B) 10

C) 25

D) 31

13

$$\frac{16^x}{4^a + 4^a + 4^a + 4^a} = \frac{1}{4}$$

Which of the following equations represents the value of x in terms of a, given the equation above?

A) $\dfrac{a}{4} = x$

B) $\dfrac{a}{2} = x$

C) $a = x$

D) $2a = x$

14

The sum of a and b is 132. If a is the square of b and the product of a and b is negative, what is a?

A) 121

B) 144

C) 169

D) 196

15

$$y = 5x^2 - 3x - 1$$
$$y + 6 = 7x$$

If (x, y) is a point where the two equations above intersect, what is the value of $\dfrac{x}{y}$?

A) -1

B) 1

C) 2

D) 3

CONTINUE

DIRECTIONS

Questions **16-20** ask you to solve a problem and enter your answer in the grid provided on your answer sheet. When completing grid-in questions:

1. You are required to bubble in the circles for your answers. It is recommended, but not required, that you also write your answer in the boxes above the columns of circles. Points will be awarded based only on whether the circles are filled in correctly.

2. Fill in only one circle in a column.

3. You can start your answer in any column as long as you can fit in the whole answer.

4. For questions 16-20, no answers will be negative numbers.

5. **Mixed numbers**, such as $4\frac{2}{5}$, must be gridded as decimals or improper fractions, such as 4.4 or as 22/5. "42/5" will be read as "forty-two over five," not as "four and two-fifths."

6. If your answer is a **decimal** with more digits than will fit on the grid, you may round it or cut it off, but you must fill the entire grid.

7. If there are **multiple correct solutions** to a problem, all of them will be considered correct. Enter only **one** on the grid.

Practice Tests | **Ivy Global**

CONTINUE

16

A stone is dropped from a height of 9 meters above the ground. If the height function can be modeled by the equation $h(t) = a - t^2$, where t is time in seconds, h is height in meters, and a is the initial height, how many seconds does it take for the stone to hit the ground?

17

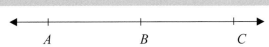

Note: Figure not drawn to scale.

A, B, and C lie on a line, as shown above. The length of $\overline{AB}$ is $x - 4$ and the length of $\overline{AC}$ is $x + 6$. What is the length of $\overline{BC}$?

18

If $f(x) = 8x + 1$ and $g(x) = 3x - 1$, what is the value of $\dfrac{f(2)}{g(f(0))}$?

19

$$\frac{d}{y} = \frac{12}{d}$$
$$y^2 = 6y - 9$$

If d is positive, what is the value of d in the system of equations above?

20

The imaginary number i is defined such that $i^2 = -1$. What is the value of $(1 - i\sqrt{5})(1 + i\sqrt{5})$?

STOP

If you complete this section before the end of your allotted time, you may check your work on this section only. Do NOT use the time to work on another section.

Math Test – Calculator

55 MINUTES, 38 QUESTIONS

Turn to Section 4 of your answer sheet to answer the questions in this section.

DIRECTIONS

Questions **1-30** ask you to solve a problem, select the best answer among four choices, and fill in the corresponding circle on your answer sheet. Questions **31-38** ask you to solve a problem and enter your answer in a grid provided on your answer sheet. There are detailed instructions on entering answers into the grid before question 31. You may use your test booklet for scratch work.

NOTES

1. You **may** use a calculator.
2. Variables and expressions represent real numbers unless stated otherwise.
3. Figures are drawn to scale unless stated otherwise.
4. Figures lie in a plane unless stated otherwise.
5. The domain of a function f is defined as the set of all real numbers x for which $f(x)$ is also a real number, unless stated otherwise.

REFERENCE

   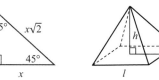

$A = \frac{1}{2}bh$ $a^2 + b^2 = c^2$ Special Triangles $V = \frac{1}{3}lwh$ $V = \frac{1}{3}\pi r^2 h$

$A = lw$ $V = lwh$ $V = \pi r^2 h$ $A = \pi r^2$ $V = \frac{4}{3}\pi r^3$

$C = 2\pi r$

There are 360° in a circle.

The sum of the angles in a triangle is 180°.

The number of radians of arc in a circle is 2π.

CONTINUE

1

A dressmaker wants to know the number of customers who will visit his shop on Tuesday. On Monday, he has 8 dresses on sale, which attracts 40 customers in addition to his 4 regular customers. On Tuesday, he has 2 dresses on sale, and only 1 of his regular customers visits. He models Monday with the equation $8c + 4 = 44$, and Tuesday with the equation $2c + 1 = n$, where c is the number of customers attracted by each dress on sale, and n is the number of customers who visit his shop on Tuesday. What is the value of n?

A) 8

B) 9

C) 10

D) 11

2

If a farmer purchases 8 pigs for every 1.5 acres of land and has 6 acres of land set aside for pigs, how many pigs will she purchase?

A) 24

B) 32

C) 40

D) 48

3

If $y = x - 2$ and $x = 2y + 4$, what is the value of x?

A) 1

B) 0

C) –2

D) –6

4

b	0	2	4	6
$S(b)$	3	4	5	6

A warehouse is calculating the total number of shelves, S, that are needed if it stores extra boxes, b. Which of the following expressions defines $S(b)$ in the table above?

A) $S(b) = b + 3$

B) $S(b) = \dfrac{1}{2}b + 3$

C) $S(b) = 3b$

D) $S(b) = 2b$

5

$$\text{Option 1: } \frac{t - 1}{3} = p$$

$$\text{Option 2: } \frac{2t - 6}{4} = p$$

Two ticket price options are offered to a person buying more than three tickets, where t is the number of tickets, and p is the total price of tickets in dollars, as shown above. For what value of t would both options be the same price?

A) 5

B) 7

C) 8

D) 16

CONTINUE

6

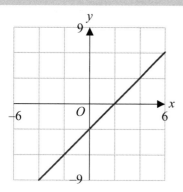

What is the slope of the line graphed above in the *xy*-plane?

A) -1

B) $\dfrac{3}{2}$

C) 1

D) $\dfrac{2}{3}$

7

The population of an invasive species of moth doubles every 5 years. If the population in 2005 was 300, what will the population be in 2020?

A) 900

B) 1,200

C) 2,000

D) 2,400

8

John fills his bag with a number of five-cent candies, v, and ten-cent candies, t. If he has a total of 54 candies and his candies are worth \$3.10 in total, which of the following must be true?

I. $\$0.05v + \$0.10t = \$3.10$
II. $54 = v + t$
III. $\$0.05 \times (54 - v) + \$0.10v = \$3.10$

A) I only

B) I and II only

C) I, II, and III

D) None of the above

9

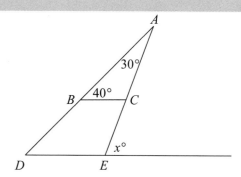

In the figure above, if $\overline{BC} \parallel \overline{DE}$, what is the value of x?

A) 30

B) 40

C) 70

D) 110

CONTINUE

10

A certain type of eel has been found to measure between 50 centimeters and 90 centimeters long. Given this information, which of the following measurements could be the length of one of these eels? (Note: 1 inch = 2.54 centimeters)

A) 19.3 inches

B) 25.2 inches

C) 35.8 inches

D) 60.0 inches

11

Two scientists are attempting to determine the age of a granite formation in the Scottish Highlands. The first scientist samples granite from 10 random sites in the Highlands and concludes that the granite is 600 ± 60 million years old. If the second scientist wants to obtain a margin of error that is smaller than the first scientist's, which of the following would be the best number of random samples to take?

A)   10

B)   60

C)   100

D) 1,000

Questions 12 and 13 refer to the following information.

A survey on coffee consumption was conducted among a random sample of students at a university. A total of 200 students were surveyed. The table below displays a summary of the results.

Student Year	Cups of Coffee (Per Day)			
	0	1	2 or more	Total
Freshman	25	9	16	50
Sophomore	5	19	26	50
Junior	10	6	50	66
Senior	0	2	32	34
Total	40	36	124	200

12

Based on the information in the table, who would be the least likely to drink any cups of coffee during the day?

A) a freshman

B) a sophomore

C) a junior

D) a senior

CONTINUE

13

Which of the following statements about the students surveyed is <u>not</u> supported by the table?

A) A higher percentage of juniors than sophomores drink 2 or more cups of coffee per day.

B) A higher percentage of juniors than seniors drink 2 or more cups of coffee per day.

C) More than 50% of students drink 2 or more cups of coffee per day.

D) 50% of freshmen do not drink coffee.

14

To ride on a roller coaster, a rider must be at least 3.5 feet tall and at most 6.5 feet tall. Which of the following inequalities represents the possible height, h, in feet, of a rider who can ride this roller coaster?

A) $h < 3.5$ or $h > 6.5$

B) $h \leq 3.5$ or $h \geq 6.5$

C) $3.5 < h < 6.5$

D) $3.5 \leq h \leq 6.5$

15

Day	Number of books
Monday	x
Tuesday	$2x$
Wednesday	$0.5x$
Thursday	x
Friday	$3.5x$

The above table outlines how many books Anthony reads per day in terms of x. What is the average daily number of books that Anthony reads, in terms of x?

A) $\dfrac{5x}{8}$

B) x

C) $\dfrac{8x}{5}$

D) $8x$

16

$$x^2 - 1 < x^3$$

For which of the following values of x is the above inequality true?

A) -3

B) -2

C) -1

D) 0

CONTINUE

Practice Tests | Ivy Global

17

Growth of Bacteria Populations

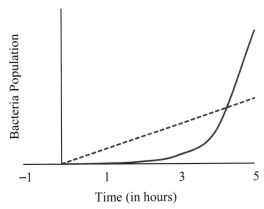

The population of Bacteria A is represented by the solid line, and the population of Bacteria B is represented by the dotted line in the graph shown above. Which of the following statements is true?

A) Bacteria A is growing linearly, but Bacteria B is growing exponentially.

B) Bacteria A is growing exponentially, but Bacteria B is growing linearly.

C) Both Bacteria A and Bacteria B are growing linearly.

D) Both Bacteria A and Bacteria B are growing exponentially.

18

$$y = -(x - 2)^2 + 4$$

Which of the following values of x results in the largest value of y in the equation above?

A) −2

B) 0

C) 2

D) 4

19

$$x = 12$$
$$3x = 4y^2$$

In the system of equations above, if $y > 0$, what is the value of x^2y?

A) 36

B) 108

C) 432

D) 1,296

20

A total of 168 fish are evenly stocked in several ponds. The number of ponds and the number of fish per pond are two consecutive even numbers. If the number of fish per pond is the larger of the two numbers, how many ponds are there?

A) 24

B) 21

C) 14

D) 12

CONTINUE

Questions 21 and 22 refer to the following information.

Number of Passengers
Using the Commuter Line

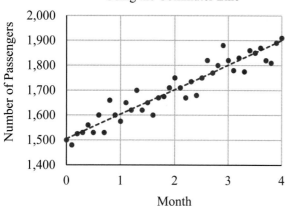

The graph above shows the number of passengers on a commuter train line over the course of 4 months.

21

If *m* is the number of months that have passed since the data started being collected, which of the following functions best represents the graph's line of best fit?

A) $f(m) = 200 + 1{,}500m$

B) $f(m) = 150 + 100m$

C) $f(m) = 1500 + 100m$

D) $f(m) = 1500 + 150m$

22

Based on the line of best fit, which of the following is the best estimate for how many passengers will be using the commuter line after one year?

A) 1,900

B) 2,000

C) 2,200

D) 2,700

23

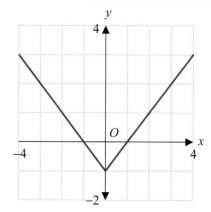

The function $f(x)$ is graphed above. If $g(x) = f(x) - 1$, which of the following statements is true?

A) $g(x)$ is always less than or equal to zero.

B) $g(x)$ is always either greater than or equal to zero, or less than or equal to negative two.

C) $g(x)$ is always greater than or equal to negative two.

D) $g(x)$ is always greater than negative one, but less than five.

CONTINUE

24

In Ms. Feldman's two science classes, approximately 3 percent of her students receive an A, and approximately 9 percent of her students receive a B. If there were 26 students in her first science class and 15 students in her second science class, which of the following is closest to the total number of students who receive either an A or a B in Ms. Feldman's two science classes?

A) 3

B) 5

C) 6

D) 9

25

The average age of 5 people in a room is 85 years. If the oldest person in the room is 100 years old, which of the following statements cannot be true?

A) The youngest person is 20 years old.

B) The range of ages in the room is 75 years.

C) The median age in the room is greater than 25 years.

D) The mode age in the room is 85 years.

26

Let j equal 925 and k equal 5,550. If a number, n, is added to j, such that the ratio of $j + n$ to k is 1:3, what is the ratio of n to $j + n$, expressed as a percentage of $j + n$?

A) 30%

B) 40%

C) 50%

D) 60%

27

$$f(t) = -2t^2 + 4t + 30$$

When Amelia goes cliff diving, her height above the water can be modelled by the function above, where t represents time in seconds. How long, in seconds, does it take for Amelia to hit the water?

A) 3

B) 4

C) 5

D) 6

28

An engineer is calculating how many planks of wood, w, and bags of cement, b, he needs to build s squares of a sidewalk. He calculates that $s:b$ is 3:1. If the sum of s and b is w, what is the value of s, in terms of w?

A) $\dfrac{4}{3}w$

B) $\dfrac{3}{4}w$

C) $w - 3$

D) $w - 4$

CONTINUE

Questions 29 and 30 refer to the following information.

Number of Foreign Language
Courses Offered in a High School

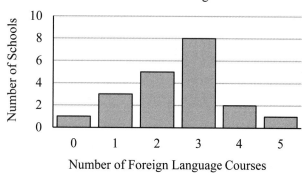

The results of a survey of 20 high schools based on the number of foreign language courses they offer are shown in the chart above.

29

How many schools offer <u>fewer</u> foreign language courses than the mean number of foreign language courses offered across the 20 schools?

A)   9

B)   10

C)   11

D)   17

30

The superintendent visits one of these 20 schools randomly for an inspection. What is the probability that the school he visits offers <u>at least</u> three foreign language courses?

A)   45%

B)   50%

C)   55%

D)   60%

CONTINUE

DIRECTIONS

Questions **31-38** ask you to solve a problem and enter your answer in the grid provided on your answer sheet. When completing grid-in questions:

1. You are required to bubble in the circles for your answers. It is recommended, but not required, that you also write your answer in the boxes above the columns of circles. Points will be awarded based only on whether the circles are filled in correctly.

2. Fill in only one circle in a column.

3. You can start your answer in any column as long as you can fit in the whole answer.

4. For questions 31-38, no answers will be negative numbers.

5. **Mixed numbers**, such as $4\frac{2}{5}$, must be gridded as decimals or improper fractions, such as 4.4 or as 22/5. "42/5" will be read as "forty-two over five," not as "four and two-fifths."

6. If your answer is a **decimal** with more digits than will fit on the grid, you may round it or cut it off, but you must fill the entire grid.

7. If there are **multiple correct solutions** to a problem, all of them will be considered correct. Enter only **one** on the grid.

CONTINUE

31

Three containers of water are poured evenly into two small pools. If the containers have 11 liters, 12 liters, and 13 liters of water each, how many liters of water are poured into one of the pools?

32

$$-15(2 + n) = -16(n - 7)$$

What is the value of n in the equation above?

33

One pizza is being shared among students and teachers. If the students take 30% of the pizza, and Rodrigo eats 60% of the students' pizza, what percent of the original pizza does Rodrigo eat? (Note: Disregard the percent symbol when entering your answer.)

34

$$8^{3x - 1} = \frac{1}{4^{3x - 21}}$$

What is the value of x in the equation above?

35

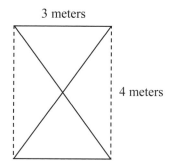

Two triangles are being sprayed onto a small rectangular playing field, with side lengths 3 meters and 4 meters, as shown in the figure above. If the solid lines represent the borders of these two triangles, what is the sum of the triangles' perimeters?

CONTINUE

36

What is the radius of the circle with the equation
$x^2 + y^2 - 7 = 9$?

Questions 37 and 38 refer to the following information.

Boyle's law states that at a constant temperature, the pressure and volume of any gas are inversely proportional. The law is written according to the equation $PV = k$, where P is the pressure of a gas, V is the volume of the gas, and k is a constant. In laboratories, a cylindrical syringe with a rubber stopper can be used to contain the gas, as shown in the diagram below.

Gas

37

Gas is contained in a syringe with a rubber stopper at one end. The gas in the syringe initially has a pressure of 78 kilopascals, and a volume of 30 cubic centimeters. If the stopper is pushed down so that the gas takes up 20 cubic centimeters, what is the new pressure of the gas, in kilopascals?

38

A scientist inserts 50 cubic centimeters of gas into syringe A and 40 cubic centimeters of the same gas into syringe B, maintaining a pressure of 15.6 kilopascals in both syringes. He then applies a rubber stopper to the syringes' ends. If the scientist compresses both syringes to a volume of 30 cubic centimeters, what is the pressure of the gas in syringe B as a percentage of the pressure of the gas in syringe A? (Disregard the percent symbol when gridding your answer.)

STOP

If you complete this section before the end of your allotted time, you may check your work on this section only. Do NOT use the time to work on another section.

Essay (Optional)

50 MINUTES

Turn to the lined pages of your answer sheet to write your essay.

DIRECTIONS

This essay is optional. It is a chance for you to demonstrate how well you can understand and analyze a written passage. Your essay should show that you have carefully read the passage and should be a concisely written analysis that is both logical and clear.

You must write your entire essay on the lines in your answer booklet. No additional paper will be provided aside from the Planning Page inside your answer booklet. You will be able to write your entire essay in the space provided if you make use of every line, keep tight margins, and write at a suitable size. Don't forget to keep your handwriting legible for the readers evaluating your essay.

You will have 50 minutes to read the passage in this booklet and to write an essay in response to the prompt provided at the end of the passage.

REMINDERS

- What you write in this booklet will not be evaluated. Write your essay in the answer booklet only.

- Essays that are off-topic will not be evaluated.

As you read the passage below, consider how Frank Pasquale uses

- evidence, like examples or facts, to support his arguments.
- logical reasoning to develop his ideas and to connect his claims to his evidence.
- stylistic or persuasive techniques, such as the choice of particular words or appeals to his readers' emotions, to give power to the ideas put forth.

Adapted from Frank Pasquale, "The Dark Market for Personal Data," © 2014 by The New York Times Company. Originally published October 16, 2014.

1   The reputation business is exploding. Having eroded privacy for decades, shady, poorly regulated data miners, brokers and resellers have now taken creepy classification to a whole new level.

2   There are lists of "impulse buyers." Lists of suckers: gullible consumers who have shown that they are susceptible to "vulnerability-based marketing." And lists of those deemed commercially undesirable because they live in or near trailer parks or nursing homes. Not to mention lists of people who have been accused of wrongdoing, even if they were not charged or convicted.

3   Typically sold at a few cents per name, the lists don't have to be particularly reliable to attract eager buyers—mostly marketers, but also, increasingly, financial institutions vetting customers to guard against fraud, and employers screening potential hires.

4   There are three problems with these lists. First, they are often inaccurate. For example, as *The Washington Post* reported, an Arkansas woman found her credit history and job prospects wrecked after she was mistakenly listed as a methamphetamine dealer. It took her years to clear her name and find a job.

5   Second, even when the information is accurate, many of the lists have no business being in the hands of retailers, bosses or banks. Having a medical condition, or having been a victim of a crime, is simply not relevant to most employment or credit decisions.

6   Third, people aren't told they are on these lists, so they have no opportunity to correct bad information. The Arkansas woman found out about the inaccurate report only when she was denied a job. She was one of the rare ones.

7   "Data-driven" hiring practices are under increasing scrutiny, because the data may be a proxy for race, class, or disability. For example, in 2011, CVS settled a charge of disability discrimination after a job applicant challenged a personality test that probed mental health issues. But if an employer were to secretly use lists based on inferences about mental health, it would be nearly impossible for an affected applicant to find out what was going on. Secrecy is discrimination's best friend: unknown unfairness can never be detected, let alone corrected.

8   These problems can't be solved with existing law. The Federal Trade Commission has strained to understand personal data markets—a $156-billion-a-year industry—and it can't find out where the data brokers get their information, and whom they sell it to. Hiding behind a veil of trade secrecy, most refuse to divulge this vital information…

9   It's unrealistic to expect individuals to inquire, broker by broker, about their files. Instead, we need to require brokers to make targeted disclosures to consumers. Uncovering problems in Big Data (or decision models based on that data) should not be a burden we expect individuals to solve on their own.

10 Privacy protections in other areas of the law can and should be extended to cover consumer data. The Health Insurance Portability and Accountability Act, or HIPAA, obliges doctors and hospitals to give patients access to their records. The Fair Credit Reporting Act gives loan and job applicants, among others, a right to access, correct and annotate files maintained by credit reporting agencies.

11 It is time to modernize these laws by applying them to all companies that peddle sensitive personal information. If the laws cover only a narrow range of entities, they may as well be dead letters. For example, protections in HIPAA don't govern the "health profiles" that are compiled and traded by data brokers, which can learn a great deal about our health even without access to medical records.

12 Congress should require data brokers to register with the Federal Trade Commission, and allow individuals to request immediate notification once they have been placed on lists that contain sensitive data. Reputable data brokers will want to respond to good-faith complaints to make their lists more accurate. Plaintiffs' lawyers could use defamation law to hold recalcitrant firms accountable.

13 We need regulation to help consumers recognize the perils of the new information landscape without being overwhelmed with data. The right to be notified about the use of one's data and the right to challenge and correct errors are fundamental. Without these protections, we'll continue to be judged by a big-data Star Chamber of unaccountable decision makers using questionable sources.

Write an essay in which you explain how Frank Pasquale builds an argument to persuade his audience that privacy laws should be updated to regulate the modern data industry. In your essay, analyze how Pasquale uses one or more of the features listed in the directions on the previous page (or features of your own choice) to strengthen the logic and persuasiveness of his argument. Be sure that your analysis focuses on the most relevant features of the passage.

Your essay should not explain whether you agree with Pasquale's claims, but rather explain how Pasquale builds an argument to persuade his audience.

Practice Test 2

SAT

Directions

- Work on just one section at a time.

- If you complete a section before the end of your allotted time, use the extra minutes to check your work on that section only. Do NOT use the time to work on another section.

Using Your Test Booklet

- No credit will be given for anything written in the test booklet. You may use the test booklet for scratch paper.

- You are not allowed to continue answering questions in a section after the allotted time has run out. This includes marking answers on your answer sheet that you previously noted in your test booklet.

- You are not allowed to fold pages, take pages out of the test booklet, or take any pages home.

Answering Questions

- Each answer must be marked in the corresponding row on the answer sheet.

- Each bubble must be filled in completely and darkly within the lines.

Correct ●   Incorrect

- Be careful to bubble in the correct part of the answer sheet.

- Extra marks on your answer sheet may be marked as incorrect answers and lower your score.

- Make sure you use a No. 2 pencil.

Scoring

- You will receive one point for each correct answer.

- Incorrect answers will NOT result in points deducted. Even if you are unsure about an answer, you should make a guess.

DO NOT BEGIN THIS TEST

UNTIL YOUR PROCTOR TELLS YOU TO DO SO

 For printable answer sheets, please visit **ivyglobal.com/study**.

Section 1

	A B C D		A B C D		A B C D		A B C D		A B C D
1	○ ○ ○ ○	12	○ ○ ○ ○	23	○ ○ ○ ○	34	○ ○ ○ ○	45	○ ○ ○ ○
2	○ ○ ○ ○	13	○ ○ ○ ○	24	○ ○ ○ ○	35	○ ○ ○ ○	46	○ ○ ○ ○
3	○ ○ ○ ○	14	○ ○ ○ ○	25	○ ○ ○ ○	36	○ ○ ○ ○	47	○ ○ ○ ○
4	○ ○ ○ ○	15	○ ○ ○ ○	26	○ ○ ○ ○	37	○ ○ ○ ○	48	○ ○ ○ ○
5	○ ○ ○ ○	16	○ ○ ○ ○	27	○ ○ ○ ○	38	○ ○ ○ ○	49	○ ○ ○ ○
6	○ ○ ○ ○	17	○ ○ ○ ○	28	○ ○ ○ ○	39	○ ○ ○ ○	50	○ ○ ○ ○
7	○ ○ ○ ○	18	○ ○ ○ ○	29	○ ○ ○ ○	40	○ ○ ○ ○	51	○ ○ ○ ○
8	○ ○ ○ ○	19	○ ○ ○ ○	30	○ ○ ○ ○	41	○ ○ ○ ○	52	○ ○ ○ ○
9	○ ○ ○ ○	20	○ ○ ○ ○	31	○ ○ ○ ○	42	○ ○ ○ ○		
10	○ ○ ○ ○	21	○ ○ ○ ○	32	○ ○ ○ ○	43	○ ○ ○ ○		
11	○ ○ ○ ○	22	○ ○ ○ ○	33	○ ○ ○ ○	44	○ ○ ○ ○		

Section 2

	A B C D		A B C D		A B C D		A B C D		A B C D
1	○ ○ ○ ○	10	○ ○ ○ ○	19	○ ○ ○ ○	28	○ ○ ○ ○	37	○ ○ ○ ○
2	○ ○ ○ ○	11	○ ○ ○ ○	20	○ ○ ○ ○	29	○ ○ ○ ○	38	○ ○ ○ ○
3	○ ○ ○ ○	12	○ ○ ○ ○	21	○ ○ ○ ○	30	○ ○ ○ ○	39	○ ○ ○ ○
4	○ ○ ○ ○	13	○ ○ ○ ○	22	○ ○ ○ ○	31	○ ○ ○ ○	40	○ ○ ○ ○
5	○ ○ ○ ○	14	○ ○ ○ ○	23	○ ○ ○ ○	32	○ ○ ○ ○	41	○ ○ ○ ○
6	○ ○ ○ ○	15	○ ○ ○ ○	24	○ ○ ○ ○	33	○ ○ ○ ○	42	○ ○ ○ ○
7	○ ○ ○ ○	16	○ ○ ○ ○	25	○ ○ ○ ○	34	○ ○ ○ ○	43	○ ○ ○ ○
8	○ ○ ○ ○	17	○ ○ ○ ○	26	○ ○ ○ ○	35	○ ○ ○ ○	44	○ ○ ○ ○
9	○ ○ ○ ○	18	○ ○ ○ ○	27	○ ○ ○ ○	36	○ ○ ○ ○		

Section 3 (No-Calculator)

	A	B	C	D			A	B	C	D			A	B	C	D			A	B	C	D			A	B	C	D
1	○	○	○	○		4	○	○	○	○		7	○	○	○	○		10	○	○	○	○		13	○	○	○	○
2	○	○	○	○		5	○	○	○	○		8	○	○	○	○		11	○	○	○	○		14	○	○	○	○
3	○	○	○	○		6	○	○	○	○		9	○	○	○	○		12	○	○	○	○		15	○	○	○	○

Only answers that are gridded will be scored. You will not receive credit for anything written in the boxes.

16   17   18   19   20

(grid-in answer bubbles for questions 16–20, each with /, ., and digits 0–9)

Section 4 (Calculator)

	A	B	C	D			A	B	C	D			A	B	C	D			A	B	C	D			A	B	C	D
1	○	○	○	○		7	○	○	○	○		13	○	○	○	○		19	○	○	○	○		25	○	○	○	○
2	○	○	○	○		8	○	○	○	○		14	○	○	○	○		20	○	○	○	○		26	○	○	○	○
3	○	○	○	○		9	○	○	○	○		15	○	○	○	○		21	○	○	○	○		27	○	○	○	○
4	○	○	○	○		10	○	○	○	○		16	○	○	○	○		22	○	○	○	○		28	○	○	○	○
5	○	○	○	○		11	○	○	○	○		17	○	○	○	○		23	○	○	○	○		29	○	○	○	○
6	○	○	○	○		12	○	○	○	○		18	○	○	○	○		24	○	○	○	○		30	○	○	○	○

Only answers that are gridded will be scored. You will not receive credit for anything written in the boxes.

31 32 33 34 35

Only answers that are gridded will be scored. You will not receive credit for anything written in the boxes.

36 37 38

Section 5 (Optional)

Important: Use a No. 2 pencil. Write inside the borders.

You may use the space below to plan your essay, but be sure to write your essay on the lined pages. Work on this page will not be scored.

Use this space to plan your essay.

START YOUR ESSAY HERE.

_____

_____

_____

_____

_____

_____

_____

_____

_____

_____

_____

_____

_____

_____

_____

_____

_____

_____

_____

_____

_____

_____

_____

_____

Continue on the next page.

Continue on the next page.

Continue on the next page.

_____

_____

_____

_____

_____

_____

_____

_____

_____

_____

_____

_____

_____

_____

_____

_____

_____

_____

_____

_____

_____

_____

_____

_____

STOP.

Reading Test

65 MINUTES, 52 QUESTIONS

Turn to Section 1 of your answer sheet to answer the questions in this section.

DIRECTIONS

Every passage or paired set of passages is accompanied by a number of questions. Read the passage or paired set of passages, then use what is said or implied in what you read and in any given graphics to choose the best answer to each question.

Questions 1-10 are based on the following passage.

This passage is adapted from Edith Wharton, *The House of Mirth*. Originally published in 1905.

Selden paused in surprise. In the afternoon rush of Grand Central Station his eyes had been refreshed by the sight of Miss Lily Bart.

Line
5   It was a Monday in early September, and he was returning to his work from a hurried dip into the country; but what was Miss Bart doing in town at that season? If she had appeared to be catching a train, he might have inferred that he had found her in the act of transition between one and another of the
10 country-houses which fought over her after the close of the Newport season; but her aimless air perplexed him. She stood apart from the crowd, letting it drift by her to the platform or the street, and wearing an air of hesitation which might, as he surmised, be the
15 mask of a very definite purpose. It struck him at once that she was waiting for someone, but he hardly knew why the idea arrested him. There was nothing new about Lily Bart, yet he could never see her without a faint movement of interest: it was
20 characteristic of her that she always roused speculation, that her simplest acts seemed the result of far-reaching intentions.

    An impulse of curiosity made him turn out of his direct line to the door, and stroll past her. He knew
25 that if she did not wish to be seen she would

contrive to elude him; and it amused him to think of putting her skill to the test.

    "Mr. Selden—what good luck!"

    She came forward smiling, eager almost, in her
30 resolve to intercept him. One or two persons, in brushing past them, lingered to look; for Miss Bart was a figure to arrest even the suburban traveler rushing to his last train.

    Selden had never seen her more radiant. Her vivid
35 head, relieved against the dull tints of the crowd, made her more conspicuous than in a ball-room, and under her dark hat and veil she regained the girlish smoothness, the purity of tint, that she was beginning to lose after eleven years of late hours and
40 indefatigable dancing. Was it really eleven years, Selden found himself wondering, and had she indeed reached the nine-and-twentieth birthday with which her rivals credited her?

    "What luck!" she repeated. "How nice of you to
45 come to my rescue!"

    He responded joyfully that to do so was his mission in life, and asked what form the rescue was to take.

    "Oh, almost any—even to sitting on a bench and
50 talking to me. One sits out a cotillion—why not sit out a train? It isn't a bit hotter here than in Mrs. Van Osburgh's conservatory—and some of the women are not a bit uglier." She broke off, laughing, to explain that she had come up to town from Tuxedo,
55 on her way to the Gus Trenors' at Bellomont, and

CONTINUE ➔

had missed the three-fifteen train to Rhinebeck. "And there isn't another till half-past five." She consulted the little jeweled watch among her laces. "Just two hours to wait. And I don't know what to do with
60 myself. My maid came up this morning to do some shopping for me, and was to go on to Bellomont at one o'clock, and my aunt's house is closed, and I don't know a soul in town." She glanced plaintively about the station. "It is hotter than Mrs. Van
65 Osburgh's, after all. If you can spare the time, do take me somewhere for a breath of air."

He declared himself entirely at her disposal: the adventure struck him as diverting. As a spectator, he had always enjoyed Lily Bart; and his course lay so
70 far out of her orbit that it amused him to be drawn for a moment into the sudden intimacy which her proposal implied.

1

Which choice best summarizes the passage?

A) Two close friends meet to spend the day together.

B) A traveler notices a woman acting suspiciously.

C) Two acquaintances unexpectedly run into one another.

D) A couple wait to board a train for a romantic getaway.

2

Selden's attitude towards Lily Bart is primarily one of

A) devotion.

B) fascination.

C) disdain.

D) pity.

3

Which choice provides the best evidence for the answer to the previous question?

A) Lines 1-3 ("In the … Bart")

B) Lines 7-12 ("If she … him")

C) Lines 17-22 ("There was … intentions")

D) Lines 24-27 ("He knew … test")

4

Over the course of the passage, the main focus of the narrative shifts from the

A) grim and suspicious attitude of one character to the gregarious behavior of another.

B) meticulous travel plans made by one character to the carefree adventures enjoyed by another.

C) appreciation of abstract beauty to the enjoyment of living in the moment.

D) private thoughts of one character about another to a friendly interaction between the two.

5

The passage suggests that Lily thinks it is good luck to run into Selden because

A) she is in danger and believes he can save her.

B) she has been meaning to talk to him for a long time.

C) she likes him better than the person she was planning to see.

D) she has nothing to do until her train arrives.

CONTINUE

6

Which choice provides the best evidence for the answer to the previous question?

A) Lines 15-17 ("It struck … him")

B) Lines 46-48 ("He responded … take")

C) Line 59-60 ("And I … myself")

D) Lines 64-65 ("It is … all")

7

The primary purpose of lines 6-12 ("but what … him") is to

A) establish that Miss Bart no longer lives in town.

B) demonstrate that Miss Bart owns many houses in Newport.

C) prove that Selden thinks Miss Bart is untrustworthy.

D) explain why Selden is surprised to see Miss Bart.

8

Selden walks toward Lily because

A) he is curious about why she is at the station.

B) he is hoping she will suggest they spend time together.

C) he wants to see if she remembers him.

D) he has missed her very much.

9

As used in line 32, "arrest" most nearly means

A) apprehend.

B) restrain.

C) impede.

D) enthrall.

10

In the context of the passage, the author's use of the phrase "eleven years of late hours and indefatigable dancing" (lines 39-40) is primarily meant to convey the idea that Lily

A) is a professional dancer.

B) prefers late parties to all daytime activities.

C) has never been very punctual.

D) spent much of her youth at lively social gatherings.

CONTINUE →

Questions 11-20 are based on the following passage.

This passage is adapted from a speech given by President Lyndon B. Johnson at the University of Michigan on May 22, 1964, announcing his plan to establish several new governmental social service organizations.

For a century we labored to settle and to subdue a continent. For half a century we called upon unbounded invention and untiring industry to create
Line an order of plenty for all of our people. The
5 challenge of the next half century is whether we have the wisdom to use that wealth to enrich and elevate our national life, and to advance the quality of our American civilization.

Your imagination and your initiative and your
10 indignation will determine whether we build a society where progress is the servant of our needs, or a society where old values and new visions are buried under unbridled growth. For in your time we have the opportunity to move not only toward the
15 rich society and the powerful society, but upward to the Great Society. The Great Society rests on abundance and liberty for all. It demands an end to poverty and racial injustice, to which we are totally committed in our time. But that is just the beginning.

20 The Great Society is a place where every child can find knowledge to enrich his mind and to enlarge his talents. It is a place where leisure is a welcome chance to build and reflect, not a feared cause of boredom and restlessness. It is a place where the city
25 of man serves not only the needs of the body and the demands of commerce but the desire for beauty and the hunger for community. It is a place where man can renew contact with nature. It is a place which honors creation for its own sake and for what it adds
30 to the understanding of the human race. It is a place where men are more concerned with the quality of their goals than the quantity of their goods.

But most of all, the Great Society is not a safe harbor, a resting place, a final objective, a
35 finished work. It is a challenge constantly renewed, beckoning us toward a destiny where the meaning of our lives matches the marvelous products of our labor. Within your lifetime, powerful forces, already loosed, will take us toward a way of life beyond the
40 realm of our experience, almost beyond the bounds of our imagination. For better or for worse, your generation has been appointed by history to deal with those problems and to lead America toward a new age. You have the chance never before afforded
45 to any people in any age. You can help build a society where the demands of morality, and the needs of the spirit, can be realized in the life of the Nation.

So, will you join in the battle to give every
50 citizen the full equality the law requires, whatever his belief, or race, or the color of his skin? Will you join in the battle to give every citizen an escape from the crushing weight of poverty? Will you join in the battle to make it possible for all nations to live in
55 enduring peace—as neighbors and not as mortal enemies? Will you join in the battle to build the Great Society, to prove that our material progress is only the foundation on which we will build a richer life of mind and spirit?

60 There are those timid souls that say this battle cannot be won, that we are condemned to a soulless wealth. I do not agree. We have the power to shape the civilization that we want. But we need your will and your labor and your hearts, if we are to build
65 that kind of society. Those who came to this land sought to build more than just a new country. They sought a new world. So I have come here today to your campus to say that you can make their vision our reality. So let us from this moment begin our
70 work so that in the future men will look back and say: it was then, after a long and weary way, that man turned the exploits of his genius to the full enrichment of his life.

CONTINUE

11

Based on the passage, what is the best description of Johnson's vision of the Great Society?

A) A time when each American has an equal share of the nation's wealth

B) A nation in which citizens continuously seek to improve themselves and society

C) A highly exclusive club for the most powerful people in the country

D) An organization dedicated to strengthening public infrastructure

12

Which choice provides the best evidence for the answer to the previous question?

A) Lines 2-4 ("For half … our people")

B) Lines 13-16 ("For in … Society")

C) Lines 35-38 ("It is … labor")

D) Lines 65-66 ("Those who … country")

13

What is the most likely reason Johnson refers to the founding of the United States in the final paragraph?

A) To link the Great Society to the original mission of the country

B) To emphasize how morally superior current generations are to previous ones

C) To decry how far Americans have fallen from their former greatness

D) To provide information about the history of the country

14

Which choice provides the best evidence for the answer to the previous question?

A) Lines 9-13 ("Your imagination … growth")

B) Lines 28-30 ("It is … race")

C) Lines 41-44 ("For better … age")

D) Lines 67-69 ("So I … reality")

15

Which of the following would Johnson probably see as a negative symptom of "unbridled growth" (line 13)?

A) A business increases its profits by forcing its employees to work much longer hours.

B) A railroad company expands its tracks across the country in a few months.

C) A higher percentage of a city's children are in school than had been previously.

D) More people purchase at least ten books in a year than ever before.

16

How does Johnson characterize the relationship between the Great Society and "abundance and liberty for all" (line 17)?

A) The Great Society will make abundance and liberty for all impossible.

B) Abundance and liberty for all are the ultimate goals of the Great Society.

C) The Great Society and abundance and liberty for all are mutually exclusive.

D) Abundance and liberty for all are the first requirements of the Great Society.

CONTINUE

17

As used in line 19, "committed" most nearly means

A) granted.

B) entrusted.

C) assigned.

D) dedicated.

18

Which best describes lines 20-32? ("The Great … goods")

A) A list of ways in which the Great Society is already a reality

B) A description of the hardships preventing Americans from realizing the Great Society

C) An explanation of how Johnson came up with the vision for the Great Society

D) A description of several aspects of Johnson's vision for the Great Society

19

As used in line 39, "loosed" most nearly means

A) unleashed.

B) relaxed.

C) extricated.

D) slackened.

20

Johnson most likely repeats the phrase "will you" (lines 49-59) in order to

A) demonstrate that his audience has many options to choose from.

B) inspire his listeners to join him in achieving his goal.

C) express his anger toward younger generations for neglecting his plans so far.

D) repeat key information to ensure that listeners can understand his ideas.

CONTINUE

Questions 21-31 are based on the following passage.

This passage is adapted from Cindi May, "The Surprising Problem of Too Much Talent." © 2014 by Scientific American.

Whether you're the owner of the Dallas Cowboys or captain of the playground dodge ball team, the goal in picking players is the same: get the top talent.
Line Hearts have been broken, allegiances tested, and
5 budgets busted as teams contend for the best athletes. The motivation for recruiting peak performers is obvious—exceptional players are the key to team success—and this belief is shared not only by coaches and sports fans, but also by corporations,
10 investors, and even whole industries. Everyone wants a team of stars.

While there is no denying that exceptional players can put points on the board and enhance team success, new research by Roderick Swaab and
15 colleagues suggests there is a limit to the benefit top talents bring to a team. Swaab and colleagues compared the amount of individual talent on teams with the teams' success, and they found striking examples of more talent hurting the team.

20 The researchers looked at three sports: basketball, soccer, and baseball. In each sport, they calculated both the percentage of top talent on each team and the teams' success over several years. For example, they identified top NBA talent using each player's
25 Estimated Wins Added (EWA), a statistic commonly employed to capture a player's overall contribution to his team, along with selection for the All-Star tournament. Once the researchers determined who the elite players were, they calculated top-talent
30 percentage at the team level by dividing the number of star players on the team by the total number of players on that team. Finally, team performance was measured by the team's win-loss record over 10 years. For both basketball and soccer, they found that
35 top talent did in fact predict team success, but only up to a point. Furthermore, there was not simply a point of diminishing returns with respect to top talent; there was in fact a cost. Basketball and soccer teams with the greatest proportion of elite athletes

40 performed worse than those with more moderate proportions of top level players.

Why is too much talent a bad thing? Think teamwork. In many endeavors, success requires collaborative, cooperative work towards a goal that is
45 beyond the capability of any one individual. When a team roster is flooded with individual talent, pursuit of personal star status may prevent the attainment of team goals. The basketball player chasing a point record, for example, may cost the team by taking risky
50 shots instead of passing to a teammate who is open and ready to score.

Two related findings by Swaab and colleagues indicate that there is in fact tradeoff between top talent and teamwork. First, Swaab and colleagues found that
55 the percentage of top talent on a team affects intrateam coordination. For the basketball study, teams with the highest levels of top performers had fewer assists and defensive rebounds, and lower field-goal percentages. These failures in strategic, collaborative play
60 undermined the team's effectiveness. The second revealing finding is that extreme levels of top talent did not have the same negative effect in baseball, which experts have argued involves much less interdependent play. In the baseball study, increasing
65 numbers of stars on a team never hindered overall performance. Together these findings suggest that high levels of top talent will be harmful in arenas that require coordinated, strategic efforts, as the quest for the spotlight may trump the teamwork needed to get
70 the job done.

The lessons here extend beyond the ball field to any group or endeavor that must balance competitive and collaborative efforts, including corporate teams, financial research groups, and brainstorming exercises.
75 Indeed, the impact of too much talent is even evident in other animals: when hen colonies have too many dominant, high-producing chickens, conflict and hen mortality rise while egg production drops. So before breaking the bank to recruit superstars, team owners
80 and industry experts might want to consider whether the goal they are trying to achieve relies on individual talent alone, or a cooperative synergy from the team. If the latter, it would be wise to reign in the talent and focus on teamwork.

CONTINUE

Coordination as a Function of Top Talent

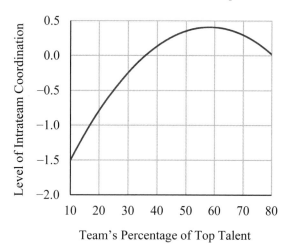

Adapted from Cindi May, "The Surprising Problem of Too Much Talent." © 2014 by Scientific American.

21

Which of the following best describes the structure of the passage as a whole?

A) A collection of anecdotes about competitive sports

B) A description of a study and its potential implications

C) A set of pieces of advice for managers in sports and business

D) A series of arguments in favor of changing athletic recruitment methods

22

Based on information in the passage, it can be inferred that the researchers' results

A) contradict most people's beliefs about team success.

B) confirm the conventional wisdom of sports recruitment.

C) provide information only about performance in a laboratory setting.

D) can be used to explain team results in all sports, as well as certain other settings.

23

Which choice provides the best evidence for the answer to the previous question?

A) Lines 12-16 ("While there … team")

B) Lines 38-41 ("Basketball and … players")

C) Lines 43-45 ("In many … individual")

D) Lines 64-66 ("In the … performance")

24

Which of the following best summarizes the researchers' findings?

A) Teamwork is the most important quality for sports teams.

B) Individual talent is the most important quality for sports teams.

C) Individual talent matters, but must be balanced against the important factor of teamwork.

D) Individual talent is more important, but strong teamwork can make up for weak talent.

CONTINUE

25

Which choice provides the best evidence for the answer to the previous question?

A) Lines 6-10 ("The motivation … industries")

B) Lines 52-54 ("Two related … teamwork")

C) Lines 64-66 ("In the … performance")

D) Lines 71-74 ("The lessons … exercises")

26

As used in line 26, "employed" most nearly means

A) occupied.

B) used.

C) appointed.

D) hired.

27

As used in line 68, "coordinated" most nearly means

A) negotiated.

B) synchronized.

C) communicated.

D) agile.

28

The passage suggests that the study observed different effects of top talent in baseball than in basketball because

A) top baseball players are better at cooperative play than top basketball players.

B) there tend to be fewer elite athletes on baseball teams than on basketball teams.

C) there are fewer team members on the court at once in basketball than are on the field at once in baseball.

D) the sport of baseball requires less cooperative play than the sport of basketball.

29

Based on lines 78-84 ("So before … teamwork"), in which of the following situations should decision makers "reign in the talent and focus on teamwork"?

A) A professor deciding which student papers to select as examples for future classes

B) A conductor auditioning singers for a choir to perform at a competition

C) A gymnastics coach helping his team members with their solo routines

D) A newspaper editor hiring journalists to cover local crime stories

30

Which of the following claims is best supported by information in the passage and graph?

A) A basketball team with no top talent will generally perform slightly better than an all-star team.

B) Basketball teams should aim to have top talent for about half of the team.

C) A struggling basketball team should replace its best players instead of its worst ones.

D) Around half of the players on an average basketball team tend to be considered top talent.

31

Information from the graph best supports which of the following statements?

A) Teams with the most talent have the highest levels of intrateam coordination.

B) Teams with the most talent have the lowest levels of intrateam coordination.

C) Teams with the least talent have the highest levels of intrateam coordination.

D) Teams with the least talent have the lowest levels of intrateam coordination.

CONTINUE

Questions 32-41 are based on the following passage.

This passage is adapted from David Noonan, "Meet the Two Scientists Who Implanted a False Memory Into a Mouse." © 2014 by Smithsonian Magazine.

Steve Ramirez, a 24-year-old doctoral student at the time, placed the mouse in a small metal box with a black plastic floor. Instead of curiously sniffing
Line around, though, the animal instantly froze in terror,
5 recalling the experience of receiving a foot shock in that same box. It was a textbook fear response, and if anything, the mouse's posture was more rigid than Ramirez had expected. Its memory of the trauma must have been quite vivid. Which was amazing,
10 because the memory was bogus: the mouse had never received an electric shock in that box. Rather, it was reacting to a false memory that Ramirez and his MIT colleague Xu Liu had planted in its brain.

The observation culminated more than two years
15 of a long-shot research effort and supported an extraordinary hypothesis: not only was it possible to identify brain cells involved in the encoding of a single memory, but those specific cells could be manipulated to create a whole new "memory" of an
20 event that never happened. What Ramirez and Liu have been able to see and control are the flickering clusters of neurons, known as engrams, where individual memories are stored. Joining forces in late 2010, the two men devised an elaborate new method
25 for exploring living brains in action, a system that combines classic molecular biology and the emerging field of optogenetics, in which lasers are deployed to stimulate cells genetically engineered to be sensitive to light.
30 In the first study, published in *Nature* in March 2012, Ramirez and Liu identified, labeled, and then reactivated a small cluster of cells encoding a mouse's fear memory, in this case a memory of an environment where the mouse had received a foot
35 shock. The feat provides strong evidence for the long-held theory that memories are encoded in engrams. Ramirez and Liu assembled a customized set of techniques to render mouse brain cells in their

target area, the dentate gyrus, sensitive to light.
40 Working with a specialized breed of genetically engineered lab mice, the team injected the dentate gyrus with a biochemical cocktail that included a gene for a light-sensitive protein, channelrhodopsin-2. Dentate gyrus cells participating in memory formation
45 would produce the protein, thus becoming light-sensitive themselves. The idea was that after the memory had been encoded, it could be reactivated by zapping those cells with a laser.

To do that, Ramirez and Liu surgically implanted
50 thin filaments from the laser through the skulls of the mice and into the dentate gyrus. Reactivating the memory—and its associated fear response—was the only way to prove they had actually identified and labeled an engram. The researchers examined the
55 brain tissues under a microscope to confirm the existence of the engrams; cells involved in a specific memory glowed green after treatment with chemicals that reacted with channelrhodopsin-2. When Ramirez and Liu looked at the treated neurons through the
60 microscope, "it was like a starry night," says Liu, "where you can see individual stars." Though these active cells were just one part of a widely distributed foot shock engram, reactivating them was enough to trigger a fear response.
65 The next step was to manipulate a specific engram to create a false memory, an elegant experiment detailed in Ramirez and Liu's second paper, published in *Science* in July 2013. They prepared the mouse, injecting the biochemical cocktail into the
70 dentate gyrus. Next, they put the mouse in a box without shocking it. As the animal explored, a memory of this benign experience was encoded as an engram. The following day, the mouse was placed in a different box, where its memory of the first (safe)
75 box was triggered by shooting the laser into the dentate gyrus. At that exact moment, the mouse received a foot shock. On the third day, the mouse was returned to the safe box—and immediately froze in fear. It had never received a foot shock there, but
80 its false memory, created by the researchers in another box, caused it to behave as if it had.

CONTINUE

Reactivating a Memory

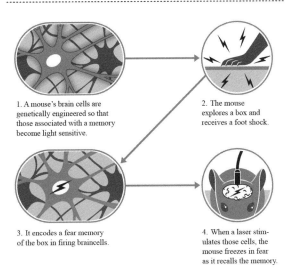

1. A mouse's brain cells are genetically engineered so that those associated with a memory become light sensitive.

2. The mouse explores a box and receives a foot shock.

3. It encodes a fear memory of the box in firing braincells.

4. When a laser stimulates those cells, the mouse freezes in fear as it recalls the memory.

Adapted from David Noonan, "Meet the Two Scientists Who Implanted a False Memory Into a Mouse." © 2014 by Smithsonian Magazine.

32

The author's attitude towards Ramirez and Liu's innovation is best described as that of

A) a zealous proponent.

B) an interested observer.

C) a wary critic.

D) a skeptical colleague.

33

Based on the passage, what is the primary significance of the research described?

A) It suggests new technologies might prevent memory loss.

B) It proves that memories cannot be tampered with.

C) It shows how specific interventions can alter memories.

D) It clarifies the purpose of the dentate gyrus.

34

Which choice provides the best evidence for the answer to the previous question?

A) Lines 16-20 ("Not only … happened")

B) Lines 37-39 ("Ramirez and … light")

C) Lines 46-48 ("The idea … laser")

D) Lines 61-64 ("Though these … response")

35

In relation to the other events described in the passage, when did the events described in the first paragraph most likely take place?

A) Before the first study

B) During the first study

C) During the second study

D) After the conclusion of the second study

36

As used in line 38, "render" most nearly means

A) provide.

B) make.

C) depict.

D) express.

37

The goal of Ramirez and Liu's first study was to

A) implant a false memory engram in a mouse.

B) study the development of fear responses in mice.

C) identify an engram storing a particular memory.

D) discover whether they could make mice more sensitive to light.

CONTINUE

38

Which choice provides the best evidence for the answer to the previous question?

A) Lines 23-25 ("Joining forces … action")

B) Lines 40-43 ("Working with … protein")

C) Lines 44-46 ("Dentate gyrus … themselves")

D) Lines 51-54 ("Reactivating the … engram")

39

As used in line 65, "manipulate" most nearly means

A) handle.

B) squeeze.

C) alter.

D) exploit.

40

Based on the passage and the graphic, the purpose of making certain cells light-sensitive is to

A) allow the researchers to reactivate a memory with a laser.

B) ensure that memories are encoded in engrams.

C) prevent the mouse from recalling the memory in a new location.

D) heighten the fear reaction in response to a foot shock.

41

Which claim about light-sensitive cells is supported by the graphic?

A) Light sensitivity allows researchers to identify particular cells.

B) Cells become light sensitive once they encode memories.

C) Stimulating cells with a laser makes them light sensitive.

D) Researchers can only stimulate light-sensitive cells.

CONTINUE

Questions 42-52 are based on the following passage.

Passage 1 is adapted from Andrew Steele, "Your phone screen just won the Nobel Prize in physics." © 2014 by Andrew Steele. Passage 2 is adapted from Sarah Zielinski, "The Potential Dark Side of Nobel-Winning LEDs: Pest Problems." © 2014 by Smithsonian Magazine.

Passage 1

Blue LEDs are important for two reasons. First, the blue light has specific applications of its own. Second, it's a vital component of the white light that
Line makes white LEDs, and therefore LED computer and
5 phone screens, possible. Blue light has a short wavelength, which allows the pits on a Blu-ray disc to be smaller and closer together than on a DVD, which is read with red light. This means we can pack over five times as much data onto a disk the same
10 size as a DVD.

Blue LEDs' biggest impact, however, is surely in giving us the ability to produce white LEDs. White light is actually a mixture of all the colors of the rainbow, as you can see if you split it up with a
15 prism, or indeed if you catch a multicolored reflection in the surface of a Blu-ray disc, DVD, or CD. However, the human eye has just three types of color receptors inside it: red, green, and blue.

We can therefore make something which looks
20 like white light using only these three colors. Combining red and green LEDs with blue ones allows us to create highly efficient white lighting, providing around 20 times as much light as an equivalent incandescent bulb. White LEDs are
25 slowly making their way onto ceilings of homes, shops, and factories around the world, but their real ubiquity today is as the back-light for computer and phone screens.

Unlock your phone or turn on a recent flat-screen
30 monitor, and red, green, and blue LEDs shining through a layer of liquid crystal allows you to browse the web and watch movies. The result is a technology which is all around us in the developed world, and making headway into the developing world, too.

Passage 2

35 The Nobel Prize in Physics was recently awarded to three scientists who invented blue light-emitting diodes. The work was crucial for producing bright white LED lighting, which is more energy-efficient than traditional incandescent bulbs. But there's a
40 possible downside to widespread use of LEDs: they could make light pollution worse. For decades, streetlights have generally used yellow, high-pressure sodium vapor lamps, which light up by sending an arc of electricity through vaporized
45 sodium metal. Now, white LEDs are quickly replacing the sodium lamps, but a study published in *Ecological Applications* shows why that might be an environmental problem.

"The main driver of the ecological impacts that
50 result from a shift to white LED lighting will be the increase in emissions of short wavelength 'blue' light," says Stephen Pawson, an entomologist at the New Zealand research institute Scion. "The behavior of many animals is influenced by light in the blue
55 portion of the spectrum. For example, insects have specific photoreceptors for blue light. Thus large-scale adoption of 'white' lighting is likely to increase the impacts of nighttime lighting on all species sensitive to 'blue' light."

60 In the study, Pawson and his Scion colleague Martin Bader looked at the effects of industrial white LEDs versus sodium lamps on insects. They set out the lamps in a field at night, placing sheets of a sticky material next to the lights to catch any insects
65 that came near. On average, the white LEDs attracted 48 percent more flying invertebrates than the sodium lamps. The researchers hypothesized that certain white LEDs might be less attractive to invertebrates than others. Unfortunately, that wasn't the case.

70 If installed as currently designed, white LEDs could exacerbate pest problems, Pawson and Bader note in their study. Midge swarms, for instance, are already known to be more attracted to white lighting.

CONTINUE

42

Passage 1 presents blue LEDs primarily as

A) a fascinating demonstration of little-understood physical principles.

B) a scientific curiosity of interest only to select groups of people.

C) a major technological breakthrough that has already proven important.

D) a promising prototype that may become highly significant in future.

43

Which choice provides the best evidence for the answer to the previous question?

A) Lines 3-5 ("Second … possible")

B) Lines 13-17 ("White light … CD")

C) Lines 17-18 ("However … and blue")

D) Lines 19-20 ("We can … colors")

44

As used in line 3, "vital" most nearly means

A) lively.

B) vigorous.

C) essential.

D) compelling.

45

According to Passage 1, blue light is important for creating white LEDs because

A) blue LEDs are cheaper to manufacture than white LEDs.

B) blue is one of the colors for which human eyes have receptors.

C) all colors must be present for humans to perceive white light.

D) blue light is the easiest to produce artificially.

46

Passage 2 primarily focuses on

A) different kinds of evidence that suggest white LEDs are beneficial.

B) what makes white LEDs different from sodium lights.

C) the author's opinion that we use too many white LEDs.

D) a study demonstrating a specific negative effect of white LEDs.

47

The researchers in Passage 2 are primarily concerned that white LEDs will

A) result in significant losses of native insects.

B) disrupt the habitats of nocturnal animals.

C) cause an increase in invertebrate populations.

D) attract more pests than sodium lamps do.

CONTINUE

48

Which choice provides the best evidence for the answer to the previous question?

A) Lines 41-45 ("For decades … metal")

B) Lines 60-62 ("In the … insects")

C) Lines 65-66 ("On average … lamps")

D) Lines 67-69 ("The researchers … others")

49

As used in line 39, "traditional" most nearly means

A) standard.

B) time-honored.

C) habitual.

D) conservative.

50

Which of the following is the best example of one of the "impacts of nighttime lighting" mentioned in line 58?

A) Insects can be caught in sheets of sticky material during experiments.

B) White LEDs are likely to emit more blue light than sodium lamps.

C) Light sources often attract unwanted pests, such as midge swarms.

D) Insects are drawn to things they have not seen before.

51

Which of the following best describes the relationship between the two passages?

A) Passage 2 describes a new application of the technology explained in Passage 1.

B) Passage 2 highlights a potential downside of the innovation described in Passage 1.

C) Passage 2 details an experiment performed to test the devices discussed in Passage 1.

D) Passage 2 criticizes the researchers profiled in Passage 1.

52

The authors of both passages would probably agree that blue LEDs

A) have significant use in producing white LEDs.

B) could be dangerous and should be used with caution.

C) would cause harm primarily to humans.

D) are too difficult to manufacture to be used widely.

STOP

If you complete this section before the end of your allotted time, you may check your work on this section only. Do NOT use the time to work on another section.

Writing and Language Test

35 MINUTES, 44 QUESTIONS

Turn to Section 2 of your answer sheet to answer the questions in this section.

DIRECTIONS

Every passage comes with a set of questions. Some questions will ask you to consider how the writer might revise the passage to improve the expression of ideas. Other questions will ask you to consider correcting potential errors in sentence structure, usage, or punctuation. There may be one or more graphics that you will need to consult as you revise and edit the passage.

Some questions will refer to a portion of the passage that has been underlined. Other questions will refer to a particular location in a passage or ask that you consider the passage in full.

After you read the passage, select the answers to questions that most effectively improve the passage's writing quality or that adjust the passage to follow the conventions of standard written English. Many questions give you the option to select "NO CHANGE." Select that option in cases where you think the relevant part of the passage should remain as it currently is.

Questions 1-11 are based on the following passage.

The Adaptive Arms Race

Every environment on Earth, from placid lakes to sunscorched deserts, **1** is populated with living beings engaged in life-and-death struggles. Predators constantly try to capture and eat prey animals, while **2** escaping predators is what prey animals try to do. Over the course of many generations, predators evolve to be better at spotting and catching their next meal, while prey animals evolve adaptations for evading and fighting off predators.

1

A) NO CHANGE
B) are populated
C) were populated
D) being populated

2

A) NO CHANGE
B) escaping predators is the goal of prey animals.
C) prey animals are trying to escape predators.
D) prey animals try to escape predators.

CONTINUE

[3] The porcupine, for instance, is covered in barbed quills that can lodge painfully in the paws or skin of any predator unwise enough to attack it. More intimidating still is the Texas horned lizard, which can fire a jet of foul-tasting blood from its eyes at a range of up to five feet. [4] This disgusting spray deter's most predators. Predators faced with noxious or dangerous defenses like these often choose to seek out easier prey.

Other prey animals avoid being eaten by blending in with their environment or imitating inedible objects. Many insects use this strategy, including stick insects and leaf insects, whose body shapes and colors resemble parts of plants. Their [5] mockery is so convincing that even people can have a hard time picking them out from surrounding vegetation. [6] Even so, such camouflage is very effective, since a prey animal that cannot be found cannot be eaten.

[3]

The writer would like to insert a sentence here to help establish the main topic of the following paragraph. Which choice most effectively conveys the main topic of this paragraph?

A) Some prey animals have evolved defensive weapons to ward off predators.

B) Every time prey evolves a new defensive trick, predators evolve a countermeasure.

C) Although prey animals defend themselves when threatened, it's clearly better to blend in and avoid being seen.

D) For many prey animals, simply running away from predators is the best solution.

[4]

A) NO CHANGE

B) This disgusting spray deters most predators.

C) This disgusting spray deters most predator's.

D) This disgusting spray deter's most predator's.

[5]

A) NO CHANGE

B) duplication

C) mimicry

D) conceit

[6]

A) NO CHANGE

B) Nevertheless,

C) Naturally,

D) Next,

CONTINUE

[1] Why, then, are some prey animals brightly colored instead? [2] It might seem like such animals would be spotted and **7** quickly devoured right away, leaving them unable to pass on their genes. [3] As it turns out, bright colors are usually part of another anti-predation strategy called "aposematism." [4] The visually distinctive patterns on animals using aposematism warn predators that their potential prey tastes bad, is poisonous, or wields a dangerous defense. [5] These warning patterns are often quite beautiful, and may ironically make the animals more appealing to humans who collect specimens. [6] For example, the striking orange and black coloration on the wings of monarch butterflies **8** had indicated that their bodies are loaded with foul-tasting poison. [7] Any bird that tries to eat a monarch butterfly quickly learns to make its next meal out of a more drab insect. **9**

Aposematism works so well that some animals have evolved to display such warnings despite being harmless, a strategy called "Batesian mimicry." Batesian mimics include the drone fly, which bears the black and yellow colors of the honey bee but lacks **10** its ability to sting. Thanks to its coloration, predators that have experienced the pain of a real bee's sting will not risk running afoul of **11** it.

7

A) NO CHANGE
B) quickly eaten up immediately,
C) immediately,
D) devoured immediately,

8

A) NO CHANGE
B) indicates
C) will indicate
D) indicated

9

The writer plans to delete a sentence to improve the focus of this paragraph. Which sentence should be deleted?

A) Sentence 2
B) Sentence 3
C) Sentence 4
D) Sentence 5

10

A) NO CHANGE
B) it's
C) their
D) they're

11

A) NO CHANGE
B) that.
C) a predator.
D) the drone fly.

CONTINUE ➡

Questions 12-22 are based on the following passage.

The Life and Legacy of Alexander III

When Alexander III inherited the throne of Macedon in the year 336 BC, he could hardly have come to power under better circumstances. He had received the best education money could buy, having been tutored by the famed scholar Aristotle, and his power over all of Greece had already been **12** secured. Through decades of war and diplomacy overseen by his father, Philip II. Alexander was well-positioned to continue his father's military expansion and earn the title "Alexander the Great."

Alexander began his conquest by invading the mighty Persian Empire. Thanks to his brilliant strategies and **13** how experienced his troops were, he quickly defeated the armies of Persia and took control of what is now the Middle East and Iran. **14** This early success encouraged him. He decided to continue pushing east despite his army's exhaustion. Threatening to mutiny, **15** he was eventually forced by his troops to turn back and end his campaign. Even so, by the time he turned thirty in 326 BC, Alexander was the ruler of the largest empire the

12

A) NO CHANGE
B) secured: through
C) secured; through
D) secured through

13

A) NO CHANGE
B) experienced troops,
C) how much experience his troops had,
D) his troops being very experienced,

14

Which choice most effectively combines the two sentences at the underlined portion?

A) This early success encouraged him; additionally, he decided to continue pushing east despite his army's exhaustion.
B) He, encouraged by his earlier success, then decided, despite his army's exhaustion, to continue pushing east.
C) Encouraged by this early success, he decided to continue pushing east despite his army's exhaustion.
D) Despite his army's exhaustion, encouragement coming from this success, he decided to continue east.

15

A) NO CHANGE
B) he eventually was forced by his troops
C) his troops eventually forced him
D) he and his troops were eventually forced

CONTINUE

world had yet 16 seen; it stretched from Egypt in the west all the way to India in the east.

Alexander had a grand vision for his new empire. He hoped to mix the cultures of Asia and Europe by transferring settlers among different regions of the empire. However, Alexander's 17 clutch of Persian customs displeased many Greek and Macedonian nobles; his decision to proclaim himself a god, as the Persian emperor had, was particularly unpopular. 18 Nevertheless, his behavior was so unpopular in some quarters that some of his former allies allegedly plotted to assassinate him.

In 323 BC, Alexander died of a sudden illness. Many historians, ancient and modern, have suggested that he was poisoned by a political rival. 19

The reading of Alexander's will showed that his death had cut short many grandiose plans. He had hoped to invade Arabia and even 20 circumnavigated Africa. His plans went unrealized as his empire quickly crumbled. Without Alexander's leadership, his generals quickly turned to fighting among themselves to carve out their own kingdoms.

16

A) NO CHANGE
B) seen, it
C) seen; it,
D) seen it

17

A) NO CHANGE
B) purchase
C) attainment
D) embrace

18

A) NO CHANGE
B) In fact,
C) In addition,
D) In spite of this,

19

Which choice, inserted here, most effectively adds support for the claim in the preceding sentence?

A) Poisons may be derived from toxic plants or animal venom, but some minerals are also toxic.
B) Macedonian nobles often poisoned their opponents to remove them from power.
C) Alexander had taken many wounds in battle, leading to an overall decline in his health.
D) Alexander's unhealthy diet and lifestyle had taken a toll on his body.

20

A) NO CHANGE
B) will circumnavigate
C) circumnavigate
D) had circumnavigated

CONTINUE

21 His conquests spread Greek culture across much of the Old World, influencing art as far away as India and establishing Greek as the language of international communication for centuries afterward. The Romans, who would later conquer much of Alexander's former territory, adopted Greek philosophy and made many **22** illusions to Greek literature in their own writings, ensuring that Greek culture would survive to influence Western thought for millennia.

Which choice, inserted here, most effectively conveys the main topic of this paragraph?

A) As a result, Alexander's work was entirely undone soon after his death.

B) Although his empire was short-lived, Alexander's conquest had an enormous impact on history.

C) Despite his early successes as a conqueror, Alexander had failed to achieve his objectives as a ruler.

D) Alexander was remembered long after his death as a fair and just ruler.

A) NO CHANGE

B) elusions

C) elisions

D) allusions

CONTINUE

Questions 23-33 are based on the following passage.

The Pressing Need for Clinical Psychologists

Clinical psychologists study, diagnose, and treat mental illnesses. Their work is vital given the high rates of mental illness among adolescents and adults. We need to train more psychologists to research mental illness and provide therapy to patients.

Mental illness is common in the United States. In 2012, the National Institutes of Mental Health estimated that almost 20% of adults in the US were diagnosed with a mental illness. Anxiety disorders, which involve excessive **23** stressing out about stuff, were the most common. Other relatively common illnesses were attention-deficit hyperactivity disorder (ADHD), which **24** involves difficulties focusing, and major depression, which saps the mood and energy of its sufferers.

If more students became **25** a psychologist, we would be better able to explore fundamental questions about mental health in our society. For instance, more people are diagnosed with mental illnesses today than in the past, and researchers are currently unsure whether mental illness is becoming more common or clinical psychologists are simply more likely to spot it. It will take broad studies of the population to address that question. **26** Without a doubt, we do not know the root causes and biological underpinnings of many disorders. To develop fuller understandings of these disorders, we will need studies of the **27** gene's and brain's of people with mental illness.

23

A) NO CHANGE
B) worry and stress,
C) uptightness,
D) difficulty taking it easy,

24

A) NO CHANGE
B) distracts
C) requires
D) brings in

25

A) NO CHANGE
B) psychologists,
C) psychologist,
D) the psychologist,

26

A) NO CHANGE
B) Furthermore,
C) Conversely,
D) Consequently,

27

A) NO CHANGE
B) gene's and brains
C) genes and brain's
D) genes and brains

CONTINUE

28 Some mental illnesses can be treated with medications, such as antidepressants for depression and stimulants for ADHD, but there are patients for whom **29** it does not work perfectly. Therapy is a vital part of recovery for these people. Even for patients who respond well to medication, regular therapy can help develop coping skills and avoid relapse. The availability of psychologists who can meet with patients to deliver therapy **30** are vital to addressing the serious public health challenge of mental illness.

28

The writer would like to insert a sentence here to help establish the main idea of the paragraph. Which choice most effectively conveys the main topic of this paragraph?

A) Though the causes of mental illnesses are not well understood, psychologists have found that many are at least partially heritable.

B) The Internet has helped people with mental illnesses form communities to support one another.

C) More psychologists are also needed to provide treatment for mental illnesses.

D) Unfortunately, mental illness is sometimes stigmatized in American society.

29

A) NO CHANGE

B) they do

C) which does

D) they does

30

A) NO CHANGE

B) were

C) is

D) are going to be

CONTINUE

Clinical psychologists have a high level of education. Most states **31** ordain that clinical psychologists have at least a Master's degree, but most practicing clinical psychologists have a Doctorate degree in Psychology.

Clinical psychologists tend to make **32** much less than other workers with Master's or Doctorate degrees. However, like most professionals with such a high level of education, clinical psychologists are quite well-paid when compared with the median American **33** worker, thus, those who pursue the career can look forward not only to making a positive difference in the lives of patients, but also to being relatively well-paid for their work.

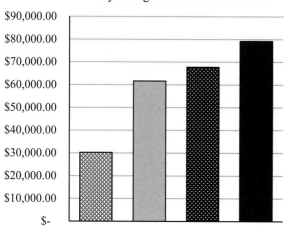

Median Incomes of Clinical Psychologists and Other Workers

⊠ Median for All American Workers
☐ Workers with a Master's Degree
▨ Clinical Psychologists
■ Workers with a Doctorate Degree

31

A) NO CHANGE
B) mandate
C) authorize
D) charge

32

Which choice most accurately and effectively represents the information in the graph?

A) NO CHANGE
B) only the same amount as the typical worker with a Doctorate degree.
C) somewhat less than the average worker with a Master's degree.
D) somewhat less than the typical worker with a Doctorate degree.

33

A) NO CHANGE
B) worker, those
C) worker, thus those
D) worker. Thus, those

CONTINUE

Questions 34-44 are based on the following passage.

The French Existentialists

In the years following World War II, France responded to its liberation from Nazi occupation with a remarkable flourishing of culture and intellectual activity. One of the foremost movements to emerge during this time was the philosophical school of Existentialism. Authors and thinkers **34** affiliating to this movement produced a formidable yet accessible body of literature that is still read by many today.

One of the pioneers of Existentialism was Jean-Paul Sartre, whose book *Existentialism is a Humanism* **35** precluded the philosophical principles of the movement. Sartre argued that human beings as individuals must define the meaning and purpose of their **36** own lives by: developing their own values and acting in accordance with them. His worldview thus emphasized the importance of individual responsibility **37** and also freedom of choice as well. Sartre's literary works explored these ideas, often by focusing on the thoughts and actions of irresponsible and immoral characters. **38**

34

A) NO CHANGE
B) affiliated in
C) affiliating by
D) affiliated with

35

A) NO CHANGE
B) preordered
C) presented
D) predicated

36

A) NO CHANGE
B) own lives by developing
C) own lives. By developing
D) own lives: by developing

37

A) NO CHANGE
B) and also freedom of choice.
C) and freedom of choice.
D) and freedom of choice as well.

38

Which choice, inserted here, most effectively provides support for the claim in the preceding sentence?

A) His short story *The Wall* depicts a captured soldier who refuses to betray his comrades.

B) In fact, despite being offered the Nobel Prize in 1964, he actually declined it.

C) For instance, his play *No Exit* portrays three people condemned to Hell and forced to reflect on their misdeeds.

D) For example, the main character of his novel *Nausea* becomes consumed by anxiety and disgust with life.

CONTINUE

39 Though he did not consider himself an existentialist, Albert Camus also addressed existentialist themes in his writings. Camus often wrote about characters struggling to find meaning in a seemingly meaningless and absurd world. In one of his best-known works, *The Stranger*, the protagonist drifts apathetically through his life and, after being sentenced to death for murder, tries to come to terms with the apparent indifference of the universe itself.

40 Camus was actually a *pied-noir*, a child of French colonists born and raised in Algeria. Camus' masterpiece, *The Plague*, depicts a group of citizens in the Algerian city of Oran as it is devastated by an outbreak of disease. This setting allows Camus to explore the existentialist themes of **41** moral responsibility the search for meaning in suffering and the importance of social ties.

39

A) NO CHANGE

B) He did not consider himself an existentialist, Albert Camus

C) Though Albert Camus did not consider himself an existentialist. He

D) Not considering himself an existentialist, though Albert Camus

40

The writer is considering deleting the underlined sentence. Should it be kept or deleted?

A) Kept, because it provides an interesting piece of information about the subject.

B) Kept, because the sentence contributes to the logical progression of the passage.

C) Deleted, because the information is not relevant and diminishes the focus of the paragraph.

D) Deleted, because the information in the sentence contradicts information provided earlier in the passage.

41

A) NO CHANGE

B) moral responsibility the search for meaning in suffering, and the importance of social ties.

C) moral responsibility, the search for meaning in suffering, and the importance of social ties.

D) moral responsibility the search for meaning in suffering, and: the importance of social ties.

CONTINUE →

Simone de Beauvoir, who maintained a lifelong romantic relationship with Sartre, united existentialist ideas with feminist convictions to write about the unique challenges that women faced in the mid-20th century. [42] However, her treatise *The Second Sex* examined how social roles and expectations [43] constrain women's choices, shape their identities, and deny them the opportunity to find their own sources of meaning. In her novel *Les Belles Images*, her character Laurence is frustrated and dissatisfied despite her seemingly ideal married life. Many critics praised de Beauvoir's frank depictions of women and felt that her female characters were more realistic and [44] relatable than Sartre. It is hardly surprising that de Beauvoir's works, like those of the other existentialists, are widely read to this day.

42

A) NO CHANGE

B) Conversely,

C) On the other hand,

D) OMIT the underlined portion and capitalize the following word.

43

A) NO CHANGE

B) bind

C) contain

D) oblige

44

A) NO CHANGE

B) relatable than was Sartre.

C) relatable than Sartre's.

D) relatable than did Sartre.

STOP

If you complete this section before the end of your allotted time, you may check your work on this section only. Do NOT use the time to work on another section.

Math Test – No Calculator

25 MINUTES, 20 QUESTIONS

Turn to Section 3 of your answer sheet to answer the questions in this section.

DIRECTIONS

Questions **1-15** ask you to solve a problem, select the best answer among four choices, and fill in the corresponding circle on your answer sheet. Questions **16-20** ask you to solve a problem and enter your answer in a grid provided on your answer sheet. There are detailed instructions on entering answers into the grid before question 16. You may use your test booklet for scratch work.

NOTES

1. You **may not** use a calculator.
2. Variables and expressions represent real numbers unless stated otherwise.
3. Figures are drawn to scale unless stated otherwise.
4. Figures lie in a plane unless stated otherwise.
5. The domain of a function f is defined as the set of all real numbers x for which $f(x)$ is also a real number, unless stated otherwise.

REFERENCE

   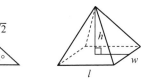

$$A = \frac{1}{2}bh \qquad a^2 + b^2 = c^2 \qquad \text{Special Triangles} \qquad V = \frac{1}{3}lwh \qquad V = \frac{1}{3}\pi r^2 h$$

$$A = lw \qquad V = lwh \qquad V = \pi r^2 h \qquad A = \pi r^2 \qquad V = \frac{4}{3}\pi r^3$$
$$C = 2\pi r$$

There are 360° in a circle.

The sum of the angles in a triangle is 180°.

The number of radians of arc in a circle is 2π.

CONTINUE

1

$$x + 6 + 2x = 5x$$

What is the value of x in the equation above?

A) 2

B) 3

C) 4

D) 5

2

If $a^2 + 3a + 1 = c$ and $-4a + 5 = d$, which of the following is equal to $c + d$?

A) $a^2 + a + 6$

B) $a^2 - a + 6$

C) $a^2 + 7a - 4$

D) 6

3

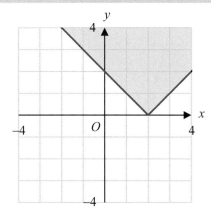

Which of the following inequalities is represented by the graph above?

A) $y \geq |x - 2|$

B) $y \geq |x + 2|$

C) $y \leq |x - 2|$

D) $y \leq |x + 2|$

4

Sophie and Jazmin have the same amount of money to invest in the stock market. If Sophie gives $15,000 to Jazmin, Jazmin has twice as much money as Sophie. How much money did Jazmin have originally?

A) $10,000

B) $30,000

C) $45,000

D) $60,000

CONTINUE

5

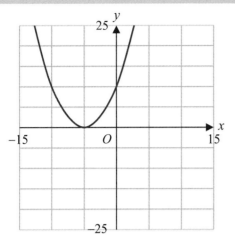

Which of the functions below could be represented by the parabola above?

A) $y = \dfrac{2}{5}(x-5)^2$

B) $y = \dfrac{2}{5}(x+5)^2$

C) $y = \dfrac{2}{5}x + 5$

D) $y = \dfrac{2}{5}x - 5$

6

Luca pays $1,195 per month for rent plus 10 cents per kilowatt hour (kWh) used for electricity. If Luca uses x kWh in one month, which expression best represents the amount of money, in dollars, that Luca needs to pay for his apartment?

A) $1195 + 0.1x$

B) $(1195 + 0.1)x$

C) $1195 + 10x$

D) $(1195 + 1)x$

7

$$ax = -y + 5$$
$$2y + 6x = 5$$

If the two equations above represent parallel lines, what is the value of a?

A) 1

B) 3

C) 5

D) 6

8

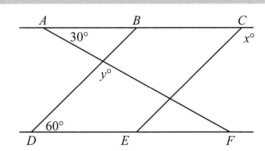

Note: figure is not drawn to scale.

In the figure above, $\overline{AC} \parallel \overline{DF}$ and $\overline{BD} \parallel \overline{CE}$. What is the value of $x - y$?

A) 30°

B) 60°

C) 90°

D) 120°

CONTINUE

9

$$8x + y = 2y + 4x$$

If $2y + 4x = 36$, what is the value of $x + y$, according to the equation above?

A) 3

B) 10

C) 12

D) 15

10

Niki is a test driver for an automobile manufacturer. Each morning, he receives a list of cars to test drive. The number of cars he has left to test drive at the end of each day can be modeled with the equation $C = 15 - 2h$, where C is the number of cars left and h is the number of hours he has worked that day. What is the meaning of the value 2 in this equation?

A) Niki starts each day with 2 cars to test drive.

B) Niki test drives cars at a rate of 2 per hour.

C) Niki test drives cars at a rate of one every 2 hours.

D) Niki cannot work more than 2 hours per day.

11

$$\frac{(x^2 - 1)(x - 1)}{x + 1}$$

If x is positive, which of the following is equivalent to the expression above?

A) $x^2 - 1$

B) $(x - 1)^2$

C) $(x + 1)^2$

D) $x^2 + 1$

12

$$f(x) = c\,(x - 3)(x + 3)$$

In the quadratic equation above, c is a nonzero constant. The graph of the equation in the xy-plane is a parabola with a vertex (h, k), where $k = -18$. Which of the following is equal to c?

A) -2

B) 2

C) 3

D) 6

CONTINUE

13

$$\frac{-28x^2 + 20x + 19}{ax} = 7x - 5 + \frac{19}{ax}$$

The equation above is true for all values of $x \neq 0$, where a is a constant. What is the value of a?

A) 7

B) 5

C) 4

D) –4

14

If the square of a negative number is decreased by 14, the result is five times the original number. What is the original number?

A) –2

B) –4

C) –5

D) –7

15

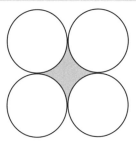

A landscape architect is creating four identical circular gardens so that each circular garden is touching two other gardens, as shown in the figure above. Each circular garden has an area of π. If these gardens are all located at an equal distance from the center of the shaded region between them, what is the area of this shaded region between the gardens?

A) $64 - \pi$

B) $4 - \pi$

C) π

D) $2 + \pi$

CONTINUE

DIRECTIONS

Questions **16-20** ask you to solve a problem and enter your answer in the grid provided on your answer sheet. When completing grid-in questions:

1. You are required to bubble in the circles for your answers. It is recommended, but not required, that you also write your answer in the boxes above the columns of circles. Points will be awarded based only on whether the circles are filled in correctly.

2. Fill in only one circle in a column.

3. You can start your answer in any column as long as you can fit in the whole answer.

4. For questions 16-20, no answers will be negative numbers.

5. **Mixed numbers**, such as $4\frac{2}{5}$, must be gridded as decimals or improper fractions, such as 4.4 or as 22/5. "42/5" will be read as "forty-two over five," not as "four and two-fifths."

6. If your answer is a **decimal** with more digits than will fit on the grid, you may round it or cut it off, but you must fill the entire grid.

7. If there are **multiple correct solutions** to a problem, all of them will be considered correct. Enter only **one** on the grid.

CONTINUE

16

If $x + y = 16$ and $x - y = -2$, what is the value of xy?

17

$$\left| 3x - 1 \right| \leq y$$
$$y = 2x$$

For the system of equations above, where $x > 0$, what is a possible value of x?

18

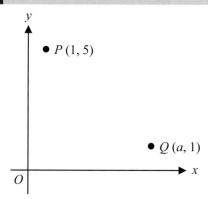

The slope of the line that passes through P and Q is $-\dfrac{2}{3}$. What is the value of a?

CONTINUE

19

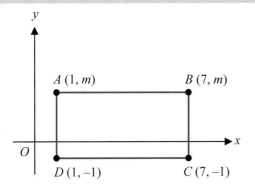

The rectangle *ABCD* is placed on a coordinate grid as shown in the figure above. If the area of the rectangle is 24, what is the value of *m*?

20

If $x + \dfrac{9}{x} = -6$, what is the value of $x^2 + \dfrac{81}{x^2}$?

STOP

If you complete this section before the end of your allotted time, you may check your work on this section only. Do NOT use the time to work on another section.

Math Test – Calculator

55 MINUTES, 38 QUESTIONS

Turn to Section 4 of your answer sheet to answer the questions in this section.

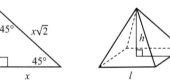

CONTINUE

1

If $a + 4 = 12$, what is $4a$?

A) 8

B) 32

C) 48

D) 64

2

Amount	100mL bottle	200mL bottle	Five 100mL bottle	Five 200mL bottle
Price	$100	$190	$450	$850

The table above shows various prices for hydrochloric acid (HCl) that a chemist needs to buy for his lab. How many dollars per hundred milliliters cheaper is it for him to buy a 200mL bottle than a 100mL bottle?

A) 5

B) 10

C) 20

D) 90

3

$$f(x) = 2x$$
$$g(x) = 5x + 1$$

Given $f(x)$ and $g(x)$ above, what is $g(f(c))$?

A) $2c$

B) $10c + 1$

C) $10c + 2$

D) $20c + 2$

4

If 75% of the employees in a company are female, and 5% of those female employees are over 6 feet tall, what percentage of the company's employees are both female and over 6 feet tall?

A) 1%

B) 3.75%

C) 10%

D) 75%

5

Activities over 24 Hours

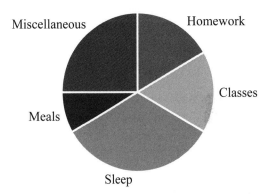

The pie chart above shows how a student spends his time in a 24-hour period. According to this chart, what fraction of his day does he spend going to classes and doing homework?

A) $\dfrac{1}{4}$

B) $\dfrac{1}{3}$

C) $\dfrac{1}{2}$

D) $\dfrac{2}{3}$

CONTINUE

6

If $f(x) = 2x + 2$ is a linear function, which of the following is true for the graph of $4f(x)$?

A) The slope is four times steeper than $f(x)$.

B) The slope is four times less steep than $f(x)$.

C) The x-intercept is four times greater than that of $f(x)$.

D) The slope changes, but the y-intercept remains the same as $f(x)$.

7

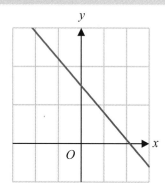

Which of the following is a possible equation for the line represented in the xy-plane above?

A) $y = -\dfrac{10x}{7} - 3$

B) $y = -\dfrac{10x}{7} + 3$

C) $y = \dfrac{10x}{7} - 3$

D) $y = \dfrac{10x}{7} + 3$

Questions 8 and 9 refer to the following information.

Career Preferences Among High School Students

Career Preference	Grade				
	9th	10th	11th	12th	Total
Healthcare	3	7	10	5	25
Education	11	8	7	12	38
Finance	1	4	6	4	15
Retail	6	3	5	4	18
Unsure	9	8	2	5	24
Total	30	30	30	30	120

8

If two different students are randomly chosen from the 11th grade, what is the probability that they both want to enter finance?

A) $\dfrac{1}{29}$

B) $\dfrac{1}{25}$

C) $\dfrac{1}{15}$

D) $\dfrac{1}{3}$

CONTINUE

9

After a lecture from a financial analyst, several 9th grade students changed their career preference. If there is now an average (arithmetic mean) of 5 students interested in finance per grade, how many 9th grade students changed their preference to finance?

A) 3

B) 5

C) 6

D) 8

10

Five students wrote a quiz and received grades of 30, 45, 75, 75, and 100. If a sixth student also writes the quiz, and her score does not change the mean score, what is her score?

A) 45

B) 50

C) 65

D) 75

11

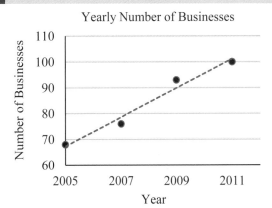

City planners in Beaufort, South Carolina, want to estimate the number of businesses in 2015 from data collected from 2005 to 2011. The number of businesses in the city during this period is graphed above. Using the line of best fit, what is the best estimate for the number of businesses in Beaufort operating in 2015?

A) 120

B) 125

C) 130

D) 140

12

If $x = a + 2b$, $y = 2a - b$, and $z = -2b$, what is $x - y + 2z$?

A) $-a - b$

B) $a - b$

C) $-a + b$

D) $-a - 3b$

CONTINUE

13

Dungeness crab and horseshoe crab populations are observed and compared by marine researchers. Researchers notice that the Dungeness population increases by 10% each year, and that the horseshoe population increases by 100 each year. If the solid line represents the Dungeness crab population, and the dotted line represents the horseshoe crab population, which of the following graphs best represents the crab populations?

A)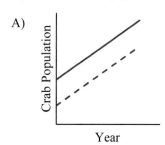

B)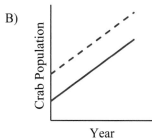

C)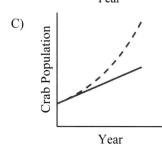

D)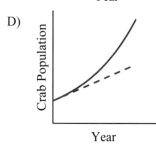

Questions 14 and 15 refer to the following information.

The graph below shows student enrollment for a psychology class and a biology class in the years 2000-2004.

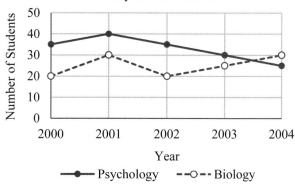
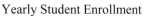

14

What is the total number of students who enrolled in the psychology class during the period from 2000 to 2002, inclusive?

A) 110

B) 130

C) 140

D) 170

CONTINUE

15

Which of the following statements is supported by the graph?

A) In 2001, there were twice as many students in the biology class than in the psychology class.

B) During the years 2001-2004, enrollment in the psychology class on average decreased by 5 students per year.

C) During the years 2002-2004, enrollment in the biology class on average increased by 10 students per year.

D) In 2003, there were more students in the biology class than in the psychology class.

16

t	0	1	2	3
$d(t)$	−3	−4	−7	−12

The table above shows the depth in feet, $d(t)$, of an anchor t seconds after it is released into the ocean. Which of the following expressions defines $d(t)$?

A) $-t^2 - 3$

B) $t^2 - 3$

C) $2t^2 - 3$

D) $t^2 - 2t - 3$

17

$$3x + 2y^2 = 3z$$

In the expression above, the value of z is 111. If $x = 15$, which of the following could be y?

A) 12

B) 30

C) 144

D) 159

18

t	$N(t)$
0	1250
1	2500
2	5000
3	10000
4	20000

The number of fruit flies, $N(t)$, in an enclosure after t hours has passed is shown in the chart above. What equation best represents the relationship between t and $N(t)$?

A) $N(t) = 1250 \times 2^t$

B) $N(t) = 1250 + 2t$

C) $N(t) = 1250 + 2t^2$

D) $N(t) = 1250^t$

CONTINUE

19

A company wants to create a solution of pure ethanol and distilled water. The density of ethanol is 0.789 grams per cubic centimeter, and the density of water is 1 gram per cubic centimeter. If the company combines 8 cubic centimeters of ethanol with 4 cubic centimeters of water, what is the resulting density of the solution, in grams per cubic centimeter, to the nearest one thousandth? (Density is mass divided by volume.)

A) 0.789

B) 0.842

C) 0.859

D) 0.895

20

$$\frac{x+1}{x+5} = \frac{1}{x-1}$$

What values of x satisfy the above equation?

A) 1 and −5

B) 2 and −3

C) 3 and −2

D) −1 and 2

21

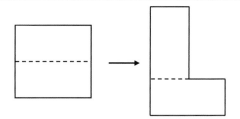

Susanne bakes a square cake with area A, and she then cuts it in half and arranges it, as shown in the diagram above. What is the perimeter of this new L-shaped cake in terms of A?

A) $\frac{5}{2}A$

B) $4A^2$

C) $4\sqrt{A}$

D) $5\sqrt{A}$

22

A colony of bacteria doubles in population every hour. Approximately how many hours will it take until the colony is 32 times its current size?

A)   5

B) 10

C) 16

D) 25

CONTINUE

23

National Park	Number of Grizzly Bears
Yellowstone	72
Glacier	90
Denali	87
North Cascades	84
Grand Teton	x

Scientists conducted a survey of the number of grizzly bears found in a small area of land in five National Parks. Their findings are shown in the table above. If the median number of grizzly bears found in the parks is 85, which of the following statements is <u>not</u> true?

A) The value of x is equal to the median number of grizzly bears.

B) The mean number of grizzly bears is greater than the median.

C) The value of x is greater than the mean number of grizzly bears.

D) If x were removed from the set, the median number of bears would increase.

24

A group of 11 people, 2 from France, 7 from England, and 2 from China, are traveling together. Unfortunately, their travel agent only booked 9 tickets, and 2 people have to leave the group. The group decides to pick 2 people at random. If the first person chosen is from England, what is the percentage chance that the second person will also be from England?

A) 30%

B) 40%

C) 50%

D) 60%

Questions 25 and 26 refer to the following information.

Isabella and Tom leave from the same location at 9:45 AM. Isabella drives north at a constant speed of 65 kilometers per hour, and Tom drives south at a constant speed of 77 kilometers per hour.

25

At what time will Isabella and Tom be 639 km apart?

A) 1:15 PM

B) 2:15 PM

C) 3:30 PM

D) 4:30 PM

26

Jorge, Tom's cousin, runs north from the same location as Isabella and Tom at 7:45 AM at a constant speed of 15 kilometers per hour. What will be the distance between Jorge and Tom by the time that Isabella catches up with Jorge, to the nearest kilometer?

A) 39

B) 85

C) 284

D) 369

CONTINUE

27

If $x \le 9$ and $x \ge 1$, which of the following statements are true?

I. $-9 \le x \le -1$
II. $1 \le x \le 9$
III. $\left| x - 5 \right| \le 4$

A) I only

B) II and III only

C) I and II only

D) I, II, and III

28

Amount of Sunlight Absorbed in One Day at Different Locations (in kilojoules)

Type of Plant	Location		
	Outside	House	Shed
Creeping Fig	25.00	z	15.00
Lavender	38.00	y	8.00
Russian Sage	32.00	22.00	9.00
New Mexico Chile	x	18.00	5.00

The table above shows the amount of energy from light that different plants absorb in different parts of Alex's property. Alex knows that if he leaves all four of his plants in the house for a day, they will absorb 78 kilojoules of energy in total. He also knows that the New Mexico Chile, if left outside, will absorb as much energy as the Creeping Fig and Lavender combined, if those plants were left in the house. How much more total energy, in kilojoules, will be absorbed by Alex's four plants if he keeps them outside rather than in the shed?

A) 33

B) 37

C) 96

D) 133

29

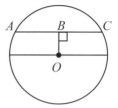

Note: The figure above is not to scale.

A circular parkette has a diameter of 10 meters. Alison and Charlie stand at the edge of the parkette (at A and C) so that they are 8 meters apart and a lamppost is between them, labeled B on the diagram above. If O is the center of the parkette, how far, in meters, is the lamppost from the center of the parkette?

A) 1

B) 2

C) 3

D) 4

30

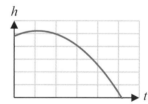

A class of physics students at W. L. Seaton Secondary School tests how long it will take a ball to fall when thrown off the top of a very tall building. The class calculates that the ball follows the function $h(t) = -2t^2 + 10t + 100$, which is graphed above, where h is the function of the height of the ball in meters, and t is the time in seconds. How many seconds does it take for the ball to reach the ground?

A) 5

B) 10

C) 12

D) 15

CONTINUE

DIRECTIONS

Questions **31-38** ask you to solve a problem and enter your answer in the grid provided on your answer sheet. When completing grid-in questions:

1. You are required to bubble in the circles for your answers. It is recommended, but not required, that you also write your answer in the boxes above the columns of circles. Points will be awarded based only on whether the circles are filled in correctly.

2. Fill in only one circle in a column.

3. You can start your answer in any column as long as you can fit in the whole answer.

4. For questions 31-38, no answers will be negative numbers.

5. **Mixed numbers**, such as $4\frac{2}{5}$, must be gridded as decimals or improper fractions, such as 4.4 or as 22/5. "42/5" will be read as "forty-two over five," not as "four and two-fifths."

6. If your answer is a **decimal** with more digits than will fit on the grid, you may round it or cut it off, but you must fill the entire grid.

7. If there are **multiple correct solutions** to a problem, all of them will be considered correct. Enter only **one** on the grid.

CONTINUE

31

If David has 7 more action figures than Michael, and Martin has 1 fewer action figure than Michael, how many more action figures does David have than Martin?

32

$$3(x - 4) - 2(8 - x) = 4(x + 1)$$

What is the value of x in the equation above?

33

Four times b is equal to 10. If c is 20 percent of b, what is the value of three times c?

34

$$\sqrt{2x + 10} = x + 5$$

What is the product of the two solutions for x in the equation above?

35

$$y + b = 5x$$
$$-2x + y = -c$$

If $b = c$, what value of x gives the same value of y in both of the equations above?

CONTINUE

36

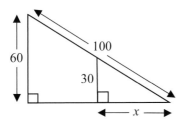

Two telephone poles are built next to each other with heights of 60 and 30 meters. A 100-meter-long wire is connected to the tops of these poles and then to the ground, as shown in the figure above. What is the length x, in meters?

Questions 37 and 38 refer to the following information.

Jennifer is conducting a series of experiments to study the effects of a drug on mouse behavior. For the duration of the experiments, she keeps the mice in cages. One cage can house up to five mice. Each cage costs a flat rate of $1.25 per day to maintain.

37

For her first experiment, Jennifer has six cages of mice at maximum capacity. If she has twice as many female mice as male mice, how many male mice does she have?

38

The animal supplies company offers a deal that will reduce the cost of maintaining each cage by half. Taking this opportunity, Jennifer decides to conduct a multi-day experiment. If she wants to test 102 mice and has a budget of 225 dollars for cage maintenance, what is the maximum length that her experiment can last, in days? (Round your answer to the nearest day.)

STOP

If you complete this section before the end of your allotted time, you may check your work on this section only. Do NOT use the time to work on another section.

Essay (Optional)

50 MINUTES

Turn to the lined pages of your answer sheet to write your essay.

DIRECTIONS

This essay is optional. It is a chance for you to demonstrate how well you can understand and analyze a written passage. Your essay should show that you have carefully read the passage and should be a concisely written analysis that is both logical and clear.

You must write your entire essay on the lines in your answer booklet. No additional paper will be provided aside from the Planning Page inside your answer booklet. You will be able to write your entire essay in the space provided if you make use of every line, keep tight margins, and write at a suitable size. Don't forget to keep your handwriting legible for the readers evaluating your essay.

You will have 50 minutes to read the passage in this booklet and to write an essay in response to the prompt provided at the end of the passage.

REMINDERS

- What you write in this booklet will not be evaluated. Write your essay in the answer booklet only.

- Essays that are off-topic will not be evaluated.

As you read the following passage, consider how Theresa Brown uses

- evidence, like examples or facts, to support her arguments.
- logical reasoning to develop her ideas and to connect her claims to her evidence.
- stylistic or persuasive techniques, such as the choice of particular words or appeals to her readers' emotions, to give power to the ideas put forth.

Adapted from Theresa Brown, "Hospitals Aren't Hotels," © 2012 by the New York Times Company. Originally published March 14, 2012.

1   "You should never do this procedure without pain medicine," the senior surgeon told a resident. "This is one of the most painful things we do."

2   She wasn't scolding, just firm, and she was telling the truth. The patient needed pleurodesis, a treatment that involves abrading the lining of the lungs in an attempt to stop fluid from collecting there.

3   I have watched patients go through pleurodesis, and even with pain medication, they suffer. We injure them in this controlled, short-term way to prevent long-term recurrence of a much more serious problem: fluid around the lungs makes it very hard to breathe.

4   A lot of what we do in medicine, and especially in modern hospital care, adheres to this same formulation. We hurt people because it's the only way we know to make them better. This is the nature of our work, which is why the growing focus on measuring "patient satisfaction" as a way to judge the quality of a hospital's care is worrisomely off the mark.

5   For several years now, hospitals around the country have been independently collecting data in different categories of patient satisfaction. More recently, the Centers for Medicare and Medicaid Services developed the Hospital Consumer Assessment of Healthcare Providers and Systems Survey and announced that by October 2012, Medicare reimbursements and bonuses were going to be linked in part to scores on the survey.

6   The survey evaluates behaviors that are integral to high-quality care: How good was the communication in the hospital? Were patients educated about all new medications? On discharge, were the instructions the patient received clear?

7   These are important questions. But implied in the proposal is a troubling misapprehension of how unpleasant a lot of actual health care is. The survey measures the "patient experience of care" to generate information important to "consumers." Put colloquially, it evaluates hospital patients' level of satisfaction.

8   The problem with this metric is that a lot of hospital care is, like pleurodesis, invasive, painful and even dehumanizing. Surgery leaves incisional pain as well as internal hurts from the removal of a gallbladder or tumor, or the repair of a broken bone. Chemotherapy weakens the immune system. We might like to say it shouldn't be, but physical pain, and its concomitant emotional suffering, tend to be inseparable from standard care.

9   What's more, recent research suggests that judging care in terms of desirable customer experiences could be expensive and may even be dangerous. A new paper by Joshua Fenton, an assistant professor at the

University of California, Davis, and colleagues found that higher satisfaction scores correlated with greater use of hospital services (driving up costs), but also with increased mortality.

10   The paper examined patient satisfaction only with physicians, rather than hospitals, and the link between satisfaction and death is obviously uncertain. Still, the results suggest that focusing on what patients want—a certain test, a specific drug—may mean they get less of what they actually need.

11   In other words, evaluating hospital care in terms of its ability to offer positive experiences could easily put pressure on the system to do things it can't, at the expense of what it should.

12   To evaluate the patient experience in a way that can be meaningfully translated to the public, we need to ask deeper questions, about whether our procedures accomplished what they were supposed to and whether patients did get better despite the suffering imposed by our care.

13   Hospitals are not hotels, and although hospital patients may in some ways be informed consumers, they're predominantly sick, needy people, depending on us, the nurses and doctors, to get them through a very tough physical time. They do not come to us for vacation, but because they need the specialized, often painful help that only we can provide. Sadly, sometimes we cannot give them the kind of help they need.

14   If the Centers for Medicare and Medicaid Services is to evaluate the patient experience and link the results to reimbursement, it needs to incorporate questions that address the complete and expected hospital experience. It's fair and even valuable to compare hospitals on the basis of how well they maintain standards of patient engagement. But a survey focused on "satisfaction" elides the true nature of the work that hospitals do. In order to heal, we must first hurt.

Write an essay in which you explain how Theresa Brown builds an argument to persuade her audience that patient satisfaction should not be a major factor in evaluating the quality of hospital care. In your essay, analyze how Brown uses one or more of the features listed in the directions above (or features of your own choice) to strengthen the logic and persuasiveness of her argument. Be sure that your analysis focuses on the most relevant features of the passage.

Your essay should not explain whether you agree with Brown's claims, but rather explain how Brown builds an argument to persuade her audience.

Practice Test 3

SAT

Directions

- Work on just one section at a time.

- If you complete a section before the end of your allotted time, use the extra minutes to check your work on that section only. Do NOT use the time to work on another section.

Using Your Test Booklet

- No credit will be given for anything written in the test booklet. You may use the test booklet for scratch paper.

- You are not allowed to continue answering questions in a section after the allotted time has run out. This includes marking answers on your answer sheet that you previously noted in your test booklet.

- You are not allowed to fold pages, take pages out of the test booklet, or take any pages home.

Answering Questions

- Each answer must be marked in the corresponding row on the answer sheet.

- Each bubble must be filled in completely and darkly within the lines.

Correct   Incorrect

- Be careful to bubble in the correct part of the answer sheet.

- Extra marks on your answer sheet may be marked as incorrect answers and lower your score.

- Make sure you use a No. 2 pencil.

Scoring

- You will receive one point for each correct answer.

- Incorrect answers will NOT result in points deducted. Even if you are unsure about an answer, you should make a guess.

DO NOT BEGIN THIS TEST

UNTIL YOUR PROCTOR TELLS YOU TO DO SO

 For printable answer sheets, please visit **ivyglobal.com/study**.

Section 1

	A	B	C	D
1	○	○	○	○
2	○	○	○	○
3	○	○	○	○
4	○	○	○	○
5	○	○	○	○
6	○	○	○	○
7	○	○	○	○
8	○	○	○	○
9	○	○	○	○
10	○	○	○	○
11	○	○	○	○

	A	B	C	D
12	○	○	○	○
13	○	○	○	○
14	○	○	○	○
15	○	○	○	○
16	○	○	○	○
17	○	○	○	○
18	○	○	○	○
19	○	○	○	○
20	○	○	○	○
21	○	○	○	○
22	○	○	○	○

	A	B	C	D
23	○	○	○	○
24	○	○	○	○
25	○	○	○	○
26	○	○	○	○
27	○	○	○	○
28	○	○	○	○
29	○	○	○	○
30	○	○	○	○
31	○	○	○	○
32	○	○	○	○
33	○	○	○	○

	A	B	C	D
34	○	○	○	○
35	○	○	○	○
36	○	○	○	○
37	○	○	○	○
38	○	○	○	○
39	○	○	○	○
40	○	○	○	○
41	○	○	○	○
42	○	○	○	○
43	○	○	○	○
44	○	○	○	○

	A	B	C	D
45	○	○	○	○
46	○	○	○	○
47	○	○	○	○
48	○	○	○	○
49	○	○	○	○
50	○	○	○	○
51	○	○	○	○
52	○	○	○	○

Section 2

	A	B	C	D
1	○	○	○	○
2	○	○	○	○
3	○	○	○	○
4	○	○	○	○
5	○	○	○	○
6	○	○	○	○
7	○	○	○	○
8	○	○	○	○
9	○	○	○	○

	A	B	C	D
10	○	○	○	○
11	○	○	○	○
12	○	○	○	○
13	○	○	○	○
14	○	○	○	○
15	○	○	○	○
16	○	○	○	○
17	○	○	○	○
18	○	○	○	○

	A	B	C	D
19	○	○	○	○
20	○	○	○	○
21	○	○	○	○
22	○	○	○	○
23	○	○	○	○
24	○	○	○	○
25	○	○	○	○
26	○	○	○	○
27	○	○	○	○

	A	B	C	D
28	○	○	○	○
29	○	○	○	○
30	○	○	○	○
31	○	○	○	○
32	○	○	○	○
33	○	○	○	○
34	○	○	○	○
35	○	○	○	○
36	○	○	○	○

	A	B	C	D
37	○	○	○	○
38	○	○	○	○
39	○	○	○	○
40	○	○	○	○
41	○	○	○	○
42	○	○	○	○
43	○	○	○	○
44	○	○	○	○

Section 3 (No-Calculator)

	A	B	C	D			A	B	C	D			A	B	C	D			A	B	C	D			A	B	C	D
1	○	○	○	○		4	○	○	○	○		7	○	○	○	○		10	○	○	○	○		13	○	○	○	○
2	○	○	○	○		5	○	○	○	○		8	○	○	○	○		11	○	○	○	○		14	○	○	○	○
3	○	○	○	○		6	○	○	○	○		9	○	○	○	○		12	○	○	○	○		15	○	○	○	○

Only answers that are gridded will be scored. You will not receive credit for anything written in the boxes.

16   17   18   19   20

(Gridded-response grids for questions 16–20, each with fraction bar /, decimal point ., and digits 0 through 9.)

Section 4 (Calculator)

	A	B	C	D			A	B	C	D			A	B	C	D			A	B	C	D			A	B	C	D
1	○	○	○	○		7	○	○	○	○		13	○	○	○	○		19	○	○	○	○		25	○	○	○	○
2	○	○	○	○		8	○	○	○	○		14	○	○	○	○		20	○	○	○	○		26	○	○	○	○
3	○	○	○	○		9	○	○	○	○		15	○	○	○	○		21	○	○	○	○		27	○	○	○	○
4	○	○	○	○		10	○	○	○	○		16	○	○	○	○		22	○	○	○	○		28	○	○	○	○
5	○	○	○	○		11	○	○	○	○		17	○	○	○	○		23	○	○	○	○		29	○	○	○	○
6	○	○	○	○		12	○	○	○	○		18	○	○	○	○		24	○	○	○	○		30	○	○	○	○

Only answers that are gridded will be scored. You will not receive credit for anything written in the boxes.

31   32   33   34   35

Only answers that are gridded will be scored. You will not receive credit for anything written in the boxes.

36   37   38

Section 5 (Optional)

Important: Use a No. 2 pencil. Write inside the borders.

You may use the space below to plan your essay, but be sure to write your essay on the lined pages. Work on this page will not be scored.

Use this space to plan your essay.

START YOUR ESSAY HERE.

_____
_____
_____
_____
_____
_____
_____
_____
_____
_____
_____
_____
_____
_____
_____
_____
_____
_____
_____
_____
_____
_____
_____
_____
_____
_____

Continue on the next page.

_____

_____

_____

_____

_____

_____

_____

_____

_____

_____

_____

_____

_____

_____

_____

_____

_____

_____

_____

_____

_____

_____

_____

_____

Continue on the next page.

Continue on the next page.

STOP.

Reading Test

65 MINUTES, 52 QUESTIONS

Turn to Section 1 of your answer sheet to answer the questions in this section.

DIRECTIONS

Every passage or paired set of passages is accompanied by a number of questions. Read the passage or paired set of passages, then use what is said or implied in what you read and in any given graphics to choose the best answer to each question.

Questions 1-10 are based on the following passage.

This passage is adapted from Alice Dunbar-Nelson, "Titee." Originally published in 1895.

It was cold that day; the great sharp north wind swept out Elysian Fields Street in blasts that made men shiver, and bent everything in its track. The
Line skies hung lowering and gloomy; the usually quiet
5 street was more than deserted, it was dismal.

Titee leaned against one of the brown freight cars for protection against the shrill norther, and warmed his little chapped hands at a blaze of chips and dry grass. "Maybe it'll snow," he muttered, casting a
10 glance at the sky that would have done credit to a practiced seaman. "Then won't I have fun! Ugh, but the wind blows!"

It was Saturday, or Titee would have been in school—the big yellow school on Marigny Street,
15 where he went every day when its bell boomed nine o'clock. He went with a run and a joyous whoop, presumably to imbibe knowledge, ostensibly to make his teacher's life a burden.

Idle, lazy, troublesome boy, she called him, to
20 herself, as day by day wore on, and Titee improved not, but let his whole class pass him on its way to a higher grade. A practical joke he relished infinitely more than a practical problem, and a good game at pin-sticking was far more entertaining than a
25 language lesson. Moreover, he was always hungry, and would eat in school before the half-past ten

intermission, thereby losing much good playtime for his voracious appetite.

But there was nothing in natural history that Titee
30 didn't know. He could dissect a butterfly or a mosquito-hawk and describe their parts as accurately as a spectacled student with a scalpel and microscope could talk about a cadaver. The entire Third District, with its swamps and canals and commons and
35 railroad sections, and its wondrous, crooked, tortuous streets, was as an open book to Titee. He knew just exactly when it was time for crawfish to be plentiful down in the Claiborne and Marigny canals; just when a poor, breadless fellow might get a job in the big
40 boneyard and fertilizing factory out on the railroad track. All these things, and more, could Titee tell of.

Titee shivered as the wind swept around the freight cars. There isn't much warmth in a bit of a jersey coat.
45 "Wish 'twas summer," he murmured, casting another sailor's glance at the sky. "Don't believe I like snow, it's too wet and cold." And, with a last parting caress at the little fire he had built for a minute's warmth, he plunged his hands in his
50 pockets, shut his teeth, and started manfully on his mission out the railroad track towards the swamps.

It was late when Titee came home, and he had performed his errand poorly, so his mother sent him to bed supperless.
55 Long walks in the teeth of a biting wind create a keen appetite. Though Titee cried himself to sleep

CONTINUE

that night, he was up bright and early the next morning, and had been to early mass, devoutly kneeling on the cold floor, blowing his fingers to
60 keep them warm, and was home almost before the rest of the family was awake.

There was evidently some great matter of business in this young man's mind, for he scarcely ate his breakfast, and had left the table, eagerly
65 cramming the remainder of his meal in his pockets.

"I wonder what he's up to now?" mused his mother as she watched his little form sturdily trudging the track in the face of the wind, his head, with the rimless cap thrust close on the shock of
70 black hair, bent low, his hands thrust deep in the bulging pockets.

"A new snake, perhaps," ventured the father. "He's a strange child."

But the next day Titee was late for school. It was
75 something unusual, for he was always the first on hand to fix some plan or mechanism to make the teacher miserable. She looked reprovingly at him this morning, when he came in during the arithmetic class, his hair all windblown, cheeks rosy from a
80 hard fight with the sharp blasts. But he made up for his tardiness by his extreme goodness all day; just think, Titee didn't even eat in school. A something unparalleled in the entire history of his school-life.

1

Which of the following best describes the structure of the passage as a whole?

A) A teacher's philosophy is outlined, and her students are briefly named.

B) A character is introduced, and hints are given that he is doing something unusual.

C) A family's history is recounted, and speculations about the youngest member are made.

D) A child's family life is described, and his school routine is outlined in detail.

2

What main effect does the description of the setting in lines 1-5 have on the mood of the passage?

A) It creates a cheerful mood, emphasizing the invigorating briskness of the wind.

B) It creates a frightful mood, implying that something sinister is lurking nearby.

C) It creates an ominous mood, highlighting the harshness of the surroundings.

D) It creates a tragic mood, focusing on the hardships faced by members of the neighborhood.

3

As used in line 2, "blasts" most nearly means

A) gusts.

B) explosions.

C) wails.

D) shockwaves.

4

Which best summarizes lines 19-28?

A) Titee works very hard in school but struggles to make good grades.

B) Titee's teacher wishes she had chosen some other profession instead.

C) Titee does well in science but has difficulty in math class.

D) Titee's teacher is frustrated with his behavior in the classroom.

CONTINUE

5

The primary purpose of lines 29-41 is to

A) imply that Titee is on his way to becoming a real troublemaker.

B) show that although Titee has problems at school, his teacher cares about him.

C) demonstrate how concerned Titee's parents are for his well-being.

D) suggest that while Titee is not a great student, he is still knowledgeable.

6

The passage most strongly suggests that one cause of Titee's bad mood is

A) the weather.

B) his teacher.

C) his parents.

D) the neighborhood.

7

Which choice provides the best evidence for the answer to the previous question?

A) Lines 13-16 ("It … nine o'clock")

B) Lines 45-46 ("Wish … the sky")

C) Line 72 ("A new … father")

D) Lines 77-80 ("She looked … blasts")

8

Titee's parents assume he's up to something they don't know about because he

A) speaks little during breakfast.

B) is late for school.

C) forgets his books at home.

D) doesn't eat much that morning.

9

Which choice provides the best evidence for the answer to the previous question?

A) Lines 47-51 ("And … swamps")

B) Lines 52-54 ("It was … supperless")

C) Lines 62-65 ("There was … pockets")

D) Line 74 ("But the … school")

10

As used in line 76, "fix" most nearly means

A) repair.

B) arrange.

C) correct.

D) secure.

CONTINUE

Questions 11-20 are based on the following passages.

The first passage is adapted from Carl Zimmer, "Reverse Engineering Birds' Beaks Into Dinosaur Bones." © 2015 by The New York Times Company. The second passage is adapted from John Noble Wilford, "Fossil with Signs of Feathers is Cited as Bird-Dinosaur Link." © 2001 by The New York Times Company.

Passage 1

Birds evolved from dinosaurs 150 million years ago. Some researchers are now trying to pinpoint the genetic changes that turned ground-running

Line dinosaurs into modern birds through experiments on
5   chicken embryos. One group, led by Bhart-Anjan Bhullar of Yale University and Arhat Abzhanov of Harvard University, reports that they have found a way to turn the beaks of chicken embryos back into dinosaur-like snouts.

10   The beak evolved fairly late in bird evolution. It originated from a pair of small, separate plates of bone sitting at the front of the upper jaw, called premaxillae. In the evolution of early birds, the premaxillae stretched out and fused together to form
15   a strong, lightweight beak.

Dr. Bhullar and Dr. Abzhanov set out to find some of the genetic changes that turned the dinosaur premaxillae into a beak. To find clues, they looked at earlier experiments on chicken embryos. The
20   scientists were struck by the fact that even before the embryo has a developed, recognizable face, a large patch of cells in the middle of what will become the bird's face makes a protein called Fgf8. Later, the region produces different proteins, called Lef1.

25   Like the embryos of chickens, those of emus produce the proteins in a single patch of cells, the scientists learned. But in animals other than birds—such as turtles, lizards, and crocodiles—the proteins are usually made in a pair of small cell patches.

30   Was it possible, the scientists wondered, that a key step in the evolution of beaks was a shift from small protein-producing patches to a single large one? That change might have allowed birds to develop big, fused premaxillae—the precursors of
35   beaks. If the hypothesis was correct, the researchers

figured, they might be able to turn back the clock on evolution. If they caused a chicken embryo to use Fgf8 and Lef1 the way other animals do, it should turn out to be a bird without a beak.

40   To reverse evolution, the scientists wedged a microscopic bead into the middle of what would become the faces of chicken embryos. The bead released chemicals into the surrounding tissue that interfere with Fgf8 and Lef1. The chicken embryos
45   failed to develop beaks and instead gained a pair of rounded, unfused bones—more like what you might have found on a dinosaur's head.

Dr. Ralph S. Marcucio, a developmental biologist, noted that the scientists used chemicals to
50   block Fgf8 and Lef1 proteins that have toxic side effects and can kill cells. The altered anatomy of the chicken skulls might not be an example of reverse evolution, he said, just dying tissue.

Passage 2

Paleontologists have discovered in China a
55   dinosaur fossil with what are reported to be clear traces of feathers from head to tail, the most persuasive evidence so far, scientists say, that feathers predated the origin of birds and that modern birds are descendants of dinosaurs. Other dinosaur
60   remains with what appear to be featherlike traces have been unearthed in recent years, but nothing as complete as this specimen, paleontologists said. Etched in the rock like a filigree decoration surrounding the skeleton are imprints of where the
65   down and feathers appear to have been.

The 130-million-year-old fossils were found a year ago by farmers in Liaoning Province in northeastern China. After an analysis by Chinese and American researchers, the fossil animal was
70   identified as a dromaeosaur, a small, fast-running dinosaur related to the velociraptor. The findings are described in the journal *Nature* by the discovery team led by Dr. Ji Qiang, director of the Chinese Academy of Geological Sciences in Beijing, and Dr.
75   Mark A. Norell, chairman of paleontology at the American Museum of Natural History in Manhattan. "This is the specimen we've been waiting for," Dr. Norell said in a statement. "It makes it indisputable

CONTINUE

that a body covering similar to feathers was present
80 in nonavian dinosaurs."

The specimen's forelimbs were too short to have supported wings, Dr. Norell said in an interview, and so it was flightless. But some of the bone structure—notably the furcula, or wishbone, and the three
85 forward-pointing toes—bears similarities to that of birds. Other recent discoveries of birdlike dinosaurs and dinosaurlike birds have encouraged support for the theory of a dinosaur-bird ancestral link.

Not that these particular dinosaurs were ancestors
90 of birds—but they may be descendants of the ancestors. Dr. Norell said the feathered fossil showed that there was "a more general distribution of feathers than in birds alone." Studying theropods that lived later than the first birds, he explained, should
95 provide insights into bird evolution, just as related "chimps and gorillas and lemurs help us understand human evolution."

11

Which best summarizes lines 10-15?

A) The beak developed into the premaxillae late in the evolution of birds.

B) The beak originated from the upper jaw bone stretching out and separating.

C) The beak evolved from a couple of small plates of bones that fused together.

D) The beak formed from lightweight tissue drawn from the mouth and throat of birds.

12

As used in line 36, "figured" most nearly means

A) computed.

B) appeared.

C) represented.

D) reasoned.

13

In Passage 1, Dr. Ralph S. Marcucio's attitude towards Dr. Bhullar and Dr. Abzhanov's research is best described as

A) cautious.

B) encouraging.

C) envious.

D) sincere.

14

Which choice provides the best evidence for the answer to the previous question?

A) Lines 16-18 ("Dr. Bhullar … beak")

B) Lines 30-33 ("Was it … one")

C) Lines 44-47 ("The chicken … head")

D) Lines 51-53 ("The altered … tissue")

15

As used in line 55, "clear" most nearly means

A) transparent.

B) vibrant.

C) unblemished.

D) obvious.

16

The primary purpose of lines 59-62 ("Other … said") is to

A) explain why the finding described in the passage is so significant.

B) offer a counterpoint to the evidence described in the rest of the passage.

C) downplay the discovery made by the researchers.

D) set forth the thesis that will be defended in the remainder of the passage.

CONTINUE

17

Passage 2 indicates that birds

A) are direct descendants of dromaeosaurs.

B) coexisted with dromaeosaurs for thousands of years.

C) share some common ancestors with dromaeosaurs.

D) have no relationship to dromaeosaurs.

18

Which choice provides the best evidence for the answer to the previous question?

A) Lines 66-68 ("The … China")

B) Lines 78-80 ("It makes … dinosaurs")

C) Lines 81-83 ("The specimen's … flightless")

D) Lines 89-91 ("Not that … ancestors")

19

Passage 2 differs from Passage 1 in that only Passage 1 describes

A) evidence from experiments on bird development.

B) the relationship between dinosaurs and birds.

C) a discovery that may link dinosaurs with birds.

D) the process of evolution as it relates to birds.

20

One difference between the findings described in the two passages is that, unlike the discovery described in Passage 2, the discovery in Passage 1

A) focused on genetic changes that occurred in the evolution of birds.

B) received widespread acceptance by the scientific community.

C) compared specific bone structures that differed in dinosaurs and birds.

D) suffered from controversy that ultimately invalidated its findings.

Questions 21-31 are based on the following passage.

This passage is adapted from Robert F. Kennedy, "Recapturing America's Moral Vision." Originally delivered in 1968.

There are millions living in the hidden places whose names and faces are completely unknown. But I have seen these other Americans. I have seen
Line children in Mississippi starving, their bodies so
5 crippled from hunger and their minds so destroyed for their whole lives that they will have no future. We haven't developed a policy so we can get enough food so that they can live, so that their lives are not destroyed. I don't think that's acceptable in
10 the United States of America, and I think we need a change.

I think we can do much, much better. And I run for the presidency because of that. I run for the presidency because I have seen proud men in the
15 hills of Appalachia, who wish only to work in dignity, but they cannot, for the mines are closed and their jobs are gone and no one—neither industry, nor labor, nor government—has cared enough to help. I think we here in this country, with
20 the unselfish spirit that exists in the United States of America, I think we can do better here also.

If we believe that we, as Americans, are bound together by a common concern for each other, then an urgent national priority is upon us. We must
25 begin to end the disgrace of this other America. And this is one of the great tasks of leadership for us, as individuals and citizens this year.

But even if we act to erase material poverty, there is another greater task: it is to confront the
30 poverty of satisfaction, purpose, and dignity that afflicts us all. Too much and for too long, we seemed to have surrendered personal excellence and community values in the mere accumulation of material things.
35 Our Gross National Product* now is over 800 billion dollars a year. But that Gross National Product—if we judge the United States of America by that—that Gross National Product counts air pollution and cigarette advertising and ambulances
40 to clear our highways of carnage. It counts special

CONTINUE

locks for our doors and the jails for the people who break them. It counts the destruction of the redwoods and the loss of our natural wonder in chaotic sprawl. It counts napalm and it counts nuclear warheads and

45 armored cars for the police to fight the riots in our cities. It counts Whitman's rifle and Speck's knife and the television programs which glorify violence in order to sell toys to our children.

Yet the Gross National Product does not allow

50 for the health of our children, the quality of their education, or the joy of their play. It does not include the beauty of our poetry or the strength of our marriages, the intelligence of our public debate or the integrity of our public officials. It measures

55 neither our wit nor our courage, neither our wisdom nor our learning, neither our compassion nor our devotion to our country. It measures everything, in short, except that which makes life worthwhile. And it can tell us everything about America except why

60 we are proud that we are Americans.

*Gross National Product refers to the total value of goods and services produced by a country in one year.

21

Kennedy's attitude toward the situation faced by "other Americans" mentioned in the passage is best described as

A) annoyed.

B) resigned.

C) outraged.

D) confused.

22

Which choice provides the best evidence for the answer to the previous question?

A) Lines 1-2 ("There are … unknown")

B) Lines 9-11 ("I don't … change")

C) Lines 31-34 ("Too much … things")

D) Lines 54-57 ("It measures … country")

23

The passage most strongly suggests that the Gross National Product

A) is essential in helping Americans escape from a life of poverty and disgrace.

B) measures economic but not personal or moral value.

C) must increase if Americans are to improve their environment, jails, and cities.

D) does not accurately represent the breakdown of industries in the American economy.

24

Which choice provides the best evidence for the answer to the previous question?

A) Lines 19-21 ("I think … also")

B) Lines 24-25 ("We must … America")

C) Lines 35-36 ("Our Gross … year")

D) Lines 57-58 ("It measures … worthwhile")

25

Based on the passage, which best describes the relationship between the "unselfish spirit" (line 20) Kennedy describes and the problems he sees in the United States?

A) The unselfish spirit exhibited by Americans can be drawn upon to resolve many of the country's problems.

B) The unselfish spirit of the men of the Appalachia must be harnessed to help avoid further problems.

C) Americans can rely on the unselfish spirit of their government to solve any problems.

D) The unselfish spirit demonstrated by industry is the cause of the United States' problems.

CONTINUE

26

As used in line 28, "erase" most nearly means

A) eliminate.

B) delete.

C) obliterate.

D) cancel.

27

Kennedy refers to "the poverty of satisfaction, purpose, and dignity" (lines 29-30) primarily to

A) urge Americans to act quickly or face economic failure.

B) suggest that Americans face more than just economic challenges.

C) inspire Americans to be more ambitious in their economic goals.

D) warn Americans that unless they fix the economy, their communities will suffer.

28

The rhetorical effect of the repetition in lines 38-48 is to

A) emphasize the various negative portions of the economy that contribute to the Gross National Product.

B) show how many areas of the economy are included in the Gross National Product.

C) reveal how economic analysts must alter their calculation of the Gross National Product.

D) demonstrate the great diversity of the American economy, as seen in the Gross National Product.

29

As used in lines 49-50, "allow for" most nearly means

A) concede.

B) ponder.

C) grant.

D) include.

30

Which of the following situations is most analogous to the problem Kennedy presents in the second to last paragraph (lines 35-48)?

A) A young woman attends the college of her choice, only to realize it doesn't live up to her expectations.

B) A woman works long hours and earns a great deal of money, but her work has a negative impact on her health.

C) A boy receives an excessive number of toys from his parents, but has no siblings with whom to share them.

D) A man lives frugally, only to find that in his old age he's unable to enjoy his accumulated riches.

31

Kennedy states that the Gross National Product does not measure

A) air pollution and environmental destruction.

B) weapons needed to fight riots in cities.

C) the honesty of public servants.

D) advertising for cigarettes and violent toys.

CONTINUE

Questions 32-41 are based on the following passage.

This passage is adapted from Scott Armstrong Elias, "First Americans lived on land bridge for thousands of years, genetics study suggests." © 2014 by Scott Armstrong Elias.

The theory that the Americas were populated by humans crossing a land bridge from Siberia to Alaska was first proposed as far back as 1590, and has been
Line generally accepted since the 1930s. However, a
5 comparison of DNA from 600 modern Native Americans with ancient DNA recovered from a late Stone Age human skeleton from Mal'ta in southern Siberia shows that Native Americans diverged genetically from their Asian ancestors around 25,000
10 years ago, just as the last ice age was reaching its peak.

Based on archaeological evidence, humans did not survive the last ice age's peak in northeastern Siberia, and yet there is no evidence they had reached
15 Alaska or the rest of the New World, either. There is evidence to suggest northeast Siberia was inhabited during a warm period about 30,000 years ago, before the last ice age peaked. After this, however, the archaeological record goes silent and only returns
20 15,000 years ago, after the last ice age ended.

So where did the ancestors of the Native Americans go for 15,000 years, after they split from the rest of their Asian relatives? As John Hoffecker, Dennis O'Rourke, and I argue, in an article for
25 *Science*, the answer seems to be that they lived on the Bering Land Bridge, the region between Siberia and Alaska that was dry land when sea levels were lower, as much of the world's freshwater was locked up in ice, but which now lies underneath the waters of the
30 Bering and Chukchi Seas. This theory has become increasingly supported by genetic evidence.

The Bering Land Bridge, also known as Central Beringia, is thought to have been up to 600 miles wide. Based on evidence from sediment cores drilled
35 into the now-submerged landscape, it seems that here and in some adjacent regions of Alaska and Siberia, the landscape at the height of the last glaciation

21,000 years ago was shrub tundra—as found in Arctic Alaska today.
40   This shrub tundra would have supported elk, perhaps some bighorn sheep, and small mammals. But it had the one resource people needed most to keep warm: wood. The wood and bark of dwarf shrubs would have been used to start fires that
45 burned large mammal bones. And there is evidence from archaeological sites that people burned bones as fuel—the charred remains of leg bones have been found in many ancient hearths. It is the heat from these fires that kept these intrepid hunter-gatherers
50 alive through the bitter cold of Arctic winter nights.

The last ice age ended, and the land bridge began to disappear beneath the sea, some 13,000 years ago. Global sea levels rose as the vast continental ice sheets melted, liberating billions of gallons of fresh water.
55 As the land bridge flooded, the entire Beringian region grew more warm and moist, and the shrub tundra vegetation spread rapidly, out-competing the steppe-tundra plants that had dominated the interior lowlands of Beringia.
60   While this spelled the end of the woolly mammoths and other large grazing animals, it probably also provided the impetus for human migration. As retreating glaciers opened new routes into the continent, humans travelled first into the
65 Alaskan interior and the Yukon, and ultimately south out of the Arctic region and toward the temperate regions of the Americas. The first definitive archaeological evidence we have for the presence of people beyond Beringia and interior Alaska comes
70 from this time, about 13,000 years ago.

These people are called Paleoindians by archaeologists. The genetic evidence records mutations in mitochondrial DNA passed from mother to offspring that are present in today's Native
75 Americans but not in the Mal'ta remains. This indicates a population isolated from the Siberian mainland for thousands of years, who are the direct ancestors of nearly all of the Native American tribes in both North and South America—the original "first
80 peoples."

CONTINUE

Gene Flow In and Out of Beringia		
Time	West to East	East to West
25,000 years ago	Initial peopling of Beringia	–
15,000 years ago	Swift peopling of the Americas	–
10,000 years ago	Later arrival of hg* D2	Back migration of C1a
<10,000 years ago	Spread of D2a	Back migration of A2a

*Stands for haplogroup: different genes across chromosomes that are often inherited together as a single line of descent

Note: D2, D2a, C1a, hg, and A2a are all genetic lineages.

32

What is the author's main point about the ancestors of Native Americans?

A) Contrary to previous theories, they are unrelated to any populations in the East.

B) They are more closely related to modern Native Americans than people from the ancient Near East.

C) They survived on Beringia for thousands of years before moving on to the Americas.

D) They crossed the Bering Land Bridge 25,000 years ago at the end of the last ice age.

33

Which choice provides the best evidence for the answer to the previous question?

A) Lines 1-4 ("The theory … 1930s")

B) Lines 15-18 ("There is … peaked")

C) Lines 23-30 ("As John … Seas")

D) Lines 32-34 ("The Bering … wide")

34

According to the passage, the shrub tundra was hospitable to early humans primarily because it

A) featured a mild, temperate climate at the time.

B) had numerous large animals that humans could hunt.

C) contained wood, an essential resource.

D) was home to a large number of bones that could be used as fuel.

35

Which choice provides the best evidence for the answer to the previous question?

A) Lines 40-41 ("This shrub … mammals")

B) Lines 42-43 ("But it … wood")

C) Lines 45-48 ("And there … hearths")

D) Lines 55-59 ("As the … Beringia")

36

As used in line 40, "supported" most nearly means

A) braced.

B) held.

C) sustained.

D) reinforced.

37

The author mentions the theory about the land bridge in lines 1-4 in order to

A) explain the theory that the rest of the passage fully supports.

B) establish the authority of the theory that the passage agrees with.

C) mention the theory that is challenged by evidence the passage will present.

D) ridicule the out-of-date theory that will be debunked in the rest of the article.

CONTINUE

38

The author indicates which of the following about the Bering Land Bridge?

A) It was inhospitable to human life until about 600 years ago.

B) It allowed early humans to cross from Siberia to Beringia.

C) It used to be a rich, forested area before the end of the ice age.

D) It disappeared once temperatures and sea levels rose.

39

As used in line 63, "retreating" most nearly means

A) retiring.

B) disappearing.

C) recoiling.

D) falling.

40

It can reasonably be inferred from the table that

A) the people of Asia and the Americas have no genetic connection.

B) the flow of people through Beringia moved in both directions.

C) the land bridge on Beringia remained isolated for hundreds of years.

D) only recently did any genetic transfer occur between modern humans.

41

Information from the table provides most direct support for which idea in the passage?

A) Humans spread rapidly through the Americas about 10-15,000 years ago.

B) Human populations moved from the Americas to Asia over the course of about 10,000 years.

C) The initial peopling of Beringia occurred about 2,500 years ago.

D) Migration of humans always flowed in one direction.

CONTINUE

Questions 42-52 are based on the following passage.

This passage is adapted from Declan Perry, "Ravens Have Social Abilities Previously Only Seen in Humans." © 2015 by Declan Perry.

A new study shows that ravens are more socially savvy than we give them credit for. They are able to work out the social dynamics of other raven groups,
Line something that previously only humans had shown
5 the ability to do. Jorg Massen and his colleagues of the University of Vienna wanted to find out more about birds' social skills, so in their study, they looked at whether ravens were intelligent enough to understand relationships in their own social groups,
10 as well as if they could figure out social groups that they had never been a part of.

Ravens within a community squabble over their ranking in the group, as higher ranked ravens have better access to food and other resources. Males
15 always outrank females, and confrontations mostly occur between members of the same sex. These confrontations are initiated by high-ranking ravens, who square up to low-ranking birds and emit a specific call to assert their dominance. Normally, the
20 lower-ranking, or submissive, raven typically makes a specific call to recognize the high-ranking raven's social superiority. Through this process, the dominant raven ensures that its social position is maintained. But sometimes, the lower-ranking bird
25 does not respond in a submissive way to a dominance call, and instead responds with a dominance reversal call. These situations often result in confrontations, and can result in changes in the social structure of raven communities.
30 Massen and his team kept a group of captive ravens and made recordings of conflicts. These included normal conflicts (in which the lower-ranking bird responded submissively to a dominance call) and dominance reversal conflicts. The same
35 method was also used to capture the calls from a different group of ravens that were housed separately. Individual ravens were then taken from the group and isolated in a separate enclosure. The recordings of different calls were then played,

40 mimicking a situation in nature where a raven overhears two other ravens in a confrontation. Massen said, "We monitored their responses to these calls to see if they reacted differently to normal dominance calls and dominance reversals. We also
45 used the recordings taken from the foreign group, to see if our ravens recognized the same behavior in other communities."

When presented with a dominance reversal recording taken from their own group, ravens
50 displayed behavior associated with stress, because they expected a disturbance in the social order. Ravens showed even higher levels of stress when they were played a dominance reversal call from members of their own sex. This makes sense,
55 because ranking disputes only occur between members of the same sex. A confrontation between two females, for example, would not have a big effect on the social status of a male raven—but would affect any females who were listening. Female
60 ravens in general were more stressed than males when they were played dominance reversal recordings. This may be because females are always lower ranked than males, so changes in community structure pose more risks to females at the bottom,
65 which have reduced access to food in the first place.

But perhaps the most impressive finding was that ravens seemed to notice dominance reversals in a foreign group of ravens, although they exhibited less stress than when they heard such calls from their own
70 social community. To be sure that the ravens weren't just recognizing that call because it was an audibly different call, Massen played calls from a different community, which weren't dominance reversal calls, and saw that the captive ravens were not stressed.
75 Massen said: "This shows that ravens are able to create a mental representation of relationship dynamics from groups they have never interacted with before. This ability has not even been observed in monkeys yet."
80 However, there are limitations to the study. Alex Thornton of the University of Exeter explained: "The results in this study are no doubt exciting, but it should be recognized that captive ravens were used.

CONTINUE

Being kept in such close proximity, with only
85 each other, may have influenced the ravens ability to
judge each other's behavior."

In addition to showing that ravens have social
abilities that were previously only seen in humans,
these findings give a clue that raven intelligence may
90 have evolved along with the development of social
communities. "Being intelligent helps the ravens play
the politics of their social group, and gain
dominance," Massen said.

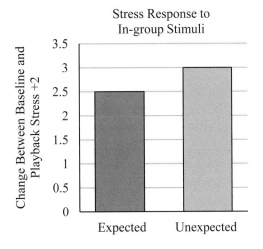

Stress Response to
In-group Stimuli

43

Which choice provides the best evidence for the
answer to the previous question?

A) Lines 37-38 ("Individual … enclosure")

B) Lines 42-44 ("We monitored … reversals")

C) Lines 66-70 ("But perhaps … community")

D) Lines 81-83 ("The results … used")

44

According to the passage, a dominance reversal call
is likely to be used by

A) a lower-ranking raven that decides to not respond
submissively to a dominance call.

B) a high-ranking raven that wishes to challenge a
lower-ranking raven.

C) a high-ranking male raven that is recognizing the
highest-ranking female in a raven social group.

D) a high-ranking female raven that is recognizing
the highest-ranked male in a raven social group.

42

The passage primarily focuses on which of the
following?

A) The difficulty of studying natural populations of
ravens in artificial settings

B) The ability of ravens to understand relationship
dynamics within their own and other social
groups

C) The various methods that ravens use in their
battle for dominance within their own social
groups

D) The limitations of a new study on ravens that
fails to take into account the birds' social natures

45

Which choice provides the best evidence for the
answer to the previous question?

A) Lines 14-16 ("Males always … sex")

B) Lines 19-22 ("Normally … superiority")

C) Lines 24-27 ("But sometimes … call")

D) Lines 30-31 ("Massen … conflicts")

CONTINUE

46

As used in line 32, "normal" most nearly means

A) unimportant.

B) mainstream.

C) average.

D) typical.

47

In lines 62-65, what is the most likely reason that the author describes females' heightened risk during changes in community structure?

A) To attempt to explain one of the results seen in the study

B) To suggest a further potential area for research in the field

C) To summarize the conclusion that the study reached

D) To provide an alternate explanation of a controversial finding

48

As used in line 66, "impressive" most nearly means

A) poignant.

B) remarkable.

C) rousing.

D) inspirational.

49

The passage indicates that ravens' social development evolved in parallel with their

A) intelligence.

B) politics.

C) dominant personalities.

D) captivity.

50

It can be most reasonably inferred that Alex Thornton

A) believes the results of the study to be erroneous for captive ravens.

B) feels that the study likely suffered from a lack of funding.

C) plans to redo the described experiment himself with a larger sample size.

D) is unsure of whether the study's results would be applicable to wild ravens.

CONTINUE

51

The graph most strongly supports which of the following conclusions?

A) Ravens are less stressed by in-group dominance calls than by dominance reversal calls from another social group.

B) Ravens are less stressed by in-group dominance reversal calls than by dominance reversal calls from another group.

C) Ravens are less stressed by in-group dominance calls than by in-group dominance reversal calls.

D) Ravens are less stressed by dominance reversal calls from other groups than by dominance calls from other groups.

52

According to the passage and the graph, which statement is true about ravens' responses to calls that violated their expectancy of normal rank relations?

A) Ravens are more likely to express surprise in these situations than when listening to calls conforming to their expectations of rank relations.

B) Female ravens are more likely than male ravens to experience a stress response when listening to these calls.

C) Ravens show a greater stress response in these situations than when listening to calls conforming to their expectations of rank relations.

D) The majority of ravens exhibit a stress response to these calls, while only a few ravens do not.

STOP

If you complete this section before the end of your allotted time, you may check your work on this section only. Do NOT use the time to work on another section.

Writing and Language Test

35 MINUTES, 44 QUESTIONS

Turn to Section 2 of your answer sheet to answer the questions in this section.

DIRECTIONS

Every passage comes with a set of questions. Some questions will ask you to consider how the writer might revise the passage to improve the expression of ideas. Other questions will ask you to consider correcting potential errors in sentence structure, usage, or punctuation. There may be one or more graphics that you will need to consult as you revise and edit the passage.

Some questions will refer to a portion of the passage that has been underlined. Other questions will refer to a particular location in a passage or ask that you consider the passage in full.

After you read the passage, select the answers to questions that most effectively improve the passage's writing quality or that adjust the passage to follow the conventions of standard written English. Many questions give you the option to select "NO CHANGE." Select that option in cases where you think the relevant part of the passage should remain as it currently is.

Questions 1-11 are based on the following passage.

Veterinarians

Many young animal lovers dream of becoming **1** a veterinarian. Veterinary medicine involves diagnosing and treating animal injuries and illnesses, and challenges its practitioners to use their creativity and intelligence to care for animals.

Veterinarians are medical professionals, but their work differs in many ways from that of doctors who treat human patients. Perhaps most obviously, veterinarians' animal patients, unlike **2** human's patients, are unable

1

A) NO CHANGE
B) veterinarian
C) veterinarians
D) the veterinarian

2

A) NO CHANGE
B) humans' patients
C) those of humans
D) human patients

CONTINUE →

to describe their symptoms. **3** As a result, veterinarians must learn how to identify illnesses based solely on objective medical signs. They rely on careful observations of their **4** patients' body's and behavior's in order to determine what is wrong. Moreover, since animals cannot understand why they are being subjected to uncomfortable or frightening procedures, veterinarians must find ways to care for patients that actively resist treatment.

Veterinarians work in many different settings. Most people are familiar with small-animal veterinarians, who tend to focus on treating common pets, such as cats, dogs, rabbits, and hamsters. Some small-animal veterinarians treat many different species of **5** animals. Whereas others work in practices that are, for example, canine-only or feline-only. Veterinarians who focus on treating pets, or "companion animals," are the most common, **6** making up half of all veterinarians. However, a number of vets work as large-animal veterinarians. These specialists might work on farms to keep livestock healthy, at racetracks to inspect and certify the health of racehorses, or even in zoos to **7** reassure that large zoo animals stay healthy in their artificial environments.

Private Practice Veterinarians by Focus

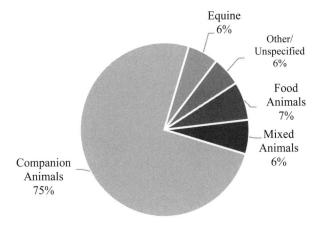

3

A) NO CHANGE

B) Conversely,

C) Regardless,

D) It would seem that

4

A) NO CHANGE

B) patient's bodies and behaviors

C) patients bodies' and behaviors'

D) patients' bodies and behaviors

5

A) NO CHANGE

B) animals, whereas others

C) animals: whereas others

D) animals. Whereas, others

6

Based on the graph, which of the following changes would complete the sentence with the most accurate information?

A) NO CHANGE

B) making up 6% of all veterinarians.

C) making up 75% of the animals that veterinarians treat.

D) making up 75% of private practice veterinarians.

7

A) NO CHANGE

B) ensure

C) assuage

D) cover

CONTINUE

8 The day-to-day challenges of being a veterinarian are formidable, but the rewards are great. Those hoping to join the field generally begin their higher education by pursuing a bachelor's degree with a strong emphasis on **9** biology, chemistry, anatomy, or other sciences. Students hoping to enter this profession in the United States also need a four-year doctoral degree in veterinary medicine. The process of applying to veterinary college is very competitive, so **10** it is of indubitably paramount significance to work hard in school to build a strong application. In veterinary college, students gain both classroom education and practical experience working with qualified veterinarians.

After graduation, veterinarians must meet some additional licensing requirements. Generally, that means successfully completing a licensing examination and satisfying continuing education requirements to maintain their licenses.

For those compassionate, hard-working individuals tenacious enough to complete the **11** ominous process of becoming a licensed veterinarian, the career offers the rewarding opportunity to promote the health and well-being of both animals and their owners.

8

Which choice most effectively sets up the examples in the following sentences?

A) NO CHANGE

B) Most students with the skills to become veterinarians could also enter other medical professions.

C) Aspiring veterinarians must complete a rigorous course of education and meet other qualifications before beginning their careers.

D) Generally speaking, veterinarians must choose to specialize in one of these subfields early in their education.

9

A) NO CHANGE

B) biology chemistry anatomy

C) biology; chemistry; anatomy

D) biology: chemistry, anatomy

10

A) NO CHANGE

B) I think it's important to

C) it seems like they probably ought to

D) aspiring veterinarians should

11

A) NO CHANGE

B) daunting

C) forbidding

D) disconcerting

CONTINUE

Questions 12-22 are based on the following passage.

Impressionism: A General Picture

The mid-1800s were a time of upheaval in France. The country's new emperor, Napoleon III, took power in 1852, launched a massive reconstruction of Paris, and went to war with other European nations. **12** This time of great political and social change also gave rise to an artistic revolution. The Impressionist Movement arose to challenge the conventions of art.

Before the arrival of the Impressionists, the conventions of visual art in France were determined by the Académie des Beaux-Arts. The Académie was an institution that set strict rules for subject matter and techniques in painting. For most of the 19th century, **13** it held that paintings should generally appear realistic, with muted colors and carefully blended brush strokes. **14** By contrast, the Académie insisted that paintings generally be about Greek or Roman myths, Biblical tales, or historical allegories. These rules stifled artistic innovation.

12

Which choice most effectively combines the underlined sentences?

A) This time gave rise to political and social change, and the Impressionist Movement was an artistic revolution.

B) This time of great political and social change, such as the Impressionist Movement, also gave rise to an artistic revolution that arose to challenge the conventions of art.

C) This time of great political and social change gave rise to the Impressionist Movement, an artistic revolution that challenged the conventions of art.

D) The Impressionist Movement, as this time of great political and social change and the rise of an artistic revolution, arose to challenge the conventions of art.

13

A) NO CHANGE

B) he

C) one

D) those

14

A) NO CHANGE

B) Moreover,

C) Suddenly,

D) Even so,

[1] In the 1860s and 1870s, the Impressionists systematically **15** broke, these stifling rules. [2] Camille Pissarro, another well-known Impressionist, produced paintings showing peasants working in fields and city-dwellers walking through streets. [3] The Impressionists painted subjects well outside the established bounds of history and mythology. [4] Many Impressionist paintings sought to **16** apprehend the beauty of fleeting moments of everyday life. [5] For instance, Claude Monet, a foundational figure in the Impressionist Movement, painted an atmospheric landscape depicting a sunrise over the harbor of Le Havre, which he named *Impression, Sunrise*. [6] Such mundane subjects would have been unthinkable even a few decades prior. **17**

15

A) NO CHANGE

B) broke these, stifling rules.

C) broke these: stifling rules.

D) broke these stifling rules.

16

A) NO CHANGE

B) imprison

C) envelop

D) capture

17

To make this paragraph most logical, sentence 2 should be placed

A) where it is now.

B) after sentence 4.

C) after sentence 5.

D) after sentence 6.

CONTINUE ⟶

The Impressionists developed new techniques of painting to accomplish their goals. They often applied wet paint onto other wet paint in thick layers with short strokes. This method created **18** a typical style with vivid colors and blurred forms. **19** While Impressionist paintings thus did not look realistic on close inspection, but they could often evoke the emotional resonance of a scene to great effect. For example, Monet's *Haystacks* series depicts a set of haystacks at different times of day and through changing **20** seasons, his repetition of the same subject matter highlights how effectively his technique could capture changing light and color.

21 The Impressionist revolution would influence art for years afterward. Many works by Post-Impressionist painters, such as Vincent van Gogh and Georges Seurat, incorporated Impressionist techniques. Such famous canvasses as van Gogh's *Starry Night* and Seurat's *Sunday Afternoon on the Island of La Grande Jatte* built on **22** their unique methods of painting to capture scenes in imaginative ways and captivate viewers.

18

A) NO CHANGE
B) an abnormal
C) a distinctive
D) an atypical

19

A) NO CHANGE
B) Impressionist
C) Although Impressionist
D) Because Impressionist

20

A) NO CHANGE
B) seasons, his,
C) seasons; his
D) seasons his

21

Which choice would most effectively sets up the information that follows?

A) NO CHANGE
B) Contemporary rivals of the Impressionists rejected some aspects of their style.
C) Few critics appreciated the Impressionists.
D) There are still Impressionist painters today.

22

A) NO CHANGE
B) his
C) the Impressionists'
D) the Post-Impressionists'

CONTINUE

Questions 23-33 are based on the following passage.

Seeing with Sound

All animals have senses that are finely tuned to deal with the challenges of their environments. Some organisms have [23] bold eyesight and use visible light to navigate and hunt. Others have sensitive noses, which enable them to sniff out food and avoid predators by scent. A few species even have the ability to navigate the world through sound, emitting clicks and listening to their echoes to locate objects. This adaptation, called echolocation, allows animals to operate in low-light environments or even total darkness.

The best known echolocators are probably [24] the *microbats.* Named for their small eyes and bodies, [25] clicks are emitted by these bats at frequencies far higher than the human ear can hear. The resulting echoes allow microbats to sense obstacles and prey, even in total darkness. Echolocation thus [26] facilitates microbats to hunt in the dead of night, when darkness keeps them safe from predators.

Interestingly, the animals they hunt, which are mainly flying insects like moths, [27] has evolved some strategies to counter the bats' echolocation. Some moths fall silent and stop beating their wings when they hear bats draw near; one species can even emit its own clicks to jam its predators' echolocation. Nevertheless, echolocation remains a highly useful ability.

23

A) NO CHANGE
B) zealous
C) serene
D) keen

24

A) NO CHANGE
B) those *microbats* that echolocate.
C) the echolocators known as *microbats*.
D) the *microbats*, a species capable of echolocation.

25

A) NO CHANGE
B) clicking by these bats occurs
C) these bats emit clicks
D) the bats' emissions of clicks are

26

A) NO CHANGE
B) endows
C) authorizes
D) enables

27

A) NO CHANGE
B) have
C) had
D) must have

CONTINUE

[1] The **28** cetaceans, members of a group of mammals, that includes dolphins and whales also use echolocation. [2] However, with echolocation they can sense objects for hundreds of meters around them in total darkness. [3] These animals dive down to depths at which there is little or no detectable light, which makes it impossible to rely on vision. [4] In addition to the high-frequency sounds used for echolocation, whales and dolphins can emit lower-frequency sounds, which travel farther, for long-distance communication. [5] Their clicks and whistles thus allow them not just to navigate and hunt, but also to identify each other and **29** coordinate there activities. **30**

28

A) NO CHANGE

B) cetaceans, members of a groups of mammals that includes dolphins and whales

C) cetaceans, members of a group of mammals that includes, dolphins and whales,

D) cetaceans, members of a group of mammals that includes dolphins and whales,

29

A) NO CHANGE

B) coordinates there

C) coordinate their

D) coordinates their

30

To make this paragraph most logical, sentence 3 should be placed

A) where it is now.

B) after sentence 1.

C) after sentence 4.

D) after sentence 5.

CONTINUE

Humans also use various forms of echolocation. 31 Without a doubt, sonar is essentially mechanical echolocation that enables boats and submarines to navigate more effectively. Medical ultrasound uses bounced sound waves to take detailed images of internal organs and structures, providing previously unavailable diagnostic information. 32

More surprisingly, some visually impaired people learn to use a kind of echolocation by clicking their tongues or tapping a cane and listening for echoes. While their abilities are not as sharp as those of animals that naturally echolocate, these people are able to 33 navigate their environment avoid hazards and even: play sports.

31

A) NO CHANGE

B) Notwithstanding this,

C) Curiously,

D) For example,

32

Which choice, inserted here, most effectively supports a claim made in the previous sentence?

A) Additionally, MRI technology also lets doctors see inside their patients' bodies.

B) For instance, ultrasound imaging, unlike X-ray photography, does not require exposing the patient to radiation.

C) For example, ultrasound imaging can reveal information about the health and sex of an unborn baby.

D) Unfortunately, ultrasound is mostly blocked by bone.

33

A) NO CHANGE

B) navigate, their environment, avoid hazards, and even, play sports.

C) navigate their environment avoid hazards and even play sports.

D) navigate their environment, avoid hazards, and even play sports.

CONTINUE

Questions 34-44 are based on the following passage.

Priming and Psychology's Replication Crisis

[1] The existence of a phenomenon called priming is one of the best-known discoveries in psychology. [2] Priming occurs when some stimulus causes unconscious changes in mindset and behavior, often in surprising ways. [3] One priming experiment revealed that research subjects who washed their hands were less judgmental **34** from moral wrongdoing afterward. [4] Another found that students who thought about a professor before taking a test performed better than students who thought about a soccer hooligan instead. **35** In another priming experiment, researchers asked subjects to watch a disgusting scene from a movie. [5] Citing these experiments, psychologists have claimed that subtle cues exert a deep influence on our behavior. **36**

34

A) NO CHANGE
B) behind
C) by
D) of

35

Which choice best provides an additional example of a priming effect?

A) NO CHANGE
B) One of the most famous priming studies found that reading words related to old age made subjects walk more slowly.
C) It's not clear what processes in the brain could cause this priming effect.
D) Many people are unnerved by the idea that priming could be used to subtly manipulate our behavior.

36

To make this paragraph most logical, sentence 2 should be placed

A) where it is now.
B) before sentence 1.
C) after sentence 4.
D) after sentence 5.

CONTINUE

Unfortunately, many priming studies have been called into question. The controversy over priming is part of a larger crisis in psychology over replication. Experimental results are not **37** considered or believed to be reliable until they are replicated by other researchers. Many results in social psychology have failed to meet this requirement. In a recent effort by social psychologists to replicate many prominent experiments, only one of seven famous priming studies **38** was successfully replicated. These disappointing findings have led some to question whether priming even exists. This "replication crisis" has seriously **39** impaired the credibility of the field, and psychologists must work quickly to understand and address the problem.

40 For example, academic psychology is a fast-paced field in which researchers must "publish or perish." This pressure can lead psychologists to tweak their statistical methods so that their experiments seem to succeed. While not fraudulent, these methods can produce misleading results. In addition, **41** researcher's samples are sometimes small and biased. Studies conducted on a handful of undergraduates are not likely to produce results that represent the broader population. The media also contribute to the problem by seizing on and reporting surprising results before they are well-supported. Together, these factors can lead psychologists to produce questionable experimental results which are reported to the public as facts.

37

A) NO CHANGE
B) considered to be regarded as reliable
C) considered reliable
D) considered

38

A) NO CHANGE
B) will be
C) were
D) had been

39

A) NO CHANGE
B) traded off
C) incapacitated
D) undermined

40

Which choice most effectively introduces the examples that follow?

A) Nevertheless, some psychologists fiercely defend the validity of the priming effect.
B) Many psychologists are also authors.
C) The replication crisis has many causes.
D) Priming is difficult to observe outside of the laboratory.

41

A) NO CHANGE
B) researchers'
C) researchers
D) researchers's

CONTINUE ➔

[42] So just what exactly are psychologists supposed to do about it? Perhaps most importantly, the nature of academic publishing must change. As long as "successful" experiments are more likely to be published than negative results or failed replications, the pressure to produce experimental success and the illusion of consensus that [43] exist around questionable studies will continue. Additionally, more funding should be made available for researchers who wish to perform replications—too few studies are ever examined and challenged in this way. Finally, the media must be more cautious in publicizing results. Responsible science [44] journalism, that avoids sensationalism will help prevent the spread of misinformation.

42

A) NO CHANGE
B) Whence a solution to this daunting dilemma?
C) How can the crisis in psychology be solved?
D) Does anyone have ideas for how to fix this?

43

A) NO CHANGE
B) have existed
C) exists
D) are existent

44

A) NO CHANGE
B) journalism: that avoids
C) journalism that avoids,
D) journalism that avoids

STOP

If you complete this section before the end of your allotted time, you may check your work on this section only. Do NOT use the time to work on another section.

Math Test – No Calculator

25 MINUTES, 20 QUESTIONS

Turn to Section 3 of your answer sheet to answer the questions in this section.

DIRECTIONS

Questions **1-15** ask you to solve a problem, select the best answer among four choices, and fill in the corresponding circle on your answer sheet. Questions **16-20** ask you to solve a problem and enter your answer in the grid provided on your answer sheet. There are detailed instructions on entering answers into the grid before question 16. You may use your test booklet for scratch work.

NOTES

1. You **may not** use a calculator.
2. Variables and expressions represent real numbers unless stated otherwise.
3. Figures are drawn to scale unless stated otherwise.
4. Figures lie in a plane unless stated otherwise.
5. The domain of a function f is defined as the set of all real numbers x for which $f(x)$ is also a real number, unless stated otherwise.

REFERENCE

$$A = \frac{1}{2}bh$$

$$a^2 + b^2 = c^2$$

Special Triangles

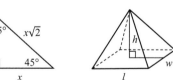

$$V = \frac{1}{3}lwh$$

$$V = \frac{1}{3}\pi r^2 h$$

$$A = lw$$

$$V = lwh$$

$$V = \pi r^2 h$$

$$A = \pi r^2$$
$$C = 2\pi r$$

$$V = \frac{4}{3}\pi r^3$$

There are 360° in a circle.

The sum of the angles in a triangle is 180°.

The number of radians of arc in a circle is 2π.

CONTINUE

Practice Tests | **Ivy Global**

1

If $3x = 15$ and $2y = 10$, which of the following values is equal to $6x + 4y$?

A) 35

B) 50

C) 65

D) 70

2

$$(2i + 3)(i + 4)$$

Which of the following is equal to the expression above? (Note: $i = \sqrt{-1}$.)

A) $12i$

B) $9 + 10i$

C) $10 + 11i$

D) $12 + 13i$

3

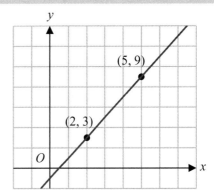

Which of the following equations represents the line in the xy-plane above?

A) $y = \dfrac{1}{4}x + 1$

B) $y = \dfrac{1}{2}x - 1$

C) $y = x + 1$

D) $y = 2x - 1$

4

A t-shirt printer can produce 40 tank tops with logos in 5 hours. At this rate, how many tank tops with logos can the printer produce in 7 hours?

A) 48

B) 56

C) 64

D) 70

CONTINUE

5

Anna paints landscapes and still-lifes. She buys canvases and paint for a cost of $3 per painting, and paints either a landscape or a still-life on each canvas. If she sells l landscapes for $20 each, and s still-lifes for $15 each, which of the following expressions represents Anna's profit, P, in dollars? (Note: Profit is equal to revenue minus cost.)

A) $P = 20l + 15s$

B) $P = 15l + 20s$

C) $P = 17l + 12s$

D) $P = 12l + 17s$

6

$$2x + y = 10$$
$$x + 2y = 35$$

According to the system of equations above, what is the value of y?

A) 20

B) 25

C) 30

D) 35

7

$$v_t = \sqrt{\frac{2mg}{C\rho A}}$$

The formula above gives the terminal velocity v_t for an object with mass m and area A falling due to the acceleration of gravity g through a medium with density ρ and a drag coefficient C. Which of the following gives A in terms of m, g, C, ρ, and v_t ?

A) $A = \sqrt{\dfrac{2mg}{C\rho v_t}}$

B) $A = \dfrac{2mg}{C\rho v_t^2}$

C) $A = \dfrac{C\rho v_t^2}{2mg}$

D) $A = v_t^2 C\rho 2mg$

8

If $y = 3x^2 + 10x - 8$, which of the following is a possible value of x when $y = 0$?

A) −4

B) 0

C) 4

D) 8

CONTINUE

9

An internet service provider charges its customers a fixed monthly fee for the first 100 gigabytes of internet use each month and a per-use charge for every additional gigabyte of use each month. The cost of the internet per month in dollars, C, can be estimated with the equation $C = 100 + 5a$, where a is the number of additional gigabytes used each month. What is the meaning of the coefficient 5 in this equation?

A) The cost per gigabyte of internet use each month.

B) The cost per additional gigabyte of internet use over 100 gigabytes.

C) The fixed monthly fee for the first 100 gigabytes of internet use.

D) The minimum number of gigabytes per month a customer must use.

10

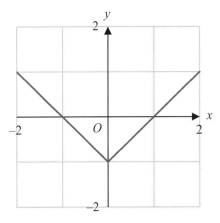

Which equation is represented by the graph above?

A) $y = |x| - 1$

B) $y = |x - 1|$

C) $y = |x + 1|$

D) $|y| = x + 1$

11

x	y
0	6
1	7
2	14
3	33

Which of the following equations best models the relationship in the table above?

A) $y = x^3 + 6$

B) $y = 2^x + 6$

C) $y = 3^x + 5$

D) $y = 4x + 4$

CONTINUE

12

$$\sqrt{5x - 5} = \sqrt{y^2 + 1}$$

Which of the following pairs (x, y) satisfies the equation above?

A) $(-1, -1)$

B) $(1, 2)$

C) $(3, 3)$

D) $(4, 1)$

13

$$ax^2 - 5x - 12 = (ax + 3)(x - 4)$$

In the quadratic equation above, a is a nonzero constant. What is the value of a?

A) 3

B) 2

C) 1

D) −1

14

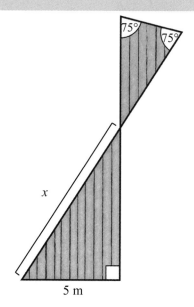

A landscape architect sketches a plan for two triangular gardens, as shown in the diagram above. What is the length x, in meters, to the nearest decimal place?

A) 8.7

B) 9.6

C) 10.0

D) 11.2

15

If $x > -4$, which of the following is equivalent to the expression $\dfrac{x^2 + 3x - 10}{x + 4}$?

A) $x - 1$

B) $(x + 5)(x - 2)$

C) $x - 1 + \dfrac{6}{x + 4}$

D) $x - 1 - \dfrac{6}{x + 4}$

CONTINUE

DIRECTIONS

Questions **16-20** ask you to solve a problem and enter your answer in the grid provided on your answer sheet. When completing grid-in questions:

1. You are required to bubble in the circles for your answers. It is recommended, but not required, that you also write your answer in the boxes above the columns of circles. Points will be awarded based only on whether the circles are filled in correctly.

2. Fill in only one circle in a column.

3. You can start your answer in any column as long as you can fit in the whole answer.

4. For questions 16-20, no answers will be negative numbers.

5. **Mixed numbers**, such as $4\frac{2}{5}$, must be gridded as decimals or improper fractions, such as 4.4 or as 22/5. "42/5" will be read as "forty-two over five," not as "four and two-fifths."

6. If your answer is a **decimal** with more digits than will fit on the grid, you may round it or cut it off, but you must fill the entire grid.

7. If there are **multiple correct solutions** to a problem, all of them will be considered correct. Enter only **one** on the grid.

CONTINUE

16

Jeff and Liz collect rain water to irrigate their garden. If they estimate that they need 2 rain barrels for every 7 square feet of land, and they have a 35 square foot garden, how many rain barrels do they need?

18

If $x = 2y + 6$ and $y = -2x - 3$, what is the value of xy?

17

$$x^2 - y^2 = 20$$
$$x - y = 4$$

If $x = a$ and $y = b$ satisfy the system of equations above, what is $a + b$?

CONTINUE

19

$$F = G\frac{m_1 \times m_2}{d^2}$$

The gravitational force between two stars is inversely proportional to the square of the distance between the two stars, as represented by Newton's universal gravitation equation shown above. G is the universal gravitation constant, d is the distance in light-years, m_1 is the mass of the first star, and m_2 is the mass of the second star. If the force of gravity between two stars that are 4 light-years apart is 64 exanewtons, what would the force of gravity be, in exanewtons, between the same two stars if they were 8 light-years apart?

20

What is the perimeter of the triangle formed by the lines $y = -\frac{4}{3}x + 16$, $x = 0$, and $y = 0$?

STOP

If you complete this section before the end of your allotted time, you may check your work on this section only. Do NOT use the time to work on another section.

Math Test – Calculator

55 MINUTES, 38 QUESTIONS

Turn to Section 4 of your answer sheet to answer the questions in this section.

Questions **1-30** ask you to solve a problem, select the best answer among four choices, and fill in the corresponding circle on your answer sheet. Questions **31-38** ask you to solve a problem and enter your answer in the grid provided on your answer sheet. There are detailed instructions on entering answers into the grid before question 31. You may use your test booklet for scratch work.

NOTES

1. You **may** use a calculator.
2. Variables and expressions represent real numbers unless stated otherwise.
3. Figures are drawn to scale unless stated otherwise.
4. Figures lie in a plane unless stated otherwise.
5. The domain of a function f is defined as the set of all real numbers x for which $f(x)$ is also a real number, unless stated otherwise.

REFERENCE

$$A = \frac{1}{2} bh$$

$$a^2 + b^2 = c^2$$

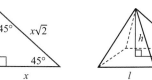

Special Triangles

$$V = \frac{1}{3} lwh$$

$$V = \frac{1}{3} \pi r^2 h$$

$$A = lw$$

$$V = lwh$$

$$V = \pi r^2 h$$

$$A = \pi r^2$$
$$C = 2\pi r$$

$$V = \frac{4}{3} \pi r^3$$

There are 360° in a circle.

The sum of the angles in a triangle is 180°.

The number of radians of arc in a circle is 2π.

CONTINUE

1

A chemist is investigating a new reaction to synthesize barite crystals. She finds that eight grams are synthesized every five minutes. If there are 111 grams of barite after an hour, how many grams of barite did the chemist start with?

A) 0

B) 8

C) 15

D) 71

2

$$3b - 2,000 = p$$

The equation above models a bakery's annual profits in dollars, p, based on the number of loaves of bread, b, that they bake. What is the meaning of the value 2,000 in this equation?

A) The bakery makes at least $2,000 per year.

B) The bakery makes 2,000 loaves of bread per year.

C) Each batch of bread costs $2,000 to bake.

D) If the company makes no bread, they will lose $2,000 per year.

3

A recipe that makes c cupcakes requires e eggs. If Grant wants to make 40 cupcakes, how many eggs will he need, in terms of c and e?

A) $\dfrac{40 \times e}{c}$

B) $\dfrac{40}{e}$

C) $\dfrac{e}{40 \times c}$

D) $\dfrac{1}{40 \times e}$

4

The points $(-2, -5)$ and $(-5, -3)$ both lie on a line. What is the slope of this line?

A) $-\dfrac{3}{2}$

B) $-\dfrac{2}{3}$

C) $\dfrac{2}{3}$

D) $\dfrac{3}{2}$

CONTINUE

5

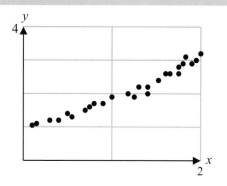

Which of the following equations best describes the line of best fit for the above scatterplot?

A) $y = x + 1$

B) $y = -x + 1$

C) $y = 2x + 1$

D) $y = 2x$

6

A chessboard has 64 squares. If one grain of sand is placed on the first square, two on the second, four on the third, and so on, with the number of grains doubling each time, how many grains of sand will be on the 64th square?

A) 64

B) 64^2

C) 2^{63}

D) 2^{64}

7

In 2014, consumers spent $31 billion on gift cards, 13.9% of which were for coffee shops. If 27% of coffee shop gift cards go unused, what is the approximate value of these unused cards, in billions of dollars?

A) 1.16

B) 4.31

C) 6.55

D) 8.37

8

The Gross Domestic Product (GDP) per capita of Country X grows by $1,000 each year. The GDP per capita of Country Y grows by 0.5% each year. Which of the following statements is true?

A) Both countries' GDP per capita are growing linearly.

B) Both countries' GDP per capita are growing exponentially.

C) The GDP per capita is growing linearly for Country X but exponentially for Country Y.

D) The GDP per capita is growing exponentially for Country X but linearly for Country Y.

CONTINUE

9

Number of Websites on the Internet

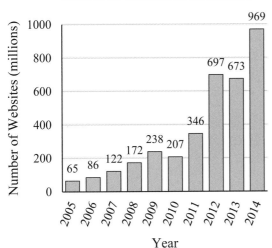

Year

The chart above displays the number of websites on the Internet from 2005 to 2014. Which of the following periods had the greatest percentage growth in number of websites?

A) 2005-2007

B) 2006-2008

C) 2007-2009

D) 2008-2010

10

Budgets of Highest Selling Films

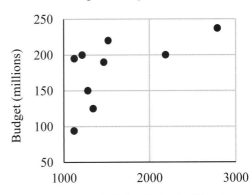

Total Ticket Sales (millions)

The total sales of films are compared to their total budgets in the graph above. What was the budget, in millions of dollars, of the film with the median total ticket sales?

A) 125

B) 190

C) 195

D) 200

11

$$f(z) = \frac{2}{z} + z \times 3$$

According to the equation above, what is the value of $f\left(\frac{2}{3}\right)$?

A) $\frac{2}{3}$

B) 1

C) 5

D) 6

CONTINUE

Questions 12 and 13 refer to the following information.

Wax Candle Specifications		
Candle Type	Height (mm)	Diameter (mm)
Tea lights	$|h - 20| \leq 4$	$|d - 30| \leq 5$
Container candles	$|h - 80| \leq 10$	$|d - 75| \leq 15$
Pillar candles	$|h - 200| \leq 18$	$|d - 75| \leq 10$

A candle-making factory produces three different types of wax candles as shown in the table above. Each candle has a standard height and a standard diameter, shown in millimeters, and a certain range of possible heights and diameters. Candles whose heights and diameters are outside these ranges cannot be sold.

12

If r_h is the range of possible heights for a candle and r_d is the range of possible diameters, for which candle is $r_h + r_d$ the greatest?

A) Tea lights

B) Container candles

C) Pillar candles

D) $r_h + r_d$ is equal for all three candles

13

What is the difference in diameter between the widest candle that can be sold and the narrowest candle that can be sold, in millimeters?

A) 45

B) 65

C) 180

D) 202

14

n	−2	−3	−4	−5
$f(n)$	4	1	−2	−5

The table above shows some values of the linear function f. In the xy-plane, if $f(n)$ is equal to y, what is the y-intercept of f?

A) −8

B) 0

C) 7

D) 10

15

If $f(x) = 3x + 7$, what is the value of $f(-1) + f(3)$?

A) 12

B) 16

C) 20

D) 24

CONTINUE

16

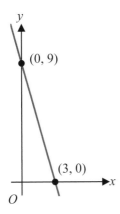

A linear function is graphed above. If this function includes the point $(a, 3)$, what is the value of a?

A) 1

B) 2

C) 3

D) 4

Questions 17 and 18 refer to the following information.

Residents of Town A and Town B who cycle, jog, do yoga, or play organized sports are represented in the table below.

Number of Active Residents in Two Towns (in hundreds)			
	Town A	Town B	Total
Cycle	6	8	14
Jog	8	9	17
Yoga	1	5	6
Sports	5	8	13
Total	20	30	50

17

According to the table above, if one of the residents who cycles is chosen at random to be surveyed for a study about exercise, what is the probability that this person is a resident of Town A?

A) $\dfrac{6}{20}$

B) $\dfrac{8}{30}$

C) $\dfrac{6}{14}$

D) $\dfrac{8}{14}$

CONTINUE

18

Four-fifths of the residents of Town A and three-quarters of the residents of Town B do not cycle, jog, do yoga, or play organized sports. To the nearest whole number, what is the total combined population of Town A and Town B?

A)   6,500

B)   14,000

C)   14,500

D)   22,000

19

$$b \leq 2a - 1$$
$$8 > a - b$$

According to the system of inequalities above, which of the following could be a value for a?

A)   −12

B)   −8

C)   −7

D)   −6

20

If x, y, a, and b are all positive integers, which of the following expressions is equivalent to $(x^a)^b \times (xy)^{ab}$?

   I. $x^{2a + 2b}y^{ab}$

  II. $(x^2y)^{ab}$

 III. $(x^2y)^{a + b}$

A)   I only

B)   II only

C)   II and III only

D)   I, II, and III

21

Which of the following graphs could represent the equation $y = 2x^3$?

A)

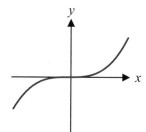

B)

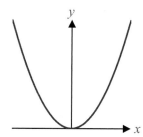

C)

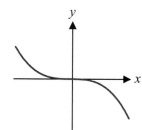

D)

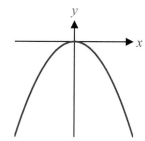

CONTINUE

Questions 22 and 23 refer to the following information.

Monthly Rent for the Year 2009	Number of Apartments Completed and Rented in 3 Months (1000s)				
	U.S.	Northeast	Midwest	South	West
Less than $950	57,400	2,700	10,200	35,700	8,800
$950 to $1,049	22,400	400	2,900	15,100	4,000
$1,050 to $1,149	13,300	1,100	1,000	7,300	3,900
$1,150 to $1,249	16,700	800	700	10,200	5,000
$1,250 to $1,349	53,200	5,000	2,500	25,000	20,700
Median Monthly Rent (dollars)	1,063	1,250	857	1,022	1,240
Total Apartments Rented (1000s)	163,000	10,000	17,200	93,300	42,400

The table above shows the number of new apartments that were completed and rented in a 3-month period in 2009 based on regional geographic location.

22

A tenant paid $1,200 per month for an apartment in the South in 2009. If this tenant moved from the South to the Midwest and paid the median monthly rate for that region as given in the table above, how much did the tenant save in annual rental costs?

A) $343

B) $1,686

C) $3,255

D) $4,116

23

Which of the following statements is true for the year 2009?

A)   The median rent for completed apartments in the U.S. is less than the median rent for these apartments in the Midwest.

B)   At least 50 percent of the newly completed apartments rented in the South cost less than the U.S. median for newly completed apartments.

C)   Apartments that cost between $1,050 and $1,149 per month make up a greater percentage of newly constructed apartments in the West than they do in the Northeast.

D)   The South was the most expensive region in which to rent apartments in the U.S., and the Midwest was the least expensive region in which to rent apartments.

CONTINUE

24

$$-5a - 4 + b = 0$$
$$a + 3 + 2b = 0$$

Which of the following linear functions intersects the point (a, b), where a and b satisfy the system of equations above?

A) $f(x) = 5x - 4$

B) $f(x) = 2x + 1$

C) $f(x) = -2x + 3$

D) $f(x) = \dfrac{1}{5}(x - 6)$

25

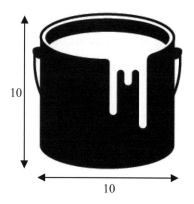

Jenish has a cylindrical paint can with a height of 10 inches and a diameter of 10 inches. If one cubic inch of paint can cover one square meter of wall, approximately how many square meters of wall space can Jenish cover with a full can of paint?

A) 250

B) 700

C) 785

D) 800

26

A bowl contains apples and oranges. After 6 oranges are eaten, there are 3 times as many apples as oranges. A short time later, 11 apples are eaten, after which there are 4 times as many oranges as apples. How many oranges were originally in the bowl?

A) 4

B) 10

C) 11

D) 12

27

A jacket is on sale for 20% off. Jamie gets a membership discount of an additional 10% off the sale price and pays 8% tax on the price after the discounts. If Jamie pays $85.73 in total, what was the original price of the jacket, to the nearest cent?

A) $102.53

B) $104.11

C) $110.25

D) $113.40

CONTINUE

28

$$\frac{3y}{x-2} = 2x + 5$$
$$y = \frac{2x^2 + x - 10}{3}$$

How many ordered pairs satisfy the system of equations shown above?

A) 0

B) 1

C) 2

D) Infinitely many

29

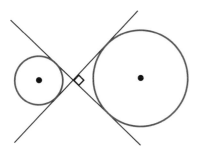

The tangents of two circles intersect at a 90° angle, as shown above. If the radius of the small circle is 1 centimeter and the radius of the large circle is 3 centimeters, what is the minimum distance, in centimeters, between the two circles?

A) $4\sqrt{2}$

B) $3(\sqrt{2}-1)$

C) $4(\sqrt{2}-1)$

D) $6(\sqrt{2}-1)$

30

Researchers A and B conduct two different surveys to determine the average score on a standardized test that is graded on a scale from 1 to 36. Researcher A randomly surveys 200 students who took the test and finds that the average score of this sample is 22 with a margin of error of 3. Researcher B randomly surveys 100 students who took the test and finds that the average score of this sample is 24 with a margin of error of 5. Based on the results of both surveys, which of the following is an appropriate conclusion?

A) Researcher A can predict with certainty that the population of all the students who took the test will have an average score of 22.

B) Researcher B can predict with certainty that the population of all the students who took the test will have an average score between 19 and 29.

C) The results that Researcher B obtained are more likely to accurately reflect the population of all the students who took the test than the results that Researcher A obtained because Researcher B randomly surveyed fewer students than Researcher A.

D) The results that Researcher A obtained are more likely to accurately reflect the population of all the students who took the test than the results that Researcher B obtained because Researcher A randomly surveyed more students than Researcher B.

CONTINUE

DIRECTIONS

Questions **31-38** ask you to solve a problem and enter your answer in the grid provided on your answer sheet. When completing grid-in questions:

1. You are required to bubble in the circles for your answers. It is recommended, but not required, that you also write your answer in the boxes above the columns of circles. Points will be awarded based only on whether the circles are filled in correctly.

2. Fill in only one circle in a column.

3. You can start your answer in any column as long as you can fit in the whole answer.

4. For questions 31-38, no answers will be negative numbers.

5. **Mixed numbers**, such as $4\frac{2}{5}$, must be gridded as decimals or improper fractions, such as 4.4 or as 22/5. "42/5" will be read as "forty-two over five," not as "four and two-fifths."

6. If your answer is a **decimal** with more digits than will fit on the grid, you may round it or cut it off, but you must fill the entire grid.

7. If there are **multiple correct solutions** to a problem, all of them will be considered correct. Enter only **one** on the grid.

CONTINUE

31

$$h : j = 6 : 7$$

The ratio of h to j is shown above. If the value of j is 21, what is the value of h?

32

Nanna has two sisters, Laurel and Jennifer. Jennifer is twice as old as Laurel, who is 4 years younger than Nanna. If Nanna is two years younger than Jennifer, what is Nanna's age, in years?

33

Rahil notices an invasive species of weed in his yard, which has an area of 243 square feet. The weed initially covers an area of 32 square feet, and takes up 50% more area each week. How many complete weeks will it take the weed to cover the entire yard?

34

When a silo is 40% empty it holds 9 more tons of grain than when it is 40% full. How many tons of grain does the silo hold when it is full?

35

A carrier pigeon flies at an average speed of 75 kilometers per hour, while a Cessna 152 propeller plane travels at an average speed of 180 kilometers per hour. A pigeon and a Cessna set off at the same time from Paris to London, a distance of 500 km. How many minutes earlier will the Cessna arrive in London than the pigeon if both fly the same route? (Round your answer to the nearest minute.)

36

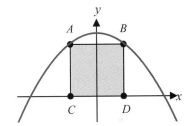

Note: figure not drawn to scale

The side CD of rectangle $ABCD$ lies along the x-axis, and the points A and B satisfy the function $y = -x^2 + 6$, as shown in the xy-plane above. If the coordinates of point D are $(1, 0)$, what is the area of rectangle $ABCD$?

CONTINUE

Questions 37 and 38 refer to the following information.

Quagga and Zebra Mussel Life Cycle and Mortality Rates			
Mussel	Population density (mussels/ square yard)	Out-of-water mortality rate (% death/day)	Water filtered (gallons/day)
Quagga	5.0×10^5	80%	5.0×10^{-2}
Zebra	7.0×10^5	60%	2.5×10^{-2}

Quagga and zebra mussels are invasive species of shellfish that damage the ecosystems and infrastructure of the fresh waterways of the United States and Canada by blocking pipes and grates, damaging boats, and filtering water, which leads to greater sunlight penetration of the water, and therefore greater microbial growth.

37

A sailboat is taken out of Lake Michigan at a Chicago port and loaded on a truck so that it can be transported to the Sacramento River in California. The underwater hull of the sailboat has a surface area of 12 square yards and is entirely covered with zebra mussels. If mussels cannot lay eggs out of water, and the trip from Chicago to California takes 5 days, how many thousands of mussels will survive the trip to live in the Sacramento River, rounded to the nearest thousand?

38

A group of scientists takes a sample consisting of some zebra and some quagga mussels from Lake Erie and puts it in a tank with a base area of 1 square yard, so that the entire base is covered with mussels. If the scientists observe that 22,000 gallons of water are filtered over the course of one day, what percentage of the area of the tank is covered by quagga mussels? (Ignore the percent sign when gridding your answer.)

STOP

If you complete this section before the end of your allotted time, check your work on this section only. Do NOT use the time to work on another section.

Essay (Optional)

50 MINUTES

Turn to the lined pages of your answer sheet to write your essay.

DIRECTIONS

This essay is optional. It is a chance for you to demonstrate how well you can understand and analyze a written passage. Your essay should show that you have carefully read the passage and should be a concisely written analysis that is both logical and clear.

You must write your entire essay on the lines in your answer booklet. No additional paper will be provided aside from the Planning Page inside your answer booklet. You will be able to write your entire essay in the space provided if you make use of every line, keep tight margins, and write at a suitable size. Don't forget to keep your handwriting legible for the readers evaluating your essay.

You will have 50 minutes to read the passage in this booklet and to write an essay in response to the prompt provided at the end of the passage.

REMINDERS

- What you write in this booklet will not be evaluated. Write your essay in the answer booklet only.

- Essays that are off-topic will not be evaluated.

As you read the following passage, consider how Stewart Brand uses

- evidence, like examples or facts, to support his arguments.
- logical reasoning to develop his ideas and to connect his claims to his evidence.
- stylistic or persuasive techniques, such as the choice of particular words or appeals to his readers' emotions, to give power to the ideas put forth.

Adapted from Stewart Brand, "Rethinking Extinction." © 2015 by Aeon Media Ltd. Originally published April 21, 2015.

1   The way the public hears about conservation issues is nearly always in the mode of "[Beloved Animal] Threatened With Extinction." That makes for electrifying headlines, but it misdirects concern. The loss of whole species is not the leading problem in conservation. The leading problem is the decline in wild animal populations, sometimes to a radical degree, often diminishing the health of whole ecosystems.

2   Viewing every conservation issue through the lens of extinction threat is simplistic and usually irrelevant. Worse, it introduces an emotional charge that makes the problem seem cosmic and overwhelming rather than local and solvable.

3   Most extinctions have occurred on oceanic islands or in restricted freshwater locations, with very few occurring on Earth's continents or in the oceans. The world's greatest conservation problem is not species extinction, but rather the precarious state of thousands of populations that are the remnants of once widespread and productive species.

4   Many new species readily emerge on ocean islands because of the isolation, but there are few other species to co-evolve with and thus they have no defense against invasive competitors and predators. The threat can be total. An endemic species under attack has nowhere to escape to. The island conservationist Josh Donlan estimates that islands, which are just 3 percent of the Earth's surface, have been the site of 95 percent of all bird extinctions since 1600, 90 percent of reptile extinctions, and 60 percent of mammal extinctions. Those are horrifying numbers, but the losses are extremely local. They have no effect on the biodiversity and ecological health of the continents and oceans that make up 97 percent of the Earth.

5   Since the majority of invasive species are relatively benign, they add to an island's overall biodiversity. The ecologist Dov Sax at Brown University in Rhode Island points out that non-native plants have doubled the botanical biodiversity of New Zealand—there are 2,104 native plants in the wild, and 2,065 non-native plants. Ascension Island in the South Atlantic, once a barren rock deplored by Charles Darwin for its "naked hideousness," now has a fully functioning cloud forest made entirely of plants and animals brought by humans in the past 200 years.

6   But the main news from ocean islands is that new methods have been found to protect the vulnerable endemic species from their worst threat, the invasive predators, thus dramatically lowering the extinction rate for the future. New Zealanders are the heroes of this story, beautifully told in *Rat Island: Predators in Paradise and the World's Greatest Wildlife Rescue* (2011) by William Stolzenburg. … In the 1980s, New Zealand conservationists were driven to desperation by the vulnerability of beloved unique creatures such as a ground-dwelling parrot called the kakapo. They decided to do whatever it took to eliminate every single rat on the kakapo's island refuge. It took many seasons of relentless poisoning and trapping, but when it was done, it was really done.

7   Conservation efforts often appear in the media like a series of defeats and retreats, but as soon as you look up from the crisis-of-the-month, you realize that, in aggregate, conservation is winning. The ecologist Stuart Pimm at Duke University in North Carolina claims that conservationists have already reduced the rate of extinction by 75 percent. Getting the world's extinction rate back down to normal is a reasonable goal for this century.

8   But a perception problem stands in the way.

9   Consider the language of these news headlines: "Fuelling Extinction: Obama Budget Is Killer For Endangered Species" (*Huffington Post*, February 2015). "'Racing Extinction' Sounds Alarm On Ocean's Endangered Creatures" (NBC News, January 2015). "'Extinction Crisis': 21,000 Of World's Species At Risk Of Disappearing" (Common Dreams, July 2013). "Australian Mammals On Brink Of 'Extinction Calamity'" (BBC, February 2015). … The headlines are not just inaccurate. As they accumulate, they frame our whole relationship with nature as one of unremitting tragedy. The core of tragedy is that it cannot be fixed, and that is a formula for hopelessness and inaction. Lazy romanticism about impending doom becomes the default view.

10   No end of specific wildlife problems remain to be solved, but describing them too often as extinction crises has led to a general panic that nature is extremely fragile or already hopelessly broken. That is not remotely the case. Nature as a whole is exactly as robust as it ever was—maybe more so, with humans around to head off ice ages and killer asteroids. Working with that robustness is how conservation's goals get reached.

Write an essay in which you explain how Stewart Brand builds an argument to persuade his audience that focusing on extinction harms the goals of the conservation movement. In your essay, analyze how Brand uses one or more of the features listed in the directions above, (or features of your own choice) to strengthen the logic and persuasiveness of his argument. Be sure that your analysis focuses on the most relevant features of the passage.

Your essay should not explain whether you agree with Brand's claims, but rather explain how Brand builds an argument to persuade his audience.

Practice Test 4

SAT

Directions

- Work on just one section at a time.

- If you complete a section before the end of your allotted time, use the extra minutes to check your work on that section only. Do NOT use the time to work on another section.

Using Your Test Booklet

- No credit will be given for anything written in the test booklet. You may use the test booklet for scratch paper.

- You are not allowed to continue answering questions in a section after the allotted time has run out. This includes marking answers on your answer sheet that you previously noted in your test booklet.

- You are not allowed to fold pages, take pages out of the test booklet, or take any pages home.

Answering Questions

- Each answer must be marked in the corresponding row on the answer sheet.

- Each bubble must be filled in completely and darkly within the lines.

Correct ●   Incorrect

- Be careful to bubble in the correct part of the answer sheet.

- Extra marks on your answer sheet may be marked as incorrect answers and lower your score.

- Make sure you use a No. 2 pencil.

Scoring

- You will receive one point for each correct answer.

- Incorrect answers will NOT result in points deducted. Even if you are unsure about an answer, you should make a guess.

DO NOT BEGIN THIS TEST

UNTIL YOUR PROCTOR TELLS YOU TO DO SO

For printable answer sheets, please visit **ivyglobal.com/study**.

Section 1

	A B C D		A B C D		A B C D		A B C D		A B C D
1	○ ○ ○ ○	12	○ ○ ○ ○	23	○ ○ ○ ○	34	○ ○ ○ ○	45	○ ○ ○ ○
2	○ ○ ○ ○	13	○ ○ ○ ○	24	○ ○ ○ ○	35	○ ○ ○ ○	46	○ ○ ○ ○
3	○ ○ ○ ○	14	○ ○ ○ ○	25	○ ○ ○ ○	36	○ ○ ○ ○	47	○ ○ ○ ○
4	○ ○ ○ ○	15	○ ○ ○ ○	26	○ ○ ○ ○	37	○ ○ ○ ○	48	○ ○ ○ ○
5	○ ○ ○ ○	16	○ ○ ○ ○	27	○ ○ ○ ○	38	○ ○ ○ ○	49	○ ○ ○ ○
6	○ ○ ○ ○	17	○ ○ ○ ○	28	○ ○ ○ ○	39	○ ○ ○ ○	50	○ ○ ○ ○
7	○ ○ ○ ○	18	○ ○ ○ ○	29	○ ○ ○ ○	40	○ ○ ○ ○	51	○ ○ ○ ○
8	○ ○ ○ ○	19	○ ○ ○ ○	30	○ ○ ○ ○	41	○ ○ ○ ○	52	○ ○ ○ ○
9	○ ○ ○ ○	20	○ ○ ○ ○	31	○ ○ ○ ○	42	○ ○ ○ ○		
10	○ ○ ○ ○	21	○ ○ ○ ○	32	○ ○ ○ ○	43	○ ○ ○ ○		
11	○ ○ ○ ○	22	○ ○ ○ ○	33	○ ○ ○ ○	44	○ ○ ○ ○		

Section 2

	A B C D		A B C D		A B C D		A B C D		A B C D
1	○ ○ ○ ○	10	○ ○ ○ ○	19	○ ○ ○ ○	28	○ ○ ○ ○	37	○ ○ ○ ○
2	○ ○ ○ ○	11	○ ○ ○ ○	20	○ ○ ○ ○	29	○ ○ ○ ○	38	○ ○ ○ ○
3	○ ○ ○ ○	12	○ ○ ○ ○	21	○ ○ ○ ○	30	○ ○ ○ ○	39	○ ○ ○ ○
4	○ ○ ○ ○	13	○ ○ ○ ○	22	○ ○ ○ ○	31	○ ○ ○ ○	40	○ ○ ○ ○
5	○ ○ ○ ○	14	○ ○ ○ ○	23	○ ○ ○ ○	32	○ ○ ○ ○	41	○ ○ ○ ○
6	○ ○ ○ ○	15	○ ○ ○ ○	24	○ ○ ○ ○	33	○ ○ ○ ○	42	○ ○ ○ ○
7	○ ○ ○ ○	16	○ ○ ○ ○	25	○ ○ ○ ○	34	○ ○ ○ ○	43	○ ○ ○ ○
8	○ ○ ○ ○	17	○ ○ ○ ○	26	○ ○ ○ ○	35	○ ○ ○ ○	44	○ ○ ○ ○
9	○ ○ ○ ○	18	○ ○ ○ ○	27	○ ○ ○ ○	36	○ ○ ○ ○		

Section 3 (No-Calculator)

	A	B	C	D		A	B	C	D		A	B	C	D		A	B	C	D		A	B	C	D
1	○	○	○	○	4	○	○	○	○	7	○	○	○	○	10	○	○	○	○	13	○	○	○	○
2	○	○	○	○	5	○	○	○	○	8	○	○	○	○	11	○	○	○	○	14	○	○	○	○
3	○	○	○	○	6	○	○	○	○	9	○	○	○	○	12	○	○	○	○	15	○	○	○	○

Only answers that are gridded will be scored. You will not receive credit for anything written in the boxes.

16 □□□□
17 □□□□
18 □□□□
19 □□□□
20 □□□□

Section 4 (Calculator)

	A	B	C	D		A	B	C	D		A	B	C	D		A	B	C	D		A	B	C	D
1	○	○	○	○	7	○	○	○	○	13	○	○	○	○	19	○	○	○	○	25	○	○	○	○
2	○	○	○	○	8	○	○	○	○	14	○	○	○	○	20	○	○	○	○	26	○	○	○	○
3	○	○	○	○	9	○	○	○	○	15	○	○	○	○	21	○	○	○	○	27	○	○	○	○
4	○	○	○	○	10	○	○	○	○	16	○	○	○	○	22	○	○	○	○	28	○	○	○	○
5	○	○	○	○	11	○	○	○	○	17	○	○	○	○	23	○	○	○	○	29	○	○	○	○
6	○	○	○	○	12	○	○	○	○	18	○	○	○	○	24	○	○	○	○	30	○	○	○	○

Only answers that are gridded will be scored. You will not receive credit for anything written in the boxes.

31   32   33   34   35

Only answers that are gridded will be scored. You will not receive credit for anything written in the boxes.

36   37   38

Important: Use a No. 2 pencil. Write inside the borders.

You may use the space below to plan your essay, but be sure to write your essay on the lined pages. Work on this page will not be scored.

Use this space to plan your essay.

START YOUR ESSAY HERE.

_____

_____

_____

_____

_____

_____

_____

_____

_____

_____

_____

_____

_____

_____

_____

_____

_____

_____

_____

_____

_____

_____

_____

Continue on the next page.

_____

_____

_____

_____

_____

_____

_____

_____

_____

_____

_____

_____

_____

_____

_____

_____

_____

_____

_____

_____

_____

_____

_____

_____

_____

_____

_____

Continue on the next page.

_____

_____

_____

_____

_____

_____

_____

_____

_____

_____

_____

_____

_____

_____

_____

_____

_____

_____

_____

_____

_____

_____

_____

_____

Continue on the next page.

STOP.

Reading Test

65 MINUTES, 52 QUESTIONS

Turn to Section 1 of your answer sheet to answer the questions in this section.

DIRECTIONS

Every passage or paired set of passages is accompanied by a number of questions. Read the passage or paired set of passages, then use what is said or implied in what you read and in any given graphics to choose the best answer to each question.

Questions 1-10 are based on the following passage.

This passage is adapted from George Eliot, *Middlemarch*. Originally published in 1872.

Will Ladislaw was struck mute for a few moments. He had never been fond of Mr. Casaubon, and if it had not been for his sense of obligation, he
Line would have laughed at him. But the idea of this
5 dried-up pedant, this elaborator of small explanations about as important as the surplus stock of false antiquities kept in a vendor's back room, having first gotten Dorothea, this adorable young creature, to marry him, stirred him with a sort of comic disgust:
10 he was divided between the impulse to laugh aloud and the equally unreasonable impulse to burst into scornful invective.

For an instant he felt that the struggle was causing a queer contortion of his features, but with a
15 good effort he resolved it into nothing more offensive than a merry smile.

Dorothea wondered; but the smile was irresistible, and shone back from her face too. Dorothea said inquiringly, "Something amuses you?"
20 "Yes," said Will, quick in finding resources. "I am thinking of the sort of figure I cut the first time I saw you, when you annihilated my poor sketch with your criticism."

"My criticism?" said Dorothea, wondering still
25 more. "Surely not. I always feel particularly ignorant about painting."

"I suspected you of knowing so much, that you knew how to say just what was most cutting. You said—I dare say you don't remember it as I do—that
30 the relation of my sketch to nature was quite hidden from you. At least, you implied that." Will could laugh now as well as smile.

"That was really my ignorance," said Dorothea, admiring Will's good humor. "I must have said so
35 only because I never could see any beauty in the pictures which my uncle told me all judges thought very fine. That always makes one feel stupid. It is painful to be told that anything is very fine and not be able to feel that it is fine—something like being
40 blind, while people talk of the sky."

"Oh, there is a great deal in the feeling for art which must be acquired," said Will. (It was impossible now to doubt the directness of Dorothea's confession.) "Art is an old language with a great
45 many artificial, affected styles, and sometimes the chief pleasure one gets out of knowing them is the mere sense of knowing."

"You mean perhaps to be a painter?" said Dorothea, with a new direction of interest. "You
50 mean to make painting your profession? Mr. Casaubon will like to hear that you have chosen a profession."

"No, oh no," said Will, with some coldness. "I have quite made up my mind against it. It is too one-
55 sided a life. I have been seeing a great deal of the German artists here: I travelled from Frankfurt with

CONTINUE ➤

one of them. Some are fine, even brilliant fellows—but I should not like to get into their way of looking at the world entirely from the studio point of view."

60   "That I can understand," said Dorothea, cordially. "But if you have a genius for painting, would it not be right to take that as a guide? Perhaps you might do better things than these—or different, so that there might not be so many pictures almost
65 all alike in the same place."

There was no mistaking this simplicity, and Will was won by it into frankness. "A man must have a very rare genius to make changes of that sort. I am afraid mine would not carry me even to the pitch of
70 doing well what has been done already, at least not so well as to make it worthwhile. And I should never succeed in anything by dint of drudgery. If things don't come easily to me I never get them."

1

Over the course of the passage, the focus of the narrative shifts from

A) Will's appraisal of Mr. Casaubon to his opinions of Dorothea.

B) Will's response to unpleasant news to a discussion with Dorothea about art and his own shortcomings.

C) Will's admiration of Dorothea from afar to a witty and flirtatious conversation between them.

D) Will's appreciation of art to his internal debate about whether he himself should become an artist.

2

In lines 1-23, Will could best be described as

A) supportive.

B) confused.

C) displeased.

D) amused.

3

Which of the following provides the best evidence for the answer to the previous question?

A) Lines 4-9 ("But the … disgust")

B) Lines 13-16 ("For an … smile")

C) Lines 18-19 ("Dorothea said … you")

D) Lines 20-23 ("I am … criticism")

4

It can be most reasonably inferred that Dorothea is

A) puzzled but pleased by Will's reaction to her news.

B) worried by Will's cold and indifferent manner.

C) startled and offended by Will's comments on art criticism.

D) dismissive of Will's artwork and opinions.

5

Which of the following provides the best evidence for the answer to the previous question?

A) Lines 10-12 ("he was … invective")

B) Lines 17-18 ("Dorothea wondered … too")

C) Lines 48-49 ("You mean … interest")

D) Lines 60-61 ("That I … cordially")

6

The passage most strongly implies which of the following about Dorothea's taste in art?

A) It arises from years of study in international venues.

B) It stems from her unschooled feelings about the pieces.

C) It is far superior to Will's own pedantic taste.

D) It is refined but too artificial to be authentic.

CONTINUE

7

As used in line 22, "annihilated" most nearly means

A) eliminated.

B) erased.

C) converted.

D) disparaged.

8

Dorothea makes a comparison in lines 37-40 ("It is ... sky") in order to

A) suggest that her sight limits her from appreciating the details in many renowned paintings.

B) illustrate her discomfort and frustration when others discuss elements in art she doesn't understand.

C) show her bored indifference toward the beauty that seems to entrance and delight others.

D) express her hope that she may one day come to understand the more enlightened perspectives of others.

9

As used in line 45, "affected" most nearly means

A) pretentious.

B) deceitful.

C) phony.

D) assumed.

10

In lines 72-73 ("If things ... them"), Will is most directly referring to

A) Dorothea's hand in marriage.

B) his potential career as a painter.

C) a proposed trip to Frankfurt.

D) his new foray into art criticism.

Questions 11-20 are based on the following passages.

Passage 1 is adapted from Huey P. Long, "Every Man a King." Originally delivered in 1934. Passage 2 is adapted from Franklin D. Roosevelt, "Commonwealth Club Address." Originally delivered in 1932.

Passage 1

I contend, my friends, that we have no difficult problem to solve in America. It is not the difficulty of the problem which we have; it is the fact that the
Line rich people of this country will not allow us to solve
5 the one little problem that is afflicting this country, because in order to cure all of our woes it is necessary to scale down the big fortunes, that we may scatter the wealth to be shared by all of the people.

We have neglected the fundamentals upon which
10 the American Government was principally predicated. The first thing that the Declaration of Independence said was: "We hold these truths to be self-evident, that there are certain inalienable rights of the people, and among them are life, liberty, and
15 the pursuit of happiness"; and it said, further, "We hold the view that all men are created equal." Now, what did they mean by that? Did they mean that someone who comes into this world without having had an opportunity to work should be born with
20 more than he and all of his children could ever dispose of, but that another one would have to be born into a life of starvation?

Read what Plato said: that you must not let any one man be too poor, and you must not let any one
25 man be too rich; that the same mill that grinds out the extra rich is the mill that will grind out the extra poor, because, in order that the extra rich can become so affluent, they must necessarily take more of what ordinarily would belong to the average man. It is a
30 very simple process of mathematics that you do not have to study, and that no one is going to discuss with you.

Now, we have organized a society, and we call it the "Share Our Wealth Society." It is a society with
35 the motto "every man a king." Every man a king, so there would be no such thing as a man or woman who did not have the necessities of life. "Every man

CONTINUE

a king." Every man to eat when there is something to
eat; all to wear something when there is something
40 to wear. That makes us all sovereign.

Passage 2

Recently a careful study was made of the
concentration of business in the United States. It
showed that our economic life was dominated by
some six hundred odd corporations who controlled
45 two-thirds of American industry. Ten million small
businessmen divided the other third. Put plainly, we
are steering a steady course toward economic
oligarchy, if we are not there already.

Just as in older times the central government was
50 first a haven of refuge, and then a threat, so now the
central and ambitious financial unit is no longer a
servant of national desire, but a danger. I would
draw the parallel one step farther. We did not think
because national government had become a threat in
55 the 18th century that therefore we should abandon
the principle of national government. Nor today
should we abandon the principle of strong economic
units called corporations, merely because their
power is susceptible to easy abuse.

60 Every man has a right to life, and this means that
he has also a right to make a comfortable living. He
may by sloth or crime decline to exercise that right;
but it may not be denied him. Every man has a right
to his own property, which means a right to be
65 assured in the safety of his savings. By no other
means can men carry the burdens of those parts of
life which afford no chance of labor: childhood,
sickness, old age.

These two requirements must be satisfied, in the
70 main, by the individuals who claim and hold control
of the great industrial and financial combinations
which dominate so large a part of our industrial life.
They have undertaken to be, not businessmen, but
princes: princes of property. I am not prepared to say
75 that the system which produces them is wrong. But
they must, where necessary, sacrifice some private
advantage, and in reciprocal self-denial must seek a
general advantage. It is here that formal government
comes in. Whenever the lone wolf, the unethical
80 competitor whose hand is against every man's,

threatens to drag the industry back to a state of
anarchy, the government may properly be asked to
apply restraint.

11

The central claim of Passage 1 is that

A) the pursuit of happiness is a fundamental right of
all American people.

B) when the rich become more rich, the poor
become more poor.

C) every man has a right to his own property, and a
right to be assured in his savings.

D) improving problems in the U.S. requires
redistributing wealth to the poor.

12

As used in line 6, "cure" most nearly means

A) improve.

B) alleviate.

C) salve.

D) preserve.

13

Long most likely included the second paragraph
(lines 9-22) to

A) call into question the moral correctness of
certain principles in the Declaration of
Independence.

B) challenge the American Government, which he
believes owns too many of the country's
corporations.

C) illustrate that the fundamental beliefs of the
country are embodied by the lives of the
American people.

D) demonstrate that Americans have failed to honor
some of the fundamental virtues of the
Declaration of Independence.

CONTINUE

14

Which choice provides the best evidence for the answer to the previous question?

A) Lines 1-2 ("I contend ... America")

B) Lines 3-5 ("it is ... country")

C) Lines 9-11 ("We have ... predicated")

D) Lines 16-17 ("Now ... by that")

15

In the second paragraph (lines 49-59) of Passage 2, Roosevelt draws a parallel between

A) municipal government and national government.

B) national government and corporations.

C) threats and principles.

D) corporations and national desire.

16

In Passage 2 Roosevelt uses the phrase "princes of property" (line 74) to

A) suggest that many of these individuals and businessmen are of royal descent.

B) indicate that these individuals often place a greater focus on property than any other asset.

C) evoke that most of the corporations owned by these individuals are inherited rather than earned.

D) emphasize that these individuals own and control an extremely large portion of the economy.

17

Which choice provides the best evidence for the answer to the previous question?

A) Lines 56-59 ("Nor today ... abuse")

B) Lines 63-65 ("Every man ... savings")

C) Lines 70-72 ("by the ... life")

D) Lines 75-78 ("But they ... advantage")

18

Which choice best describes the relationship between Passage 1 and Passage 2?

A) Passage 1 claims that too much money is under the control of too few people; Passage 2 claims that too much of the economy is under the control of too few corporations.

B) Passage 1 focuses on a discussion about corporations and economic control; Passage 2 focuses on a discussion about money and wealth distribution.

C) Both Passage 1 and Passage 2 argue that for society and the economy to improve, the government must strictly limit the financial power of wealthy elites.

D) Both Passage 1 and Passage 2 argue that wealth is unfairly concentrated, but that veering toward more equal distribution could be dangerous for the economy.

CONTINUE →

19

Long would most likely respond to the discussion of rights in the third paragraph of Passage 2 (lines 60-68) by stating that

A) the right to one's own property is the most important right of all.

B) such rights, and all rights to basic necessities, are deserved by every man.

C) offering every man these rights can lead to unequal and unsustainable wealth distribution.

D) while such rights are important, none are as important as the right to vote.

20

Passage 2 differs from Passage 1 in that only Passage 2

A) makes explicit mention of the role of corporations.

B) references the work of reputable economic experts.

C) refers to the rights of Americans to support its argument.

D) identifies an urgent problem afflicting the country.

Questions 21-31 are based on the following passage and supplementary material.

This passage is adapted from Chau Tu, "Can Music Be Used as Medicine?" © 2015 by Chau Tu, as first published by The Atlantic Company.

Current research shows that music affects the body and brain to at least some degree, physically and psychologically. For instance, research
Line published in 2005 by Theresa Lesiuk at the
5 University of Windsor, Canada, concluded that music helped to improve the quality and timeliness of office work, as well as increase overall positive attitudes while people were working on those tasks. A review in 2012 by Costas Karageorghis found
10 there was "evidence to suggest that carefully selected music can promote ergogenic and psychological benefits during high-intensity exercise." Meanwhile, Stefan Koelsch in Berlin has found "music can evoke activity changes in the core
15 brain regions that underlie emotion," and physically, "happy" music triggers zygomatic muscle activity—that is, smiling—and "sad" music "leads to the activation of the corrugator muscle"—the frowning muscle in the brow.
20　　However, the long-term effects still need to be parsed more thoroughly, and it's still unclear if and how, exactly, music might be used as treatment. "Just because music—or anything else—acts upon a part of the brain, does not mean that mental health
25 can be influenced," Robert Zatorre, a neurologist at McGill University, wrote in an email. "We need far more sophisticated understandings of what is going on in a given disease before we can really answer" the question of whether music can definitively affect
30 mental or physical health. "That said, there are a few promising avenues that people are trying with particular disorders, and hopefully that work will accelerate in future."

One such condition is Parkinson's disease.
35 Jessica Grahn is a neuroscientist at Western University in Ontario who's been studying the relationship between music and movement, and she points to research that has shown that even when people don't seem to be physically responding to
40 music—by tapping their foot or dancing—fMRI

CONTINUE →

scans reveal that their brains' motor systems are responding internally. "When we look at what happens when someone appears to be very passively listening to music, and they're not doing anything to
45 it, we see quite a lot of the brain responding," she says.

People in these studies, done by Grahn and others, seem to be responding to a song's rhythm. The rhythm, Grahn says, really drives responses in
50 the brain's movement areas, and these responses tend to be stronger with music that has a clear beat that people can follow. Now, the next step for researchers is to find out if rhythm can be used to activate motor brain areas in people who have
55 problems there.

Parkinson's patients, for example, often experience "breaks" or "freezing," and have trouble initiating movement. "It's not entirely clear why freezing happens," Grahn says. But "one thing that
60 people have observed is that if you play music that has a steady beat, or sometimes even just a metronome with a steady beat, these patients seem to have improvements in their walking." Grahn has also observed music seeming effective in elongating
65 and improving the gait of Parkinson's patients, which is often jerky and unsteady.

Still, there are a lot of variables that haven't been studied yet, from figuring out the strength and duration of these apparent effects to whether an
70 individual's musical abilities have an impact. A major boon, Grahn says, would be obtaining data—much, much more of it, and from patients in real-world situations.

"Patients really vary; some have a very fast
75 progression in the disease, some have a slow progression," she says. "It's impossible to test enough patients to really capture every kind of patient with every kind of musical ability in the lab."

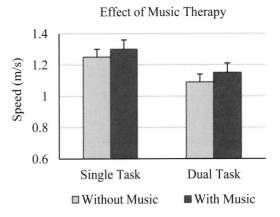

Effect of Music Therapy

This graph shows the walking speed of a group of patients with Parkinson's disease, first while walking without music then while walking with music. The patients either walked (single task), or walked while simultaneously doing something else (dual task).

21

The passage primarily focuses on which of the following aspects of music?

A) Its physiological effects on facial musculature in humans

B) Its impressive ability to improve productivity in office settings

C) Its potential effects on patients with health conditions

D) Its lasting impact on the moods of people with Parkinson's disease

CONTINUE

22

Which of the following best describes the structure of the passage as a whole?

A) An overview of diverse research findings followed by a discussion of a particular avenue of research

B) A series of related anecdotes followed by a scientific theory that unites them all

C) An interview with a doctor conducting research followed by descriptions of her patients

D) An explanation of a basic problem followed by an exploration of multiple potential solutions

23

As used in line 7, "positive" most nearly means

A) favorable.

B) definite.

C) unequivocal.

D) practical.

24

How do the studies in the first paragraph (lines 1-19) relate to the rest of the passage?

A) They outline the prevailing scientific consensus about music and the body, while the rest of the passage argues that new evidence suggests the truth is more complicated.

B) They introduce the topic of music's effects on the body, while the rest of the passage discusses a potential manifestation of that phenomenon.

C) They demonstrate the wide range of opinions that exists about Parkinson's treatment, while the rest of the passage advocates a specific treatment for the illness.

D) They emphasize the difficulty of securing funding for scientific research, while the rest of the passage talks about the benefits of well-funded experiments.

25

As used in line 34, "condition" most nearly means

A) illness.

B) situation.

C) environment.

D) requirement.

26

The passage most strongly suggests that

A) music therapy is a potential cure for Parkinson's patients.

B) the effects of music on the brain are confusing and difficult to study.

C) while some support researching the effects of music on the brain, others are scornful.

D) music may have significant effects for some patients, but it's too early to tell.

27

Which choice provides the best evidence for the answer to the previous question?

A) Lines 26-30 ("We need … health")

B) Lines 47-48 ("People in … rhythm")

C) Lines 58-59 ("It's not … says")

D) Lines 74-76 ("Patients really … says")

CONTINUE

28

It is reasonable to conclude that one reason Grahn would like significantly more data about the effect of music on Parkinson's patients is that more data would

A) make her argument more convincing to scientific authorities.

B) allow her to improve the gait of all Parkinson's patients.

C) clarify how individual factors might affect patients' responses to music.

D) demonstrate her need for significantly more funding to conduct her research.

29

Which choice provides the best evidence for the answer to the previous question?

A) Lines 35-37 ("Jessica Grahn … movement")

B) Lines 49-52 ("The rhythm … follow")

C) Lines 63-66 ("Grahn has … unsteady")

D) Lines 67-70 ("Still … impact")

30

Based on the graph, Parkinson's patients who listened to music while walking moved

A) faster than patients who did not listen to music.

B) faster than they did without listening to music.

C) slower than patients who did not listen to music.

D) slower than they did without listening to music.

31

Data in the graph provide most direct support for which assertion in the passage?

A) Lines 13-19 ("Meanwhile ... the brow")

B) Lines 42-46 ("When we ... says")

C) Lines 59-63 ("But ... their walking")

D) Lines 74-76 ("Patients really ... says")

Questions 32-42 are based on the following passage and supplementary material.

This passage is adapted from Kelly McGonigal, "Use Stress to Your Advantage." © 2015 by Dow Jones and Company.

When Harvard Business School professor Alison Wood Brooks asked hundreds of people if they should try to calm down or try to feel excited in
Line stressful situations, the responses were nearly
5 unanimous: 91% thought that the best advice was to try to calm down. But is it true?

Prof. Brooks designed an experiment to find out. For a research paper published last year in the *Journal of Experimental Psychology*, she recruited
10 140 people to give a speech. She told part of the group to relax and to calm their nerves by saying to themselves, "I am calm." The others were told to embrace their anxiety and to tell themselves, "I am excited."
15 Members of both groups were still nervous before the speech, but the participants who had told themselves "I am excited" felt better able to handle the pressure and were more confident in their ability to give a good talk. Not only that, but observers who
20 rated the talks found the excited speakers more persuasive, confident, and competent than the participants who had tried to calm down. With this one change in mindset, the speakers had transformed their anxiety into energy that helped them to perform
25 under pressure.

"We're bombarded with information about how bad stress is," says Jeremy Jamieson, a professor of psychology at the University of Rochester who specializes in stress. But the conventional view, he
30 says, fails to appreciate the many ways in which physical and psychological tension can help us to perform better.

In research published in the *Journal of Experimental Social Psychology* in 2010, Prof.
35 Jamieson tested his theory with college students who were preparing to take the Graduate Record Examination (GRE). He invited 60 students to take a practice GRE and collected saliva samples from them beforehand to get baseline measures of their
40 levels of alpha-amylase, a hormonal indicator of

CONTINUE

stress. He told them that the goal of the study was to examine how the physiological stress response affects performance.

He then gave half the students a brief pep talk to
45 help them rethink their pre-exam nervousness. "People think that feeling anxious while taking a standardized test will make them do poorly," he told them. "However, recent research suggests that stress doesn't hurt performance on these tests and can even
50 help performance. People who feel anxious during a test might actually do better… If you find yourself feeling anxious, simply remind yourself that your stress could be helping you do well."

It worked: students who received the mindset
55 intervention scored higher on the practice exam than those in the control group. The difference in GRE scores could not be attributed to differences in ability: students had been randomly assigned to the two groups and didn't differ, on average, in their
60 SAT scores or college GPAs.

Prof. Jamieson wondered about another possible explanation: perhaps his pep talk had simply calmed the students down instead of helping them to use their stress. To test this proposition, he took a second
65 saliva sample from students after the exam. The group that had received the mindset message showed higher, not lower, levels of salivary alpha-amylase— in other words, they were more stressed after the exam, not less.

70 Interestingly, he also found that stress by itself, as measured by the saliva sample, was not the key to better performance. For students who had received the pep talk, a stronger physical stress response was associated with higher scores. In contrast, there was
75 no relationship between stress hormones and performance in the control group. The stress response by itself had not helped or hurt their test-taking in any predictable way.

What makes such mindset interventions so
80 promising, says Prof. Jamieson, is that when they work, they do not just have an immediate, one time effect—they stick. He delivered his pep talk days before the actual exam, but the students had somehow internalized its message.

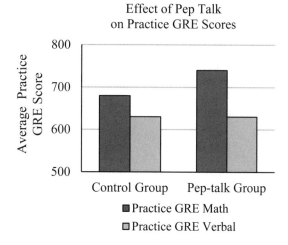

Effect of Pep Talk on Practice GRE Scores

■ Practice GRE Math
□ Practice GRE Verbal

32

The passage is written from the perspective of someone who is

A) an expert on physiological symptoms of stress in humans.

B) interested in recent research about different ways people respond to stress.

C) an advocate for decreasing the stressfulness of graduate school admissions.

D) passionate about helping young people lower their stress levels.

33

As used in line 13, "embrace" most nearly means

A) hold.

B) adopt.

C) accept.

D) support.

CONTINUE

34

Which statement best summarizes lines 1-25?

A) A researcher found that the best strategy for dealing with stress was counterintuitive to most of the people she surveyed.

B) A student discovered that she would need to learn to manage her stress better in order to keep her GPA at a satisfactory level.

C) A pair of experts provided their opinions on how to deal with stress and agreed that stress can be beneficial.

D) A public speaking coach offered tips on handling anxiety gleaned from a long career of helping others succeed.

35

Professor Brooks found that participants who were told to embrace their anxiety

A) rated themselves as more confident but performed at their usual level.

B) received higher ratings from observers of the talks.

C) remained anxious, but impressed viewers with their apparent calm.

D) varied too much in their responses to provide conclusive evidence.

36

Which choice provides the best evidence for the answer to the previous question?

A) Lines 5-6 ("91% … calm down")

B) Line 7 ("Prof. Brooks … out")

C) Lines 12-14 ("The others … excited")

D) Lines 19-22 ("Not only … down")

37

As used in line 29, "conventional" most nearly means

A) ritual.

B) plain.

C) standard.

D) routine.

38

Professor Jamieson's study suggests that encouraging students to embrace their anxiety

A) stabilizes their test scores.

B) decreases their nervousness.

C) has long-lasting effects.

D) affects everyone differently.

39

Which choice provides the best evidence for the answer to the previous question?

A) Lines 33-37 ("In research … Examination")

B) Lines 46-48 ("People think … them")

C) Lines 70-72 ("Interestingly … better performance")

D) Lines 79-82 ("What makes … stick")

40

The passage most strongly suggests that

A) typical beliefs about stress may limit performance.

B) stress is the best predictor of test scores.

C) all individuals experience stress in the same way.

D) most mindset interventions lead to lower stress levels.

CONTINUE

41

Which statement best summarizes the information presented in the graph?

A) On average, students who were more stressed did better on the practice GRE.

B) On average, students who were less stressed did better on the practice GRE.

C) On average, students who were told to think of their anxiety positively did better on the practice GRE.

D) On average, students who were told to think of their anxiety positively did worse on the practice GRE.

42

Which of the following is supported by the passage and the graph?

A) Studying harder before the test was linked to more stress while taking it, but made no difference in scores.

B) Being told to embrace anxiety was linked to much higher scores on the practice GRE math section than on the verbal.

C) A strong physiological stress response was predictive of top scores on the practice GRE verbal section, but not on the math.

D) People think stress is only harmful, but its positive effects tend to outweigh any negative effects.

Questions 43-52 are based on the following passage.

This passage is adapted from "Exploring our moon today to learn more about Earth's youth billions of years ago" by Augusto Carballido. © 2015 by Augusto Carballido.

The surface of the Earth preserves little or no information about its distant past. Constant tectonic activity has recycled Earth's crust and shifted
Line landmasses. Rainfall, wind, ice, and snow have
5 weathered away surface features over billions of years. Most of the craters formed by the impacts of asteroids and comets have been erased from the geologic record, with just over 100 known craters remaining on the continents.
10   But there is a place where we can go to learn more about the past of our own planet: the moon. In sharp contrast to Earth's surface, that of the moon is covered with thousands of craters of all sizes, many of them produced shortly after the moon was born.
15 The moon doesn't have the winds, rivers, or plate tectonics capable of erasing these marks of ancient impacts.
       For that reason, the surface of the moon is like a window into the early history of our solar system.
20 By studying the chemical composition of rocks and soil on our natural satellite, we could obtain a glimpse of the Earth's own geological infancy—including the emergence of life.
       The Earth formed 4.54 billion years ago, after
25 ancient asteroids known as planetesimals piled up into a single, planet-sized body as they orbited the Sun. Scientists think the moon formed roughly 70 million years later, when a planet about the size of Mars collided with the young Earth. With the aid of
30 sophisticated computer models, experts have shown that this huge collision created a donut-shaped envelope of molten rock and hot gas around the Earth. By calculating how this scorching disk would lose its heat, they've deduced that the moon
35 condensed from all this hot material in less than 100 years.
       Fast forward some 500 million years. Around this time, the giant planets Jupiter, Saturn, Uranus, and Neptune likely underwent a rearrangement of
40 their orbits around the Sun, as a result of complex

CONTINUE

gravitational interactions with myriad planetesimals. This rearrangement sent many asteroids on a collision course with Earth. When they crashed into our planet, their impacts launched terrestrial
45　fragments into Earth's orbit. A very exciting possibility is that some of those Earth rocks might have landed on the moon.

If those pieces of Earth did make it to the moon, they're probably still lying somewhere on the lunar
50　surface. Some studies predict a large concentration of impacts near the moon's poles. In some regions, there may be as much as a golf cart's mass worth of terrestrial material spread over an area equivalent to 140 soccer fields. Whether this mass is in the form
55　of rocks or tiny dust particles depends on, among other things, how hard Earth's fragments hit the lunar ground.

Regardless of their size, terrestrial remnants could contain invaluable information about our
60　planet's early years. For example, those terrestrial meteorites may hold a record of the chemical composition of the Earth's ancient mantle, the hot layer of rock between the crust and the core. Learning about the composition of the Earth billions
65　of years ago would allow us to make comparisons with our present-day planet. With more historical data, we could infer how a habitable planet evolves over time and potentially catch a glimpse of the emergence of life; this would also enable us to
70　understand extrasolar planetary systems.
We are still a long way from obtaining a clear understanding of our home planet. But the possibility of lunar exploration by private ventures, in addition to those carried out by national space
75　agencies, raises the odds of mind-blowing discoveries that can shed light on Earth's mysteries. We may well end up repeating the words of Apollo 8 astronaut Bill Anders: "We came all this way to explore the moon, and the most important thing is
80　that we discovered the Earth."

43

Based on the passage, the lunar surface reveals more valuable information about

A) the Earth's distant past than the Earth's surface does.

B) the planetary orbits than the Earth's surface does.

C) the Sun's formation than the Earth's surface does.

D) planetesimals than the Earth's surface does.

44

The passage indicates that the discovery of terrestrial remnants on the moon could provide valuable insight into

A) the patterns of tectonic activity on the moon 4.54 billion years ago.

B) the rearrangement of the orbits of Earth and other planets over time.

C) the force at which fragments of the moon collided with the Earth.

D) the evolution of our planet and the emergence of life.

45

Which choice provides the best evidence for the answer to the previous question?

A) Lines 37-41 ("Around this ... planetesimals")

B) Lines 54-57 ("Whether this ... ground")

C) Lines 66-70 ("With more ... systems")

D) Lines 72-76 ("But the ... mysteries")

CONTINUE

46

The passage most clearly suggests that the moon can provide important information because it

A) formed more recently, and is therefore less damaged than the Earth.

B) undergoes minimal surface activity, and is therefore more susceptible to tectonic shifts.

C) formed more recently, and is therefore more similar to the state of Earth today.

D) undergoes minimal surface activity, and is therefore rich with historical information.

47

Which choice provides the best evidence for the answer to the previous question?

A) Lines 4-6 ("Rainfall … years")

B) Lines 15-17 ("The moon … impacts")

C) Lines 27-29 ("Scientists think … Earth")

D) Lines 50-51 ("Some studies … poles")

48

The primary purpose of the second paragraph (lines 10-17) is to

A) introduce studying the lunar surface as an alternative way to understand the geological history of Earth.

B) provide a counterargument against the claim that Earth provides minimal information about its geological history.

C) present a problem with research into the evolution of planets and the solar system.

D) define key terms and describe the experimental setup of research into the moon's surface features.

49

The author most likely uses the phrase "geological infancy" (line 22) to refer to the

A) surprisingly small size of the Earth.

B) underdevelopment of the planet today.

C) early stage of the Earth's life.

D) fragility of the Earth's rock formations.

50

Which situation is most similar to the one described in lines 10-11 ("But there … moon")?

A) An interview with a politician's assistant yields more information about the politician than an interview with the politician herself.

B) A musician's autobiography does not include as much detail about his songwriting as his fans had hoped.

C) A travel guide for a major city focuses on current attractions rather than its history and culture.

D) A biologist is able to gather more data by studying a bird in its natural habitat than by studying it in her lab.

CONTINUE

51

As used in line 5, "weathered away" most nearly means

A) overcome.

B) eroded.

C) exhausted.

D) frayed.

52

What function does the fifth paragraph (lines 37-47) serve in the passage as a whole?

A) It provides background for why terrestrial fragments could be located on the moon.

B) It outlines the development of planetary orbits, and their effect on the evolution of planets.

C) It summarizes the details of the computer modeling that is explored in the rest of the passage.

D) It describes how ancient asteroids pile up into a single body to form new planets.

STOP

If you complete this section before the end of your allotted time, you may check your work on this section only. Do NOT use the time to work on another section.

Writing and Language Test

35 MINUTES, 44 QUESTIONS

Turn to Section 2 of your answer sheet to answer the questions in this section.

DIRECTIONS

Every passage comes with a set of questions. Some questions will ask you to consider how the writer might revise the passage to improve the expression of ideas. Other questions will ask you to consider correcting potential errors in sentence structure, usage, or punctuation. There may be one or more graphics that you will need to consult as you revise and edit the passage.

Some questions will refer to a portion of the passage that has been underlined. Other questions will refer to a particular location in a passage or ask that you consider the passage in full.

After you read the passage, select the answers to questions that most effectively improve the passage's writing quality or that adjust the passage to follow the conventions of standard written English. Many questions give you the option to select "NO CHANGE." Select that option in cases where you think the relevant part of the passage should remain as it currently is.

Questions 1-11 are based on the following passage.

What Do Professors Do?

There is no such thing as a "typical day" in the life of a college professor. That's part of the appeal of this **1** career each day offers unique opportunities and challenges. Add in the fact that **2** most universities today try to admit students from a broad range of backgrounds and many professors feel that they've won the career lottery.

1

A) NO CHANGE
B) career each,
C) career, each
D) career: each

2

Which detail best supports the assertion at the end of this sentence?

A) NO CHANGE
B) most professors teach a subject that they love
C) teaching is harder than it looks
D) many professors struggle to balance academic and administrative responsibilities

CONTINUE

Becoming a professor requires many years of study in a specific [3] discipline. A master's degree is the minimum educational requirement, but most tenure-track positions require a doctoral degree. Anne Swanson, who teaches English at a small independent university, explains, "to become a professor, I first earned a B.A. in English, followed by a Ph.D. in Rhetoric and Composition." That took Anne six years of advanced studies, which included becoming [4] coherent in two foreign languages.

While most of Prof. Swanson's students only see her lecture a few times a week and assign some homework, that's not all she [5] had done. "The reality is that for every hour I spend in the classroom, I spend a minimum of two hours on planning and grading," she says. This planning begins well before the semester does. Over the summer, when most students are visiting family, studying abroad, or taking summer jobs, [6] she works on syllabi, along with reviewing the textbook and developing a preliminary schedule of lesson plans and assignments.

3

A) NO CHANGE
B) discipline, however, a master's
C) discipline, a master's
D) discipline, for example, a master's

4

A) NO CHANGE
B) vivid
C) fluent
D) fluid

5

A) NO CHANGE
B) does
C) did
D) would do

6

A) NO CHANGE
B) she is working on syllabi, reviewing the textbook, and developing
C) she is working to create syllabi, and she reviews the textbook and develops
D) she reviews the textbook and is developing syllabi and

CONTINUE

[1] Once the semester begins, Prof. Swanson works on her lectures, reviews and revises the lesson plans and assignments, and holds office hours. [2] "During office hours, I meet with students to review assignments," she says. [3] She also advises students about their courses and even what major to choose. [4] Her advice isn't limited to academic subjects, though; "Sometimes a student comes in to talk about something class-related and we end up talking about time management or even a problem with a roommate," she says. **7**

When she's not meeting with students, participating in committees, and planning, Prof. Swanson is grading papers submitted by her students **8** with the online classroom through the Internet. "Sometimes I wish I taught math because there the answers are just right or wrong," **9** she says. "Grading writing assignments means I make note of such issues as incorrect punctuation and grammar, but I spend far more time writing comments in the margins. The good news is I can grade papers anywhere I have access to the website."

7

To make this paragraph most logical, sentence 1 should be placed

A) where it is now.

B) after sentence 2.

C) after sentence 3.

D) after sentence 4.

8

A) NO CHANGE

B) using the university's online classroom

C) that are submitted using her university's virtual classroom

D) online through the virtual online classroom on the Internet

9

A) NO CHANGE

B) one says

C) I say

D) they say

CONTINUE

Her job also includes participating in English department meetings and **10** <u>staging</u> other services for the university. Prof. Swanson is on her institution's faculty salary committee and a committee devoted to social justice issues. These committees meet year-round, even during the summer.

During most weeks, Prof. Swanson spends just nine hours in the classroom and another nine creating lesson plans and lectures. **11** "The bottom line is that I work all year long, and I work a lot more than 40 hours a week. But I love being a professor. It's the best job ever."

10

A) NO CHANGE

B) achieving

C) discharging

D) performing

11

At this point the writer is considering adding the following sentence

> Office hours and committee and faculty meetings take up about eighteen hours, and she can spend as much as sixteen hours grading papers.

Should the writer make this addition here?

A) Yes, because it supports the statement about how many hours Prof. Swanson works.

B) Yes, because it explains what all professors have to do in addition to teaching.

C) No, because the number of hours Prof. Swanson spends on grading is only approximate.

D) No, because Prof. Swanson doesn't always teach summer classes.

CONTINUE

Questions 12-22 are based on the following passage.

The Midnight Ride of Sybil Ludington

Paul Revere's midnight ride is legendary, but the story of a similar ride made by a teenage girl named Sybil Ludington is less well-known. **12** Her journey through the rough countryside of Putnam County, New York, was of equal importance to the Continental Army during the Revolutionary War. General George Washington even visited her family farm to personally thank the brave girl, **13** though her bravery helped win an important battle.

Before the Revolutionary War **14** set sail, Sybil Ludington led a fairly stable and secure life. Her father, Henry Ludington, was a successful farmer and businessman. He had served the British crown in the French and Indian War, and he remained a Loyalist **15** until 1773, when he joined the rebel cause. Because of his extensive military experience, Henry Ludington was named a Colonel and commissioned to lead a regiment of the Continental Army made up of local men.

12

Which choice would most effectively develop the main topic of this passage?

A) NO CHANGE

B) Sybil Ludington rode a horse named "Star," married a man named Edmund Ogden, and lived to the age of 77.

C) During the Revolutionary War, a number of people rode through the night to warn about impending battles.

D) Paul Revere went on to serve in the militia and become a successful entrepreneur.

13

A) NO CHANGE

B) whereas

C) insofar as

D) because

14

A) NO CHANGE

B) sprouted

C) broke out

D) blew up

15

A) NO CHANGE

B) until 1773 when he

C) until 1773. When he

D) until, 1773, when he

CONTINUE

[1] In late April 1777, British General William Tryon led a company of 2,000 men in an attack on Danbury, Connecticut, more than 20 miles away from the Ludington home. [2] Riders were dispatched to find help battling Tryon's soldiers. [3] The British destroyed the munitions stored **16** they're by the Continental Army before setting all the homes owned by revolutionaries on fire. [4] On the night of April 26, 1777, one of these riders arrived at the Ludington farm. [5] Because it was planting season, Colonel Ludington's regiment had disbanded; someone would have to spread the order to regroup. [6] The rider from Danbury was exhausted and the Colonel had to prepare for battle, so it was decided that Sybil, then 16, would go. **17**

She saddled her horse, Star, and set off into a **18** night: darkened by a powerful rainstorm. Riding over muddy roads that ran through deep woods, Sybil stopped at the farmhouses of the militiamen and **19** shouts, "The British are burning Danbury; muster at Ludington's!" By the time Sybil returned home the next morning, she had ridden 40 miles, and most of the 400 members of her

16

A) NO CHANGE
B) their
C) there
D) they are

17

For the sake of cohesion of the paragraph, sentence 2 should be placed

A) where it is now.
B) after sentence 3.
C) after sentence 4.
D) after sentence 5.

18

A) NO CHANGE
B) night darkened by:
C) night darkened, by
D) night darkened by

19

A) NO CHANGE
B) shouting
C) to shout
D) shouted

CONTINUE

father's regiment were assembled at the farm. [20] By this time, Sybil's clothes were completely wet and muddy. They set off in pursuit of Tryon's troops, whom they encountered in Ridgefield, Connecticut. As a result of that battle, Tryon withdrew his troops from Connecticut, never to return. Shortly thereafter, General Washington visited the Ludington home to thank Sybil for [21] one's courageous ride.

Although Sybil rode twice as far as Paul Revere, she never became as famous as he did. However, she has still been honored for her role in history: the Daughters of the American Revolution erected a statue of her in New York, and the U.S. Postal Service [22] issued a stamp in her likeness bearing her image.

[20]

The writer is considering deleting this sentence. It should be

A) kept, because it makes sense that Sybil would have been soaked after riding through the rain.

B) kept, because it helps to explain why Sybil rode so quickly and how she inspired the assembled troops.

C) deleted, because it interrupts the transition from information about assembled troops to their action.

D) deleted, because there's no clear explanation in the passage of why Sybil's clothes would be wet or muddy.

[21]

A) NO CHANGE

B) her

C) she

D) their

[22]

A) NO CHANGE

B) issued a stamp bearing her likeness.

C) issued a stamp bearing her image and likeness.

D) also honored her by issuing a stamp with her image and likeness.

CONTINUE

Questions 23-33 are based on the following passage.

After "The Fall"

Sometime around 1560, the Dutch Renaissance painter Pieter Bruegel the Elder painted a work that would become known as "The Fall of Icarus." The painting depicts the fate of Icarus, a character from Greek mythology who flew too close to the sun.

According to the myth, [23] Icarus, and his father, Daedalus were imprisoned after Daedalus betrayed King Minos of Crete. [24] Although Daedalus warned his son not to fly too close to the sun, Icarus was overcome with the thrill of flight and flew too high. The wax melted, rendering the wings useless, and the Icarus fell into the sea and drowned.

23

A) NO CHANGE
B) Icarus and his father, Daedalus,
C) Icarus; and his father, Daedalus
D) Icarus—and his father, Daedalus

24

Which sentence, inserted here, would most effectively develop the series of events described in the paragraph?

A) Icarus was unjustly accused for a crime he didn't commit, which made his father absolutely furious.
B) To escape, the father and son built wings from bird feathers held together with wax and flew to freedom.
C) King Minos was a cruel man who imprisoned a number of his subjects for no reason.
D) Fortunately, Daedalus was an inventor, and he was able to use his skills to hatch a plan for escape.

CONTINUE

"The Fall of Icarus" has **25** induced the work of poets and captured the imagination of countless art scholars. Despite that fact—or perhaps because of it—there is disagreement about how to interpret the painting. In spite of the title, the painting does not focus on **26** Icarus spectacular fall into the sea. **27** The central figure is a farmer plowing his field. Some of the other prominent figures are a shepherd, a fisherman, and a merchant ship. All of these figures are simply going about their day, paying no attention to the drowning Icarus. All we see of this tragic youth are his legs flailing just above the water's surface.

25

A) NO CHANGE
B) driven
C) provoked
D) inspired

26

A) NO CHANGE
B) Icaruses
C) Icarus's
D) that of Icarus

27

Which choice most effectively combines the underlined sentences?

A) A farmer, a shepherd, a fisherman, and a merchant ship are included among the prominent figures, with the farmer being the central figure, plowing his field.

B) The central figure of a farmer is accompanied by other prominent figures, including the following: a shepherd, a fisherman, and a merchant ship.

C) The central figure is a farmer plowing his field; other prominent figures include a shepherd, a fisherman, and a merchant ship.

D) Three prominent figures and the central figure are actually, respectively, a shepherd, a fisherman, a merchant ship, and a farmer who is plowing his fields.

CONTINUE

[1] After viewing the painting in 1938, W. H. Auden was inspired to write his poem "Musée des Beaux Arts." [2] **28** <u>They</u> wrote, "... how everything turns away quite leisurely from the disaster; the ploughman may have heard the splash, the forsaken cry, but for him it was not an important failure. ..." **29** <u>It's so sad!</u> **30** <u>As an allegory, Auden clearly interpreted the painting as</u> about the nature of suffering and our indifference to the suffering of others.

William Carlos Williams also composed a poem about the painting, entitled "Landscape with the Fall of Icarus." The last lines of the poem discuss the fall: "unsignificantly, off the coast, there was a splash, quite unnoticed. This was Icarus drowning." **31** <u>By adding the word "Landscape" as an addition to</u> the title of the painting, Williams subordinates the fall, just as Bruegel did.

28

A) NO CHANGE
B) He
C) Him
D) One

29

The writer is considering deleting the underlined sentence. Should the writer make this deletion?

A) Yes, because the sentence contradicts the main idea of the paragraph.

B) Yes, because the sentence is not consistent with the overall style and tone of the passage.

C) No, because the sentence serves to emphasize the main idea of the paragraph.

D) No, because information in the sentence supports the argument that follows.

30

A) NO CHANGE
B) Auden clearly interpreted the painting as an allegory
C) Auden, as an allegory, clearly interpreted the painting as
D) Clearly, Auden interpreted as an allegory the painting

31

A) NO CHANGE
B) By revising the name of
C) By adding the word "Landscape" to
D) By adding to the title the word "landscape"

CONTINUE

Though they are both commenting on Bruegel's work, Auden and Williams offer different interpretations. While Auden recognizes the human tendency to become preoccupied by the demands of everyday life, Williams emphasizes the lack of concern and seems almost to protest against privileging the ordinary over the catastrophic. **32** Each artist offers his own view. Because Bruegel remained **33** moot about his intentions for this painting, each viewer is free to offer his or her own interpretation.

32

The writer is considering deleting the underlined sentence. Should the sentence be kept or deleted?

A) Kept, because it provides a detail that supports the main topic of the paragraph.

B) Kept, because it supports the main argument of the passage.

C) Deleted, because it unnecessarily repeats information that has been provided earlier in the paragraph.

D) Deleted, because it fails to support the main argument of the passage as introduced in the first paragraph.

33

A) NO CHANGE

B) mood

C) mute

D) mused

Questions 34-44 are based on the following passage.

Frozen Smoke

What is 1,000 times less dense than **34** glass has been used as insulation on the Mars Exploration Rover and thermal sports bottles, and can collect interstellar dust? The answer is aerogel, a mixture of one or more solid materials—silica, carbon, iron oxide, organic polymers, semiconductor nanostructures, gold, or copper—and up to 99.8% air. Aerogels made from graphene are among the least dense materials in the world, but aerogels made of other substances are also very light and have other remarkable properties.

Though it sounds like **35** an impossible invention in some book somewhere, aerogel is real. Aerogel is made by **36** creating a gel in a solution, then the slow removal of the liquid component using high temperatures, drying the gel while maintaining its shape. The liquid is then replaced by air. The resulting foam is as light as a cloud, but **37** rich enough to survive the force of a rocket launch.

34

A) NO CHANGE
B) glass, has
C) glass; has
D) glass. Has

35

A) NO CHANGE
B) the preposterous product of pure fancy
C) it's some stuff that's just plain made up
D) something out of science fiction

36

A) NO CHANGE
B) creation of a gel in a solution, then the slow removing of
C) creating a gel in a solution, then slowly removing
D) creating a gel in a solution, then you remove

37

A) NO CHANGE
B) burly
C) stern
D) robust

CONTINUE

NASA used aerogel for its "Stardust" mission, **38** which collected dust from the "Wild 2" comet. Thanks to its incredibly low density, the aerogel was able to trap the fragile dust particles without damaging them, even though the dust travels through space at about 6 times the speed of a rifle bullet. The gel is so porous that it gradually slows the dust particles without creating heat that could alter them.

[1] This insulation can be either injected into existing cavities in older buildings or **39** it is manufactured as insulating boards for new construction. [2] Aerogel also has some remarkable thermal properties. [3] "R-value" is a standard measure of thermal resistance, and **40** aerogel's r-value is higher than those of all other forms of insulation. [4] Because it has such high thermal resistance, aerogel is a valuable form of insulation. [5] An aerogel-based plaster has even been developed for use in historic buildings to make them more energy-efficient while preserving their appearance. **41**

R-Values of Various Insulators

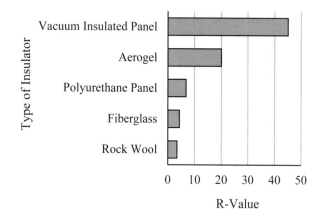

38

A) NO CHANGE

B) who

C) what

D) whom

39

A) NO CHANGE

B) is manufactured

C) by manufacturing it

D) manufactured

40

Which choice most accurately and effectively represents the information in the graph?

A) NO CHANGE

B) the r-value of aerogel is lower than that of either rock wool or fiberglass.

C) aerogel has a higher r-value than do traditional insulators like rock wool and fiberglass.

D) aerogel is a better choice of insulation than vacuum insulated panels for most buildings.

41

For the sake of cohesion of the paragraph, sentence 1 should be placed

A) where it is now.

B) after sentence 2.

C) after sentence 3.

D) after sentence 4.

CONTINUE

[42] The researchers at University of Wisconsin-Madison know how to freeze-dry cellulose and use safer polymers. Researchers at the University of Wisconsin-Madison are currently exploring ways that aerogels may be developed for cleaning up oil and chemical spills. The specific aerogel these researchers are working with is made of cellulose nanofibrils and an environmentally friendly polymer. Even the process is environmentally friendly, using freeze-drying to [43] avoid the use of potentially harmful organic solvents.

The wide range of applications for aerogels promises to become even wider as ongoing improvements to the manufacturing process produce [44] aerogels with greater strength, lower density, or other novel properties.

42

Which choice most effectively establishes the main point of the paragraph?

A) NO CHANGE

B) Beyond its use as an effective insulator, aerogel may have additional environmentally beneficial uses.

C) Aerogel is made in Wisconsin using eco-friendly materials like polymers and nanofibrils.

D) The way aerogel is currently manufactured makes it hard on the environment and useless for tasks like cleaning up oil spills.

43

A) NO CHANGE

B) dodge

C) evade

D) resist

44

A) NO CHANGE

B) aerogels; with greater strength; lower density; or other

C) aerogels with: greater strength, lower density, or other

D) aerogels with greater strength lower density or other

STOP

If you complete this section before the end of your allotted time, you may check your work on this section only. Do NOT use the time to work on another section.

Math Test – No Calculator

25 MINUTES, 20 QUESTIONS

Turn to Section 3 of your answer sheet to answer the questions in this section.

DIRECTIONS

Questions **1-15** ask you to solve a problem, select the best answer among four choices, and fill in the corresponding circle on your answer sheet. Questions **16-20** ask you to solve a problem and enter your answer in the grid provided on your answer sheet. There are detailed instructions on entering answers into the grid before question 16. You may use your test booklet for scratch work.

NOTES

1. You **may not** use a calculator.
2. Variables and expressions represent real numbers unless stated otherwise.
3. Figures are drawn to scale unless stated otherwise.
4. Figures lie in a plane unless stated otherwise.
5. The domain of a function f is defined as the set of all real numbers x for which $f(x)$ is also a real number, unless stated otherwise.

REFERENCE

$$A = \frac{1}{2}bh$$

$$a^2 + b^2 = c^2$$

Special Triangles

$$V = \frac{1}{3}lwh$$

$$V = \frac{1}{3}\pi r^2 h$$

$$A = lw$$

$$V = lwh$$

$$V = \pi r^2 h$$

$$A = \pi r^2$$
$$C = 2\pi r$$

$$V = \frac{4}{3}\pi r^3$$

There are 360° in a circle.

The sum of the angles in a triangle is 180°.

The number of radians of arc in a circle is 2π.

CONTINUE

1

If 20 less than $3x$ is 40, what is the value of x?

A) 3

B) 20

C) 30

D) 40

2

If $\dfrac{x-5}{4} = y$ and $y = 6$, what is the value of x?

A) 5

B) 10

C) 29

D) 36

3

An anthropologist proposes that the change in a certain population can be modeled by the expression $\sqrt{9x^2} - 7x$. If x is positive, which of the following is equivalent to this expression?

A) $2x$

B) $-4x$

C) $3x^2 - 7x$

D) $3x - \sqrt{7x}$

4

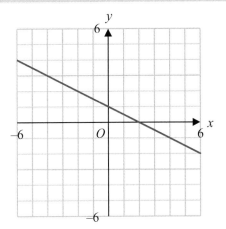

What is the slope of the function in the graph above?

A) -2

B) $-\dfrac{1}{2}$

C) $\dfrac{1}{2}$

D) 2

CONTINUE

5

A line in the *xy*-plane passes through the point $(1, 1)$ and has a slope of $\frac{1}{3}$. Which of the following points lies on the line?

A) $(0, 0)$

B) $(4, 3)$

C) $(6, 3)$

D) $(7, 3)$

8

$$(n^3 - 3n^2 + 5)(n^2 - n)$$

Which of the following is equivalent to the above expression?

A) $n^5 - 4n^4 + 3n^3 + 5n^2 - 5n$

B) $n^5 - n^4 - 3n^3 + 8n^2 - 5n$

C) $n^5 - 3n^4 + 5n^2$

D) $n^5 - 4n^4 + 3n^3$

6

What is the value of i^8? (Note: $i = \sqrt{-1}$).

A) -1

B) $-i$

C) 1

D) i

9

$$x - 8 = y$$
$$x = y^2 + 16y + 64$$

Which of the following values of y gives the same value of x in the system of equations above?

A) 8

B) 4

C) -4

D) -8

7

A computer programmer can write 3 pages of HTML code in 5 hours and 2 pages of JavaScript code in 3 hours. How many hours will it take her to create 6 new websites, each consisting of one page of HTML code and one page of JavaScript?

A) 18

B) 19

C) 20

D) 21

CONTINUE

10

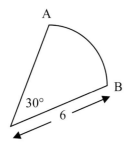

Note: figure is not drawn to scale.

What is the length of arc AB in the figure above?

A) 2π

B) $\dfrac{3\pi}{2}$

C) π

D) $\dfrac{\pi}{2}$

11

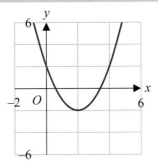

If $f(x) = (x - 2)^2$, which of the following equations represents the graph shown above?

A) $y = f(x) - 2$

B) $y = f(x - 2)$

C) $\dfrac{f(x)}{2}$

D) $y = f(x) + 2$

12

$$y = 5n + 6$$
$$y = n^2 - 2n - 24$$

Which value of n gives the same value of y in both of the above equations?

A) 0

B) 5

C) 10

D) 15

CONTINUE

13

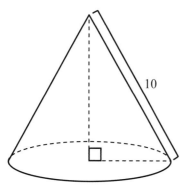

Note: figure is not drawn to scale.

What is the volume of the cone in the diagram above if the diameter of the base is 16?

A) 32π

B) 96π

C) 128π

D) 192π

14

$$y = \frac{3x^2 + 14x - 25 + 3x^2 - 2x - 23}{3x^2 + 3x - 18}$$

Based on the equation above, for which of the following values of x is y undefined?

A) -3

B) -2

C) 3

D) 6

15

The electrostatic force, F, between two charged particles can be modeled by the equation $F = k_e \frac{q_1 q_2}{r^2}$, where k_e is Coulomb's constant, q_1 and q_2 are the magnitudes of the charges, and r is the distance between them. If the distance between the two charges were doubled, what would happen to the electrostatic force between them?

A) It would double.

B) It would decrease by half.

C) It would quadruple.

D) It would decrease by three quarters.

CONTINUE

DIRECTIONS

Questions **16-20** ask you to solve a problem and enter your answer in the grid provided on your answer sheet. When completing grid-in questions:

1. You are required to bubble in the circles for your answers. It is recommended, but not required, that you also write your answer in the boxes above the columns of circles. Points will be awarded based only on whether the circles are filled in correctly.

2. Fill in only one circle in a column.

3. You can start your answer in any column as long as you can fit in the whole answer.

4. For questions 16-20, no answers will be negative numbers.

5. **Mixed numbers,** such as $4\frac{2}{5}$, must be gridded as decimals or improper fractions, such as 4.4 or as 22/5. "42/5" will be read as "forty-two over five," not as "four and two-fifths."

6. If your answer is a **decimal** with more digits than will fit on the grid, you may round it or cut it off, but you must fill the entire grid.

7. If there are **multiple correct solutions** to a problem, all of them will be considered correct. Enter only **one** on the grid.

CONTINUE

16

$$y = -\frac{2}{3}x + 1$$

Line L is represented by the equation above in the xy-plane. If Line M is perpendicular to line L, what is the slope of Line M?

17

Truck drivers for a delivery company received a total of $2,000 in bonuses. Truck drivers who completed their deliveries early received a bonus of $200, and truck drivers who completed their deliveries on time received a bonus of $100. If at least one truck driver received a bonus for completing a delivery on time, what is the largest possible number of bonuses that were received for completing deliveries early?

18

If $f(x) = x^2 - 5x + 1$ and $g(x) = f(2x)$, what is $g(3)$?

19

$$\sqrt{4x^2 - 16} = 3$$

If $x > 0$, what is the solution of the equation above?

20

A person's basal metabolic rate, BMR, is the minimum energy the person requires to survive. BMR depends on a person's age, gender, height, and weight. A twenty-five year old man who is six feet tall and weighs 150 pounds has a BMR of 1700 kilocalories per day. A twenty-five year old man who is six feet tall and weighs 190 pounds has a BMR of 1940 kilocalories per day. For every additional 10 pounds gained, BMR increases by k kilocalories per day, where k is a constant. What is the value of k?

STOP

If you complete this section before the end of your allotted time, you may check your work on this section only. Do NOT use the time to work on another section.

Math Test – Calculator

55 MINUTES, 38 QUESTIONS

Turn to Section 4 of your answer sheet to answer the questions in this section.

DIRECTIONS

Questions **1-30** ask you to solve a problem, select the best answer among four choices, and fill in the corresponding circle on your answer sheet. Questions **31-38** ask you to solve a problem and enter your answer in the grid provided on your answer sheet. There are detailed instructions on entering answers into the grid before question 31. You may use your test booklet for scratch work.

NOTES

1. You **may** use a calculator.
2. Variables and expressions represent real numbers unless stated otherwise.
3. Figures are drawn to scale unless stated otherwise.
4. Figures lie in a plane unless stated otherwise.
5. The domain of a function f is defined as the set of all real numbers x for which $f(x)$ is also a real number, unless stated otherwise.

REFERENCE

      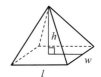

$$A = \frac{1}{2}bh \qquad a^2 + b^2 = c^2 \qquad \text{Special Triangles} \qquad V = \frac{1}{3}lwh \qquad V = \frac{1}{3}\pi r^2 h$$

$$A = lw \qquad V = lwh \qquad V = \pi r^2 h \qquad A = \pi r^2 \qquad V = \frac{4}{3}\pi r^3$$
$$C = 2\pi r$$

There are 360° in a circle.

The sum of the angles in a triangle is 180°.

The number of radians of arc in a circle is 2π.

CONTINUE

1

Research shows that every thirty minutes, a certain virus infects 16 more organisms. If the virus has infected 47 organisms after one hour, how many organisms were originally infected?

A) 0

B) 8

C) 15

D) 71

2

Day	Number of Manuscripts Edited
Tuesday	m
Wednesday	$2.5m$
Thursday	$3.5m$
Friday	$4m$

Bartleby edits manuscripts at a rate according to m, as defined in the chart above. If he works every day, begins editing on Tuesday, and edits 33 manuscripts by the end of the day on Friday, what is the value of m?

A) 2

B) 3

C) 4

D) 5

3

Skye spends $1.75 per day on online newspaper subscriptions. How much does she spend for the months of July, August, and September combined? (July and August each have 31 days and September has 30 days).

A) $52.50

B) $108.50

C) $161.00

D) $161.50

4

If $\dfrac{x}{y} = 4$, what is the value of $\dfrac{6x}{y}$?

A) 6

B) 16

C) 24

D) 36

5

$$3(x + 5) + 7 = 22$$

What is the value of x in the equation above?

A) 0

B) $\dfrac{3}{7}$

C) $\dfrac{7}{3}$

D) 11

CONTINUE

6

Traffic Regulation Survey Results					
Age	18-34	35-54	55-74	75 and older	Total
Support	24	62	71	44	201
Oppose	53	32	32	18	135
Total	77	94	103	62	336

A city is considering a new traffic regulation. City planners conducted a survey of a random sample of adult residents about their position on the new regulation, and the results of the survey are summarized in the chart above. Which of the following statements is supported by the chart's data?

A) A person between 35 and 54 years old is less likely to oppose the regulation than a person between 55 and 74 years old.

B) A person between 35 and 54 years old is equally likely to oppose the regulation as a person between 55 and 74 years old.

C) A person between 18 and 34 years old is more likely to oppose the regulation than a person between 55 and 74 years old.

D) The data is insufficient to support any of the statements above.

7

$$y = x^2 + 5x - 4$$
$$y = 6x + 2$$

If (x, y) is a solution to the system of equations above, which of the following is a possible value of xy?

A) −200

B) −20

C) 6

D) 60

8

In the xy-plane, the line $kx - 6y = 24$ passes through the point $(3, 6)$. What is the value of k?

A) 6

B) 12

C) 20

D) 60

9

Which of the expressions below are equivalent to $5x^2 + 13x - 6$?

  I. $(5x - 2)(x + 3)$
 II. $(x - 2)(5x + 3)$
III. $5(x - 2)(x + 3)$

A) I only

B) II only

C) III only

D) I, II, and III

10

$$|x - 4| \leq 6$$

Which of the following inequalities is equivalent to the inequality above?

A) $-2 \leq x \leq 10$

B) $-4 \leq x \leq 10$

C) $x \leq 4$ or $x \geq 10$

D) $x \leq -10$ or $x \geq 2$

CONTINUE

11

x	0	3	6	9
$f(x)$	2	6	10	14

Which of the following equations defines $f(x)$ in the table above?

A) $f(x) = \dfrac{4}{3}x + 2$

B) $f(x) = \dfrac{3}{4}x + 1$

C) $f(x) = -\dfrac{4}{3}x$

D) $f(x) = 4x + 2$

12

$$y = t^2 + 4t + 10$$

Which of the following scenarios could be modeled by y in the equation above, where t represents time?

A) A population of ladybugs that doubles every four weeks.

B) The height of a rock that is dropped off a ten-foot cliff.

C) The height of a hot air balloon that accelerates as it rises.

D) The value of an investment that increases by 5% every quarter.

13

Employment Status of Residents in Franklin County			
Education Level	Employed	Unemployed or Not in Labor Force	Total
Less than High School Diploma	198	164	362
High School Graduate	510	318	828
Some College	367	153	520
College Graduate	707	216	923
Total	1782	851	2633

The table above shows data from a survey of the employment status of residents in Franklin County. The participants were randomly selected from all residents over the age of 25 years old. Based on the given data, what is the likelihood that an employed worker over the age of 25 has not attended college, to the nearest tenth of a percent?

A) 28.6%

B) 39.7%

C) 54.7%

D) 59.5%

CONTINUE

14

Genetic Divergence of Species

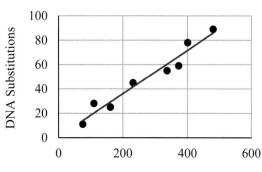

Time (millions of years)

The number of differences in two species' DNA sequences can be used to estimate when those species branched off from a common ancestor. The plot above shows the number of substitutions, S, in the DNA sequence of bonobos compared to the DNA sequence of humans. If the time, T, since the species shared a common ancestor is measured in millions of years, which of the following equations is the best estimate for the plot's line of best fit?

A) $S = 0.2T$

B) $S = 0.2T + 10$

C) $S = 5.5T$

D) $S = 5.5T + 10$

15

$$x^2 + 2x - 2$$
$$3x^2 - x - 1$$

What is the product of the two expressions above?

A) $3x^4 + 5x^3 - 9x^2 + 2$

B) $3x^4 + 5x^3 - 9x^2 + 2x$

C) $3x^4 + 5x^3 - 8x^2 + 2x$

D) $3x^4 + 5x^3 - 8x^2 + 2x + 2$

Questions 16 and 17 refer to the following information.

The nine-banded armadillo, frequently found in the southern United States, eats roughly 500 different kinds of foods. Around 10% of its daily intake consists of plants. Female armadillos over 1 year of age commonly give birth to quadruplets and may give birth to over 50 young in a lifetime. The chart below shows the population of the nine-banded armadillo in a rural district from 2012–2014. The population counts were taken at the beginning of each year.

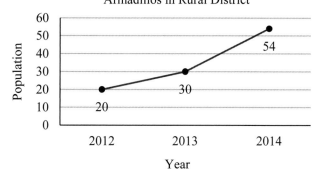

Armadillos in Rural District

16

If the average nine-banded armadillo eats 3 pounds of food per day, what is the approximate weight of plant matter, in pounds, consumed by 3 armadillos in one week?

A) 2.1

B) 6.3

C) 21

D) 63

CONTINUE

17

There were 5 females that had litters in 2012, and 12 females had litters in 2013. Assuming that 4 baby armadillos were born with every litter, how many armadillos did not survive between 2012 and 2014?

A) 24

B) 34

C) 40

D) 54

18

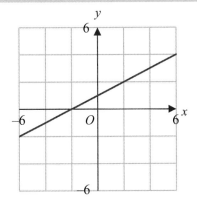

If $f(x)$ is equal to y in the xy-coordinate plane, which of the following functions represents the graph above?

A) $f(x) = \dfrac{1}{2}x + 1$

B) $f(x) = -\dfrac{1}{2}x + 1$

C) $f(x) = 2x - 1$

D) $f(x) = -\dfrac{1}{2}x - 1$

19

Data Set A: 1, 1, 2, 4, 4, 6
Data Set B: 2, 2, 3, 3, 5

Which of the following statements is supported by the information provided above?

A) Data Set A has a larger mean than Data Set B; Data Set A has a larger standard deviation than Data Set B.

B) Data Set A has a larger mean than Data Set B; Data Set A has a smaller standard deviation than Data Set B.

C) Data Set A and Data Set B have the same mean; Data Set A has a larger standard deviation than Data Set B.

D) Data Set A and Data Set B have the same mean; Data Set A has a smaller standard deviation than Data Set B.

CONTINUE

20

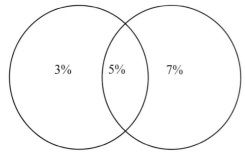

Affected Directly   Affected Indirectly

3%   5%   7%

The chart above shows data on how an increase in the number of school music programs affects students in schools. At Shelby High School, 56 students, 8% of the total student population, have indicated that they are directly affected by an increase in the school's music programs. Based on the data above, what is the best estimate for the number of students who are only affected indirectly by an increase in the school's music programs?

A)   49

B)   79

C)   84

D)   141

21

An auto dealership is offering a deal on used cars. The final sale price of each car is 5% off the pre-sale price, plus an additional 1% off the pre-sale price for every 10,000 miles on the car's odometer. Kara is considering two cars at the dealership. Car 1 has a pre-sale price of $4,500 with 80,000 miles on its odometer, and Car 2 has a pre-sale price of $5,200 with 20,000 miles on its odometer. What is the difference, rounded to the nearest dollar, between the sale prices of Car 1 and Car 2?

A) $903

B) $908

C) $921

D) $926

22

$$2y = \frac{x}{5} - 1$$

$$y = \frac{2x + 8}{3}$$

What is the solution to the system of equations above?

A)   There are no solutions.

B) $\left(-\frac{95}{17}, -\frac{18}{17}\right)$

C) $\left(-\frac{85}{19}, -\frac{18}{19}\right)$

D)   There are infinitely many solutions.

CONTINUE

23

Package 1   Package 2

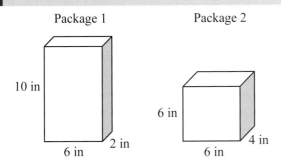

10 in

6 in   2 in

6 in

6 in   6 in   4 in

The figures above show two options for packaging. The material required for Package 1 is 184 square inches, and the material required for Package 2 is 168 square inches. A company measures package efficiency as package volume per square inch of packaging material. Which of the following statements is true?

A) Package 1 is more efficient than Package 2 by approximately 0.20 cubic inches per square inch.

B) Package 1 is more efficient than Package 2 by approximately 0.37 cubic inches per square inch.

C) Package 2 is more efficient than Package 1 by approximately 0.20 cubic inches per square inch.

D) Package 2 is more efficient than Package 1 by approximately 0.37 cubic inches per square inch.

24

If you flip 2 fair coins at the same time, what is the probability that exactly one will come up tails?

A) $\frac{3}{4}$

B) $\frac{1}{2}$

C) $\frac{1}{4}$

D) 0

25

Change in Teens' Physical Activity

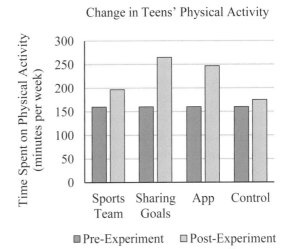

A psychologist conducted a study to compare different methods of encouraging teenagers to participate in physical activities. The three methods studied were obligatory participation on a sports team, sharing personal goals with a friend, and recording physical activity on an interactive smartphone app. Participants were randomly assigned to one of these methods or a control group. The study measured the participants' increase in physical activity one month after the experiment. The results are shown in the bar graph above. Which of the following statements is supported by the graph?

A) Participation on a sports team was the most effective of the methods studied for increasing physical activity.

B) When compared with the control group, every method that was studied improved the teens' physical activity at the time of the post-study measurement.

C) Teens' physical activity will decline over time if no method is employed to encourage it.

D) Joining a sports team helped teens improve their cardiovascular stamina.

CONTINUE

Questions 26 and 27 refer to the following information.

Results from the 2007 census for the Mining, Quarrying, and Oil and Gas Extracting sector of the U.S. economy are compared to census results from 1997 and 2002. The comparison of the sector based on establishments with more than one employee is summarized in the table below.

Mining, Quarry, and Oil and Gas Extracting Economic Sector for the U.S.			
	1997	2002	2007
Number of Establishments	25,000	24,087	22,667
Value of Shipments ($ Millions)	173,985	182,911	413,525
Annual Payroll ($ Millions)	20,798	21,174	40,687
Total Employment	509,006	477,840	730,433
Payroll Per Employee ($)	40,861	44,312	55,703
US Total Population	272,646,925	287,625,193	301,231,207
US Population Per Establishment	10,906	11,941	13,289

26

Which of the following statements is true for the period from 2002 to 2007?

A) Value of shipments decreased because number of establishments decreased.

B) Value of shipments increased by more than 100%.

C) Payroll per employee decreased because total employment increased.

D) Total employment decreased by more than 5%.

27

An analyst compared the ratio of the value of shipments to annual payroll in 1997 to that same ratio in 2007. What is the approximate percentage growth, to the nearest tenth of a percent, of this ratio during this period?

A)   21.5%

B)   95.6%

C)   237.7%

D)   836.5%

CONTINUE

4

4

28

Salbutamol, a chemical used to treat asthma, has a biological half-life of 1.6 hours, which means that after 1.6 hours in the body, salbutamol loses half of the value of its therapeutic activity. If salbutamol's therapeutic activity starts at a value of 480, what is its value of therapeutic activity after the chemical has been in the body for 480 minutes?

A) 7

B) 15

C) 30

D) 60

29

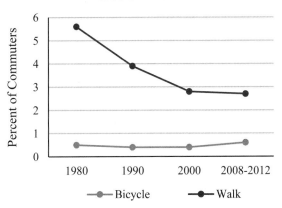

Walking and Bicycling to Work:
1980 to 2008-2012

Researchers conducted a study on commuters' choices of transportation to work. The chart above displays some of the data they collected. Which of the following statements is supported by the chart?

A) Walking was the most popular mode of transportation for commuters between 1980 and 2012.

B) The number of commuters who bicycled to work decreased from 1980 to 2000.

C) The percentage of commuters who walked to work decreased more slowly between 1980 and 1990 than between 1990 and 2000.

D) In 2000, about 6 times as many commuters walked to work as biked to work.

CONTINUE

30

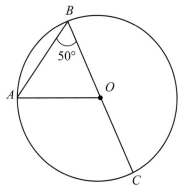

Note: figure is not drawn to scale.

In the diagram above, what is the length of arc AC if the radius of the circle is 10 and BC is the diameter?

A) $\dfrac{25\pi}{18}$

B) $\dfrac{25\pi}{9}$

C) $\dfrac{50\pi}{9}$

D) $\dfrac{100\pi}{9}$

CONTINUE

DIRECTIONS

Questions **31-38** ask you to solve a problem and enter your answer in the grid provided on your answer sheet. When completing grid-in questions:

1. You are required to bubble in the circles for your answers. It is recommended, but not required, that you also write your answer in the boxes above the columns of circles. Points will be awarded based only on whether the circles are filled in correctly.

2. Fill in only one circle in a column.

3. You can start your answer in any column as long as you can fit in the whole answer.

4. For questions 31-38, no answers will be negative numbers.

5. **Mixed numbers**, such as $4\frac{2}{5}$, must be gridded as decimals or improper fractions, such as 4.4 or as 22/5. "42/5" will be read as "forty-two over five," not as "four and two-fifths."

6. If your answer is a **decimal** with more digits than will fit on the grid, you may round it or cut it off, but you must fill the entire grid.

7. If there are **multiple correct solutions** to a problem, all of them will be considered correct. Enter only **one** on the grid.

CONTINUE

31

$$y = 0.25x + 5$$

In the equation above, what is the value of x if $y = 6$?

32

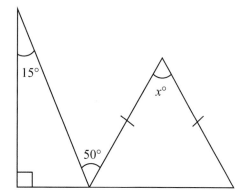

Note: figure is not drawn to scale.

In the diagram above, what is the value of x?

33

A farmer transports oranges in crates that each contain 5 pounds of oranges. The farmer can fit 16 crates in her truck, and the total revenue from one truckload of oranges is $96. What is the revenue, in dollars, from one pound of oranges?

34

If $f(x) = 6x + 1$ and $g(x) = 2x - 1$, what is the value of $\dfrac{f(3)}{g(f(0))}$?

35

A day is the amount of time it takes the Earth to rotate around its axis, and a year is the amount of time it takes the Earth to orbit the sun. The speed of the Earth's rotation has been slowly decreasing. Assume that 900 million years ago, one day was 18 hours long, whereas today it is 24 hours long and there are 365 days in a year. Assuming the Earth has always taken the same amount of time to orbit the sun as it does today, how many days did one year contain 900 million years ago? Round your answer to the nearest whole number.

CONTINUE

36

An object's mass in kilograms, m, is represented by the equation $3\sqrt{m} - \sqrt{162} = 0$. What is the object's mass in kilograms?

38

Susan would like to run 26 miles in 3 hours and 54 minutes. Currently, she can run 26 miles at a pace of 11 minutes/mile. If she plans on improving her pace by 15 seconds/mile every week, how many weeks will it take Susan to reach her goal?

Questions 37 and 38 refer to the following information.

Susan is training for a marathon. To track her progress, she has been keeping a record of her recent practice runs. The table below summarizes her training progress.

Time For Practice Runs		
Week	Distance (in miles)	Time (in minutes)
1	10	100
2	12	108
3	8	68
4	10	87
5	12	105

37

How much faster, in seconds, did Susan run each mile in Week 3 compared to Week 4?

STOP

If you complete this section before the end of your allotted time, you may check your work on this section only. Do NOT use the time to work on another section.

Essay (Optional)

50 MINUTES

Turn to the lined pages of your answer sheet to write your essay.

DIRECTIONS

This essay is optional. It is a chance for you to demonstrate how well you can understand and analyze a written passage. Your essay should show that you have carefully read the passage and should be a concisely written analysis that is both logical and clear.

You must write your entire essay on the lines in your answer booklet. No additional paper will be provided aside from the Planning Page inside your answer booklet. You will be able to write your entire essay in the space provided if you make use of every line, keep tight margins, and write at a suitable size. Don't forget to keep your handwriting legible for the readers evaluating your essay.

You will have 50 minutes to read the passage in this booklet and to write an essay in response to the prompt provided at the end of the passage.

REMINDERS

- What you write in this booklet will not be evaluated. Write your essay in the answer booklet only.

- Essays that are off-topic will not be evaluated.

As you read the following passage, consider how Christine Porath uses

- evidence, like examples or facts, to support her arguments.
- logical reasoning to develop her ideas and to connect her claims to her evidence.
- stylistic or persuasive techniques, such as the choice of particular words or appeals to her readers' emotions, to give power to the ideas put forth.

Adapted from Christine Porath, "No Time to Be Nice at Work." © 2015 by The New York Times Company. Originally published June 19, 2015.

1   Rudeness and bad behavior have all grown over the last decades, particularly at work. For nearly 20 years I've been studying, consulting, and collaborating with organizations around the world to learn more about the costs of this incivility. How we treat one another at work matters. Insensitive interactions have a way of whittling away at people's health, performance, and souls.

2   Robert M. Sapolsky, a Stanford professor and the author of *Why Zebras Don't Get Ulcers*, argues that when people experience intermittent stressors like incivility for too long or too often, their immune systems pay the price. We also may experience major health problems, including cardiovascular disease, cancer, diabetes, and ulcers.

3   Intermittent stressors—like experiencing or witnessing uncivil incidents or even replaying one in your head—elevate levels of hormones called glucocorticoids throughout the day, potentially leading to a host of health problems, including increased appetite and obesity. A study published in 2012 that tracked women for 10 years concluded that stressful jobs increased the risk of a cardiovascular event by 38 percent.

4   I've surveyed hundreds of people across organizations spanning more than 17 industries, and asked people why they behaved uncivilly. Over half of them claim it is because they are overloaded, and more than 40 percent say they have no time to be nice. But respect doesn't necessarily require extra time. It's about how something is conveyed; tone and nonverbal manner are crucial.

5   Incivility also hijacks workplace focus. According to a survey of more than 4,500 doctors, nurses, and other hospital personnel, 71 percent tied disruptive behavior, such as abusive, condescending, or insulting personal conduct, to medical errors, and 27 percent tied such behavior to patient deaths.

6   My studies with Amir Erez, a management professor at the University of Florida, show that people working in an environment characterized by incivility miss information that is right in front of them. They are no longer able to process it as well or as efficiently as they would otherwise.

7   In one study, the experimenter belittled the peer group of the participants, who then performed 33 percent worse on anagram word puzzles and came up with 39 percent fewer creative ideas during a brainstorming task focused on how they might use a brick. In our second study, a stranger—a "busy professor" encountered en route to the experiment—was rude to participants by admonishing them for bothering her. Their performance was 61 percent worse on word puzzles, and they produced 58 percent fewer ideas in the brick task than those who had not been treated rudely. We found the same pattern for those who merely witnessed incivility: they performed 22 percent worse on word puzzles and produced 28 percent fewer ideas in the brainstorming task.

8   Even though a growing number of people are disturbed by incivility, I've found that it has continued to climb over the last two decades. A quarter of those I surveyed in 1998 reported that they were treated rudely at work at least once a week. That figure rose to nearly half in 2005, then to just over half in 2011.

9   Although in surveys people say they are afraid they will not rise in an organization if they are really friendly and helpful, the civil do succeed. My recent studies with Alexandra Gerbasi and Sebastian Schorch at the Grenoble École de Management, published in the *Journal of Applied Psychology*, show that behavior involving politeness and regard for others in the workplace pays off. In a study in a biotechnology company, those seen as civil were twice as likely to be viewed as leaders.

10   Civility pays dividends. J. Gary Hastings, a retired judge in Los Angeles, told me that when he informally polled juries about what determined their favor, he found that respect—and how attorneys behaved—was crucial. Juries were swayed based on thin slices of civil or arrogant behavior.

11   Across many decisions—whom to hire, who will be most effective in teams, who will be able to be influential—civility affects judgments and may shift the balance toward those who are respectful.

12   Given the enormous cost of incivility, it should not be ignored. We all need to reconsider our behavior. You are always in front of some jury. In every interaction, you have a choice: Do you want to lift people up or hold them down?

Write an essay explaining how Christine Porath builds her argument to persuade her audience that civility should be more highly valued than it currently is. Analyze how Porath utilizes at least one of the features in the box above, or features of your own choosing, to make her argument more logical and persuasive. Your analysis should focus on the most relevant features of the passage.

You should not explain whether you agree with Porath's argument; rather, your essay should explain how Porath builds an argument to persuade her readers.

Practice Test 5

SAT

Directions

- Work on just one section at a time.

- If you complete a section before the end of your allotted time, use the extra minutes to check your work on that section only. Do NOT use the time to work on another section.

Using Your Test Booklet

- No credit will be given for anything written in the test booklet. You may use the test booklet for scratch paper.

- You are not allowed to continue answering questions in a section after the allotted time has run out. This includes marking answers on your answer sheet that you previously noted in your test booklet.

- You are not allowed to fold pages, take pages out of the test booklet, or take any pages home.

Answering Questions

- Each answer must be marked in the corresponding row on the answer sheet.

- Each bubble must be filled in completely and darkly within the lines.

Correct ●   Incorrect

- Be careful to bubble in the correct part of the answer sheet.

- Extra marks on your answer sheet may be marked as incorrect answers and lower your score.

- Make sure you use a No. 2 pencil.

Scoring

- You will receive one point for each correct answer.

- Incorrect answers will NOT result in points deducted. Even if you are unsure about an answer, you should make a guess.

DO NOT BEGIN THIS TEST

UNTIL YOUR PROCTOR TELLS YOU TO DO SO

For printable answer sheets, please visit **ivyglobal.com/study**.

Section 1

	A B C D		A B C D		A B C D		A B C D		A B C D
1	○ ○ ○ ○	12	○ ○ ○ ○	23	○ ○ ○ ○	34	○ ○ ○ ○	45	○ ○ ○ ○
2	○ ○ ○ ○	13	○ ○ ○ ○	24	○ ○ ○ ○	35	○ ○ ○ ○	46	○ ○ ○ ○
3	○ ○ ○ ○	14	○ ○ ○ ○	25	○ ○ ○ ○	36	○ ○ ○ ○	47	○ ○ ○ ○
4	○ ○ ○ ○	15	○ ○ ○ ○	26	○ ○ ○ ○	37	○ ○ ○ ○	48	○ ○ ○ ○
5	○ ○ ○ ○	16	○ ○ ○ ○	27	○ ○ ○ ○	38	○ ○ ○ ○	49	○ ○ ○ ○
6	○ ○ ○ ○	17	○ ○ ○ ○	28	○ ○ ○ ○	39	○ ○ ○ ○	50	○ ○ ○ ○
7	○ ○ ○ ○	18	○ ○ ○ ○	29	○ ○ ○ ○	40	○ ○ ○ ○	51	○ ○ ○ ○
8	○ ○ ○ ○	19	○ ○ ○ ○	30	○ ○ ○ ○	41	○ ○ ○ ○	52	○ ○ ○ ○
9	○ ○ ○ ○	20	○ ○ ○ ○	31	○ ○ ○ ○	42	○ ○ ○ ○		
10	○ ○ ○ ○	21	○ ○ ○ ○	32	○ ○ ○ ○	43	○ ○ ○ ○		
11	○ ○ ○ ○	22	○ ○ ○ ○	33	○ ○ ○ ○	44	○ ○ ○ ○		

Section 2

	A B C D		A B C D		A B C D		A B C D		A B C D
1	○ ○ ○ ○	10	○ ○ ○ ○	19	○ ○ ○ ○	28	○ ○ ○ ○	37	○ ○ ○ ○
2	○ ○ ○ ○	11	○ ○ ○ ○	20	○ ○ ○ ○	29	○ ○ ○ ○	38	○ ○ ○ ○
3	○ ○ ○ ○	12	○ ○ ○ ○	21	○ ○ ○ ○	30	○ ○ ○ ○	39	○ ○ ○ ○
4	○ ○ ○ ○	13	○ ○ ○ ○	22	○ ○ ○ ○	31	○ ○ ○ ○	40	○ ○ ○ ○
5	○ ○ ○ ○	14	○ ○ ○ ○	23	○ ○ ○ ○	32	○ ○ ○ ○	41	○ ○ ○ ○
6	○ ○ ○ ○	15	○ ○ ○ ○	24	○ ○ ○ ○	33	○ ○ ○ ○	42	○ ○ ○ ○
7	○ ○ ○ ○	16	○ ○ ○ ○	25	○ ○ ○ ○	34	○ ○ ○ ○	43	○ ○ ○ ○
8	○ ○ ○ ○	17	○ ○ ○ ○	26	○ ○ ○ ○	35	○ ○ ○ ○	44	○ ○ ○ ○
9	○ ○ ○ ○	18	○ ○ ○ ○	27	○ ○ ○ ○	36	○ ○ ○ ○		

Section 3 (No-Calculator)

	A	B	C	D		A	B	C	D		A	B	C	D		A	B	C	D		A	B	C	D
1	○	○	○	○	4	○	○	○	○	7	○	○	○	○	10	○	○	○	○	13	○	○	○	○
2	○	○	○	○	5	○	○	○	○	8	○	○	○	○	11	○	○	○	○	14	○	○	○	○
3	○	○	○	○	6	○	○	○	○	9	○	○	○	○	12	○	○	○	○	15	○	○	○	○

Only answers that are gridded will be scored. You will not receive credit for anything written in the boxes.

16   17   18   19   20

Section 4 (Calculator)

	A	B	C	D		A	B	C	D		A	B	C	D		A	B	C	D		A	B	C	D
1	○	○	○	○	7	○	○	○	○	13	○	○	○	○	19	○	○	○	○	25	○	○	○	○
2	○	○	○	○	8	○	○	○	○	14	○	○	○	○	20	○	○	○	○	26	○	○	○	○
3	○	○	○	○	9	○	○	○	○	15	○	○	○	○	21	○	○	○	○	27	○	○	○	○
4	○	○	○	○	10	○	○	○	○	16	○	○	○	○	22	○	○	○	○	28	○	○	○	○
5	○	○	○	○	11	○	○	○	○	17	○	○	○	○	23	○	○	○	○	29	○	○	○	○
6	○	○	○	○	12	○	○	○	○	18	○	○	○	○	24	○	○	○	○	30	○	○	○	○

Only answers that are gridded will be scored. You will not receive credit for anything written in the boxes.

31

32

33

34

35

Only answers that are gridded will be scored. You will not receive credit for anything written in the boxes.

36

37

38

Important: Use a No. 2 pencil. Write inside the borders.

You may use the space below to plan your essay, but be sure to write your essay on the lined pages. Work on this page will not be scored.

Use this space to plan your essay.

START YOUR ESSAY HERE.

Continue on the next page.

_____

_____

_____

_____

_____

_____

_____

_____

_____

_____

_____

_____

_____

_____

_____

_____

_____

_____

_____

_____

_____

_____

Continue on the next page.

Continue on the next page.

STOP.

Reading Test

65 MINUTES, 52 QUESTIONS

Turn to Section 1 of your answer sheet to answer the questions in this section.

DIRECTIONS

Every passage or paired set of passages is accompanied by a number of questions. Read the passage or paired set of passages, then use what is said or implied in what you read and in any given graphics to choose the best answer to each question.

Questions 1-10 are based on the following passage.

This passage is adapted from Benjamin L. Farjeon, *Devlin the Barber*. Originally published in 1880.

In an agony of horror and despair, he had flown from the printing office to my house. I cannot say whether he chose my house premeditatedly; it is
Line likely that it was done without distinct intention, but it
5 was proof that he regarded my friendship as genuine, and that he knew he could depend upon my sympathy in times of trouble. As indeed he could. My heart bled as I gazed upon him. The words issued with difficulty from his trembling lips; his features were convulsed;
10 he shook like a man in an ague.
"Oh, my Lizzie!" he moaned. "My poor, poor Lizzie! Oh, my child, my child!"
I took in regularly a penny daily newspaper, and I had read it this morning, but there was no mention
15 in its columns of the dreadful occurrence. The discovery had been made too late for the first editions of the daily journals.
Mr. Melladew's story being told, disjointedly, and in fragments which I had to piece together in
20 order to arrive at an intelligible comprehension of it, the unhappy man sat before me, moaning.
"Oh, my Lizzie! Oh, my poor child!"
"Was she at home?" I asked gently. "Was she at home when you went from here last night?" I did
25 not attempt to console him—of what avail were mere words at such a moment?

"Yes, she was there," he moaned. "When she went to bed I kissed her. For the last time! For the last, last time!"
30 And then he broke down utterly. I could get nothing further from him.
When she went to bed, he kissed her. What kind of riddle was here, in the midst of the horrible tragedy, that the hapless girl should have wished her parents
35 good-night and retired to rest, and be found ruthlessly murdered a few hours afterwards? With such joyful news as Mr. Melladew had to communicate to his daughter, the probability was that they had kept up later than usual, talking of the brighter future that then
40 seemed spread before them. It made the tragic riddle all the more difficult.
There came a knock at the street-door, and a gentleman was admitted, upon most urgent business, he said. It turned out that he was a newspaper
45 reporter, who, in advance of the police, had tracked Mr. Melladew to my house, and had come to obtain information from him for his newspaper. I pointed out to him the condition of Mr. Melladew, and said something to the effect that it was scarcely decent to
50 intrude upon him at such a time.
The reporter, who evidently felt deeply for the bereaved father, and whose considerate manner was such as to completely disarm me, said aside to me, "Pray do not think that I am devoid of feeling; I am a
55 father myself, and have a daughter of the age of his poor girl. My mission is not one of idle curiosity.

CONTINUE →

A ruthless murder has been committed, and the
murderer is at large. I am not working only for my
paper; I am assisting the cause of justice. Every
60 scrap of information we can obtain will hasten the
arrest of the wretch who has been guilty of a crime
so diabolical."

"He can tell you nothing," I said, compelled to
admit that he was right. "Look at him as he sits
65 there, crushed and broken down by the blow."

"I pity him from my heart," said the reporter.

1

Which choice best summarizes the passage?

A) A small town is distraught following the murder
of a little girl.

B) A detective gathers information to piece together
a terrible crime.

C) A man seeks support from a friend following his
daughter's murder.

D) A young woman is killed as an act of revenge in
a small town.

2

Based on the passage, which choice best describes the
relationship between the narrator and Mr. Melladew?

A) The narrator is a good friend of Mr. Melladew.

B) The narrator is a distant relative of Mr.
Melladew.

C) The narrator is a newspaper reporter at Mr.
Melladew's office.

D) The narrator is an inquisitive neighbor of Mr.
Melladew.

3

As used in line 1, "flown" most nearly means

A) fluttered.

B) strolled.

C) soared.

D) dashed.

4

The passage indicates that the narrator did not attempt
to console Mr. Melladew because

A) the narrator did not understand what had happened.

B) the narrator was also grieving deeply over the death.

C) the narrator knew nothing he could say would help.

D) the narrator could not sympathize with the
grieving father.

5

Which choice provides the best evidence for the
answer to the previous question?

A) Lines 13-15 ("I took … occurrence")

B) Lines 24-26 ("I did … moment")

C) Lines 63-64 ("He can … right")

D) Line 66 ("I pity … reporter")

6

The author uses the word "riddle" in line 33 to
indicate that the situation is

A) terribly puzzling.

B) meticulously organized.

C) oddly amusing.

D) highly problematic.

7

According to the narrator, what made the "tragic
riddle all the more difficult" (line 41)?

A) Mr. Melladew had kissed his daughter for the last
time before going to bed.

B) Mr. Melladew and his daughter had been
discussing their bright future late into the evening.

C) Mr. Melladew's daughter had just returned home
after a long time away.

D) Mr. Melladew and his wife had loved their
daughter deeply.

CONTINUE

8

Which choice best describes the narrator's initial view of the newspaper reporter?

A) The reporter was sensible for wanting to quickly make sense of a terrible crime.

B) The reporter was compassionate for coming to comfort Mr. Melladew.

C) The reporter was clever for tracking Mr. Melladew to the narrator's house.

D) The reporter was inconsiderate for disturbing Mr. Melladew in that moment.

9

Which choice provides the best evidence for the answer to the previous question?

A) Lines 44-46 ("It turned … house")

B) Lines 47-50 ("I pointed … time")

C) Lines 54-56 ("Pray do … girl")

D) Lines 59-62 ("Every scrap … diabolical")

10

As used in line 56, "idle" most nearly means

A) unoccupied.

B) pointless.

C) unemployed.

D) sluggish.

Questions 11-21 are based on the following passage and supplementary material.

This passage and graphic are adapted from Moshe Y. Vardi, "Are Robots Taking Our Jobs?". © 2016 by Moshe Y. Vardi.

Automation, driven by technological progress, has been increasing for the past several decades. Two schools of economic thought have for many years
Line been engaged in a debate about the potential effects of
5 automation on jobs, employment, and human activity: will new technology spawn mass unemployment as robots take jobs away from humans? Or will the jobs robots take over release or unveil—or even create—a demand for new human jobs? Are today's modern
10 technological innovations like those of the past, which made obsolete the job of buggy maker, but created the job of automobile manufacturer? Or is there something about today that is markedly different?
15   This is not a new concern. Dating back at least as far as the Luddites of early 19th-century Britain, new technologies cause fear about the inevitable changes they bring. It may seem easy to dismiss today's concerns as unfounded in reality, but economists
20 Jeffrey Sachs and Laurence Kotlikoff ask, "What if machines are getting so smart, thanks to their microprocessor brains, that they no longer need unskilled labor to operate?" There is considerable evidence that this concern may be justified.
25 Researchers Eric Brynjolfsson and Andrew McAfee recently wrote, "For several decades after World War II, the economic statistics we care most about all rose together here in America as if they were tightly coupled. At the same time, we created millions of
30 jobs, and many of these were the kinds of jobs that allowed the average American worker to enjoy a high and rising standard of living. GDP grew, and so did productivity—our ability to get more output from each worker. But … productivity growth and
35 employment growth started to become decoupled from each other."
     The U.S. economy has been performing quite poorly for the bottom 90 percent of Americans for the past 40 years. Technology is driving productivity
40 improvements, which grow the economy. But the

CONTINUE ➤

rising tide is not lifting all boats; most people are not seeing any benefit from this growth. While the U.S. economy is still creating jobs, it is not creating enough of them. The labor force participation rate,
45 which measures the active portion of the labor force, has been dropping since the late 1990s.

While manufacturing output is at an all-time high, manufacturing employment is today lower than it was in the later 1940s. Wages for private
50 nonsupervisory employees have stagnated since the late 1960s, and the wages-to-GDP ratio has been declining since 1970. Long-term unemployment is trending upwards, and inequality has become a global discussion topic.

55 Is automation, driven by progress in technology in general, and artificial intelligence and robotics in particular, the main cause for the economic decline of working Americans? In economics, it is easier to agree on the data than to agree on causality. Many
60 other factors can be in play, such as globalization, deregulation, decline of unions, and the like. Nevertheless, in a 2014 poll of leading academic economists, forty-three percent agreed with the statement that "information technology and
65 automation are a central reason why median wages have been stagnant in the U.S. over the decade, despite rising productivity," while only twenty-eight percent disagreed. Similarly, a 2015 study concluded that technological progress is a major
70 factor in the increase of inequality over the past decades.

The bottom line is that while automation is eliminating many jobs in the economy that were once done by people, there is no sign that the
75 introduction of technologies in recent years is creating an equal number of well-paying jobs to compensate for those losses. A 2014 Oxford study found that the number of U.S. workers shifting into newly created industries has been strikingly small:
80 in 2010, only 0.5 percent of the labor force was employed in industries that did not exist in 2000. The discussion about humans, machines, and work tends to be a discussion about some undetermined point in the far future, but it is time to face reality—
85 the future is now.

Economic Productivity and Average Real Earnings

The graphic is adapted from "Are Robots Taking Our Jobs?" by Moshe Y. Vardi. ©2016 by Moshe Y. Vardi.

11

The passage best supports which of the following conclusions about changes in the economy?

A) Automation has led to increased long-term unemployment in all industries.

B) Automation has led to revolutionary and beneficial change for all workers.

C) Automation has led to a fall in workers' wages below the poverty line.

D) Automation has led to decreased employment opportunities despite increased productivity.

12

Which of the following best supports the answer to the previous question?

A) Lines 9-12 ("Are today's … manufacturer")

B) Lines 15-18 ("Dating back … bring")

C) Lines 49-52 ("Wages for … 1970")

D) Lines 72-77 ("The bottom … losses")

CONTINUE

13

Which of the following situations is most similar to the problem described in the passage?

A) A restaurant fires servers after implementing an online ordering service.

B) Upon spotting a butterfly in the garden, a child drops her toys to chase after it.

C) A farmer sells his old tractor to a neighbor when he buys a larger one.

D) The creation of faster airplanes allows for easier international travel.

14

Which of the following does the author cite as a potential contributing factor to the economic decline of working Americans?

A) Workplace inequality

B) The collapse of major industries

C) The rise of unions

D) Globalization

15

As used in line 3, "schools" most nearly means

A) institutes.

B) foundations.

C) groups.

D) universities.

16

The author includes the series of questions at the end of the first paragraph (lines 6-14) in order to

A) define the perspectives of both sides of the debate.

B) emphasize the author's concern about technological progress.

C) urge readers to identify their own opinions on the subject.

D) pique readers' interest in the negative effects of automation.

17

Which choice provides the best evidence for the answer to the previous question?

A) Lines 1-2 ("Automation … decades")

B) Lines 2-5 ("Two schools … activity")

C) Lines 7-9 ("Or will … jobs")

D) Line 15 ("This is … concern")

18

As used in line 39, "driving" most nearly means

A) steering.

B) propelling.

C) hustling.

D) transporting.

CONTINUE

19

The author includes data from a poll and a study in the fifth paragraph (lines 55-71) to support his claim that

A) forty-three percent of Americans believe they are not paid enough.

B) automation is a major contributor to the economic decline of working Americans.

C) the American economy is unable to keep up with technological progress.

D) technological progress is the reason for wage inequality in America.

20

Data in the graphic provide most direct support for which idea in the passage?

A) Despite the increase in worker productivity in recent years, there has been a continuous decline in workers' wages.

B) Up until the 1970s, economic productivity and the employment rate increased concurrently.

C) Automation is eliminating jobs once done by people, and is not creating enough jobs to compensate for those losses.

D) In recent years, economic productivity has increased, but workers' wages have not.

21

According to the data in the graphic, the highest average wages most clearly occurred in what year?

A) 1965

B) 1975

C) 1985

D) 1987

Questions 22-31 are based on the following passages.

Passage 1 is adapted from "Why You Should Dispense With Antibacterial Soaps" by Sarah Ades and Kenneth Keiler. ©2016 by Sarah Ades and Kenneth Keiler. Passage 2 is adapted from "Cleaning Your Hands May Be More Complicated Than You Think" by Christine Carson. ©2014 by Christine Carson.

Passage 1

A recent US Food and Drug Administration ruling banned the use of triclosan, triclocarban, and seventeen other antiseptics from household soaps
Line because they have not been shown to be safe or even
5 to have any benefit. Today, an estimated 40 percent of soaps use at least one of these chemicals.

Despite the fact that soap and water are sufficient to remove pathogens, manufacturers in the 1990s began to incorporate triclosan and triclocarban into
10 products for the average consumer, and many people were attracted by claims that these products killed more bacteria. Triclosan became so prevalent in household products that a 2003 nationwide survey of healthy individuals found the chemical in the urine of
15 75 percent of the 2,517 people tested. Laboratory tests show the addition of these chemicals can reduce the number of bacteria in some situations. However, studies in a range of environments, including urban areas in the United States, have shown that the
20 addition of antibacterials in soap does not reduce the spread of infectious disease.

As a matter of fact, the effect of triclosan on antibiotic resistance in bacteria is a serious concern. Bacteria evolve resistance to nearly every threat they
25 face, and some of the common mechanisms that bacteria use to evade triclosan also help them evade antibiotics that are needed to treat disease. Following the introduction of triclosan into the market, bacteria with these resistance mechanisms grow stronger,
30 causing an increase of bacteria resistant to medical antibiotics and a potential spread of multi-drug resistance.

As resistance spreads, we will not be able to kill as many pathogens with existing drugs. Removing
35 triclosan from consumer products will help protect

CONTINUE

antibiotic drugs. To a large extent, this ruling is a victory of science over advertising.

Passage 2

Triclosan is a potent antibacterial agent that can kill most types of bacteria, both beneficial bacteria
40 and disease-causing ones. Its use in hospital hand washes has undoubtedly saved millions of lives by preventing infection. But it is also used at much lower concentrations in hundreds of household products including antibacterial liquid soaps—
45 concentrations at which they are often no more effective than plain soap and water.

Adding triclosan at such low levels in these products may even encourage bacteria to become resistant to antibiotics. Exposing bacteria to low
50 levels of germ-killing chemicals can activate the mechanisms they have to protect themselves against such chemicals—bacteria can thicken their outer walls, turn on pumps designed to expel toxic chemicals, and even produce enzymes to inactivate
55 the chemicals. Low levels of exposure that don't kill the bacteria entirely can prepare them to successfully defend themselves against later challenges.

Questions about the safety of triclosan have been
60 raised recently because evidence suggests some chemicals used widely in personal care products, including triclosan, can mimic or interfere with hormones, at least in laboratory-based experiments. If these endocrine-disrupting compounds have a
65 similar effect on humans, they could disrupt our bodies' delicately balanced endocrine systems.

In laboratory tests and animal models, triclosan has been shown to behave like the human hormone estrogen. It can dock at estrogen receptors on human
70 cells (maintained in the lab) and start a chain of cellular events in the same way that natural estrogen does. So far, there's no evidence showing that triclosan can do the same in humans, but new research shows very low daily doses of triclosan can
75 encourage cancer progression in mice that already have estrogen-dependent breast cancer.

This doesn't prove that triclosan is an endocrine-disrupting compound that mimics estrogen or that it

can promote breast cancer in humans, but it does
80 emphasize the critical need for more research into the effects of triclosan in humans, given its widespread use. In the meantime, plain soap and water may be the way to go for safe, clean hands.

22

The author of Passage 1 makes which of the following claims about triclosan?

A) Triclosan soap can reduce bacteria, but not as effectively as alcohol.

B) Triclosan soap is marketed as a more effective disinfectant than other soap.

C) Triclosan has directly caused the spread of multi-drug-resistant bacteria.

D) Triclosan was found in 75% of household soaps in a 2003 survey.

23

Which choice provides the best evidence for the answer to the previous question?

A) Lines 7-12 ("Despite … bacteria")

B) Lines 12-15 ("Triclosan … tested")

C) Lines 17-21 ("However … disease")

D) Lines 24-27 ("Bacteria … disease")

24

Which choice best describes the developmental pattern of Passage 1?

A) It introduces a ruling on a chemical, then explores reasons for the ruling.

B) It describes the history of a drug, then considers recent findings on the drug.

C) It discusses the serious dangers of an ingredient, then mentions possible benefits.

D) It raises an issue of sanitation, then investigates an issue of drug resistance.

CONTINUE

25

As used in line 12, "prevalent" most nearly means

A) flourishing.

B) pervasive.

C) accepted.

D) infamous.

26

The authors of Passage 1 most likely include the phrase "this ruling is a victory of science over advertising" (lines 36-37) in order to

A) illustrate the lack of respect they have for the sales strategies of large corporations.

B) repeat their approval for the FDA decision to ban triclosan from household soaps.

C) indicate that the ruling was triggered by controversy around the marketing of antibacterial soaps.

D) suggest that advertising of household products often conflicts with scientific research.

27

As used in line 71, "natural" most nearly means

A) ecological.

B) unprocessed.

C) biological.

D) humanistic.

28

The authors of both passages would most likely view antibacterial hand washes as

A) impractical, because of the unstable nature of the chemical triclosan.

B) acceptable, because they are effective and efficient in hospital settings.

C) advantageous, because they can kill more bacteria than regular soap.

D) problematic, because of their widespread use despite safety concerns.

29

Passage 1 differs from Passage 2 in that only Passage 2

A) mentions the marketing strategies of antibacterial soap manufacturers.

B) provides an in-depth examination of the chemical triclosan.

C) discusses safety concerns that pertain to human biological systems.

D) explores possible effects of triclosan on the endocrine system.

30

The author of Passage 2 would most likely respond to the FDA ruling in Passage 1 (lines 1-3) by saying that

A) triclosan need not be banned in household soaps because the safety concerns have yet to be proven true.

B) the ruling was prudent, given the unanswered safety questions that have been raised about triclosan.

C) the ruling was an effective start to the needed removal of estrogen from all household items.

D) no steps should be taken to avoid triclosan until more research is conducted.

31

Which choice provides the best evidence for the answer to the previous question?

A) Lines 40-42 ("Its use … infection")

B) Lines 55-58 ("Low levels … challenges")

C) Lines 69-72 ("It can … does")

D) Lines 79-82 ("It does … use")

CONTINUE

Questions 32-41 are based on the following passage.

This passage is adapted from Ada Deer's address to the Alaska Native Review Commission, delivered in 1984 in Anchorage, Alaska. Deer discusses the passage of the Menominee Termination Act, a 1961 law which stripped her tribe of its status, and which she helped to overturn in 1973 with the passage of the Menominee Restoration Act.

The Menominee Termination Act was passed in 1954, and it did not become final until 1961. Termination is a cultural, economic, and political

Line disaster, and my people, the Menominee people,
5   suffered great injustice as a result of this act. Many people today still do not understand the details of termination. They have only suffered the hardships and the injustices. One of the myths that has followed the Menominees over the years is that the
10 Menominees consented to termination, and I wish to correct that because that is not really true.

First of all, termination began as a simple piece of legislation in Congress. The Menominees had carried out a suit against the federal government for
15 mismanagement of their timber trust. They had won and had been awarded a sum of money, approximately eight and a half million dollars. Our congressman at that time was Congressman Melvin Laird. He introduced a simple per capita bill that
20 required that a fifteen hundred dollar per capita payment be given to each enrolled Menominee. The bill got through the House in that form, but when it got to the Senate, it was changed. Senator Arthur V. Watkins stated that if the Menominees wanted their
25 money, they would have to agree to termination.

There was a meeting out in our area. Most of our people showed their opposition and their displeasure and their lack of understanding by not even going to the meeting. Nonetheless, 169 people voted for the
30 idea of termination, and 5 people voted against it. However, this was only after Senator Watkins threatened that termination was going to happen no matter what the Menominees wanted. A few weeks later, after more of this matter had become
35 disseminated and people had a better idea of what this could mean, another meeting was called and, again, many people did not go because they did not

understand the importance of it. The vote was 159 to 0 against it.
40   However, Senator Watkins took that first vote to Congress and said that there was approval by the Menominees. At this point, there were approximately 3,000 people in our tribe; 169 to 5 or 159 to 0 is a very small percentage of people, and they certainly
45 were not well informed. The Termination Act became final in 1961.

The Menominees were no longer a federally-recognized tribe, no longer eligible for health and education services, and our rolls were to be closed. It
50 was a devastating act to the people of the tribe. A great social disorganization and psychological devastation resulted from termination. Many of our youngsters could not go on to vocational school and could not go on to college. Our hospital was closed,
55 and access to medical services became a serious problem. Many people suffered serious illnesses, and I'm certain that a number of people died because of the lack of medical care.

All the major policies on American Indians have
60 come from the top down. They have not come from the bottom up. They have not been based on the needs, the wishes, and the aspirations of the informed people at the grassroots level. In contrast, the Menominee Restoration Act came from the people,
65 came from the bottom up, and I'm very proud to say that it's my tribe that worked to demonstrate what can be done by a small group of people who utilize the political process and who keep in mind their convictions, their dedication, and their desires.
70   We formed a movement called D.R.U.M.S., Determination of Rights and Unity for Menominee Shareholders, and our thrust was to stop the land sales, to work for restoration, and to have Menominees in positions of power. This movement
75 started in about 1969 or 1970, and when you think about how long it takes to get a law through Congress, it was a very short time. Our Menominee restoration legislation was signed into law on December 22, 1973.
80   We set up a whole new tribal governmental structure. We have a nine-member tribal legislature with three people elected each year so we have

CONTINUE

continuity. We have the tribal legislature electing the
chair of the tribe on a one-year basis, so it's not a
85 popularity contest among the tribal members. We
have a trust and management agreement—we
decided not to call it a treaty—that spells out what
the Secretary of the Interior can and can't do, and
we are on the road now toward community
90 development.

32

The passage is written from the perspective of
someone who is

A) an active participant.

B) a detached observer.

C) a curious journalist.

D) a sympathetic outsider.

33

The author indicates that the Menominee
Termination Act began as a bill introduced in

A) the Senate by Melvin Laird.

B) the Senate by Arthur Watkins.

C) Congress by Melvin Laird.

D) Congress by Arthur Watkins.

34

Which situation is most similar to the one described
in lines 40-45 ("However … informed")?

A) A family unanimously agrees to go to their
favorite restaurant for dinner.

B) A census-taker visits every house in a
community to ensure accuracy.

C) A scientist uses a small sample size to yield a
desired result.

D) A university conducts a community dialogue in
response to an unpopular policy.

35

The central idea of the fifth paragraph (lines 47-58) is
that termination

A) caused the community's hospital to be relocated.

B) negatively impacted Menominee health,
education, and society.

C) ended a scholarship program that had helped
Menominee youth.

D) set a dangerous precedent for the government's
dealings with tribes.

36

As used in line 63, the phrase "people at the
grassroots level" most nearly means

A) members of farming communities.

B) nearby politicians and judges.

C) lawmakers in the federal government.

D) local community members.

37

In comparison to previous U.S. policies affecting
Native Americans, the creation of the Menominee
Restoration Act was

A) more participatory.

B) more secretive.

C) more sudden.

D) more exclusive.

38

Which choice provides the best evidence for the
answer to the previous question?

A) Lines 8-11 ("One of … true")

B) Lines 15-17 ("They had … dollars")

C) Lines 63-69 ("In contrast … desires")

D) Lines 77-79 ("Our Menominee … 1973")

CONTINUE

39

As used in line 70, "movement" most nearly means

A) political organization.

B) cultural trend.

C) deliberate march.

D) charitable cause.

40

The passage most strongly suggests that the process of passing laws in Congress is usually

A) lengthy.

B) expensive.

C) efficient.

D) exciting.

41

Which choice provides the best evidence for the answer to the previous question?

A) Lines 19-21 ("He introduced … Menominee")

B) Lines 31-33 ("However, this … wanted")

C) Lines 59-60 ("All the … down")

D) Lines 74-77 ("This movement … time")

Questions 42-52 are based on the following passage and supplementary material.

This passage is adapted from "Pollen Genetics Can Help with Forensic Investigations" by Karen L. Bell, Berry Brosi, and Kevin Burgess. ©2016 by Karen L. Bell, Berry Brosi, and Kevin Burgess.

Forensic palynology is the application of palynology—the study of pollen—to crime investigation. While usually unnoticeable, pollen is
Line essentially ubiquitous in terrestrial habitats and is
5 extremely tough. In fact, pollen is so durable that paleontologists can examine fossilized pollen grains in ancient sediments to see what plants grew during prehistoric times. And the "signature" of pollen grains is specific to a particular place (because different
10 plant species occur in different areas) and time (because different plant species blossom at different times).

Forensic palynology has been particularly useful in cases where there is suspected movement of
15 evidence, or where a crime has occurred in a location with distinct plant species. For example, following the Bosnian war, investigators uncovered mass graves where bodies had been moved from different locations. Pollen was one of the lines of evidence
20 used to trace bodies to their original burial sites. In a case in New Zealand, a burglar was tracked to the scene of the crime when pollen grains on his clothing were matched to an uncommon plant species growing in front of the victim's house.

25 While pollen is an ideal biomarker for linking people and objects to particular places and times, forensic palynology has been underutilized because of its reliance on experts to meticulously identify pollen under the microscope. Furthermore, it's often
30 impossible to determine the exact species of a grain by mere observation; identification is typically limited to a genus or a family of plants—a group of related species. This reduces the technique's effectiveness because while many plant species occur
35 in a small geographic range, the genus or family to which they belong may cover a much broader area.

But researchers have recently developed a new technique for identifying pollen, using genetics. Since it makes identification much easier and faster for

CONTINUE

40 large numbers of pollen samples, we believe this
development has the potential to transform forensic
palynology, allowing us to harness the power of
pollen to solve crimes.

DNA barcoding is a technique to identify species
45 using their specific genetic signatures. There are two
parts to the standardized sequence we use for plant
DNA barcoding. One is a section of the large
subunit of a gene called ribulose-1,5-bisphosphate
carboxylase/oxygenase (rbcL); the other is a gene
50 called maturase-K (matK). Once an investigator
sequences these gene regions from a sample, they
can be compared against a database containing all
the known DNA sequences of rbcL and matK to
identify the species.

55 To DNA barcode pollen, the first step is to
extract the DNA. Each pollen grain has a tough,
protective outer layer called the exine. In order to
release the DNA inside, we break the exine by
putting the pollen grains in a tube filled with small
60 silica beads and shaking vigorously for several
minutes. Once the cells release their DNA, it can be
purified and then sequenced.

High-throughput DNA sequencing is a
methodological advance that has made pollen DNA
65 barcoding feasible. This new method allows
researchers to sequence multiple pieces of DNA at
the same time, without separating them first. It's a
key innovation because forensic pollen samples
typically contain a mixture of species. Without high-
70 throughput sequencing, these species would first
need to be painstakingly separated—and then we'd
be back to the same efficiency problems of
traditional morphological analysis. With high-
throughput sequencing, the whole mixture of pollen
75 grains can be ground up in one sample, the DNA
isolated and sequenced, and matched to a
database. This technique is known as DNA
metabarcoding.

We still need to optimize and standardize these
80 methods before official use in forensic
investigations; we also need to expand the reference
databases and include more species that may be of
interest to forensic specialists. While there are still
hurdles to overcome, pollen DNA barcoding could

85 become a commonly used and scientifically rigorous
technique in law enforcement and national security.

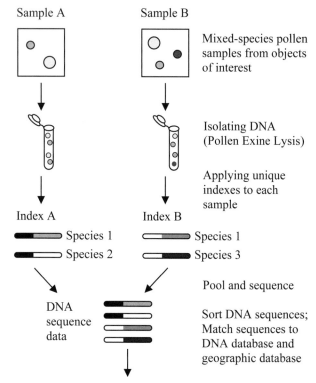

Inferred origin of objects of interests

Adapted from "Review and future prospects for DNA barcoding
methods in forensic palynology." © 2015 by Elesvier Ireland.

42

The passage is primarily concerned with establishing
that

A) pollen exine analysis should be used as evidence
in forensic investigations around the world.

B) identifying pollen species is more labor-intensive
and time-consuming than identifying pollen
families.

C) a new technique could increase the usefulness of
pollen genetics in forensic investigations.

D) despite technological advances, observation
under the microscope remains the most reliable
technique for examining pollen.

CONTINUE

43

Which choice provides the best evidence for the answer to the previous question?

A) Lines 1-3 ("Forensic palynology … investigation")

B) Lines 25-29 ("While pollen … microscope")

C) Lines 44-45 ("DNA barcoding … signatures")

D) Lines 83-86 ("While there … security")

44

Which choice best describes the structure of the passage as a whole?

A) It explains a new scientific field, then analyzes practical applications of research in that field.

B) It introduces the evolution of a plant species, then lists the uses of that plant species.

C) It identifies a problem with an existing technique, then describes a potential solution to the problem.

D) It describes a new field of work, then explores the history of related fields of work.

45

It can be reasonably inferred that the authors view forensic palynology with

A) frustration.

B) relief.

C) concern.

D) optimism.

46

Which choice provides the best evidence for the answer to the previous question?

A) Lines 8-12 ("And the … times")

B) Lines 33-36 ("This reduces … area")

C) Lines 37-38 ("But researchers … genetics")

D) Lines 38-43 ("Since it … crimes")

47

As used in line 20, "trace" most nearly means

A) draw.

B) track.

C) copy.

D) transport.

48

What function does the fifth paragraph (lines 44-54) serve in the passage as a whole?

A) To describe the scientific background of the DNA of pollen

B) To contrast mundane, traditional techniques of the past

C) To explain the DNA barcoding technique

D) To provide evidence for the labor-intensive nature DNA barcoding

49

As used in line 65, "feasible" most nearly means

A) likely.

B) suitable.

C) possible.

D) beneficial.

50

Information from the graphic supports which of the following statements?

A) Pollen grains must be initially separated in samples in order to identify species.

B) Pollen samples often contain two or three different species.

C) During DNA barcoding, pollen DNA must be sequenced before it can be isolated.

D) Multiple pollen species can share a single DNA barcode.

CONTINUE

51

According to the passage and the graphic, the purpose of searching a geographic database is to

A) determine where the object of study came from.

B) study the geographic range where a specific plant genus occurs.

C) identify species-specific genetic signatures.

D) obtain pollen samples from plants in their natural habitat.

52

Based on the graphic and the passage, what is the purpose of the first step in barcoding?

A) To amplify the barcoding marker

B) To sequence DNA

C) To identify pollen species

D) To isolate the DNA

STOP

If you complete this section before the end of your allotted time, you may check your work on this section only. Do NOT use the time to work on another section.

Writing and Language Test

35 MINUTES, 44 QUESTIONS

Turn to Section 2 of your answer sheet to answer the questions in this section.

DIRECTIONS

Every passage comes with a set of questions. Some questions will ask you to consider how the writer might revise the passage to improve the expression of ideas. Other questions will ask you to consider correcting potential errors in sentence structure, usage, or punctuation. There may be one or more graphics that you will need to consult as you revise and edit the passage.

Some questions will refer to a portion of the passage that has been underlined. Other questions will refer to a particular location in a passage or ask that you consider the passage in full.

After you read the passage, select the answers to questions that most effectively improve the passage's writing quality or that adjust the passage to follow the conventions of standard written English. Many questions give you the option to select "NO CHANGE." Select that option in cases where you think the relevant part of the passage should remain as it currently is.

Questions 1-11 are based on the following passage.

If You Build It...

By the time Anne Hamilton turned 20, she was one of the most powerful women in Scotland. Her father, Sir James Hamilton, first Duke of **1** Hamilton and an advisor to King Charles I, had been executed during Britain's Wars of the Three Kingdoms. **2** Because Anne was James's true heir, James felt that a man would be better able to represent the political and financial interests of the family, so he left his titles and estates to

1

A) NO CHANGE

B) Hamilton, and an,

C) Hamilton and, an

D) Hamilton, and an

2

A) NO CHANGE

B) Although

C) As

D) In order that

CONTINUE ➤

his younger [3] brother William! However, when William died from wounds sustained at the Battle of Worcester in 1651, he left [4] the entire kit and kaboodle to Anne. She became Duchess of Hamilton, Marchioness of Clydesdale, Countess of Arran, Lanark, and Cambridge, and the Lady Aven, Innerdale, Machanshire, and Polmont.

Along with the titles, Anne inherited enormous debts, which led to the confiscation of many of the family estates. [5] Anne was also responsible for her younger sister, Susanna, and for the children of her uncle William. Anne moved the family into a barn near the family palace. Despite her reduced circumstances, Anne found a suitable [6] husband, William Douglas, the Earl of Selkirk, whom she married in 1656, when she was 24.

[3]

A) NO CHANGE
B) brother, William,
C) brother William.
D) brother William?

[4]

A) NO CHANGE
B) a bunch of stuff
C) everything
D) the whole nine yards

[5]

At this point the writer is considering adding the following sentence.

> Confiscation is sometimes still used to resolve debts today.

Should the writer make this addition here?

A) Yes, because it clarifies the meaning of an important concept.
B) Yes, because it shows that the estates were not taken by force.
C) No, because it contradicts information from earlier in the paragraph.
D) No, because the information is unnecessary and irrelevant.

[6]

A) NO CHANGE
B) husband William Douglas the Earl of Selkirk
C) husband William Douglas, the Earl of Selkirk,
D) husband William, Douglas the Earl of Selkirk;

CONTINUE

Together, they [7] raise money to pay off the family debt, and Anne asked King Charles II to make her husband the Duke of Hamilton, [8] which secured the title for generations to come and ownership of the estates.

[9] Anne ignored the future, choosing instead to focus on the family's glorious history. In 1684, she and her husband began a major home renovation project that they called their "Great Design." They demolished three sides of the palace and built two new wings. The palace was finished in about 1701, following William's death in 1694. Eventually, under Anne and William's descendants, Hamilton Palace would become the largest private residence in the western hemisphere. Anne died in 1716 at the age of 84.

7

A) NO CHANGE

B) were raising

C) had raised

D) raised

8

A) NO CHANGE

B) which secured the title and ownership of the estates for generations to come.

C) which secured the title and ownership for generations to come of the estates.

D) which secured for generations the title and ownership of the estates to come.

9

Which choice provides the most appropriate introduction to the paragraph?

A) NO CHANGE

B) The titles that Anne had secured were not purely honorific: they conferred real social and legal advantages.

C) After securing the estates, Anne made sure that the family would have a palace worthy of its position.

D) Anne had finally saved the family's home and the family's honor.

CONTINUE

[1] Despite Anne's efforts to ensure that Hamilton Palace would endure, it was sold in 1921, and the new owners decided to demolish it. [2] The demolition took over a decade to complete; by the time it was finished, only the family mausoleum still stood. [3] Parts of the **10** home, were sold off. [4] Now, however, the drawing room has been returned to Scotland, where part of it is on display in the National Museum in Edinburgh. [5] Thus, 300 years after her death, Anne Hamilton's legacy persists. [6] In fact, the American press tycoon William Randolph Hearst bought eleven rooms, including Anne's drawing room, and had them installed in his California castle. **11**

10

A) NO CHANGE

B) home were

C) home: were

D) home; were

11

To make this paragraph most logical, sentence 6 should be placed

A) where it is now.

B) before sentence 2.

C) before sentence 4.

D) before sentence 5.

CONTINUE

Questions 12-22 are based on the following passage and supplementary material.

Radiocarbon Dating

　　Radiocarbon dating, which [12] help scientists to calculate the age of organic material, has revolutionized archaeology and geology. [13] Since it's invention in the 1940s, it has helped to establish the age of numerous specimens, including a prehistoric forest and a body frozen for millennia in the Alps.

　　Radiocarbon dating operates on fairly simple principles. Its originator, Willard Libby, realized that living things contain not only carbon but also the radioactive isotope carbon-14. When a plant or an animal is [14] lively, the proportion of carbon-14 to other isotopes of carbon in its body is the same as in the atmosphere. However, when the organism dies, the carbon-14 begins to decay. Because carbon-14 breaks down [15] of a predictable rate, it's possible to tell how old a preserved sample is by measuring how much of the isotope remains in the sample.

12

A) NO CHANGE
B) are helping
C) helps
D) have helped

13

A) NO CHANGE
B) It's
C) Its
D) Since its

14

A) NO CHANGE
B) alive,
C) enlivened,
D) livid,

15

A) NO CHANGE
B) for
C) of
D) at

CONTINUE

Of course, this procedure can't tell us everything, and the results often need careful interpretation. Since carbon-14 **16** gains half of its total amount every 5,700 years, any object older than 50,000 years won't have enough carbon-14 to test. The process also typically has about a 200-year margin of error, meaning that we still can't know the precise moment of the organism's death. **17** Before the ban on above-ground nuclear testing in 1963, there was a spike in the levels of carbon-14 in the air. Finally, because the amount of carbon-14 in the atmosphere has fluctuated over time, scientists must correct for external factors to get an accurate result.

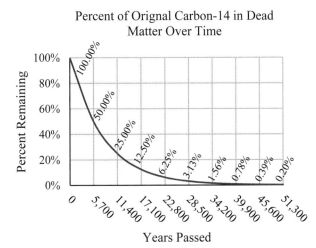

Percent of Orignal Carbon-14 in Dead Matter Over Time

16

Which choice offers the most correct interpretation of the data in the graph?

A) NO CHANGE

B) loses half of its total amount every 5,700 years,

C) loses half of its total amount every 10,000 years,

D) loses half of its total amount every 500 years,

17

Which of the following choices best supports the paragraph's claim that carbon-14 dating isn't always completely accurate?

A) NO CHANGE

B) Carbon takes other forms, too, including "allotypes" like diamonds and graphite; it's remarkable just how multifaceted this element is.

C) Furthermore, since isotope decay begins at the death of the biological organism, an artifact made from old wood (to name one example) might be newer than the test indicates.

D) Many other scientific procedures also have some margin of error, however small; the same applies for political polling.

CONTINUE

Scientists typically use radiocarbon dating in concert with other kinds of analysis. [18] After hikers found "Ötzi," a mummy preserved in ice, on the alpine border between Italy and Austria in 1991, investigators initially assumed he had perished in an avalanche in recent times. However, his [19] handmade clothing sewn at home and copper axe suggested to the archaeologist Konrad Spindler that he had died perhaps four thousand years earlier. Radiocarbon dating supported the idea that the mummy was very old, and gave an even closer range: he had died between 3350 and 3100 BCE.

When dating nonhuman objects, radiocarbon dating can be used alongside other evidence, like sedimentary deposits. A fossilized forest in Wisconsin, destroyed during the last glacial advance before the end of the Pleistocene epoch, [20] is originally thought to be up to 24,000 years old based on sedimentary evidence. [21] For this reason, a series of radiocarbon tests concluded that the forest was actually destroyed around 13,550 years ago. Though radiocarbon dating isn't [22] correct, when used alongside other techniques it can be a useful tool: a skeleton key to unlock some of time's deepest secrets.

18

A) NO CHANGE

B) After hikers, preserved in ice, found "Ötzi," a mummy, on the alpine border between Italy and Austria in 1991,

C) After, on the alpine border between Italy, preserved in ice, and Austria, a mummy, "Ötzi," hikers found,

D) In 1991, after hikers found, between Italy and Austria, "Ötzi," preserved in ice, a mummy on the alpine border

19

A) NO CHANGE

B) handmade clothing that he had

C) handmade clothing

D) handmade, hand-sewn clothing

20

A) NO CHANGE

B) will be

C) was

D) is being

21

A) NO CHANGE

B) As such,

C) Thus,

D) However,

22

A) NO CHANGE

B) perfect,

C) unspoiled,

D) consummate,

CONTINUE

Questions 23-33 are based on the following passage.

Social Media Coordinator

It can sometimes be hard to remember just how new many of our most popular social media platforms, such as Twitter and Snapchat, actually 23 is. Most took off only recently: Twitter around 24 2010 Instagram around 2012 and Snapchat around 2014. In the early days of these platforms, public figures usually managed their own accounts, sometimes with disastrous results. For example, in 2011 a British Member of Parliament became famous online by accidentally tweeting his own name while attempting to search for it. Around the same time, many commentators expressed skepticism about the new "social media experts" starting to offer their services.

23

A) NO CHANGE

B) are

C) was

D) be

24

A) NO CHANGE

B) 2010 Instagram, around 2012 and,

C) 2010, Instagram around 2012, and

D) 2010, Instagram around 2012 and,

CONTINUE

25 Five years later, though, these jobs are probably here to stay. This is because **26** an amateurish social media presence can have significant consequences for both public figures and companies. A celebrity whose social media presence is just a flood of impersonal promotional notices may turn off his or her followers. **27** Nevertheless, a company that tries to participate in important cultural **28** conversations; without having a clear, pre-existing **29** stake around them risks seeming opportunistic and insincere.

Which choice effectively conveys the main point of the essay?

A) NO CHANGE

B) Their skepticism was often directed at the perceived vagueness of the term.

C) They expressed their doubts on blogs and in magazine articles.

D) It was even a topic for comedians and satirists.

A) NO CHANGE

B) an unproven

C) a basic

D) a raw

A) NO CHANGE

B) Instead,

C) Likewise,

D) As such,

A) NO CHANGE

B) conversations—

C) conversations:

D) conversations

A) NO CHANGE

B) stake in

C) stakeholder of

D) sweepstake for

CONTINUE

It's also important that companies handle their social media pratfalls gracefully when they do happen. When an employee of the American Red Cross accidentally sent out a good-natured but decidedly off-message tweet at a party using the official **30** Red Cross account the 130-year-old organization reacted with gentle humor rather than shame. The gaffe ended up encouraging many Twitter users to make friendly donations to the charity. **31**

Given these high stakes, organizations increasingly acknowledge the need for real expertise and specific qualifications. Those with social media jobs tend to study either marketing, journalism, or communications in school. These degrees can help students acquire the imaginative and verbal skills they'll need to make **32** expedient social media posts.

The writing skills and business strategies that social media coordinators learn as undergraduates are sometimes supplemented by a certificate in digital marketing or search-engine optimization. Search-engine optimization, or "SEO," is the technical side of social media work. It involves the use of keywords to boost a brand's profile by making it more prominent in search results. SEO strategies often require a lot of number-crunching, statistics, and a moment-to-moment awareness of what competitors are doing **33** minute-by-minute.

In the years since flubs by The Red Cross and that British Member of Parliament, social media strategies have become more polished, and the workers responsible for executing them have acquired greater legitimacy. As social media becomes more integral to commercial, cultural, and civic communication, fewer people doubt the value of having competent professionals behind the digital wheel.

30

A) NO CHANGE
B) Red Cross account, the 130-year-old
C) Red Cross account. The 130-year-old
D) Red Cross account the 130-year-old,

31

At this point, the author is considering adding the following sentence:

> The Red Cross and Red Crescent Movement exists in almost every country on Earth; most of these national chapters have their own Twitter accounts.

Should the author make this addition here?

A) Yes, because it relates to Twitter and the Red Cross.
B) Yes, because it supports the paragraph's central claim.
C) No, because it repeats information stated already.
D) No, because it does not relate to the paragraph's main idea.

32

A) NO CHANGE
B) effective
C) majestic
D) okay

33

A) NO CHANGE
B) day-by-day.
C) hour-to-hour.
D) OMIT the underlined portion.

CONTINUE

Questions 34-44 are based on the following passage.

Are Video Games Art?

Are video games art? The film critic Roger Ebert famously said they weren't. No game, he claimed, had anything like the power of a great book or movie, and none ever would. Mike Krahulik, a prominent voice in video games, [34] disagreed: since illustration, music, and writing are all art, he argued, a game that is a combination of those things must also be art.

Both of these arguments, [35] consequently, are too broad. Although Ebert is right that many games can't compete with great books or movies, that doesn't mean that no game can or ever will. Krahulik's claim that anything composed of artworks must itself be an artwork is also [36] saccharine: I could pile paintings on the floor and sleep on them, but that wouldn't make my bed a work of art.

34

A) NO CHANGE

B) disagreed, since—illustration, music, and writing are all art:

C) disagreed, since: illustration, music, and writing are all art,

D) disagreed: since illustration music and writing are all art

---

35

A) NO CHANGE

B) similarly

C) likewise

D) however

36

A) NO CHANGE

B) sanctimonious

C) simplistic

D) unpretentious

CONTINUE

Games *are* art, but for not for the reason Krahulik [37] suggests. Games are art because they do what all art does: take a human experience and distill it into something that moves us and teaches us a universal lesson about that experience. Shakespeare's *Hamlet*, for instance, shows us a young man paralyzed by depression and struggling with [38] terrible choices. Should he: trust his vision of his father's ghost? Should he kill his stepfather to avenge his father? Although his specific experience isn't the same as [39] ourselves, his struggles are extreme versions of the ethical and emotional challenges that we all face. His story reminds us of our own, which makes it moving, and because it is so extreme and concentrated, [40] it expresses to us revelations about things about ourselves that aren't as obvious in our everyday lives.

37

A) NO CHANGE
B) suggest
C) are suggesting
D) have suggested

38

A) NO CHANGE
B) terrible choices, should he
C) terrible choices. Should he
D) terrible choices should he:

39

A) NO CHANGE
B) us
C) ours
D) oneself

40

A) NO CHANGE
B) it shows us things
C) this revelatory process conveys to us things
D) OMIT the underlined portion.

CONTINUE

Games also capture experience, but they do it in a unique way: not through a story, but through mechanics, the rules that define the world of the game and the actions available to the player.

Consider *Depression Quest*, a text-based game that captures the inertia of depression by showing healthy things you could do for your character—but making it impossible to actually click on those options. **41** Or consider *This War of Mine*, which puts you in charge of a household of civilians trapped in a war-torn city. **42** You confront this game with terrible choices. Will you steal from an elderly couple to feed your characters? If you don't, your characters could get sick and even die. But if you do, your characters might be so **43** haggled by guilt that they become unable to perform other tasks.

41

At this point, the writer is considering adding the following sentence:

> Your character in this game has a partner named Alex, who is very concerned about your mental health.

Should the writer make this addition here?

A) Yes, because it provides an example of the principle presented by the preceding sentence.

B) Yes, because it helps establish a contrast between *Depression Quest* and *This War of Mine*.

C) No, because it distracts from the paragraph's focus on the choices available to players.

D) No, because Roger Ebert does not think games can accurately represent relationships.

42

A) NO CHANGE

B) This game, confronting you with terrible choices.

C) Terrible choices confront themselves to you with this game.

D) This game confronts you with terrible choices.

43

A) NO CHANGE

B) stumped

C) crippled

D) miffed

CONTINUE

Struggling with these games' mechanics forces us to engage with depression and ethical anxiety first-hand. It's a different way of learning about those feelings than watching *Hamlet*, but it's very powerful. **44**

Which choice provides the most appropriate conclusion to this paragraph and the passage as a whole?

A) However, it is also different from how painting, music, and literature affect us.

B) By teaching us fundamental truths about the human experience, these games do what all art strives to do.

C) Who knew that *Hamlet* and *Depression Quest* had so much in common?

D) If only Krahulik and Ebert had understood how important games are.

STOP

If you complete this section before the end of your allotted time, you may check your work on this section only. Do NOT use the time to work on another section.

Math Test – No Calculator

25 MINUTES, 20 QUESTIONS

Turn to Section 3 of your answer sheet to answer the questions in this section.

DIRECTIONS

Questions **1-15** ask you to solve a problem, select the best answer among four choices, and fill in the corresponding circle on your answer sheet. Questions **16-20** ask you to solve a problem and enter your answer in the grid provided on your answer sheet. There are detailed instructions on entering answers into the grid before question 16. You may use your test booklet for scratch work.

NOTES

1. You **may not** use a calculator.
2. Variables and expressions represent real numbers unless stated otherwise.
3. Figures are drawn to scale unless stated otherwise.
4. Figures lie in a plane unless stated otherwise.
5. The domain of a function f is defined as the set of all real numbers x for which $f(x)$ is also a real number, unless stated otherwise.

REFERENCE

$$A = \frac{1}{2}bh$$

$$a^2 + b^2 = c^2$$

Special Triangles

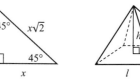

$$V = \frac{1}{3}lwh$$

$$V = \frac{1}{3}\pi r^2 h$$

$$A = lw$$

$$V = lwh$$

$$V = \pi r^2 h$$

$$A = \pi r^2$$
$$C = 2\pi r$$

$$V = \frac{4}{3}\pi r^3$$

There are 360° in a circle.

The sum of the angles in a triangle is 180°.

The number of radians of arc in a circle is 2π.

CONTINUE

1

Ivan's Ice Cream Store sells both regular cones and waffle cones. The price for a regular cone is $2 and the price for a waffle cone is $3. If Ivan sold r regular cones and w waffle cones on a given day, which of the following expressions represents the total revenue, in dollars, made by Ivan on that day?

A) $2r + 3w$

B) $2w + 3r$

C) $5rw$

D) $6rw$

2

The population of Japan from 2007 to 2016 can be modeled by the equation $P(x) = 127.8 - 0.15x$, where P is the population of Japan in millions and x is the number of years since 2007. Which of the following best describes the meaning of the number 0.15 in this equation?

A) The percent change in the population of Japan per year.

B) The decrease in the population of Japan per year.

C) The decrease, in millions, of the population of Japan per year.

D) The difference, in millions, between the population of Japan in 2007 and in 2016.

3

How many cubic centimeters are in one cubic meter?

A)   100

B)   1,000

C)   10,000

D) 1,000,000

4

Which of the following is equivalent to the difference between $4x^2 + 3x - 9$ and $7x^3 - 12x^2 - 8x$?

A) $-7x^3 + 16x^2 + 11x - 9$

B) $-7x^3 + 15x^2 + 17x - 4$

C) $7x^3 + 16x^2 - 17x - 5$

D) $7x^3 + 15x^2 - 11x + 9$

5

If Raquel has 50 balloons and additional balloons come in packs of 10, which of the following equations describes the number of packs, p, Raquel will need to buy in order to have b balloons?

A) $50b = 10p$

B) $b = 50p - 10$

C) $b = 15p - 10$

D) $b = 10p + 50$

CONTINUE

6

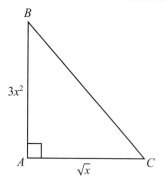

In the triangle $\triangle ABC$ above, which of the following expressions represents the length of $\overline{BC}$?

A) $3x^2 + \sqrt{x}$

B) $9x^4 + x$

C) $\sqrt{3x^2 + \sqrt{x}}$

D) $\sqrt{9x^4 + x}$

7

$$2y + x + 3 = 0$$

Which of the following equations represents a line that is perpendicular to the line represented by the above equation?

A) $y = 2x + 3$

B) $y = -2x - 3$

C) $y = \frac{1}{2}x + 3$

D) $y = \frac{-1}{2}x + 3$

8

$$s = 200 - 10x$$
$$l = 320 - 20x$$

In the equations above, s and l represent the number of bacteria in colonies of staphylococcus and listeria, respectively, that survive after the temperature is raised $x°C$ above 40°C. If there are as many surviving staphylococcus bacteria as surviving listeria bacteria, how many listeria bacteria are there?

A) 240

B) 120

C) 80

D) 60

9

Which of the following is a solution for x in the equation $\dfrac{x^2 + x - 6}{x + 3} = 0$?

A) −3

B) 0

C) 1

D) 2

CONTINUE

10

$$v = \frac{1}{4}(y-4)^2 + 2$$

The value of a book, in dollars, is calculated according to the equation above, where y is the number of years since it was printed and v is its value. If the book is printed when $y = 0$, what is the dollar difference in the value of the book between when it is printed and when it is worth the least?

A) 0

B) 4

C) 6

D) 18

11

Jake is submitting 48 pieces of art to a competition. If he makes 3 pieces every week, and he has 5 pieces of art in storage, how many weeks does Jake need to complete his submission to the competition?

A) 16

B) 15

C) 14

D) 13

12

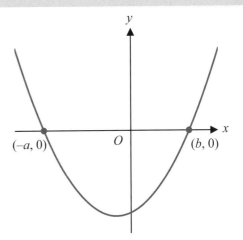

The x-coordinates $-a$ and b for the equation $y = x^2 + 2x - 24$ are plotted on an xy-graph, as shown above. What is the value of $a - b$?

A) −2

B) 0

C) 2

D) 10

CONTINUE

13

If $5x + 4 = 19$, what is the value of a if $2^a = \dfrac{4^{2x}}{2^x}$?

A)   3

B)   4

C)   9

D)   12

14

If there is no real solution for the equation $0 = 2x^2 + 3x + c$, what is a possible value for c?

A) -10

B) -5

C) 1

D) 5

15

$$\frac{x-5}{x+2} - \frac{7}{x-2}$$

Which of the following is equivalent to the above expression?

A) $\dfrac{x - 12}{x^2 - 4}$

B) $1 - \dfrac{14x}{x^2 - 4}$

C) $1 + \dfrac{14x}{x^2 - 4}$

D) $\dfrac{14x}{x^2 - 4}$

CONTINUE

DIRECTIONS

Questions **16-20** ask you to solve a problem and enter your answer in the grid provided on your answer sheet. When completing grid-in questions:

1. You are required to bubble in the circles for your answers. It is recommended, but not required, that you also write your answer in the boxes above the columns of circles. Points will be awarded based only on whether the circles are filled in correctly.

2. Fill in only one circle in a column.

3. You can start your answer in any column as long as you can fit in the whole answer.

4. For questions 16-20, no answers will be negative numbers.

5. **Mixed numbers,** such as $4\frac{2}{5}$, must be gridded as decimals or improper fractions, such as 4.4 or as 22/5. "42/5" will be read as "forty-two over five," not as "four and two-fifths."

6. If your answer is a **decimal** with more digits than will fit on the grid, you may round it or cut it off, but you must fill the entire grid.

7. If there are **multiple correct solutions** to a problem, all of them will be considered correct. Enter only **one** on the grid.

CONTINUE

16

If $10 = 15x - 5$, what is $2x$?

17

$$h(t) = -a(t - 3)^2 + 5$$

The equation above gives the height in feet, h, of a ball given the number of seconds, t, that it has been in the air. If the ball's height is 2 feet when it has been in the air for 4 seconds, what is the value of a?

18

$$6y + 4x = 32$$
$$2y + x^2 = 12$$

According to the system of equations above, if x is a positive integer, what is the value of $y - x$?

19

$$x^2 + y^2 - 6x + 12y + 44 = 0$$

In the xy-plane, if the coordinates of the center of the circle defined by the equation above are $(h, -k)$, what is the value of hk?

20

A laboratory is calculating the amount of energy, in Joules, that is required to heat a sample of mercury. To do this, the laboratory uses the equation $E = Sm\Delta T$, where E is the energy required in Joules, S is the specific heat capacity of the substance, m is the mass of the sample in grams, and ΔT is the change in temperature in degrees Celsius. If it takes 50 Joules to increase the temperature of 1 gram of iron from 50°C to 100°C, and the specific heat capacity of iron is 5 times the specific heat capacity of mercury, how much energy, in Joules, would it take to increase the temperature of 10 grams of mercury from 50°C to 100°C?

STOP

If you complete this section before the end of your allotted time, check your work on this section only. Do NOT use the time to work on another section.

Math Test – Calculator

55 MINUTES, 38 QUESTIONS

Turn to Section 4 of your answer sheet to answer the questions in this section.

DIRECTIONS

Questions **1-30** ask you to solve a problem, select the best answer among four choices, and fill in the corresponding circle on your answer sheet. Questions **31-38** ask you to solve a problem and enter your answer in a grid provided on your answer sheet. There are detailed instructions on entering answers into the grid before question 31. You may use your test booklet for scratch work.

NOTES

1. You **may** use a calculator.
2. Variables and expressions represent real numbers unless stated otherwise.
3. Figures are drawn to scale unless stated otherwise.
4. Figures lie in a plane unless stated otherwise.
5. The domain of a function f is defined as the set of all real numbers x for which $f(x)$ is also a real number, unless stated otherwise.

REFERENCE

$A = \frac{1}{2}bh$ $a^2 + b^2 = c^2$ Special Triangles $V = \frac{1}{3}lwh$ $V = \frac{1}{3}\pi r^2 h$

$A = lw$ $V = lwh$ $V = \pi r^2 h$ $A = \pi r^2$ $V = \frac{4}{3}\pi r^3$

$C = 2\pi r$

There are 360° in a circle.

The sum of the angles in a triangle is 180°.

The number of radians of arc in a circle is 2π.

CONTINUE

1

If $4x + 7 = 15$, what is the value of $6x - 5$?

A)   3

B)   7

C)   11

D)   15

2

The base fee to take a taxi is $3.25. There is an additional charge of $0.75 for every kilometer driven. If the total cost of Victoria's taxi ride was $12.25, how long was her ride, in kilometers?

A)   4

B)   8

C)   12

D)   22

3

20, 21, 28, 28, 18, 31, 22, 24

An elementary school has 8 different Grade 1 classrooms. The number of students in each classroom is given in the list above. What is the average (arithmetic mean) number of students in a Grade 1 classroom?

A)   23.5

B)   24

C)   28

D)   31

4

If $x = \dfrac{y}{2}$, which of the following is equivalent to the expression $3x - 11 + 11x + 74$?

A) $\dfrac{y}{2} + 49$

B) $14y + 85$

C) $7(y + 9)$

D) $11\left(\dfrac{3y}{2} + 8\right)$

Questions 5-6 refer to the following information.

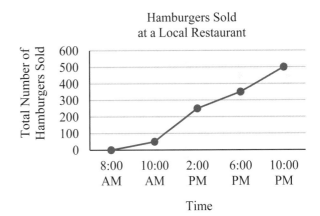

Hamburgers Sold
at a Local Restaurant

The graph above shows the cumulative sales of hamburgers at a local restaurant throughout the day.

5

Approximately how many hamburgers were sold between 6:00 PM and 10:00 PM?

A)   100

B)   150

C)   350

D)   500

CONTINUE

6

During what time period was the restaurant selling hamburgers the fastest?

A) 8:00 AM to 10:00 AM

B) 10:00 AM to 2:00 PM

C) 2:00 PM to 6:00 PM

D) 6:00 PM to 10:00 PM

7

Coffee	Tea	Neither
24	10	6

In an office of 200 people, 40 employees were randomly selected and surveyed about whether they drank coffee or tea. The results are displayed in the table above. Based on the results of this survey, how many employees in the entire office most likely drink coffee?

A) 20

B) 60

C) 96

D) 120

8

Liu is testing a new motor for a dirt bike. To determine the fuel efficiency of the bike, he needs to run the motor at a speed no more than 20 kilometers per hour above or below the target speed of 100 kilometers per hour. Which of the following inequalities represents the range of speeds, x, in kilometers per hour, that he should aim for when testing his dirt bike?

A) $20 < x < 120$

B) $20 \leq x \leq 120$

C) $80 < x < 120$

D) $80 \leq x \leq 120$

9

A survey was taken at a children's arcade in which children were asked which superhero was their favorite. The surveyors would like to extend their results to a more general population. To which of the following populations could the results of the survey be reasonably applied?

A) Children living in the neighborhood of the arcade

B) Parents living in the neighborhood of the arcade

C) Children from around the world

D) Comic book writers

CONTINUE

10

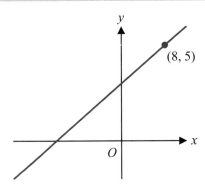

A line, shown in the graphic above, has a slope of $\frac{1}{4}$ and passes through the point (8, 5). What is the y-intercept of this line?

A) 2

B) 3

C) 4

D) 5

Questions 11-12 refer to the following information.

The graph below shows the census data for City H from 1960 to 2005.

Population of City H from 1960 to 2005

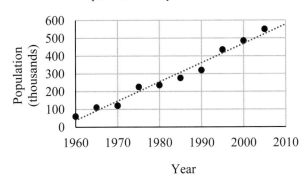

11

According to the line of best fit in the figure above, which of the following best approximates the year in which the population of City H was estimated to be 400,000 people?

A) 1993

B) 1995

C) 1998

D) 2003

12

If the slope of the line of best fit is 10,000, which of the following is a reasonable interpretation?

A) City H had approximately 10,000 people in 1955.

B) City H has a maximum yearly population change of approximately 10,000 people.

C) City H has been growing by approximately 10,000 people every 5 years.

D) City H has been growing by approximately 10,000 people every year.

CONTINUE

13

At a certain high school, Grade 9 students can choose to take either Drama or Music. The number of students taking each of these courses is summarized in the table below.

	Male	Female	Total
Drama	48	71	119
Music	98	77	175
Total	146	148	294

If a music student is selected at random, what is the probability that they are female?

A) $\dfrac{77}{175}$

B) $\dfrac{77}{294}$

C) $\dfrac{98}{175}$

D) $\dfrac{175}{294}$

14

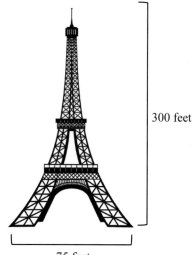

300 feet

75 feet

A replica of the Eiffel Tower is 300 feet tall and each side of its square base has a length of 75 feet, as shown in the picture above. Stan wants to build a model of this tower that is 40 centimeters tall. How long should each side of the square base be, in centimeters, if Stan wants to ensure that his model is to scale?

A) 10

B) 12.5

C) 25

D) 30

CONTINUE

15

A group of scientists is testing a new skin cream to cure rashes. There are 100 people with rashes who have volunteered to take part in the study. The scientists must select 50 of the 100 people to take the treatment; the remaining people make up the control group and do not take the treatment. What method of selecting these groups will be the most likely to lead to meaningful results from the trials?

A) The volunteers with the most severe rashes will receive the treatment.

B) The volunteers with the least severe rashes will receive the treatment.

C) The volunteers will choose whether they will receive the treatment.

D) The groups will be selected randomly.

16

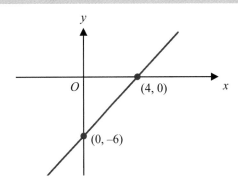

Which of the following equations is graphed in the figure above?

A) $y = \dfrac{3}{2}x + 6$

B) $y = \dfrac{2}{3}x + 6$

C) $y = \dfrac{3}{2}x - 6$

D) $y = \dfrac{2}{3}x - 6$

17

Andre needs to write an essay that is between 1,000 and 1,500 words long. If he writes 8 words per minute, which of the following is an amount of time that he could spend writing?

A) 2 hours

B) 2 hours and 10 minutes

C) 3 hours and 10 minutes

D) 3 hours and 30 minutes

CONTINUE

18

The rainfall in two cities, X and Y, was recorded over a period of 58 days. The amount of rainfall was rounded to the nearest 5mm and is displayed in the histograms below.

Rainfall in City X

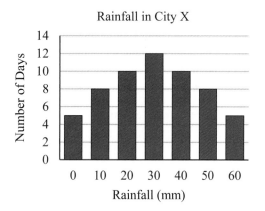

Rainfall in City Y

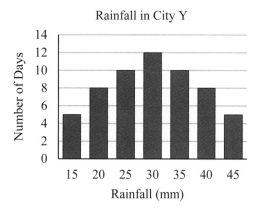

Which of the following statements is true about the rainfall in these cities during this time period?

A) They have the same mean, and City X has a greater standard deviation.

B) They have the same mean, and City Y has a greater standard deviation.

C) City X has a greater mean and a greater standard deviation.

D) City Y has a greater mean and a greater standard deviation.

19

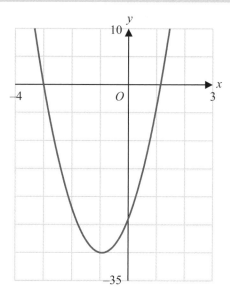

Which of the following functions is represented by the above graph?

A) $f(x) = -7x^2 - 29x - 24$

B) $f(x) = -7x^2 + 29x - 24$

C) $f(x) = 7x^2 - 13x - 24$

D) $f(x) = 7x^2 + 13x - 24$

CONTINUE

20

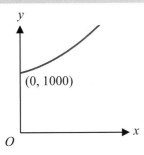

A client opens a savings account with a bank and graphs the approximate amount of money in their account over time, as shown above. If the client makes an initial deposit of $1,000 and does not make any further deposits or withdrawals, which of the following scenarios could be represented by this graph?

A) The client's account offers a $30 yearly bonus, which is deposited directly into the account every year.

B) The client's account offers a 3% yearly rate of interest, which is deposited directly into the account every year.

C) The bank offers to eliminate all banking fees as long as the client maintains an account balance of $1,000, but does not offer any additional incentives.

D) The bank charges a monthly banking fee on the client's account, and does not offer any additional incentives.

21

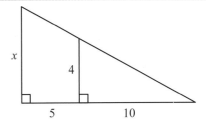

In the diagram above, what is the length of the side x? (Note: Diagram is not to scale.)

A) 6

B) 7

C) 8

D) 10

22

Two quantities, a and b, are related by the formula $a = 16b^2$. Which of the following expressions is equal to b?

A) $\pm \dfrac{a^2}{16}$

B) $\pm \dfrac{a}{4}$

C) $\pm \dfrac{\sqrt{a}}{4}$

D) $\pm \dfrac{\sqrt{a}}{16}$

CONTINUE

23

If $(3^x)(9^y) = 243$, what is the value of $x + 2y$?

A) 3

B) 4

C) 5

D) 7

24

The water level in a pond rises at a constant rate as water drains into it from a nearby lake. If the water level in the pond is 3 feet and 6 inches at 8:20, and 3 feet and 9 inches at 8:40, what will the water level be at 10:00?

A) 3 feet and 10 inches

B) 4 feet and 6 inches

C) 4 feet and 9 inches

D) 5 feet and 3 inches

25

If $\sqrt{3k^2 + 9} - m = 0$ and $m = 6$, which of the following is a possible value for k?

A) 1

B) 2

C) 3

D) 4

26

Cat Only	7
Dog Only	9
Both	5

The above table shows how many people in a class own a cat, a dog, or both. If 25% of the people in the class own neither a cat nor a dog, how many total students are there in the class?

A) 21

B) 24

C) 25

D) 28

27

$$\frac{4(2y - 6)}{6} = \frac{3x + 2}{3}$$

$$2y = 4x - 13$$

What is the solution (x, y) to the system of equations above?

A) $\left(8, \frac{19}{2}\right)$

B) $\left(9, \frac{17}{4}\right)$

C) $\left(\frac{5}{2}, 7\right)$

D) $\left(9, \frac{7}{2}\right)$

CONTINUE

28

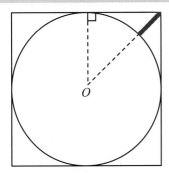

In the figure above, a circle is inscribed in a square. Point O is the center of the circle, and the side length of the square is 2 units. What is the length of the shaded line segment?

A) $\dfrac{1}{\sqrt{2}}$

B) $\sqrt{2} - 1$

C) $\dfrac{1}{4}$

D) $\dfrac{2}{5}$

29

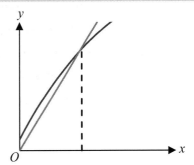

A segment of a particular comet's orbit can be modeled by the expression $y = \sqrt{31x + 8}$, as shown in the figure above. A nearby satellite follows a trajectory modeled by $y = 2x$. If the comet and the satellite are traveling in the same plane, at approximately what value of x will they collide?

A) $\dfrac{1}{4}$

B) 4

C) 8

D) 16

30

Let a quadratic equation be defined as $ax^2 + bx + c = 0$, where there is one possible solution for x. Which of the following must be true?

  I. $b = \pm\sqrt{4ac}$

  II. $x = -\dfrac{b}{2a}$

  III. $x = \sqrt{b^2 - 4ac}$

A) I only

B) I and II only

C) II and III only

D) I, II, and III

CONTINUE

DIRECTIONS

Questions **31-38** ask you to solve a problem and enter your answer in the grid provided on your answer sheet. When completing grid-in questions:

1. You are required to bubble in the circles for your answers. It is recommended, but not required, that you also write your answer in the boxes above the columns of circles. Points will be awarded based only on whether the circles are filled in correctly.

2. Fill in only one circle in a column.

3. You can start your answer in any column as long as you can fit in the whole answer.

4. For questions 31-38, no answers will be negative numbers.

5. **Mixed numbers,** such as $4\frac{2}{5}$, must be gridded as decimals or improper fractions, such as 4.4 or as 22/5. "42/5" will be read as "forty-two over five," not as "four and two-fifths."

6. If your answer is a **decimal** with more digits than will fit on the grid, you may round it or cut it off, but you must fill the entire grid.

7. If there are **multiple correct solutions** to a problem, all of them will be considered correct. Enter only **one** on the grid.

CONTINUE

31

A truck drives at 80 kilometers per hour between two towns that are 360 kilometers apart. How many hours will the trip take?

32

The equation of a line is given by $y = 2x - k$. If the point (7, 5) lies on the line, what is the value of k?

33

There are approximately 2.5 centimeters in an inch, and there are 12 inches in 1 foot. Milan is 6.5 feet tall. What is Milan's height, in centimeters?

34

A laser reflects off a mirror as shown below, according to the equation $y = |8x - 5|$. At what value of x does the laser strike the mirror?

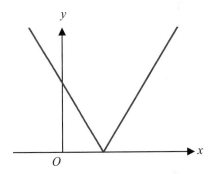

CONTINUE

35

Lucy makes $9.00 per hour. She earns 1.5 times her normal pay while she works overtime, and 2 times her normal pay when she works holidays. The day before a holiday, Lucy works eight hours at regular pay and 120 minutes overtime. How many complete hours does she need to work the next day to earn at least $153 in total?

36

$$x^2 + 2x + y^2 - 8y + 8 = 0$$

What is the radius of the circle described by the above equation?

CONTINUE

Questions 37 and 38 refer to the following information.

The graph below shows the stock price for a company in the first 24 days of April.

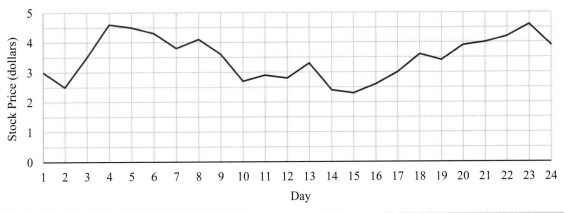

37

On what day of the month was the company's stock worth the least?

38

By what percentage did the price of the stock increase from the 2nd of April to the 5th of April? (Disregard the % sign when gridding-in your answer.)

STOP

If you complete this section before the end of your allotted time, you may check your work on this section only. Do NOT use the time to work on another section.

Essay (Optional)

50 MINUTES

Turn to the lined pages of your answer sheet to write your essay.

DIRECTIONS

This essay is optional. It is a chance for you to demonstrate how well you can understand and analyze a written passage. Your essay should show that you have carefully read the passage and should be a concisely written analysis that is both logical and clear.

You must write your entire essay on the lines in your answer booklet. No additional paper will be provided aside from the Planning Page inside your answer booklet. You will be able to write your entire essay in the space provided if you make use of every line, keep tight margins, and write at a suitable size. Don't forget to keep your handwriting legible for the readers evaluating your essay.

You will have 50 minutes to read the passage in this booklet and to write an essay in response to the prompt provided at the end of the passage.

REMINDERS

- What you write in this booklet will not be evaluated. Write your essay in the answer booklet only.

- Essays that are off-topic will not be evaluated.

As you read the passage below, consider how Mark Bittman uses

- evidence, such as facts or examples, to support claims.
- reasoning to develop ideas and to connect claims and evidence.
- stylistic or persuasive elements, such as word choice or appeals to emotion, to add power to the ideas expressed.

Adapted from Mark Bittman, "Don't Ask How to Feed the 9 Billion," © 2014 by The New York Times Company. Originally published November 11, 2014.

1   At dinner with a friend the other night, I mentioned that I was giving a talk this week debunking the idea that we need to grow more food on a large scale so we can "feed the nine billion"—the anticipated global population by 2050.

2   She looked at me, horrified, and said, "But how are you going to produce enough food to feed the hungry?"

3   I suggested she try this exercise: "Put yourself in the poorest place you can think of. Imagine yourself in the Democratic Republic of Congo, for example. Now. Are you hungry? Are you going to go hungry? Are you going to have a problem finding food?"

4   The answer, obviously, is "no." Because she—and almost all of you reading this—would be standing in that country with some $20 bills and a wallet filled with credit cards, and you would go buy yourself something to eat.

5   The difference between you and the hungry is not production levels; it's money. There are no hungry people with money; there isn't a shortage of food, nor is there a distribution problem. There is an I-don't-have-the-land-and-resources-to-produce-my-own-food, nor-can-I-afford-to-buy-food problem.

6   And poverty and the resulting hunger aren't matters of bad luck; they are often a result of people buying the property of traditional farmers and displacing them, appropriating their water, energy and mineral resources, and even producing cash crops for export while reducing the people growing the food to menial and hungry laborers on their own land.

7   If poverty creates hunger, it teams up with the food system to create another form of malnourishment: obesity. If you define "hunger" as malnutrition, and you accept that overweight and obesity are forms of malnutrition as well, then almost half the world is malnourished.

8   The solution to malnourishment isn't to produce more food. The solution is to eliminate poverty.

9   Look at the most agriculturally productive country in the world: the United States. Is there hunger here? Yes, quite a bit. We have the highest percentage of hungry people of any developed nation, a rate closer to that of Indonesia than that of Britain.

10 Is there a lack of food? You laugh at that question. It is, as the former Food and Drug Administration commissioner David Kessler likes to call it, "a food carnival." It's just that there's a steep ticket price.

11 A majority of the world is fed by hundreds of millions of small-scale farmers, some of whom are themselves among the hungry. The rest of the hungry are underpaid or unemployed workers, but boosting yields does nothing for them.

12   So we should not be asking, "How will we feed the world?" but "How can we help end poverty?" Claiming that increasing yield would feed the poor is like saying that producing more cars or private jets would guarantee that everyone had one.

13   And how do we help those who have malnutrition from excess eating? We can help them, and help preserve the Earth's health, if we recognize that the industrial model of food production is neither inevitable nor desirable. The best method of farming for most people is probably traditional farming boosted by science. The best method of farming for those in highly productive agricultural societies would be farming made more intelligent and less rapacious. That is, the kind of farming we can learn from people who still have a real relationship with the land and are focused on quality rather than yield. The goal should be food that is green, fair, healthy, and affordable.

14   It's not news that the poor need money and justice. If there's a bright side here, it's that it might be easier to make the changes required to fix the problems created by industrial agriculture than those created by inequality.

15   There's plenty of food. Too much of it is going to feed animals, too much of it is being converted to fuel, and too much of it is being wasted. We don't have to increase yield to address any of those issues; we just have to grow food more smartly than with the brute force of industrial methods, and we need to address the circumstances of the poor. Our slogan should not be "let's feed the world," but "let's end poverty."

Write an essay in which you explain how Mark Bittman builds an argument to persuade his audience that we don't have a food production problem, but rather a poverty problem. In your essay, analyze how Bittman uses one or more of the features listed in the directions above, (or features of your own choice) to strengthen the logic and persuasiveness of his argument. Be sure that your analysis focuses on the most relevant features of the passage.

Your essay should not explain whether you agree with Bittman's claims, but rather explain how Bittman builds an argument to persuade his audience.

Practice Test 6

SAT

Directions

- Work on just one section at a time.

- If you complete a section before the end of your allotted time, use the extra minutes to check your work on that section only. Do NOT use the time to work on another section.

Using Your Test Booklet

- No credit will be given for anything written in the test booklet. You may use the test booklet for scratch paper.

- You are not allowed to continue answering questions in a section after the allotted time has run out. This includes marking answers on your answer sheet that you previously noted in your test booklet.

- You are not allowed to fold pages, take pages out of the test booklet, or take any pages home.

Answering Questions

- Each answer must be marked in the corresponding row on the answer sheet.

- Each bubble must be filled in completely and darkly within the lines.

Correct ●   Incorrect

- Be careful to bubble in the correct part of the answer sheet.

- Extra marks on your answer sheet may be marked as incorrect answers and lower your score.

- Make sure you use a No. 2 pencil.

Scoring

- You will receive one point for each correct answer.

- Incorrect answers will NOT result in points deducted. Even if you are unsure about an answer, you should make a guess.

DO NOT BEGIN THIS TEST

UNTIL YOUR PROCTOR TELLS YOU TO DO SO

For printable answer sheets, please visit **ivyglobal.com/study**.

Section 1

	A B C D		A B C D		A B C D		A B C D		A B C D
1	○ ○ ○ ○	12	○ ○ ○ ○	23	○ ○ ○ ○	34	○ ○ ○ ○	45	○ ○ ○ ○
2	○ ○ ○ ○	13	○ ○ ○ ○	24	○ ○ ○ ○	35	○ ○ ○ ○	46	○ ○ ○ ○
3	○ ○ ○ ○	14	○ ○ ○ ○	25	○ ○ ○ ○	36	○ ○ ○ ○	47	○ ○ ○ ○
4	○ ○ ○ ○	15	○ ○ ○ ○	26	○ ○ ○ ○	37	○ ○ ○ ○	48	○ ○ ○ ○
5	○ ○ ○ ○	16	○ ○ ○ ○	27	○ ○ ○ ○	38	○ ○ ○ ○	49	○ ○ ○ ○
6	○ ○ ○ ○	17	○ ○ ○ ○	28	○ ○ ○ ○	39	○ ○ ○ ○	50	○ ○ ○ ○
7	○ ○ ○ ○	18	○ ○ ○ ○	29	○ ○ ○ ○	40	○ ○ ○ ○	51	○ ○ ○ ○
8	○ ○ ○ ○	19	○ ○ ○ ○	30	○ ○ ○ ○	41	○ ○ ○ ○	52	○ ○ ○ ○
9	○ ○ ○ ○	20	○ ○ ○ ○	31	○ ○ ○ ○	42	○ ○ ○ ○		
10	○ ○ ○ ○	21	○ ○ ○ ○	32	○ ○ ○ ○	43	○ ○ ○ ○		
11	○ ○ ○ ○	22	○ ○ ○ ○	33	○ ○ ○ ○	44	○ ○ ○ ○		

Section 2

	A B C D		A B C D		A B C D		A B C D		A B C D
1	○ ○ ○ ○	10	○ ○ ○ ○	19	○ ○ ○ ○	28	○ ○ ○ ○	37	○ ○ ○ ○
2	○ ○ ○ ○	11	○ ○ ○ ○	20	○ ○ ○ ○	29	○ ○ ○ ○	38	○ ○ ○ ○
3	○ ○ ○ ○	12	○ ○ ○ ○	21	○ ○ ○ ○	30	○ ○ ○ ○	39	○ ○ ○ ○
4	○ ○ ○ ○	13	○ ○ ○ ○	22	○ ○ ○ ○	31	○ ○ ○ ○	40	○ ○ ○ ○
5	○ ○ ○ ○	14	○ ○ ○ ○	23	○ ○ ○ ○	32	○ ○ ○ ○	41	○ ○ ○ ○
6	○ ○ ○ ○	15	○ ○ ○ ○	24	○ ○ ○ ○	33	○ ○ ○ ○	42	○ ○ ○ ○
7	○ ○ ○ ○	16	○ ○ ○ ○	25	○ ○ ○ ○	34	○ ○ ○ ○	43	○ ○ ○ ○
8	○ ○ ○ ○	17	○ ○ ○ ○	26	○ ○ ○ ○	35	○ ○ ○ ○	44	○ ○ ○ ○
9	○ ○ ○ ○	18	○ ○ ○ ○	27	○ ○ ○ ○	36	○ ○ ○ ○		

Section 3 (No-Calculator)

	A	B	C	D		A	B	C	D		A	B	C	D		A	B	C	D		A	B	C	D
1	○	○	○	○	4	○	○	○	○	7	○	○	○	○	10	○	○	○	○	13	○	○	○	○
2	○	○	○	○	5	○	○	○	○	8	○	○	○	○	11	○	○	○	○	14	○	○	○	○
3	○	○	○	○	6	○	○	○	○	9	○	○	○	○	12	○	○	○	○	15	○	○	○	○

Only answers that are gridded will be scored. You will not receive credit for anything written in the boxes.

16　17　18　19　20

Section 4 (Calculator)

	A	B	C	D		A	B	C	D		A	B	C	D		A	B	C	D		A	B	C	D
1	○	○	○	○	7	○	○	○	○	13	○	○	○	○	19	○	○	○	○	25	○	○	○	○
2	○	○	○	○	8	○	○	○	○	14	○	○	○	○	20	○	○	○	○	26	○	○	○	○
3	○	○	○	○	9	○	○	○	○	15	○	○	○	○	21	○	○	○	○	27	○	○	○	○
4	○	○	○	○	10	○	○	○	○	16	○	○	○	○	22	○	○	○	○	28	○	○	○	○
5	○	○	○	○	11	○	○	○	○	17	○	○	○	○	23	○	○	○	○	29	○	○	○	○
6	○	○	○	○	12	○	○	○	○	18	○	○	○	○	24	○	○	○	○	30	○	○	○	○

Only answers that are gridded will be scored. You will not receive credit for anything written in the boxes.

31   32   33   34   35

Only answers that are gridded will be scored. You will not receive credit for anything written in the boxes.

36   37   38

■ Section 5 (Optional)

Important: Use a No. 2 pencil. Write inside the borders.

You may use the space below to plan your essay, but be sure to write your essay on the lined pages. Work on this page will not be scored.

Use this space to plan your essay.

START YOUR ESSAY HERE.

_____

_____

_____

_____

_____

_____

_____

_____

_____

_____

_____

_____

_____

_____

_____

_____

_____

_____

_____

_____

_____

_____

_____

_____

_____

_____

Continue on the next page.

_____

_____

_____

_____

_____

_____

_____

_____

_____

_____

_____

_____

_____

_____

_____

_____

_____

_____

_____

_____

_____

_____

_____

_____

_____

Continue on the next page.

_____

_____

_____

_____

_____

_____

_____

_____

_____

_____

_____

_____

_____

_____

_____

_____

_____

_____

_____

_____

_____

_____

_____

_____

Continue on the next page.

STOP.

Reading Test

65 MINUTES, 52 QUESTIONS

Turn to Section 1 of your answer sheet to answer the questions in this section.

DIRECTIONS

Every passage or paired set of passages is accompanied by a number of questions. Read the passage or paired set of passages, then use what is said or implied in what you read and in any given graphics to choose the best answer to each question.

Questions 1-10 are based on the following passage.

This passage is adapted from Suzanne Metcalf, *Annabel*. First published in 1906.

Will Carden walked slowly up the lane, his basket on his arm and his hands thrust deep into his pockets. Once out of sight of the Williams' grounds,
Line his proud bearing relaxed and great tears welled in
5 his gray eyes. The scornful words uttered by Mrs. Williams had struck him like a blow and humiliated him beyond measure—her children were rich, and he was poor. There was a gulf between them, and the fine lady did not wish for her children to play with
10 the "vegetable boy." It brought to Will's heart a bitterness such as he had never known in all his brief lifetime.

He liked the Williams boys and girls. They had always been good comrades, and not one of them
15 had ever hinted that there was any difference in their positions; but of course they did not know, as their mother did, how far beneath them was the poor "vegetable boy."

Will glanced down at the worn shoes upon his
20 feet. The leather was the same color as the earth upon the path, for he worked in the garden with them. His trousers were too short; he knew that well enough, but hadn't cared about it until then. They were patched in places too, because his mother
25 had an old-fashioned idea that patches were more

respectable than rags, while Will knew well enough that both were evidence of a poverty that could not be concealed. His gray shirt, although of coarse material, was clean, and lots of the village boys wore
30 the same cheap straw hat as his.

The Williams children didn't wear such hats, though. Will tried to think what they did wear, but he had never noticed particularly, although it was easy to remember that the boys' clothes were of fine
35 cloths and velvets, and he had heard Flo speak of the pretty puffs and tucks in the Williams girls' dresses. Yes, they were rich, and no one knew so well as Will how very poor and needy the Cardens were. Perhaps Mrs. Williams was quite right, but oh, how hard his
40 rejection was to bear!

The Cardens' cottage stood upon the south edge of the village, and with it were two acres of excellent land, where Will and Egbert, assisted at times by their mother and little Florence, raised the vegetables
45 on which their living depended. Egbert was two years older than Will, who was now fifteen, and Florence—or "Flo," as everybody called her—was a little elf of ten.

Will tried hard to bear up under the humiliation
50 he had suffered; but there was no one near to see him and for a few minutes he gave way and let his tears flow unrestrained. Yet he kept on his way, with bent head and stooping shoulders, a very different boy from the merry, lighthearted youth who had carried
55 the heavy basket to the big house only an hour ago.

CONTINUE

Suddenly, to the eyes blurred with tears, a dark form loomed up in the road just ahead of him. Will hastily wiped away the unmanly drops and tried to whistle. He shifted his path to the edge of the road; 60 but the other did the same, and the boy stopped abruptly knowing that he had been purposely halted.

Then he glanced timidly up at a round, bearded face and two shrewd but kindly eyes that were looking at him from beneath a slouched felt hat.

1

Which choice best summarizes the passage?

A) A character undergoes an unpleasant experience and reflects on his harsh reality.

B) A character works on a vegetable farm to support his impoverished family.

C) A character is scolded for behaving in a socially inappropriate manner.

D) A character walks home downcast and discouraged after a disastrous argument.

2

The passage most clearly implies that Mrs. Williams

A) regards her family as one of high status.

B) often invites Will over for dinner.

C) had been upset with Will for lying.

D) is good friends with Mrs. Carden.

3

According to the passage, Will's emotions after the incident with Mrs. Williams are best described as

A) understanding and forgiving.

B) furious and resentful.

C) wounded and troubled.

D) casual and indifferent.

4

Which choice provides the best evidence for the answer to the previous question?

A) Lines 1-3 ("Will Carden … pockets")

B) Lines 23-28 ("They were … concealed")

C) Lines 41-45 ("The Cardens' … depended")

D) Lines 49-52 ("Will tried … unrestrained")

5

The passage most clearly indicates that Will views the Williams children as

A) ignorant and careless.

B) privileged and pompous.

C) respectable, but his equals.

D) friends, but not equals.

6

Which choice provides the best evidence for the answer to the previous question?

A) Lines 5-8 ("The scornful … poor")

B) Lines 13-18 ("They had … boy")

C) Lines 32-36 ("Will tried … dresses")

D) Lines 38-40 ("Perhaps Mrs. Williams … bear")

7

The author uses the word "gulf" in line 8 to indicate that between Will and the Williams children, there is a

A) large body of water.

B) significant social disparity.

C) difference in moral standards.

D) considerable age difference.

CONTINUE

8

As used in line 4, the phrase "proud bearing" most nearly means

A) arrogant air.

B) dignified demeanor.

C) ignorant attitude.

D) satisfied expression.

9

As used in line 16, "positions" most nearly means

A) beliefs.

B) stances.

C) locations.

D) statuses.

10

In the context of the passage, the description of the Williams children's clothing in the fourth paragraph mainly serves to

A) emphasize the source of the Williams family's wealth.

B) contrast with the description of Will's less extravagant clothing.

C) present the fashion styles and trends of the time period.

D) show that the Williams children were embarrassed by their luxury.

Questions 11-20 are based on the following passage.

This passage and graphic are adapted from, "More Women Are Running the World, so Why Aren't More Men Doing the Dishes?" © 2016 by Alice Evans.

Globally, women are triumphing in historically male-dominated areas. Slowly and incrementally, support is growing for women's employment and public
Line leadership. But social change seems curiously one-sided.
5 While women have taken on more work outside the home, men's share of care work—cooking, cleaning, and caring for children and elderly relatives—has not increased at the same rate.

Rising employment for women partly reflects
10 macroeconomic changes. Processes such as deindustrialization, demechanization, deregulation, and trade liberalization have reduced the number of working class men's jobs in rich countries—and their wages. In the U.S., women's employment increased as young
15 men's median wages declined from $41,000 in 1973 to $23,000 in 2013.

Similar changes have occurred as far away as Zambia. From the mid-1980s, families' economic security worsened due to trade liberalization, factory
20 closures, public sector contraction, user fees for health and education, and the devastating toll of HIV/AIDS. Families could no longer rely solely on a male breadwinner. Many came to perceive women's employment as advantageous.
25 Globally, there has also been a growth in sectors demanding stereotypically "feminine" characteristics: health, education, public administration, and financial services in Britain, and export-oriented manufacturing in Bangladesh. These changes have increased the
30 opportunity cost of women staying at home.

Resulting exposure to a critical mass of women performing socially valued, masculine roles appears to have steadily undermined gender stereotypes. Increasingly, people are seeing women as equally
35 competent and deserving of status. This ideological change has fostered a positive feedback loop, with more women pursuing historically male-dominated fields. However, the initial trigger (the rising opportunity cost of women staying at home) has not occurred in all
40 countries.

CONTINUE

In the oil-producing countries of the Middle East and North Africa, growth is concentrated in male-dominated sectors. The consequent lack of women in socially-valued positions reinforces widely-shared
45 beliefs that men are more competent and deserving of status. This impedes the positive feedback loop that is occurring in Bangladesh, Britain, the U.S., and Zambia. Globally, rising female employment and leadership seem contingent upon shifts in
50 perceived interests, and exposure to women demonstrating their equal competence.

Exposure to men sharing care work appears to undermine people's internalized gender ideologies—their beliefs about what men and women can and
55 should do. For instance, men who cooked and cleaned in their youth (or saw other men doing so) did not regard it as "women's work." Instead, they took pride in their cooking, cleanliness, and capacity to wash shirts. Seeing men sharing care work also
60 seems to affect people's norm perceptions—their beliefs about what others think and do. Women who had grown up sharing care work with brothers were commonly more optimistic about social change. Besides wanting to share care work, they also
65 anticipated social support for their behavior.

But exposure to men sharing care work remains limited. This is partly because care work is typically performed behind closed doors, leading many to assume that such practices are uncommon. These
70 perceptions discourage others from sharing care work. Bana Collins, a market trader supporting an unemployed husband, exemplifies this: "Here in Zambia, a woman doesn't have time to rest … We were born into this system. Every woman must be
75 strong. It's just tradition. We are all accustomed to it. We can't change it."

Egalitarian social change is slowest when it is not publicly visible. Supportive work-family policies are important, but their acceptance is conditional on
80 norm perceptions. Even if people become privately critical, this does not seem sufficient for behavioral change. To amplify the ongoing progress toward gender equality, we need to increase exposure to both women as professionals and men as care
85 workers.

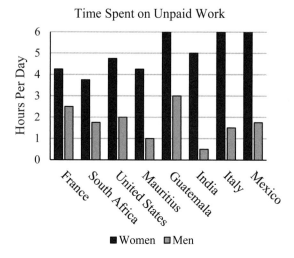

Time Spent on Unpaid Work

Adapted from, "More Women Are Running the World, so Why Aren't More Men Doing the Dishes?" © 2016 by Alice Evans.

11

The central claim of the passage is that

A) more women are in positions of leadership around the world, and this is reflected by the distribution of care work.

B) growing equality for women in some areas has not been accompanied by equality in others.

C) there are not enough role models for men who wish to make care work their career.

D) the rising cost of living has encouraged more women around the world to work outside the home.

12

The author makes use of which of the following to support her argument?

A) Evidence from recent works of art, television, and literature

B) Statistics from the U.S. Department of Labor

C) Comparisons among different nations and regions in the world

D) Analysis from feminist scholars at the University of Zambia

CONTINUE

13

Based on the passage, which choice best describes the relationship between young men's median wages and women's employment?

A) As young men's wages decreased, so did employment for women.

B) As young men's wages increased, so did employment for women.

C) As young men's wages went up, employment for women went down.

D) As young men's wages went down, employment for women went up.

14

Which choice provides the best evidence for the answer to the previous question?

A) Lines 14-16 ("In the … 2013")

B) Lines 36-39 ("This ideological … fields")

C) Lines 42-44 ("In the … sectors")

D) Lines 53-56 ("Exposure to … do")

15

As used in line 20, "contraction" most nearly means

A) muscle spasm.

B) abbreviation.

C) shrinkage.

D) squeezing.

16

The passage states that in some North African and Middle Eastern countries, women have not entered the workforce in greater numbers because

A) economic growth is focused in male-dominated fields.

B) men who perform care work do not do so in the public eye.

C) feedback loops give women in the oil industry greater acceptance.

D) governmental policies have not kept pace with changing attitudes.

17

Which choice best supports the conclusion that policies favorable to working women are insufficient to improve public perceptions of care work?

A) Lines 47-49 ("This impedes … Zambia")

B) Lines 60-62 ("Seeing men … do")

C) Lines 68-70 ("This is … uncommon")

D) Lines 79-81 ("Supportive … perceptions")

18

As used in line 83, "amplify" most nearly means

A) make louder.

B) boost.

C) make easier.

D) magnify.

CONTINUE

19

Which claim about unpaid work is supported by the data in the graph?

A) Men didn't average over four unpaid hours a day in any country studied.

B) Men in Guatemala and Italy did the same amount of unpaid work.

C) Women in France worked as much as women in Mauritius.

D) No countries studied showed a difference of less than two hours between men and women.

20

The author would most likely attribute the particularly high hourly disparities between men and women in Italy, India, and Mexico, as represented in the graph, to

A) national media narratives which undervalue work done by women.

B) the lack of changing perceptions about men performing care work.

C) the decline in median wages for young men since 1970.

D) the absence of government programs supporting women in the workforce.

Questions 21-31 are based on the following passage.

Passage 1 is adapted from Tim Crowe, "Health Check: Can Vitamins Supplement a Poor Diet?". ©2016 by Tim Crowe. Passage 2 is adapted from "Taking High Doses of Vitamins Can Do More Harm Than Good" by Peter McCaffery. ©2016 by Peter McCaffery.

Passage 1

Vitamins and minerals are essential for maintaining good health. While eating a varied diet should give us all the nutrients we need, recent diet and health surveys
Line show the typical diet is far from varied. The argument
5 that we need to supplement for best health has some truth, but primarily because of our poor eating habits.

There are groups of people for whom vitamin and mineral supplements may be recommended. Women planning pregnancy can benefit from folic acid and
10 iodine to reduce the risk of birth defects. People with limited exposure to sunlight would be advised to consider a vitamin D supplement. And, of course, people with a clinically diagnosed deficiency could benefit from taking supplements.

15 Most people think to take supplements "just in case," but this nutritional insurance policy may be an issue for more than just your wallet. Seeing a supplement as a solution may contribute to neglecting healthy food choices, which has consequences in the long-term.
20 Food is a complex mix of vitamins, minerals, and phytochemicals (plant chemicals that help reduce risk of health conditions). Supplements do not provide the same benefits of phytochemicals and other components found in food, such as fiber. Whole foods usually contain
25 vitamins and minerals in different forms. For example, vitamin E occurs in eight different forms, but supplements contain only one of these forms.

In a study of habits linked to long-term health, eating plenty of plant-based foods proved more effective than
30 taking supplements. In fact, these trials failed to find any benefit of improved life-expectancy or reduced risk of disease from taking supplements.

The promise of possible benefits from supplements distracts from what really promotes better health and
35 reduces chronic disease: eating a varied diet of minimally-processed and plant- based foods, exercising regularly,

CONTINUE

and refraining from smoking. If you feel you could
be lacking in certain vitamins and minerals, it is
better to look at changing your diet and lifestyle,
40　rather than reaching for supplements.

Passage 2

Without vitamins in our diet we wouldn't
survive, but taking too many can be harmful.
However, since the discovery of vitamins, the idea
that more is better has been promoted, much to the
45　benefit of manufacturers in this billion-dollar
industry. Driven by health-conscious consumers and
skeptics of mainstream medicine, the worldwide
market is huge.

One driving force behind the high doses of
50　vitamins came from the support of two-time Nobel
Prize winner Linus Pauling. In the 1970s, he
strongly promoted the work of American biochemist
Irwin Stone, who claimed that high amounts of
vitamin C could treat the common cold. Despite the
55　excitement, several trials have shown little effect of
vitamin C as an agent to relieve cold symptoms.

Worse still, for a number of years, the antioxidant
properties of vitamin C, vitamin E, and the beta-
carotene form of vitamin A were considered anti-
60　cancer agents. After a series of trials, however, these
supposed cancer-fighters have shown either no
effect, or actually an increase in the occurrence of
cancer. Vitamin E supplements were not found to
reduce prostate cancer, but rather led to a significant
65　increase of the disease.

The aim of these trials was to explore whether
taking more vitamins was beneficial, but perhaps a
more important task is exploring how these vitamins
operate. Beta-carotene is suggested to prevent cancer
70　and delay aging effects, but it can also be broken
down in the body into a molecule that interferes with
the body's own cancer prevention system.

We need to know more about the function of
vitamins and the consequences of high doses—
75　especially since we take so many without
considering their possible harm. A more complete
understanding of vitamins could help us find a better
balance. Until then, my advice would be to get all

your vitamins and nutrients from a balanced diet that
80　includes fruit and vegetables.

21

What is the author's central claim in Passage 1?

A) People should take vitamin supplements as a
preventative measure against sudden illness.

B) Eating a strictly vegetarian diet is more effective
than taking vitamins in maintaining overall
health.

C) Supplements can help those with insufficient
exposure to the sun by raising their levels of
vitamin D.

D) The health benefits people seek from
supplements are better achieved through diet.

22

Which of the following situations is most analogous
to the problem presented in lines 4-6?

A) A government enacts a policy that remedies one
symptom of a problem rather than addressing its
root cause.

B) An animal adapts to environmental changes
caused primarily by human actions.

C) A nonfiction author revises an earlier edition of
her book and releases a newer one to account for
new developments.

D) A television program encourages its viewers to
pursue more active lifestyles.

CONTINUE

23

The author of Passage 1 recognizes counterclaims to the position he takes in the passage by

A) acknowledging some studies that showed that vitamin B could protect against autoimmune diseases.

B) citing trials that did not show any link between supplements and increased life expectancy.

C) accepting that vitamin supplements can help some groups, like people with limited exposure to the sun.

D) conceding that eating vegetables and exercising vigorously are unpleasant activities.

24

Which choice best supports the claim in Passage 1 that it's better to get vitamins from foods than from supplements?

A) Lines 2-4 ("While eating … varied")

B) Lines 20-22 ("Food is … conditions")

C) Lines 28-30 ("In a … supplements")

D) Lines 33-35 ("The promise … disease")

25

As used in line 16, the phrase "nutritional insurance policy" is primarily meant to convey the idea that

A) some Americans enroll in private insurance policies that cover diseases of malnutrition.

B) people who take vitamin supplements often do so for additional assurance that they will remain healthy.

C) insurance premiums have become more expensive because more people take vitamin supplements.

D) doctors have advocated for a national subsidy to make vitamin supplements more affordable.

26

The author of Passage 2 indicates that, in comparison to vitamin supplements, a balanced diet is

A) less effective.

B) less likely to cause harm.

C) easier to obtain.

D) no more or less effective.

27

Which choice provides the best evidence for the answer to the previous question?

A) Lines 43-46 ("However … industry")

B) Lines 51-54 ("In the … cold")

C) Lines 57-60 ("Worse still … agents")

D) Lines 78-80 ("Until then … vegetables")

28

According to Passage 2, which of the following is true of beta-carotene?

A) It is an antioxidizing form of vitamins C and E with several healthy properties.

B) It is a supplement that generates billions of dollars in sales each year in the U.S. alone.

C) It has the potential to both increase and reduce the body's ability to fight cancer.

D) It has cold-curing properties discovered by Irwin Stone and promoted by C. Everett Koop.

CONTINUE

29

As it is used in line 49, the phrase "driving force" most nearly means

A) steering ability.

B) significant strength.

C) powerful influence.

D) effective action.

30

On which of the following points would the authors of both passages most likely agree?

A) For most otherwise healthy people, a balanced diet is preferable to vitamin supplements.

B) Clinical studies should further investigate the risks of high doses of vitamins.

C) Vitamins have several important cancer-fighting properties.

D) People with clinically diagnosed vitamin deficiencies should not take supplements.

31

Which best describes the overall relationship between Passage 1 and Passage 2?

A) Passage 1 advocates a different role for vitamin supplements than Passage 2, but both articles use the same studies as evidence.

B) Passage 1 doubts that vitamin supplements do much good, while Passage 2 suggests that they may actively cause harm.

C) Passage 1 recommends the use of vitamin supplements, while Passage 2 does not.

D) Passage 1 disputes the work of Stone and Pauling, while Passage 2 accepts it.

Questions 32-42 are based on the following passage.

This passage is adapted from a hearing featuring Archbishop Desmond Tutu before a subcommittee of the U.S. House of Representatives in 1984 in which he addresses the oppressive apartheid system in South Africa. Apartheid was a policy of segregation and political and economic discrimination against non-European groups in the Republic of South Africa.

Mr. Chairman and members of this committee, may I add a special word of appreciation to those who have been participating in the protests at the South African
Line Embassy and the South African consulates throughout
5 the United States in the Free South Africa Movement. I hope that we note this is a peaceful, nonviolent strategy to effect changes in the policies of the U.S. Government and within South Africa.

The oppressed in South Africa and the lovers of
10 freedom there are deeply thankful for this demonstration of solidarity with the exploited, the voiceless, and the powerless. The protest is not, might I point out, anti-South Africa. It is decidedly anti-apartheid, anti-injustice, and anti-oppression, which are not the same
15 thing. It is one of the ironies of the South African situation that I can be here, in this great and free land, the land of the brave and home of the free, to address so august a body as this; and yet, in my own country, the land of my birth, I would not be able to speak to a
20 comparable body because I and nearly 23 million other black South Africans are victims of the politics of exclusion.

Seventy-three percent of South Africa's population, the blacks, have no part in their nation's constitution,
25 which mentions them—quite incredibly—only once. How could this be seen as a step in the right direction? How could this be regarded as even remotely democratic? Its three chambers are racially defined. Consequently, racism and ethnicity are entrenched and
30 hallowed in the constitution.

The oppressed have protested these politics of exclusion, and they have done so peacefully. They have staged stayaways and demonstrations against the new constitution, against sham black local government,
35 against increases in rent, against increases in the general

CONTINUE

sales tax, and against the inferior education foisted on blacks. The South African Government has reacted violently and with a mailed fist—against a popular and mass movement of peaceful protest it
40 has reacted with violence. The problem of South Africa is the system, the repressive and unjust system of apartheid.

Mr. Chairman, our people are peace-loving to a fault. They have sought to change South Africa's
45 racist policies by peaceful means since 1912 at the very least, using conventional peaceful methods of demonstrations, petitions, delegations, and even a passive resistance campaign. As a tribute to this commitment of our people to peaceful change, the
50 only two South Africans to have won Nobel Peace Prizes are both black.

Mr. Chairman, we are talking about a moral issue. You are either for or against apartheid, and not by rhetoric. You are either in favor of evil, or you
55 are in favor of good. You are either on the side of the oppressed, or on the side of the oppressor. You cannot be neutral. Apartheid is evil and immoral, without remainder. It uses evil and immoral methods. If you had supported the Nazis against the
60 Jews, you would have been accused of adopting an immoral position. Apartheid is an evil as immoral in my view as Nazism, and in my view, the Reagan administration's support and collaboration with it is equally immoral, evil, and without remainder.

65 In court you are guilty as an accessory before or after the fact. Why should this administration respond so quickly and so decisively when something is done against Solidarity in Poland, applying sanctions at the drop of a hat, and yet when
70 similar treatment is meted out to black trade unions in South Africa, all we get is convoluted, deceptive arguments?

America is a great country, with great traditions of freedom and equality. I hope this great country
75 will be true to its history and its traditions, and will unequivocally and clearly take its stand on the side of right and justice in South Africa.

32

The main purpose of the passage is to

A) propose a new form of government in South Africa.

B) ask for America's support in abolishing apartheid in South Africa.

C) explain some of the benefits of the Free South Africa Movement.

D) ask for America's assistance in supporting apartheid in South Africa.

33

Desmond Tutu's tone is best described as

A) passionate.

B) remorseful.

C) skeptical.

D) inquisitive.

34

According to the passage, the anti-apartheid protests in the Free South Africa Movement had been

A) unorganized and violent.

B) unsupported by South African consulates.

C) supported by the Polish government.

D) without violence.

CONTINUE

35

Which choice provides the best evidence that South Africans are aware of some responses to apartheid in the United States?

A) Lines 6-8 ("I hope … Africa")

B) Lines 9-12 ("The oppressed … powerless")

C) Lines 43-44 ("Mr. Chairman … fault")

D) Lines 48-51 ("As a … black")

36

As used in line 11, "solidarity" most nearly means

A) harmony.

B) consensus.

C) federation.

D) support.

37

Desmond Tutu most strongly suggests that he

A) is displeased with the lack of support from the United States Government to abolish apartheid.

B) believes apartheid to be more evil and immoral than Nazism.

C) is angered that Poland supports the apartheid system.

D) believes the United States Government is more supportive of South Africa than Poland.

38

Which choice provides the best evidence for the answer to the previous question?

A) Lines 53-54 ("You are … rhetoric")

B) Lines 59-61 ("If you … position")

C) Lines 61-64 ("Apartheid is … remainder")

D) Lines 73-74 ("America is … equality")

39

Desmond Tutu uses the words "evil" and "immoral" in line 61 in order to emphasize the

A) dehumanizing and oppressive nature of apartheid.

B) growing strength of his movement's dissenters.

C) inner fortitude of the apartheid system's supporters.

D) challenge of using peaceful protest as a political tactic.

40

As it is used in line 64, "accessory" most nearly means

A) attaché.

B) collaborator.

C) adjunct.

D) subsidiary.

CONTINUE

41

In lines 15-22, what is the most likely reason that Desmond Tutu addresses the irony of his ability to speak before a sub-committee of the U.S. Congress?

A) To underscore the lack of civil rights in South Africa due to the apartheid system

B) To encourage Americans to reflect on their history and the abolition of slavery

C) To force Congress to answer and admit they were ignorant of South African realities

D) To stress the importance of peaceful protests against the apartheid system

42

The final paragraph (lines 73-77) serves to

A) support the claim in the previous paragraph with a historical example of apartheid.

B) praise the United States and ask again for their support.

C) direct attention to the listener's attention to the United States' tradition of compromise.

D) illustrate how superior South Africa is to the United States.

Questions 43-52 are based on the following passage.

This passage is adapted from "Testing ancient human hearing via fossilized ear bones" by Rolf Quam. ©2015 by Rolf Quam.

The internal anatomy of the ear influences its hearing abilities. Using CT scans and careful virtual reconstructions of fossilized bones from the ears of our
Line ancient human relatives, researchers have demonstrated
5 how our ancient ancestors heard the world. Hearing abilities are closely tied with verbal communication, so by figuring out when certain hearing capacities emerged during our evolutionary history, we might be able to shed some light on when spoken language started to
10 evolve. This is one of the most debated questions in paleoanthropology, since many researchers consider the capacity for spoken language a defining feature unique to humans.

Modern human beings are generally able to hear
15 sounds very well between 1.0-6.0 kHz, a range that includes many of the sounds of spoken language. Most vowels fall below 2.0 kHz, while consonants are mainly at higher frequencies. In contrast, lab tests show that chimpanzees—our closest living relative—and most
20 other primates aren't as sensitive in that same range. Chimpanzee hearing shows a loss in sensitivity between 1.0-4.0 kHz.

Researchers investigated when this human hearing pattern first emerged during our evolutionary history. In
25 particular, if they could find a similar pattern of good hearing between 1.0-6.0 kHz in a fossil human species, they could argue that language was present.
To study hearing capacities of fossils, they measured a large number of dimensions of the ancient ears—
30 including the length of the ear canal and the size of the ear drum—using virtual reconstructions of the fragile skulls on a computer. They then inputted all the data into a computer model that predicts hearing capacity based on ear anatomy. The model studies the capacity of the
35 ear as a receiver of a signal, similar to an antenna. The results show how efficiently the ear transmits sound energy from the environment to the brain.

Previously, studies investigated the hearing abilities in several fossilized hominin individuals from the site

CONTINUE

of the Sima de los Huesos ("Pit of the Bones") in
40 northern Spain. These fossils were about 430,000
years old, and anthropologists consider them
representative of ancestors of the later Neanderthals.
The computer model calculated that hearing abilities
45 in the Sima hominins were nearly identical to living
humans in showing a broad region of good hearing.

   In their current study, researchers are working
with much earlier hominin individuals, representing
the species *Australopithecus africanus* and
50 *Paranthropus robustus*. These fossils were
excavated at the sites of Sterkfontein and Swartkrans
in South Africa, and likely date to around two
million years ago.

   After measuring their ear structures and
55 modeling their hearing, these species were found to
have a hearing pattern that was more similar to a
chimpanzee—but slightly modified in the human
direction. In fact, these early hominins showed better
hearing than either chimpanzees or modern humans
60 from about 1.0-3.0 kHz, and the region of best
hearing was shifted toward slightly higher
frequencies compared with chimpanzees.

   This auditory pattern may have been a particular
advantage for living on the savanna. *A. africanus*
65 and *P. robustus* regularly occupied the savanna,
since as much as half of their diet was made up of
resources found in open environments, based on
measurements of isotopes in their teeth. In such open
environments, sound waves didn't travel as far as
70 they did in the rain forest canopy. Sound signals
tended to fade out sooner, and short-range
communication was favored. The hearing pattern of
these early hominins would have worked well in
these conditions.

75   There is a general consensus among
anthropologists that the small brain size and ape-like
cranial anatomy and vocal tract in these early
hominins indicate they likely did not have the
capacity for language. However, they certainly
80 could communicate vocally. Many primates
regularly emit a variety of vocalizations including
grunts, screams, and howls.

   These South African fossils have provided
another data point as we try to puzzle out the
85 emergence of language. Two million years ago, it
seems these early hominins didn't have language
capacity. But 430,000 years ago, it looks like the
Sima de los Huesos hominins did. Researchers
suspect that sometime between these early South
90 African forms and the later—more human-like—
Sima forms, language emerged.

(A)

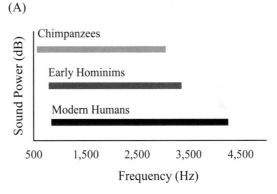

(B)

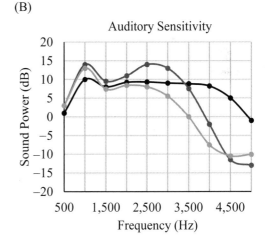

Graph (A) represents region of maximum sensitivity. Graph (B)
represents hearing sensitivity, with points higher on the curve
indicating greater sensitivity. Adapted from "Testing ancient
human hearing via fossilized ear bones" by Rolf Quam. ©2015
by Rolf Quam.

CONTINUE

43

Which one of the following best describes the overall structure of the passage?

A) Facts are provided, a prediction is made, and a potential experiment is outlined.

B) A common misconception is explained and refuted with evidence.

C) Disparate scientific facts are joined together by a central story.

D) A question is introduced, research is presented, and a conclusion is formed.

44

The first paragraph primarily serves to

A) describe a question that has long interested researchers.

B) make an unexpected accusation that the rest of the passage will explain.

C) lay out a hypothesis that the passage will prove to be false.

D) prove that a surprising comparison is indeed accurate.

45

According to the passage, early hominins from South Africa

A) had the capacity for language.

B) did not have the capacity for language.

C) could not communicate vocally.

D) had human-like cranial anatomy.

46

As used in line 28, "capacities" most nearly means

A) abilities.

B) volumes.

C) readiness.

D) magnitudes.

47

The passage most strongly suggests that *A. africanus* and *P. robustus's* greater hearing sensitivity

A) in the 1.0-3.0 kHz range would have helped them communicate in the rain forest.

B) in the 1.0-3.0 kHz range would have helped them communicate in the savanna.

C) in the 4.0-4.5 kHz range would have helped them communicate in the rain forest.

D) in the 4.0-4.5 kHz range would have helped them communicate in the savanna.

48

Which choice provides the best evidence for the answer to the previous question?

A) Lines 28-32 ("To study ... computer")

B) Lines 54-58 ("After measuring ... direction")

C) Lines 72-74 ("The hearing ... conditions")

D) Lines 83-85 ("These South ... language")

CONTINUE

49

As used in line 85, "emergence" most nearly means

A) elevation.

B) appearance.

C) coming.

D) approach.

50

Which choice provides the best evidence that factors other than hearing ability can suggest the capacity for language?

A) Lines 44-46 ("The computer … hearing")

B) Lines 58-62 ("In fact … with chimpanzees")

C) Lines 75-79 ("There is … language")

D) Lines 80-82 ("Many primates … howls")

51

Which choice is supported by the data in the second graphic?

A) Modern humans, chimpanzees, and early hominins have equal audio sensitivity at 3500 Hz.

B) Chimpanzees have greater audio sensitivity at 3500 Hz than humans and early hominins.

C) Modern humans have greater audio sensitivity at 4000 Hz than chimpanzees and early hominins.

D) Chimpanzees have greater audio sensitivity at 4000 Hz than modern humans and early hominins.

52

Data from both graphics best support which idea in the passage?

A) Sima hominins had the capacity for language.

B) Early hominins had better hearing than chimpanzees at 3.0 kHz.

C) Hearing abilities in the Sima hominins were identical to living humans.

D) Modern human beings are able to hear sounds very well between 3.0-10.0 kHz.

STOP

If you complete this section before the end of your allotted time, you may check your work on this section only. Do NOT use the time to work on another section.

Writing and Language Test

35 MINUTES, 44 QUESTIONS

Turn to Section 2 of your answer sheet to answer the questions in this section.

DIRECTIONS

Every passage comes with a set of questions. Some questions will ask you to consider how the writer might revise the passage to improve the expression of ideas. Other questions will ask you to consider correcting potential errors in sentence structure, usage, or punctuation. There may be one or more graphics that you will need to consult as you revise and edit the passage.

Some questions will refer to a portion of the passage that has been underlined. Other questions will refer to a particular location in a passage or ask that you consider the passage in full.

After you read the passage, select the answers to questions that most effectively improve the passage's writing quality or that adjust the passage to follow the conventions of standard written English. Many questions give you the option to select "NO CHANGE." Select that option in cases where you think the relevant part of the passage should remain as it currently is.

Questions 1-11 are based on the following passage.

Storyteller Without Words

When we talk about great graphic novels, **1** people usually point to Art Spiegelman's *Maus* (1991) as the defining early work. But the story of visual novels goes back much further than that. Lynd Ward, an American artist specializing in woodcuts, **2** induced a series of novels without words from 1929 to 1937 that match *Maus* for power, expressive ability, and political resonance.

1
A) NO CHANGE
B) one usually points
C) you usually point
D) we usually point

2
A) NO CHANGE
B) produced
C) reduced
D) adduced

CONTINUE

[1] Woodcutting is a form of engraving in which an artist carves an image into the flat side of a wooden block, which is then used as a stamp. [2] In *Wild Pilgrimage* (1932), he experimented with different colored inks, using black to represent reality and red to illustrate dreams. [3] Lynd Ward pushed the boundaries of this difficult technique throughout his career. [4] In his next work, *Prelude to a Million Years* (1933), he stopped drawing rectangular outlines and let his images fit the shape of whatever they represented. [5] In *Vertigo*, his 1937 classic, Ward shifted between page-filling images and tiny frames like a movie director alternating wide shots and close-ups. **3**

Thematically, Ward's work focuses on the alienation individuals face in a harsh, money-driven society. Sometimes these individuals are artists. The protagonist of *Gods' Man* (1929) is a painter exploited by businessmen and **4** whom policemen beat. *Prelude to a Million Years* tells the story of an art-obsessed sculptor who ignores the abusive relationship between his neighbors and finally burns to death in a fire caused by their fighting. **5**

3

To make this paragraph most logical, sentence 3 should be placed

A) where it is now.

B) before sentence 1.

C) before sentence 2.

D) before sentence 5.

4

A) NO CHANGE

B) beaten by policemen.

C) who is beaten by policemen.

D) policemen beat him.

5

At this point, the author is thinking of adding the following sentence:

> Although Ward himself was never caught in a fire, he did suffer from tuberculosis as a child.

Should the writer add this sentence here?

A) No, because it does not fit into this paragraph's list of characters alienated from society.

B) No, because none of Ward's characters are children.

C) Yes, because it adds biographical information that helps contextualize the scene from *Prelude to a Million Years*.

D) Yes, because it shows that authors' lives do not necessarily mirror events in their books.

CONTINUE

At other times, these individuals are members of the working class. **6** Factory workers and labor organizers are recurring characters in Ward's work. Some of his most powerful images show police assaulting workers on strike. One of the characters in *Vertigo* refuses to take a job when he realizes he has been **7** hired: as a scab, a non-union worker brought in to replace striking employees.

8 Unlike modern graphic novels, Ward's books do not include any dialogue or narrative text. One way they make up for this is through highly symbolic images. *Song Without Words* (1936) is a symbolic journey through a pregnant woman's fears of bringing a child into a world dominated by fascism. The key image of this book shows the woman shaking her fists **9** deferentially at a huge skull whose eyes are Nazis and whose teeth are tombstones.

6

A) NO CHANGE

B) Recurrence is made of characters who are factory workers and labor organizers.

C) Ward's work recurs with factory workers and labor organizers as characters.

D) Regarding characters, in Ward's work, factory workers and labor organizers recur.

7

A) NO CHANGE

B) hired, as a scab; a non-union worker

C) hired as a scab—a non-union worker

D) hired, as: a scab, a non-union worker

8

A) NO CHANGE

B) Unlike modern graphic novels, Ward did not include any dialogue or narrative text in his books.

C) Unlike modern graphic novels, no dialogue or narrative text is included in Ward's books.

D) Ward's books, unlike modern graphic novelists, do not include any dialogue or narrative text.

9

A) NO CHANGE

B) definitely

C) defiantly

D) deviantly

CONTINUE

Thematically rich and visually breathtaking, Lynd Ward's work deserves to be remembered as a milestone of visual storytelling. Happily, **10** they are seeing renewed attention in the 21st century. His six woodcut novels have been collected in a new edition by the Library of America, **11** prefaced with an introduction by Art Spiegelman himself.

10

A) NO CHANGE

B) it is seeing

C) one is seeing

D) you are seeing

11

A) NO CHANGE

B) preceded by a prefatory introduction composed by none other than Art Spiegelman himself.

C) and the Library of America engaged Art Spiegelman himself to write the introduction.

D) Art Spiegelman himself providing the introduction that precedes the six novels.

CONTINUE

Questions 12-22 are based on the following passage.

The Albatross

The albatross has long held a special place in the human imagination [12] for a long time and continues to do so. In Samuel Taylor Coleridge's 1798 poem *The Rime of the Ancient Mariner*, the bird plays a central role in conveying the poem's message of care for nonhuman life. [13] In works as enduring as Herman Melville's 1851 novel *Moby Dick* and those as recent as the 2005 sci-fi film *Serenity*, the albatross has retained its power as a metaphor. The real birds are no less remarkable than this powerful metaphor: albatrosses circled the whole earth on their huge wings millions of years before any humans could do so in ships.

[14] While we might imagine the albatross to be just one species, when there are actually 22 recognized albatross species. The biggest, the wandering albatross, has a wingspan that can reach up to 11 feet, 6 inches—the largest of any bird on earth. The range of most albatross species, including that of the wandering albatross, is restricted to the Southern Hemisphere, from South America to Africa to Australia, but four species live in the Northern Hemisphere, in the Pacific Ocean.

12

A) NO CHANGE
B) for many years
C) time and again
D) DELETE the underlined portion.

13

Which choice most effectively supports the idea that the albatross has long captured the human imagination?

A) NO CHANGE
B) Herman Melville's *Moby Dick* ends with the mention of "small fowls . . . screaming over the yet yawning gulf."
C) The titular Mariner in Coleridge's poem makes a grave mistake when he shoots an albatross with a crossbow.
D) Coleridge and other poets of the Romantic period were keenly interested in nature.

14

A) NO CHANGE
B) We might imagine the albatross to be just one species,
C) While we might imagine the albatross to be just one species,
D) While we might imagine the albatross to be just one species, but

CONTINUE

[1] Unlike land-based birds, which spend much of their time perched on trees or buildings, or coastal seabirds like gulls, which like to sit on docksides and shores, albatrosses spend most of their time in the air, landing only when they need to eat or breed. [2] Much like a glider, an albatross can use the rise and fall of the winds for propulsion, barely even flapping its wings. [3] Each bird has a special tendon that keeps its wings extended without using any energy. [4] In fact, the heart rate of a flying albatross is close to its heart rate on the ground. [5] Albatrosses are able to spend so much time aloft because their bodies have evolved to **15** accessorize extremely long flights. **16**

17 The most strenuous part of the flight for an albatross is taking off. Albatrosses have long **18** lifespans perhaps 50 or 60 years but they cannot breed until they are 5 or 6 years old. Once mature, they spend two or more years learning and preparing a special mating dance.

15

A) NO CHANGE
B) accommodate
C) acclimatize
D) accelerate

16

To make this paragraph most logical, Sentence 5 should be placed

A) where it is now.
B) after sentence 1.
C) after sentence 2.
D) after sentence 3.

17

Which choice most effectively conveys the main topic of the paragraph?

A) NO CHANGE
B) Human-sized gliders also make use of the currents in the air.
C) While the albatross spends most of its life in the air, it must land to breed.
D) Albatrosses range in size, but are large birds as a rule.

18

A) NO CHANGE
B) lifespans—perhaps 50 or 60 years—but
C) lifespans, perhaps; 50 or 60 years, but
D) lifespans, perhaps 50—or 60—years but

CONTINUE

These dances cement the [19] bound between [20] partner's and make it easier for them to recognize one another as they look after their egg. The egg incubates for up to 80 days, and it can take another 280 days before the chick is ready to fly; the larger the species of albatross, the longer it takes for chicks to learn to fly.

[21] Despite the albatross's incredible flying abilities, it's no wonder that [22] they have inspired so many poets. As it soars effortlessly above the remotest waters on earth, it almost seems to us like a visitor from another world.

19

A) NO CHANGE
B) bond
C) pact
D) vow

20

A) NO CHANGE
B) partners'
C) partner
D) partners

21

A) NO CHANGE
B) Given
C) Instead of
D) Notwithstanding

22

A) NO CHANGE
B) they are having
C) it have
D) it has

CONTINUE

Questions 23-33 are based on the following passage.

Flour Power

The tray in your hands is heavy with chocolate bonbons oozing cherry liqueur. Behind you, the smell of meringues and warm doughnuts wafts out of the kitchen. Your mouth is still sticky from the creamy éclair that wasn't quite pretty enough to serve. If you were a pastry cook, this would be a normal day on the **23** job? However, just because the work tastes good doesn't mean it's easy. Baking is exhausting and places demands on every **24** faculty—focus, precision, timing, and artistic sense, to name a few. Still, for many pastry cooks, the effort is worth the sweet reward.

Pastry chefs and pastry cooks work in a wide range of environments. Part of this range is captured in their titles. A pastry chef is specifically someone in charge of other people. A pastry cook might work alone at **25** a small establishment—a dessert station at a neighborhood restaurant, for example. A pastry chef might lead a whole team of pastry cooks at a dessert shop or in the kitchen of a resort, hotel, or private catering business. The size of the establishment **26** effects the kind of work a given cook will do: cooks in a larger kitchen are split up among preparation, production, and service duty, while a solo cook **27** had to fill all those roles.

23
A) NO CHANGE
B) job…
C) job,
D) job.

24
A) NO CHANGE
B) staff
C) notion
D) inquiry

25
A) NO CHANGE
B) a small establishment. A dessert station
C) a small establishment a dessert station
D) a small establishment; a dessert station

26
A) NO CHANGE
B) affect
C) affects
D) effect

27
A) NO CHANGE
B) has
C) has had
D) having

CONTINUE

[28] Whether one works as a pastry cook or as a pastry chef, baking is a deeply rewarding career. Many aspiring pastry cooks go to culinary school, where [29] you work methodically through categories of desserts like literature students work through novels: this month's unit is cakes, next month's is chocolates, and so on. Students in these programs combine in-class lessons with an "externship," a stint working in a real restaurant kitchen. [30] Since preparing desserts is a hands-on process, it's very important that cooks in training practice in a live environment. In fact, this real-world experience is so important that some pastry cooks forgo culinary school entirely, working their way up through kitchens without any formal training.

28

Which choice most effectively sets up the information that follows?

A) NO CHANGE

B) A pastry cook must attend culinary school to become a well-rounded baker.

C) Just as there are many places a pastry cook can work, there are multiple ways to become a cook in the first place.

D) Although most careers require an internship, baking usually involves an externship.

29

A) NO CHANGE

B) one works

C) he or she works

D) they work

30

A) NO CHANGE

B) Although

C) Nevertheless,

D) While

CONTINUE

31 They might start as line cooks, gradually become sous-chefs or assistant cooks, and finally take on a leadership role after many years.

[1] Once they complete their training, whether in school or out of school, pastry cooks find themselves in a moderately competitive market. [2] Because preparing desserts requires such specialized skills, pastry cooks have fewer qualified competitors than conventional cooks; however, there are also fewer positions for pastry cooks. [3] To become more attractive candidates, it's a good idea for pastry cooks to gain experience in other kinds of food preparation beyond baking. [4] For a **32** predictive employer, if a pastry cook can help out elsewhere in the kitchen—well, that's icing on the cake. **33**

31

At this point, the writer is considering adding the following sentence:

> Students at a culinary school have the benefit of a structured environment and supervision by prestigious instructors.

Should the writer make this addition here?

A) Yes, because structure is an important part of any pastry cook's success.

B) Yes, because it emphasizes how different an education cooks receive in and out of school.

C) No, because only some culinary schools have prestigious instructors.

D) No, because it interrupts the description of the alternative career path that does not involve culinary school.

32

A) NO CHANGE

B) constructive

C) prospective

D) anticipatory

33

To make this paragraph most logical, sentence 2 should be placed

A) where it is now.

B) before sentence 1.

C) after sentence 3.

D) after sentence 4.

CONTINUE

Questions 34-44 are based on the following passage and supplemental material.

A la Carte: How Restaurant Menus Might Influence Your Order

Well-run restaurants manage their customers' experiences as carefully as stage managers control theater productions. It's all about the little choices. Is the restaurant the kind of place where the servers will **34** loudly, noisily sing you "Happy Birthday," surrounded by baseball memorabilia? Is it the kind of place where servers carefully explain complicated dishes to you with impeccable French pronunciation, wearing crisp white aprons that match the crisp white tablecloths?

One surprisingly impactful choice relates to menu design. A 2009 Cornell University study found that menus that render prices as numerals without dollar signs, as in "8.75," encourage customers to spend more than menus which either use dollar signs, as in "$8.75," or **35** wrote out everything in words, as in "eight dollars and seventy-five cents."

The study took place over three months at the Culinary Institute of America's restaurant in Hyde Park, New York. The customers were a broad mix of **36** tourists, locals, and friends, and family, of culinary

34

A) NO CHANGE
B) loudly and noisily
C) loudly, at high volume
D) loudly

35

A) NO CHANGE
B) written
C) write
D) writes

36

A) NO CHANGE
B) tourists locals and friends and family
C) tourists, locals, and friends and family
D) tourists, locals, and friends and family,

CONTINUE

students and staff. **37** Servers **38** <u>erratically</u> gave their tables one of three menu types: a menu that used dollar signs and numerals, a menu that used numerals without dollar signs, and a menu that spelled out the numbers using words and wrote out "dollars."

At this point, the writer is considering adding the following sentence:

> In order to avoid biasing the customers, the researchers did not tell them the purpose of the study.

Should the writer include this sentence?

A) Yes, because the sentence provides relevant additional information about the experiment.

B) Yes, because the sentence explains the importance of the broad mix of customers previously mentioned.

C) No, because the paragraph is about what experimenters did, but this sentence only explains what they did not do.

D) No, because the information in this sentence contradicts information elsewhere in the paragraph.

A) NO CHANGE

B) randomly

C) oddly

D) haphazardly

CONTINUE

To isolate the effects of menu prices, it wasn't enough for the researchers to simply identify which tables spent the most. They also had to take into consideration additional factors like the size of the parties, the location of the tables, and the length of time that each group stayed in the restaurant. **39** Once these factors were controlled for, once the researchers concluded that menu styles affected how much customers spent. **40** Specifically, they discovered that the numerals-only menu correlated with an 8.15 percent increase in the amount that individuals paid. **41** The diners with menus that had no dollar signs paid an average total of $3.70—and over $5.00 more than what either of the other groups paid.

Change in Total Party Check, From Average

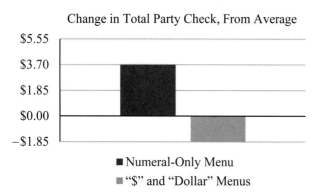

■ Numeral-Only Menu
■ "$" and "Dollar" Menus

This result was unexpected. The researchers had assumed that the menus with words only—as in "eight dollars"—would correlate with the biggest spending increases, because we aren't used to seeing prices represented that way. But ultimately, changing dollar signs to the word "dollars" had no **42** affect on the amount that parties spent.

39

A) NO CHANGE

B) These factors were controlled for, the researchers concluded

C) Once these factors were controlled for, the researchers concluded

D) Once these factors were controlled for, after the researchers concluded

40

A) NO CHANGE

B) Nevertheless,

C) Instead,

D) However,

41

Which of the following choices offers the most accurate interpretation of the graph?

A) NO CHANGE

B) The diners with "$" and "Dollar" menus paid more than any other group

C) Items on the menu with no dollar signs cost $3.70 more on average than items on other menus

D) The parties with menus that had no dollar signs paid an average total that was $3.70 more than the average for all parties

42

A) NO CHANGE

B) affect to

C) effect to

D) effect on

CONTINUE

43 Anecdotally, servers who sing birthday songs as part of their job don't always enjoy doing so. Given the highly specific circumstances of this experiment, it would be fascinating to replicate it in different **44** circumstances, perhaps the results would surprise us yet again.

43

Which of the following choices best establishes the main idea of the paragraph?

A) NO CHANGE

B) Ultimately, the Cornell study suggests that the ways that restaurant customers interact with text aren't always the most intuitive ones.

C) To make restaurant-going a more appealing experience, managers must do more to anticipate what customers want.

D) French cuisine is no longer the only kind of food people think of when they hear "fine dining," but it has a long history in the United States.

44

A) NO CHANGE

B) circumstances perhaps

C) circumstances. Perhaps

D) circumstances? Perhaps

STOP

If you complete this section before the end of your allotted time, you may check your work on this section only. Do NOT use the time to work on another section.

Math Test – No Calculator

25 MINUTES, 20 QUESTIONS

Turn to Section 3 of your answer sheet to answer the questions in this section.

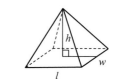

CONTINUE

1

Given $y - 4 = m(x - 3)$, where m is a non-zero constant, for what value of x does $y = 4$?

A) -3

B) 3

C) 4

D) 7

4

Which of the following expressions is negative for some value of x?

A) $|x + 4|$

B) $|x - 4|$

C) $|x - 4| + 1$

D) $|x - 4| - 2$

2

Which of the following inequalities describes the range of values of x shown in the number line above?

A) $-4 < x < 1$

B) $-4 \leq x < 1$

C) $-4 < x \leq 1$

D) $-4 \leq x \leq 1$

5

If y is four more than six times x, and y is also two more than four times x, what is y?

A) -2

B) 1

C) 2

D) 4

6

Which of the following is a solution to the equation $-x + 2(3x^2 + 3x) = 36 - x$?

A) -6

B) -2

C) 2

D) 6

3

Andrea makes chess pieces from stones she finds in her yard. She sells the pieces for \$5 each if they are sold individually and for \$2 each if they are sold in a set of 8. Which of the following expressions represents the amount, in dollars, that Andrea makes if she sells a individual chess pieces and s sets of 8?

A) $5a + 2s$

B) $5a + 16s$

C) $5s + 2a$

D) $5s + 8a$

CONTINUE

7

If $n^{3-x}(n^2) = n^7$ for every integer n, what is x?

A) -2

B) 2

C) 4

D) 5

8

Which of the following points is an x-intercept of the parabola given by $y = x^2 - 5x - 6$?

A) $(0, 5)$

B) $(0, 6)$

C) $(5, 0)$

D) $(6, 0)$

9

$$\frac{4 + 2i}{1 - i}$$

If $i = \sqrt{-1}$, which of the following is equivalent to the expression above?

A) $1 + 3i$

B) $3 + i$

C) 3

D) $3i$

10

For a function f, if $f(3) = 0$ and $f(8) = 0$, which of the following expressions could be equal to $f(x)$?

A) $x^2 + 3x + 8$

B) $x^2 - 11x + 24$

C) $x^2 + 9x + 64$

D) $x^2 - 3x - 8$

11

$$y = ax + 5$$
$$y = 6x + 3$$

If the system of equations above has no solution, and $a = 6k + 3$, what is the value of $2k$?

A) -4

B) 0

C) 1

D) 6

12

The function $y = (x - a)^2 - 1$ has two x-intercepts: $(2, 0)$ and $(4, 0)$. What is the value of a?

A) 2

B) 3

C) 4

D) 5

CONTINUE

13

If the sine of angle x is $\dfrac{4}{5}$, what is the cosine of x?

A) $\dfrac{3}{5}$

B) $\dfrac{4}{5}$

C) $\dfrac{4}{3}$

D) $\dfrac{3}{4}$

14

$$3x(x-3)(x+4)=0$$

Which of the following values of x is <u>not</u> a solution to the equation above?

A) -4

B) -3

C) 0

D) 3

15

$$N = \dfrac{K}{\dfrac{K-I}{I}(rt)}$$

The equation above models the population, N, of bacteria in fluid over time, t, in hours, where K is the maximum possible population, I is the initial population, and r is the population growth rate in bacteria per hour. Which of the following equations gives the growth rate in terms of N, t, K, and I?

A) $r = \dfrac{IK}{Nt(K-I)}$

B) $r = \dfrac{K(K-I)+IN}{Nt(K-I)}$

C) $r = \dfrac{KIt}{N(K-I)}$

D) $r = \dfrac{Nt(K-I)}{KI}$

CONTINUE

DIRECTIONS

Questions **16-20** ask you to solve a problem and enter your answer in the grid provided on your answer sheet. When completing grid-in questions:

1. You are required to bubble in the circles for your answers. It is recommended, but not required, that you also write your answer in the boxes above the columns of circles. Points will be awarded based only on whether the circles are filled in correctly.

2. Fill in only one circle in a column.

3. You can start your answer in any column as long as you can fit in the whole answer.

4. For questions 16-20, no answers will be negative numbers.

5. **Mixed numbers,** such as $4\frac{2}{5}$, must be gridded as decimals or improper fractions, such as 4.4 or as 22/5. "42/5" will be read as "forty-two over five," not as "four and two-fifths."

6. If your answer is a **decimal** with more digits than will fit on the grid, you may round it or cut it off, but you must fill the entire grid.

7. If there are **multiple correct solutions** to a problem, all of them will be considered correct. Enter only **one** on the grid.

Grid example answers:

`5 / 1 1`	`8 . 4`	`3 / 7`
`. 4 2 2`	`. 3 2 6`	`. 1 2 5`

CONTINUE →

16

$$4(x - 4) = 4$$

What is the solution to the equation above?

17

What is the slope of the line that passes through the points $(-2, -4)$ and $(3, 6)$?

18

$$f(x) = \frac{2x^3 + 5}{x^2 - 7x + 10}$$

What is one value of x that would make $f(x)$ undefined?

19

A satellite orbiting Earth begins a launch sequence to move its orbit to the moon. As it accelerates toward the moon, its speed in kilometers per second is given by the function $f(t) = 30 + 10t$, where t is the time in seconds that has passed since it changed course. If the satellite's maximum velocity is 150 kilometers per second, for how many seconds does it accelerate before hitting its maximum velocity?

20

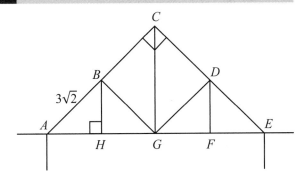

A Waddell "A" truss bridge is built across a river, as represented by the diagram above. If point H is the midpoint of $\overline{AG}$, point G is the midpoint of $\overline{AE}$, and point B is the midpoint of $\overline{AC}$, what is the length of the bridge, $\overline{AE}$, in meters?

STOP

If you complete this section before the end of your allotted time, you may check your work on this section only. Do NOT use the time to work on another section.

Math Test – Calculator

55 MINUTES, 38 QUESTIONS

Turn to Section 4 of your answer sheet to answer the questions in this section.

DIRECTIONS

Questions **1-30** ask you to solve a problem, select the best answer among four choices, and fill in the corresponding circle on your answer sheet. Questions **31-38** ask you to solve a problem and enter your answer in a grid provided on your answer sheet. There are detailed instructions on entering answers into the grid before question 31. You may use your test booklet for scratch work.

NOTES

1. You **may** use a calculator.
2. Variables and expressions represent real numbers unless stated otherwise.
3. Figures are drawn to scale unless stated otherwise.
4. Figures lie in a plane unless stated otherwise.
5. The domain of a function f is defined as the set of all real numbers x for which $f(x)$ is also a real number, unless stated otherwise.

REFERENCE

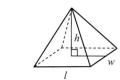

$$A = \frac{1}{2}bh \qquad a^2 + b^2 = c^2 \qquad \text{Special Triangles} \qquad V = \frac{1}{3}lwh \qquad V = \frac{1}{3}\pi r^2 h$$

$$A = lw \qquad V = lwh \qquad V = \pi r^2 h \qquad A = \pi r^2 \qquad V = \frac{4}{3}\pi r^3$$
$$C = 2\pi r$$

There are 360° in a circle.

The sum of the angles in a triangle is 180°.

The number of radians of arc in a circle is 2π.

CONTINUE

1

A total of 50 students are surveyed about their preferred sport. If 25 students prefer hockey, 10 prefer baseball, 10 prefer basketball, and 5 prefer football, what is the ratio of students who prefer hockey to students who prefer football?

A) 5:1

B) 5:2

C) 2:1

D) 1:5

2

Javed notices that a flock of birds flies close to the ground for a long time before flying upwards very quickly. Which of the following could be a graph of the birds' altitude over time?

A)
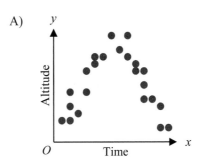

B)
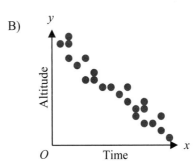

C)
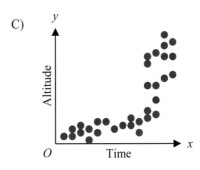

D)
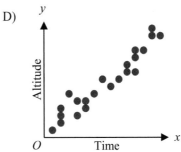

CONTINUE

3

Snails travel at a speed of about 13 millimeters per second. To the nearest minute, how long would it take for a snail to climb the Washington Monument, which is 169 meters tall? (1 millimeter = 0.001 meters)

A) 36

B) 77

C) 130

D) 217

4

$$6 < -3x$$

Which of the following is equivalent to the inequality above?

A) $x < -2$

B) $x > -2$

C) $x < 2$

D) $x > 2$

5

Restaurant Customers by Month

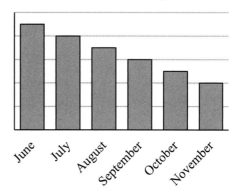

The number of customers per month in a restaurant is shown on the graph above. Which of the following statements best describes the change in the number of customers from June to November for this restaurant?

A) From June to November there was a steady increase in the number of customers.

B) From June to November there was neither an increase nor a decrease in the number of customers.

C) From June to November there was a sudden decrease, followed by a gradual decrease in the number of customers.

D) From June to November there was a steady decrease in the number of customers.

CONTINUE

Questions 6 and 7 refer to the following information.

A city has a number of cats and dogs in its shelters. A random selection of the animals from these shelters are surveyed, and are shown below.

	Dogs	Cats	Total
Male	35	32	67
Female	43	29	72
Total	78	61	139

6

The city wants to estimate the number of female cats and dogs they have in shelters. If there are 12,482 total animals in the city's shelters, which of the following changes would most likely improve the accuracy of the survey?

A) Survey more animals

B) Survey fewer animals

C) Conduct the survey a second time

D) Conduct the survey in a different city

7

Based on the data above, if a pet is selected from a city shelter at random, what is the probability that it will be a female dog?

A) $\dfrac{43}{72}$

B) $\dfrac{72}{139}$

C) $\dfrac{43}{78}$

D) $\dfrac{43}{139}$

8

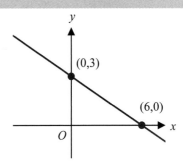

What is the slope of the line in the graph above?

A) 2

B) 1

C) $\dfrac{1}{2}$

D) $-\dfrac{1}{2}$

9

A chemist is pouring a 36 fluid ounce solution of NaCl mixed with purified water from a beaker. If she pours one-twelfth of the original solution into a second beaker and one-ninth of the original solution into a third beaker, what is the sum total of the solution, in fluid ounces, that the chemist pours into the second and third beakers?

A) 3

B) 4

C) 7

D) 21

CONTINUE

10

$$\frac{19}{4}x + \frac{11}{2} = \frac{3}{4}x + \frac{7}{2}$$

What value of x satisfies the equation above?

A) –5

B) $-\dfrac{5}{2}$

C) –2

D) $-\dfrac{1}{2}$

Questions 11 and 12 refer to the following information.

The following chart shows the number of minutes that each member of a family has spent communicating on their mobile devices.

Family Member	Texting	Calling	Instant Messaging
Janet	30	130	0
Rick	45	110	10
Evan	60	15	180
Lucy	75	30	160

11

On average, how many minutes per person were spent on texting and instant messaging?

A) 120

B) 130

C) 140

D) 150

12

How many additional minutes of texting did Lucy use compared to Janet, as a percentage of Janet's texting minutes?

A) 45%

B) 50%

C) 100%

D) 150%

13

$$4x < 8$$
$$-3x \leq 3$$

What is the range of all values of x that satisfy the system of inequalities above?

A) $1 \leq x < 2$

B) $-2 < x \leq -1$

C) $-1 \leq x < 2$

D) $-2 < x \leq 1$

14

If one Canadian dollar is worth 75 U.S. cents, how many Canadian dollars is $60 U.S. worth?

A) 45

B) 60

C) 75

D) 80

CONTINUE

15

Yearly Pollination Rate

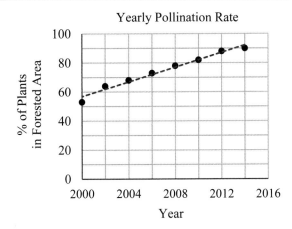

The graph above shows the pollination rate of plants in a certain forested area. Based on the line of best fit, what is the average annual increase in the pollination rate?

A)   5%

B)   3.8%

C)   2.5%

D)   1.5%

16

If the graph of a linear function passes through (2, 2) and (4, 6), which of the following is an expression of the function?

A) $f(x) = -2x + 2$

B) $f(x) = -2x - 2$

C) $f(x) = 2x + 2$

D) $f(x) = 2x - 2$

17

Ellie starts walking from her house toward her school, six miles away. She walks at three miles per hour. Her sister will leave the house on a bike, heading toward the school at nine miles per hour. How many minutes after Ellie should her sister leave so that they get to school at the same time?

A) 20

B) 40

C) 60

D) 80

18

Which of the following is a solution to $2x^2 + 9x + 7 = 0$?

A) $-\dfrac{9}{2}$

B) -1

C) 0

D) $\dfrac{9}{2}$

CONTINUE

Questions 19 and 20 refer to the following information.

A hockey team plays 30 games in a season. Their goal differential was recorded for each game, and that data is displayed on the histogram below. (Goal differential = goals scored – goals against.)

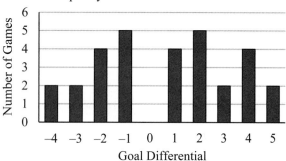

Frequency of Goal Differentials in a Season

19

What is the team's goal differential for the entire season?

A)   0

B)   11

C)   13

D)   19

20

What percentage of its games did the team win, to the nearest tenth of a percent?

A)   50.0%

B)   56.7%

C)   63.3%

D)   69.3%

21

$$y = -x^2 - 4x + 12$$

The shape of an arch is given by the equation above. The ground is where $y = 0$. What is the distance between the two places where the arch touches the ground?

A)   2

B)   6

C)   8

D)   12

22

$$-2y = 3x + 5$$
$$4y + kx = 4$$

In the system of equations above, k is a constant. If the system has no solution, what is the value of k?

A)   4

B)   5

C)   6

D)   7

CONTINUE

23

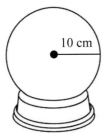

The glass snow globe shown in the diagram above weighs 2,000 grams when empty. The snow globe is filled 90% full with a mixture of water and white plastic particles. If this mixture has a density of 1.268 grams/cubic centimeter, what is the mass of the filled snow globe, to the nearest gram? (Note: Mass is equal to the product of density and volume.)

A) 4,780

B) 5,310

C) 6,780

D) 7,310

24

What is the y-coordinate of the vertex of the parabola given by the equation $y = x^2 - 10x + 29$?

A) 4

B) 5

C) 10

D) 29

25

$$\frac{3\sqrt{x+1}}{2} = \frac{3}{\sqrt{6x+1}}$$

According to the equation above, which of the following expressions must be equal to 0?

A) $3x^2 + 5x - 3$

B) $3x^2 + 7x + 3$

C) $6x^2 + 5x + 5$

D) $6x^2 + 7x - 3$

26

Probability Tree of Genetic Traits

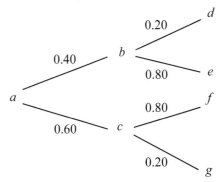

The probability tree above represents the probability of the outcome of two biology experiments, where the second experiment depends on the results of the first experiment. The first experiment begins with trait a and has a 40% chance of producing trait b and a 60% chance of producing trait c. What is the probability that the experiment will produce trait g?

A) 12%

B) 20%

C) 48%

D) 60%

CONTINUE

27

Line L passes through the points $(-3, 1)$ and $(1, 3)$. Line M passes through the points $(2, -4)$ and $(7, 11)$. If L and M intersect at the point (x, y), what is the value of $x + y$?

A)   4

B)   5

C)   6

D)   10

29

How many real solutions exist for the equation $0 = x^2 + 4x + 15$?

A)   0

B)   1

C)   2

D)   Cannot be determined

28

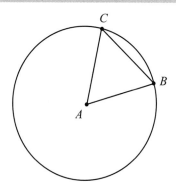

In the figure above, point A is the center of the circle, and line segments $\overline{AB}$, $\overline{AC}$, and $\overline{BC}$ form the equilateral triangle $\triangle ABC$ as shown. If minor arc $\overset{\frown}{BC}$ is $\dfrac{\pi}{3}$ units long, what is the area of the circle, in square units?

A) $\dfrac{\pi}{9}$

B) $\dfrac{\pi^2}{9}$

C) π

D) 3π

30

$$f(x) = \frac{(x+2)^2}{6}$$
$$g(x) = 2x - 2$$

Given functions f and g above, which of the following could be a line that passes through the intersection of $f(x)$ and $g(x)$ and is perpendicular to $g(x)$ in the xy-plane?

A) $y = -\dfrac{1}{2}x + 8$

B) $y = -\dfrac{1}{2}x + 4$

C) $y = -2x + 6$

D) $y = -2x + 8$

CONTINUE

DIRECTIONS

Questions **31-38** ask you to solve a problem and enter your answer in the grid provided on your answer sheet. When completing grid-in questions:

1. You are required to bubble in the circles for your answers. It is recommended, but not required, that you also write your answer in the boxes above the columns of circles. Points will be awarded based only on whether the circles are filled in correctly.

2. Fill in only one circle in a column.

3. You can start your answer in any column as long as you can fit in the whole answer.

4. For questions 31-38, no answers will be negative numbers.

5. **Mixed numbers**, such as $4\frac{2}{5}$, must be gridded as decimals or improper fractions, such as 4.4 or as 22/5. "42/5" will be read as "forty-two over five," not as "four and two-fifths."

6. If your answer is a **decimal** with more digits than will fit on the grid, you may round it or cut it off, but you must fill the entire grid.

7. If there are **multiple correct solutions** to a problem, all of them will be considered correct. Enter only **one** on the grid.

CONTINUE

31

If Spencer can read one comic book every 45 minutes, how many hours would it take Spencer to read 8 comic books?

32

In a small town, the ratio of cars to people is always 1:3. If the town's population increases from 270 to 360, how many more cars will there be?

33

x	3	4	5	6
$f(x)$	12	15	18	21

Based on the table above, if f is a linear function, what is $f(-1)$?

34

Sebastian's bill at a restaurant is $50 before taxes. There is a tax of 13%, and Sebastian wants to leave a tip equal to 15% of the before-tax price. How much, in dollars, should Sebastian pay in total? (Disregard the dollar sign when gridding your answer.)

35

If $\dfrac{x^3 - 12x + 16}{x + 4} = 0$, what is a possible value of x?

CONTINUE

36

$$\frac{2}{1+i}$$

If the expression above is written in the form $a + bi$, where a and b are real numbers, what is the value of $a + b$? (Note: $i = \sqrt{-1}$)

Questions 37 and 38 refer to the following information.

Students in a science class found several ladybugs and counted the number of spots on each one. Their findings are displayed in the following table:

Number of Spots	Number of Ladybugs Found
9	1
10	4
11	6
12	8
13	2

37

What was the median number of spots on the ladybugs the students found?

38

After collecting the data in the table, one student found three more ladybugs, all with the same number of spots. When these ladybugs were added to the data set, the mean number of spots on a ladybug was exactly 12. How many spots did each of the newly found ladybugs have?

STOP

If you complete this section before the end of your allotted time, you may check your work on this section only. Do NOT use the time to work on another section.

Essay (Optional)

50 MINUTES

Turn to the lined pages of your answer sheet to write your essay.

DIRECTIONS

This essay is optional. It is a chance for you to demonstrate how well you can understand and analyze a written passage. Your essay should show that you have carefully read the passage and should be a concisely written analysis that is both logical and clear.

You must write your entire essay on the lines in your answer booklet. No additional paper will be provided aside from the Planning Page inside your answer booklet. You will be able to write your entire essay in the space provided if you make use of every line, keep tight margins, and write at a suitable size. Don't forget to keep your handwriting legible for the readers evaluating your essay.

You will have 50 minutes to read the passage in this booklet and to write an essay in response to the prompt provided at the end of the passage.

REMINDERS

- What you write in this booklet will not be evaluated. Write your essay in the answer booklet only.

- Essays that are off-topic will not be evaluated.

Adapted from Jamie T. Mullins, "What causes asthma? Clues from London's Great Smog with implications for air pollution today," © 2016 by Jamie T. Mullins. Originally published on www.theconversation.com, July 26, 2016.

1   Asthma is a chronic respiratory condition with no known cure. It impacts people of all ages through episodic constrictions of the airways, which may be even worse than it sounds. Approximately 334 million people worldwide suffer from asthma, including 24 million Americans and 5.4 million residents of the U.K., and the average annual cost of each case has been estimated to be between $2,300 and $4,000.

2   In a recent study, my coauthors and I used an unexpected exposure to a major air pollution event—the Great London Smog of 1952—to demonstrate that air pollution exposure in early life leads to higher incidence of asthma during both childhood and adulthood. While London's air is much cleaner today than it was 60 years ago, our findings have major implications for the many countries that continue to struggle with high levels of urban air pollution.

3   The Great Smog took place in London over five days in early December 1952. During that time, a layer of warm air settled over the city, trapping colder air near ground level. The cold air drove Londoners to pile coal on their fires to keep warm, and the upper layer of warm air trapped the resulting smoke near the ground where it mixed with a heavy fog.

4   Ultimately, some 3,000 to 4,000 "extra" deaths—that is, deaths above the normal rates, which are attributed to the abnormal conditions—occurred during the Great Smog. Approximately 8,000 more cardiac and respiratory deaths over the next several months have also been linked to the smog. The toll of the Great Smog was so large that it ultimately served as a major impetus for the passage of the 1956 and 1968 U.K. Clean Air Acts.

5   In our analysis, we found that people who were exposed to the Great Smog during the first year of life were four to five times more likely to develop asthma as a child and three times more likely to report asthma as an adult, compared to baseline rates. We also found evidence suggesting that children who were exposed to the Great Smog in utero suffered twice the normal rate of childhood asthma. Our results indicate that early exposure to air pollution has significant long-term impacts on health, and contributes to the development of asthma.

6   Our results suggest that reducing exposure to extreme air pollution events, especially among the young, may be an effective means of combating the initial development of asthma. By improving air quality and protecting young children from air pollution, policy makers and doctor-parent teams may be able to meaningfully reduce the likelihood of asthma in individual children and the incidence of asthma in the population as a whole.

7   Our findings also dramatically illustrate the long-term effects of air pollution exposure. While there is a strong consensus that exposure to air pollution negatively affects health, our work presents some of the

first evidence that such exposure has lifelong consequences. The London Smog took place more than 60 years ago, but some of those that lived through it are still feeling its impacts today.

8   Such long-term effects have ominous implications for the millions of people around the world who are exposed regularly to extreme air pollution. In a recent article, Douglas Dockery and Arden Pope—two of the foremost researchers on air pollution and health—noted that conditions during a 2013 air pollution event in Harbin, China were "remarkably similar to those from London during the 1952 Great Smog."

9   Unfortunately, such extreme air pollution is both a widespread and growing problem. Beijing suffered some of its worst recorded air pollution at the end of 2015. And for all of the attention that air quality in China has received since the Beijing Olympics, none of its cities even makes the list of the top 20 most polluted in the world. Much of the urban population in emerging Asia, the Middle East and Africa regularly face more extreme levels of air pollution. Our results suggest that the negative health impacts of these exposures will last for many years to come.

Write an essay in which you explain how Jamie T. Mullins builds an argument to persuade his audience that air pollution is a serious problem with severe impacts on human health. In your essay, analyze how Mullins uses one or more of the features listed in the directions on the previous page (or features of your own choice) to strengthen the logic and persuasiveness of his argument. Be sure that your analysis focuses on the most relevant features of the passage.

Your essay should not explain whether you agree with Mullins's claims, but rather explain how Mullins builds an argument to persuade his audience.

Answers and Scoring
Chapter 3

Practice Test Answers

Test 1

For answer explanations, please visit **ivyglobal.com/study**.

Reading

1. A	12. B	23. B	34. B	45. A
2. B	13. A	24. D	35. C	46. C
3. A	14. A	25. B	36. D	47. A
4. B	15. D	26. A	37. A	48. B
5. B	16. B	27. A	38. C	49. C
6. D	17. C	28. C	39. A	50. D
7. C	18. D	29. B	40. A	51. D
8. B	19. C	30. D	41. C	52. C
9. D	20. D	31. D	42. D	
10. D	21. A	32. B	43. B	
11. C	22. B	33. B	44. C	

Writing

1. A	10. C	19. C	28. A	37. D
2. C	11. D	20. D	29. D	38. B
3. D	12. C	21. D	30. B	39. A
4. C	13. C	22. A	31. A	40. D
5. D	14. B	23. B	32. B	41. D
6. B	15. C	24. C	33. B	42. C
7. B	16. A	25. C	34. B	43. B
8. B	17. D	26. B	35. A	44. B
9. C	18. C	27. D	36. C	

Math – No Calculator

1. C	5. D	9. C	13. B	17. 10
2. C	6. B	10. A	14. B	18. 17/2 or 8.5
3. B	7. A	11. B	15. B	19. 6
4. C	8. B	12. A	16. 3	20. 6

Math – Calculator

1. D	9. C	17. B	25. A	33. 18
2. B	10. B	18. C	26. C	34. 3
3. B	11. D	19. C	27. C	35. 16
4. B	12. A	20. D	28. B	36. 4
5. B	13. B	21. C	29. A	37. 117
6. B	14. D	22. D	30. C	38. 80
7. D	15. C	23. C	31. 18	
8. B	16. D	24. B	32. 142	

For live scoring and scaling, please visit **cloud.ivyglobal.com**.

Practice Test Answers

Test 2

For answer explanations, please visit **ivyglobal.com/study**.

Reading

1. C	12. C	23. A	34. A	45. B
2. B	13. A	24. C	35. C	46. D
3. C	14. D	25. B	36. B	47. D
4. D	15. A	26. B	37. C	48. C
5. D	16. D	27. B	38. D	49. A
6. C	17. D	28. D	39. C	50. C
7. D	18. D	29. B	40. A	51. B
8. A	19. A	30. B	41. A	52. A
9. D	20. B	31. D	42. C	
10. D	21. B	32. B	43. A	
11. B	22. A	33. C	44. C	

Writing

1. A	10. A	19. B	28. C	37. C
2. D	11. D	20. C	29. B	38. C
3. A	12. D	21. B	30. C	39. A
4. B	13. B	22. D	31. B	40. C
5. C	14. C	23. B	32. D	41. C
6. C	15. C	24. A	33. D	42. D
7. D	16. A	25. B	34. D	43. A
8. B	17. D	26. B	35. C	44. C
9. D	18. B	27. D	36. B	

Math – No Calculator

1. B	5. B	9. D	13. D	17. $1/5 \leq x \leq 1$
2. B	6. A	10. B	14. A	18. 7
3. A	7. B	11. B	15. B	19. 3
4. C	8. A	12. B	16. 63	20. 18

Math – Calculator

1. B	9. B	17. A	25. B	33. 1.5
2. A	10. C	18. A	26. B	34. 15
3. B	11. A	19. C	27. B	35. 0
4. B	12. A	20. C	28. C	36. 40
5. B	13. D	21. D	29. C	37. 10
6. A	14. A	22. A	30. B	38. 17
7. B	15. B	23. B	31. 8	
8. A	16. A	24. D	32. 32	

For live scoring and scaling, please visit **cloud.ivyglobal.com**.

Practice Test Answers

Test 3

For answer explanations, please visit **ivyglobal.com/study**.

Reading

1. B	12. D	23. B	34. C	45. C
2. C	13. A	24. D	35. B	46. D
3. A	14. D	25. A	36. C	47. A
4. D	15. D	26. A	37. C	48. B
5. D	16. A	27. B	38. D	49. A
6. A	17. C	28. A	39. B	50. D
7. B	18. D	29. D	40. B	51. C
8. D	19. A	30. B	41. A	52. C
9. C	20. A	31. C	42. B	
10. B	21. C	32. C	43. C	
11. C	22. B	33. C	44. A	

Writing

1. C	10. D	19. B	28. D	37. C
2. D	11. B	20. C	29. C	38. A
3. A	12. C	21. A	30. B	39. D
4. D	13. A	22. C	31. D	40. C
5. B	14. B	23. D	32. C	41. B
6. D	15. D	24. A	33. D	42. C
7. B	16. D	25. C	34. D	43. C
8. C	17. C	26. D	35. B	44. D
9. A	18. C	27. B	36. A	

Math – No Calculator

1. B	5. C	9. B	13. B	17. 5
2. C	6. A	10. A	14. C	18. 0
3. D	7. B	11. A	15. D	19. 16
4. B	8. A	12. C	16. 10	20. 48

Math – Calculator

1. C	9. B	17. C	25. C	33. 5
2. D	10. A	18. D	26. B	34. 45
3. A	11. C	19. D	27. C	35. 233
4. B	12. C	20. B	28. D	36. 10
5. A	13. B	21. A	29. C	37. 86
6. C	14. D	22. D	30. D	38. 60
7. A	15. C	23. B	31. 18	
8. C	16. B	24. B	32. 10	

For live scoring and scaling, please visit **cloud.ivyglobal.com**.

Practice Test Answers

Test 4

For answer explanations, please visit **ivyglobal.com/study**.

Reading

1. B	12. B	23. A	34. A	45. C
2. C	13. D	24. B	35. B	46. D
3. A	14. C	25. A	36. D	47. B
4. A	15. B	26. D	37. C	48. A
5. B	16. D	27. A	38. C	49. C
6. B	17. C	28. C	39. D	50. A
7. D	18. A	29. D	40. A	51. B
8. B	19. B	30. B	41. C	52. A
9. A	20. A	31. C	42. B	
10. B	21. C	32. B	43. A	
11. D	22. A	33. C	44. D	

Writing

1. D	10. D	19. D	28. B	37. D
2. B	11. A	20. C	29. B	38. A
3. A	12. A	21. B	30. B	39. D
4. C	13. D	22. B	31. C	40. C
5. B	14. C	23. B	32. C	41. D
6. B	15. A	24. B	33. C	42. B
7. A	16. C	25. D	34. B	43. A
8. B	17. B	26. C	35. D	44. A
9. A	18. D	27. C	36. C	

Math – No Calculator

1. B	5. D	9. D	13. C	17. 9
2. C	6. C	10. C	14. A	18. 7
3. B	7. B	11. A	15. D	19. 5/2 or 2.5
4. B	8. A	12. C	16. 3/2 or 1.5	20. 60

Math – Calculator

1. C	9. A	17. B	25. B	33. 1.2 or 6/5
2. B	10. A	18. A	26. B	34. 19
3. C	11. A	19. C	27. A	35. 487
4. C	12. C	20. A	28. B	36. 18
5. A	13. B	21. C	29. D	37. 12
6. C	14. A	22. B	30. C	38. 8
7. D	15. A	23. C	31. 4	
8. C	16. B	24. B	32. 70	

 For live scoring and scaling, please visit **cloud.ivyglobal.com**.

Practice Test Answers

Test 5

For answer explanations, please visit **ivyglobal.com/study**.

Reading

1. C	12. D	23. A	34. C	45. D
2. A	13. A	24. A	35. B	46. D
3. D	14. D	25. B	36. D	47. B
4. C	15. C	26. B	37. A	48. C
5. B	16. A	27. C	38. C	49. C
6. A	17. B	28. D	39. A	50. B
7. B	18. B	29. D	40. A	51. A
8. D	19. B	30. B	41. D	52. D
9. B	20. D	31. D	42. C	
10. B	21. B	32. A	43. D	
11. D	22. B	33. C	44. C	

Writing

1. A	10. B	19. C	28. D	37. A
2. B	11. C	20. C	29. B	38. C
3. C	12. C	21. D	30. B	39. C
4. C	13. D	22. B	31. D	40. B
5. D	14. B	23. B	32. B	41. C
6. A	15. D	24. C	33. D	42. D
7. D	16. B	25. A	34. A	43. C
8. B	17. C	26. A	35. D	44. B
9. C	18. A	27. C	36. C	

Math – No Calculator

1. A	5. D	9. D	13. C	17. 3
2. C	6. D	10. B	14. D	18. 2
3. D	7. A	11. B	15. B	19. 18
4. A	8. C	12. C	16. 2	20. 100

Math – Calculator

1.	B	9.	A	17.	B	25.	C	33.	195
2.	C	10.	B	18.	A	26.	D	34.	0.625 or 5/8
3.	B	11.	A	19.	D	27.	A	35.	3
4.	C	12.	D	20.	B	28.	B	36.	3
5.	B	13.	A	21.	A	29.	C	37.	15
6.	B	14.	A	22.	C	30.	B	38.	80
7.	D	15.	D	23.	C	31.	4.5 or 9/2		
8.	D	16.	C	24.	C	32.	9		

 For live scoring and scaling, please visit **cloud.ivyglobal.com**.

Practice Test Answers

Test 6

For answer explanations, please visit **ivyglobal.com/study**.

Reading

1. A	12. C	23. C	34. D	45. B
2. A	13. D	24. C	35. B	46. A
3. C	14. A	25. B	36. D	47. B
4. D	15. C	26. B	37. A	48. C
5. D	16. A	27. D	38. C	49. B
6. B	17. D	28. C	39. A	50. C
7. B	18. B	29. C	40. B	51. C
8. B	19. A	30. A	41. A	52. B
9. D	20. B	31. B	42. B	
10. B	21. D	32. B	43. D	
11. B	22. A	33. A	44. A	

Writing

1. D	10. B	19. B	28. C	37. A
2. B	11. A	20. D	29. D	38. B
3. C	12. D	21. B	30. A	39. C
4. B	13. A	22. D	31. D	40. A
5. A	14. C	23. D	32. C	41. D
6. A	15. B	24. A	33. A	42. D
7. C	16. B	25. A	34. D	43. B
8. A	17. C	26. C	35. C	44. C
9. C	18. B	27. B	36. C	

Math – No Calculator

1. B	5. A	9. A	13. A	17. 2
2. B	6. C	10. B	14. B	18. 2 or 5
3. B	7. A	11. C	15. A	19. 12
4. D	8. D	12. B	16. 5	20. 12

Math – Calculator

1.	A	9.	C	17.	D	25.	D	33.	0
2.	C	10.	D	18.	B	26.	A	34.	64
3.	D	11.	C	19.	D	27.	D	35.	2
4.	A	12.	D	20.	B	28.	C	36.	0
5.	D	13.	C	21.	C	29.	A	37.	11
6.	A	14.	D	22.	C	30.	A	38.	17
7.	D	15.	C	23.	C	31.	6		
8.	D	16.	D	24.	A	32.	30		

For live scoring and scaling, please visit **cloud.ivyglobal.com**.

Answers and Scoring | **Ivy Global**

The Scoring System
Part 2

The new SAT will have three test scores on a scale from 10 to 40. There will be one test score for each test: the Reading Test, the Writing and Language Test, and the Math Test. The Reading Test score and the Writing and Language Test score will be added together and converted to a single area score in Evidence-Based Reading and Writing; there will also be an area score in Math-based on the Math Test Score.

The area scores will be on a scale from 200 to 800. Added together, they will form the composite score for the whole test, on a scale from 400 to 1600. The Essay will be scored separately and will not affect your scores in other areas.

SAT Scoring	
Test Scores (10 to 40)	• Reading Test • Writing and Language Test • Math Test
Area Scores (200 to 800)	• Evidence-Based Reading and Writing • Math
Composite Score (400 to 1600)	• Math (Area Score) + Evidence-Based Reading and Writing (Area Score)
Essay Scores (1 to 4)	• Reading • Analysis • Writing

The College Board will also be reporting new types of scores. **Cross-test scores** for **Analysis in Science** and **Analysis in History/Social Studies** will be based on performance on specific questions across different tests relating to specific types of content. For example, your cross-test score in Analysis in Science will be based on your performance on questions relating to science passages on the Reading Test as well as questions using scientific data on the Math Test. These scores will be on a scale from 10 to 40.

There will also be seven **subscores** based on particular question types within each test section. Subscores will be reported on a scale from 1 to 15. Four will be related to particular questions in the Reading and Writing and Language Test: Words in Context, Command of Evidence, Expression of Ideas, and Standard English Conventions. The other three relate to specific types of questions on the Math Test: Heart of Algebra, Problem Solving and Data Analysis, and Passport to Advanced Math.

Cross-Test Scores and Subscores

You will receive **cross-test scores** for Analysis in Science and Analysis in History/Social Studies. The scores are based on your performance on questions in their respective subject domains across all sections of the exam. These scores will be reported on a scale of 10-40.

You will also receive **subscores** based on your performance on certain question types within each test section. Subscores will be reported on a scale of 1-15. There will be seven subscores, for the following areas:

- **Words in Context:** this subscore will be based on your performance on questions related to determining the meanings of words in the context of a passage in the Reading and Writing and Language tests.

- **Command of Evidence:** this subscore will be based on your performance on questions that ask you to identify the best evidence in the Reading and Writing and Language tests.

- **Expression of Ideas:** this subscore will be based on your performance on questions that ask you to identify clear, stylistically appropriate choices in Writing passages.

- **Standard English Conventions:** this subscore will be based on your performance on questions that ask you to identify and correct errors of grammar, punctuation, usage, and syntax in Writing passages.

- **Heart of Algebra:** this subscore will be based on your performance on Math questions testing key concepts in Algebra.

- **Problem Solving and Data Analysis**: this subscore will be based on your performance on Math questions testing your ability to analyze sets of data, the meanings of units and quantities, and the properties of different objects and operations.

- **Passport to Advanced Math:** this subscore will be based on your performance on Math questions that test the skills you'll build on as you continue to learn more advanced math including rewriting expressions, solving quadratic equations, working with polynomials and radicals, and solving systems of equations.

You can calculate these scores online using our free scoring tools.

  For live scoring and scaling, please visit **cloud.ivyglobal.com**.

Scoring Your Tests

Part 3

You can score your tests online using our free scoring tools, or you can use the tables below to help you calculate your scores.

 For live scoring and scaling, please visit **cloud.ivyglobal.com**.

To score your tests manually, first use the answer key to mark each of your responses right or wrong. Then, calculate your **raw score** for each section by counting up the number of correct responses.

Section	Raw Score (# of Questions Correct)					
	Test 1	Test 2	Test 3	Test 4	Test 5	Test 6
1. Reading	___	___	___	___	___	___
2. Writing and Language	___	___	___	___	___	___
3. Math: No-Calculator	___	___	___	___	___	___
4. Math: Calculator	___	___	___	___	___	___
Raw Score for Reading (Section 1)	___	___	___	___	___	___
Raw Score for Writing and Language (Section 2)	___	___	___	___	___	___
Raw Score for Math (Section 3 + 4)	___	___	___	___	___	___

Scaled Scores

Once you have found your raw score for each section, convert it into an approximate **scaled test score** using the following chart. To find a scaled test score for each section, find the row in the Raw Score column which corresponds to your raw score for that section, then check the column for the section you are scoring in the same row. For example, if you had a raw score of 48 for Reading, then your scaled Reading test score would be 39. Keep in mind that these scaled scores are estimates only. Your actual SAT score will be scaled against the scores of all other high school students taking the test on your test date.

Raw Score	Math Scaled Score	Reading Scaled Score	Writing Scaled Score	Raw Score	Math Scaled Score	Reading Scaled Score	Writing Scaled Score
58	40			28	23	26	25
57	40			27	22	25	24
56	40			26	22	25	24
55	39			25	21	24	23
54	38			24	21	24	23
53	37			23	20	23	22
52	36	40		22	20	22	21
51	35	40		21	19	22	21
50	34	40		20	19	21	20
49	34	39		19	18	20	20
48	33	39		18	18	20	19
47	33	38		17	17	19	19
46	32	37		16	16	19	18
45	32	36		15	15	18	18
44	31	35	40	14	14	17	17
43	30	34	39	13	13	16	16
42	30	34	38	12	12	16	15
41	29	33	37	11	11	14	14
40	29	33	35	10	10	13	13
39	28	32	34	9	10	12	12
38	28	31	33	8	10	11	11
37	27	31	32	7	10	10	10
36	27	30	31	6	10	10	10
35	26	30	30	5	10	10	10
34	26	29	29	4	10	10	10
33	25	29	28	3	10	10	10
32	25	28	27	2	10	10	10
31	24	28	27	1	10	10	10
30	24	27	26	0	10	10	10
29	23	26	26				

Use the table below to record your scaled scores:

	Scaled Scores					
Section	Test 1	Test 2	Test 3	Test 4	Test 5	Test 6
Reading (Out of 40)	_____	_____	_____	_____	_____	_____
Writing and Language (Out of 40)	_____	_____	_____	_____	_____	_____
Math (Out of 40)	_____	_____	_____	_____	_____	_____

Essay Score

Estimate your essay score by assigning your essay a score out of 1-4 in each scoring area listed below. Have a trusted reader check your work. For more information on essay scoring criteria, see Chapter 4 of Ivy Global's New SAT Guide.

	Essay Score					
Scoring Area	Reading		Analysis		Writing	
	Reader 1	Reader 2	Reader 1	Reader 2	Reader 1	Reader 2
Test 1	_____	_____	_____	_____	_____	_____
Test 2	_____	_____	_____	_____	_____	_____
Test 3	_____	_____	_____	_____	_____	_____
Test 4	_____	_____	_____	_____	_____	_____
Test 5	_____	_____	_____	_____	_____	_____
Test 6	_____	_____	_____	_____	_____	_____

Area Score Conversion

You can look up your area score out of 800 below. To find your overall score, combine your area score for Reading + Writing with your area score for Math to get your total score out of 1600.

Reading + Writing

Scaled Score	Area Score	Scaled Score	Area Score	Scaled Score	Area Score
80	760-800	59	550-630	39	350-430
79	750-800	58	540-620	38	340-420
78	740-800	57	530-610	37	330-410
77	730-800	56	520-600	36	320-400
76	720-800	55	510-590	35	310-390
75	710-790	54	500-580	34	300-380
74	700-780	53	490-570	33	290-370
73	690-770	52	480-560	32	280-360
72	680-760	51	470-550	31	270-350
71	670-750	50	460-540	30	260-340
70	660-740	49	450-530	29	250-330
69	650-730	48	440-520	28	240-320
68	640-720	47	430-510	27	230-310
67	630-710	46	420-500	26	220-300
66	620-700	45	410-490	25	210-290
65	610-690	44	400-480	24	200-280
64	600-680	43	390-470	23	200-270
63	590-670	42	380-460	22	200-260
62	580-660	41	370-450	21	200-250
61	570-650	40	360-440	20	200-240
60	560-640				

Math

Total Points	Area Score	Total Points	Area Score
40	760-800	24	440-520
39	740-800	23	420-500
38	720-800	22	400-480
37	700-780	21	380-460
36	680-760	20	360-440
35	660-740	19	340-420
34	640-720	18	320-400
33	620-700	17	300-380
32	600-680	16	280-360
31	580-660	15	260-340
30	560-640	14	240-320
29	540-620	13	220-300
28	520-600	12	200-280
27	500-580	11	200-260
26	480-560	10	200-240
25	460-540		

Use the table below to record your area scores and to calculate your overall score:

	Reading + Writing Area Score	Math Area Score	Overall Score (400-1600)
Test 1	_____ +	_____ =	_____
Test 2	_____ +	_____ =	_____
Test 3	_____ +	_____ =	_____
Test 4	_____ +	_____ =	_____
Test 5	_____ +	_____ =	_____
Test 6	_____ +	_____ =	_____

SAT Tutoring

Ivy Global's SAT Tutoring Program is a premium test prep resource for students looking to increase their test scores and confidence.

This program brings students together with experienced tutors for one-on-one instruction. Each student is provided a custom curriculum, which seamlessly interweaves test strategies and assignments to address their individual strengths and weaknesses.

Why Ivy Global?

Top Tutors
Trust their 99th percentile scores and extensive experience

Mentorship
Discover an academic mentor in your tutor

Long-Term Skills
Master concepts and develop effective study habits

Expert Understanding
Work with prep materials created by SAT experts

How does it work?

1. Student is paired with a tutor based on their needs

2. Sessions are scheduled in-office, online, or, if available, in-home

3. Student meets tutor weekly, writes diagnostic tests, and improves scores

Learn more

For pricing and other inquiries, visit our website at www.ivyglobal.com.

About Ivy Global

Since 2007, Ivy Global has provided premium consulting services for prospective students applying to top private schools and US colleges. With offices in New York, Silicon Valley and Toronto, we have helped thousands of students maximize their educational opportunities in North America and abroad.

To set up a free initial consultation, contact us at 1-888-588-7955 or info@ivyglobal.com, or visit www.ivyglobal.com for more information.